CASEBOOK SERIES

JANE AUSTEN: *Emma* (Revised) David Lodge
JANE AUSTEN: *'Northanger Abbey' & 'Persuasion'* B. C. Southam
JANE AUSTEN: *'Sense and Sensibility', 'Pride and Prejudice' & 'Mansfield Park'* B. C. Southam
BECKETT: *Waiting for Godot* Ruby Cohn
WILLIAM BLAKE: *Songs of Innocence and Experience* Margaret Bottrall
CHARLOTTE BRONTE: *'Jane Eyre' & 'Villette'* Miriam Allott
EMILY BRONTE: *Wuthering Heights* (Revised) Miriam Allott
BROWNING: *'Men and Women' & Other Poems* J. R. Watson
CHAUCER: *The Canterbury Tales* J. J. Anderson
COLERIDGE: *'The Ancient Mariner' & Other Poems* Alun R. Jones & W. Tydeman
CONRAD: *'Heart of Darkness', 'Nostromo' & 'Under Western Eyes'* C. B. Cox
CONRAD: *The Secret Agent* Ian Watt
DICKENS: *Bleak House* A. E. Dyson
DICKENS: *'Hard Times', 'Great Expectations' & 'Our Mutual Friend'* Norman Page
DICKENS: *'Dombey and Son' & 'Little Dorrit'* Alan Shelston
DONNE: *Songs and Sonnets* Julian Lovelock
GEORGE ELIOT: *Middlemarch* Patrick Swinden
GEORGE ELIOT: *'The Mill on the Floss' & 'Silas Marner'* R. P. Draper
T. S. ELIOT: *'Prufrock', 'Gerontion' & 'Ash Wednesday'* B. C. Southam
T. S. ELIOT: *The Waste Land* C. B. Cox & Arnold P. Hinchliffe
T. S. ELIOT: *Plays* Arnold P. Hinchliffe
HENRY FIELDING: *Tom Jones* Neil Compton
E.M. FORSTER: *A Passage to India* Malcolm Bradbury
WILLIAM GOLDING: *Novels 1954–64* Norman Page
HARDY: *The Tragic Novels* (Revised) R. P. Draper
HARDY: *Poems* James Gibson & Trevor Johnson
HARDY: *Three Pastoral Novels* R. P. Draper
GERARD MANLEY HOPKINS: *Poems* Margaret Bottrall
HENRY JAMES: *'Washington Square' & 'The Portrait of a Lady'* Alan Shelton
JONSON: *Volpone* Jonas A. Barish
JONSON: *'Every Man in his Humour' & 'The Alchemist'* R. V. Holdsworth
JAMES JOYCE: *'Dubliners' & 'A Portrait of the Artist as a Young Man'* Morris Beja
KEATS: *Odes* G.S. Fraser
KEATS: *Narrative Poems* John Spencer Hill
D.H. LAWRENCE: *Sons and Lovers* Gamini Salgado
D.H. LAWRENCE: *'The Rainbow' & 'Women in Love'* Colin Clarke
LOWRY: *Under the Volcano* Gordon Bowker
MARLOWE: *Doctor Faustus* John Jump
MARLOWE: *'Tamburlaine the Great', 'Edward II' & 'The Jew of Malta'* J. R. Brown
MARLOWE: *Poems* Arthur Pollard
MAUPASSANT: *In the Hall of Mirrors* T. Harris
MILTON: *Paradise Lost* A. E. Dyson & Julian Lovelock
O'CASEY: *'Juno and the Paycock', 'The Plough and the Stars' & 'The Shadow of a Gunman'* Ronald Ayling
EUGENE O'NEILL: *Three Plays* Normand Berlin
JOHN OSBORNE: *Look Back in Anger* John Russell Taylor
PINTER: *'The Birthday Party' & Other Plays* Michael Scott
POPE: *The Rape of the Lock* John Dixon Hunt
SHAKESPEARE: *A Midsummer Night's Dream* Antony Price
SHAKESPEARE: *Antony and Cleopatra* (Revised) John Russell Brown
SHAKESPEARE: *Coriolanus* B. A. Brockman

SHAKESPEARE: *Early Tragedies* Neil Taylor & Bryan Loughrey
SHAKESPEARE: *Hamlet* John Jump
SHAKESPEARE: *Henry IV Parts I and II* G.K. Hunter
SHAKESPEARE: *Henry V* Michael Quinn
SHAKESPEARE: *Julius Caesar* Peter Ure
SHAKESPEARE: *King Lear* (Revised) Frank Kermode
SHAKESPEARE: *Macbeth* (Revised) John Wain
SHAKESPEARE: *Measure for Measure* C. K. Stead
SHAKESPEARE: *The Merchant of Venice* John Wilders
SHAKESPEARE: *'Much Ado About Nothing' & 'As You Like It'* John Russell Brown
SHAKESPEARE: *Othello* (Revised) John Wain
SHAKESPEARE: *Richard II* Nicholas Brooke
SHAKESPEARE: *The Sonnets* Peter Jones
SHAKESPEARE: *The Tempest* (Revised) D. J. Palmer
SHAKESPEARE: *Troilus and Cressida* Priscilla Martin
SHAKESPEARE: *Twelfth Night* D. J. Palmer
SHAKESPEARE: *The Winter's Tale* Kenneth Muir
SPENSER: *The Faerie Queene* Peter Bayley
SHERIDAN: *Comedies* Peter Davison
STOPPARD: *'Rosencrantz and Guildenstern are Dead', 'Jumpers' & 'Travesties'*
T. Bareham
SWIFT: *Gulliver's Travels* Richard Gravil
SYNGE: *Four Plays* Ronald Ayling
TENNYSON: *In Memoriam* John Dixon Hunt
THACKERAY: *Vanity Fair* Arthur Pollard
TROLLOPE: *The Barsetshire Novels* T. Bareham
WEBSTER: *'The White Devil' & 'The Duchess of Malfi'* R. V. Holdsworth
WILDE: *Comedies* William Tydeman
VIRGINIA WOOLF: *To the Lighthouse* Morris Beja
WORDSWORTH: *Lyrical Ballads* Alun R. Jones & William Tydeman
WORDSWORTH: *The 1807 Poems* Alun R. Jones
WORDSWORTH: *The Prelude* W. J. Harvey & Richard Gravil
YEATS: *Poems 1919–35* Elizabeth Cullingford
YEATS: *Last Poems* Jon Stallworthy

Issues in Contemporary Critical Theory Peter Barry
Thirties Poets: 'The Auden Group' Ronald Carter
Tragedy: Developments in Criticism R.P. Draper
The Epic Ronald Draper
Poetry Criticism and Practice: Developments since the Symbolists A.E. Dyson
Three Contemporary Poets: Gunn, Hughes, Thomas A.E. Dyson
Elizabethan Poetry: Lyrical & Narrative Gerald Hammond
The Metaphysical Poets Gerald Hammond
Medieval English Drama Peter Happé
The English Novel: Developments in Criticism since Henry James Stephen Hazell
Poetry of the First World War Dominic Hibberd
The Romantic Imagination John Spencer Hill
Drama Criticism: Developments since Ibsen Arnold P. Hinchliffe
Three Jacobean Revenge Tragedies R.V. Holdsworth
The Pastoral Mode Bryan Loughrey
The Language of Literature Norman Page
Comedy: Developments in Criticism D.J. Palmer
Studying Shakespeare John Russell Brown
The Gothic Novel Victor Sage
Pre-Romantic Poetry J.R. Watson

Shakespeare:

King Lear

A CASEBOOK
EDITED BY

FRANK KERMODE

Revised Edition

MACMILLAN

First published 1969
Reprinted twelve times
Revised edition 1992

Published by
MACMILLAN PRESS LTD
Houndmills, Basingstoke, Hampshire RG21 6XS
and London
Companies and representatives
throughout the world

ISBN 0–333–53357–7 hardcover
ISBN 0–333–53358–5 paperback

A catalogue record for this book is available
from the British Library.

11   10   9   8   7   6   5   4   3
04   03   02   01   00   99   98   97   96

Printed in Hong Kong

CONTENTS

ACKNOWLEDGEMENTS

The editor and publisher wish to thank the following for permission to use copyright material:
Maynard Mack, 'Actors and Redactors', from *King Lear in Our Time* (University of California Press); A. C. Bradley, *Shakespearean Tragedy* (the representatives of the late A. C. Bradley); G. Wilson Knight, *The Wheel of Fire* (Methuen & Co. Ltd); Enid Welsford, *The Fool* (Curtis Brown Ltd); George Orwell, 'Lear, Tolstoy and the Fool', from *Shooting an Elephant* (Miss Sonia Brownell, Secker & Warburg and Harcourt, Brace & World Inc.; © Sonia Brownell Orwell 1945, 1946, 1950); Robert B. Heilman, 'The Unity of *King Lear*', from *Sewanee Review*, LVI i (Winter 1948); Barbara Everett, 'The New *King Lear*', from *Critical Quarterly*, Winter 1960 (Mrs Barbara Jones); John Holloway, *The Story of the Night* (University of Nebraska Press); William R. Elton, 'Double Plot', chapter 9 of *King Lear and the Gods* (Henry E. Huntington Library and Art Gallery, San Marino); Stanley Cavell, *Disowning Knowledge in Six Plays of Shakespeare* (Cambridge University Press, 1987), pp. 39–84; Stephen Greenblatt, *Shakespearian Negotiations: The Circulation of Social Energy in Renaissance England* (Berkeley, University of California Press, 1988), pp. 94–128, 184–92.

Every effort has been made to trace all the copyright holders but if any have been inadvertently overlooked the publishers will be pleased to make the necessary arrangement at the first opportunity.

GENERAL EDITOR'S PREFACE

The Casebook series, launched in 1968, has become a well-regarded library of critical studies. The central concern of the series remains the 'single-author' volume, but suggestions from the academic community have led to an extension of the original plan, to include occasional volumes on such general themes as literary 'schools' and genres.

Each volume in the central category deals either with one well-known and influential work by an individual author, or with closely related works by one writer. The main section consists of critical readings, mostly modern, collected from books and journals. A selection of reviews and comments by the author's contemporaries is also included, and sometimes comment from the author himself. The Editor's Introduction charts the reputation of the work or works from the first appearance to the present time.

Volumes in the 'general themes' category are variable in structure but follow the basic purpose of the series in presenting an integrated selection of readings, with an Introduction which explores the theme and discusses the literary and critical issues involved.

A single volume can represent no more than a small selection of critical opinions. Some critics are excluded for reasons of space, and it is hoped that readers will pursue the suggestions for further reading in the Select Bibliography. Other contributions are severed from their original context, to which some readers may wish to turn. Indeed, if they take a hint from the critics represented here, they certainly will.

A. E. DYSON

INTRODUCTION

The entry for *King Lear* in the Stationer's Register is dated 26 November 1607, and it mentions that the play had been performed 'uppon S. Stephans night at Christmas last', that is, 26 December 1606. The play as we have it cannot have been written before March 1603, the date of publication of Samuel Harsnett's *Declaration of Egregious Popish Impostures*, from which Shakespeare borrowed several elements, including the names of Edgar's devils. (There is an exploration of the relationship between these two works in the essay of Stephen Greenblatt reprinted below.)

The old play *King Leir*, probably written about 1590, which he also used, was published on 8 May 1605, possibly in the hope that customers would mistake the long-disused chronicle for Shakespeare's new play. Its claim on its title page to have been 'sundry times lately acted' may therefore suggest that Shakespeare's work was in production early in 1605, or perhaps it was performed even earlier, for a sonnet by William Strachey, published with Jonson's *Sejanus* in November 1604, seems to have Shakespearian echoes. Some scholars have argued that Gloucester's reference to 'these late eclipses' [I ii 112] alludes to the lunar and solar eclipses of September and October 1605, but the prevailing view is that *Lear* appeared originally in late 1604.

Publication as a Quarto followed in 1608. This was the Pied Bull Quarto, so called because it was printed, by Nathaniel Butter, at the sign of the Pied Bull. It is a notoriously messy text. Recently it has been argued that it represents an earlier version of the play than the text in the Folio of 1623, which is thought to be based on Shakespeare's own rewriting of the piece some years later. In this belief the Oxford editors attempt 'to emend Q – where emendation seems desirable – as though F did not exist ...' And they offer as two distinct versions *The History of King Lear* (Quarto) and *The Tragedy of King Lear* (Folio). This view has won a good deal of support, but there are difficulties in the way of treating the evidence thus, as for example when a reading that stands in Q is evidently a sophistication of a reading preserved in F; and the problems facing a modern editor of *King Lear*, which have been recognised as exceptionally difficult ever since the birth of modern bibliographical techniques, seem as knotty as ever.

There is no direct evidence as to the contemporary reception of Shakespeare's play, whether on the stage or as a book. Like *Hamlet*, it took an existing work on the same theme and utterly transformed it, in such a manner that, like *Hamlet*, it seems to have presupposed a high degree of sophistication in its audience. But that audience, though fit for great tragedy, lacked the desire, or perhaps the terminology, to record its reactions. And by the time the desire was felt and the terminology current, the whole situation had altered. The issue now was not whether the audience was fit, but whether the play was; it had to fit the rules. And the rules of tragedy were not deduced from such plays as *King Lear*. Restoration playwrights, conscious of their own knowledge of *art*, and crediting their Jacobean predecessors, Jonson apart, only with *nature*, saw no reason why they should not 'improve' Shakespeare, introduce regularity into his chaos, polish his rough stones into jewels. Nahum Tate's version of *Lear*, of which the prefatory matter is printed in this collection, is only one of many such. Published in 1681, it was the basis of all stage performances for almost a century and a half until Macready restored most of Shakespeare's text in 1838.

Maynard Mack, whose essay gives the gist of Tate's highly adulterate version, rightly insists on the extraordinary resilience of Shakespeare's play, its power to suffer interpretation, to speak, through veils of prejudice and distortion, to the predominant interests of various persons and periods. Though Tate seems absurd to us, it was possible to condone his version and still think nobly of Shakespeare. Dr Johnson, who believed that there was always an appeal open from the rules to nature, accepted 'Tatification' not because he found Shakespeare too irregular but because he found him too painful. In particular, he thought the conclusion of the play 'contrary to the natural ideas of justice'.

This is no superficial judgement. We know that Johnson dreaded the task of re-reading *Lear* for his edition. He saw that Shakespeare, whose sources provide a happy ending, brought Lear to an apparent end of his torment and then, with the death of Cordelia, denied him the restoration afforded his prototype Job and made him suffer beyond the limit of pain. Johnson rightly believed that Shakespeare had done this with deliberation; and, holding a higher view than we perhaps can of the ultimate justice of providence, he found this as much in conflict with a truth to which he desperately held as those jaunty explanations of pain and evil he condemned in Jenyns and Pope. Lear is like a felon, hanged and then cut down and revived for further torment; and to Johnson, behind whose criticism is the force of a venerable intellect and a temperament subject to strong agitation at the idea of punishment without mercy, this was intolerable. For him to prefer Tate to Shakespeare is not a failure of attention or taste but a great critic's despairing choice.

As time went by, the discrepancy between what could be seen on the stage, and what Shakespeare himself wrote, grew more troublesome, and gave rise to the opinion that the play was unactable, or anyway ought not to be acted. This view is, of course, consistent with a very high opinion of its merits, as may be gathered from Lamb's essay, and also from Bradley's. Since Bradley's day the stage has regained some of the flexibility it had when Shakespeare was writing, and it no longer seems sensible to call a play 'too great for the stage'; the modern praise of *King Lear* is not subject to such conditions. Nor are we likely to think of it as violating some established faith in order and justice. For these reasons we tend to think of ourselves as understanding the play better than the generations between Shakespeare's and our own.

We should not be too confident of this. As Mr Mack implies, *King Lear* has many 'subtexts', is patient of many interpretations. It suffered Jan Kott's apocalyptic Absurdity, it sustained Mr Peter Brook's cruel production. In choosing the Absurd or the Cruel one asks the play to complement one's own interests, and it patiently does so, for us as it did for Tate. In Shakespeare's Quarto text the servants of Cornwall are horrified by the putting out of Gloucester's eyes, and one undertakes to 'fetch some flax and whites of eggs / To apply to his bleeding face' [III vii]; but in Mr Brook's production they pushed the old man off the stage. And in explaining this change Mr Brook, who might have defended it (however unconvincingly) by arguing that the lines were cut in the Folio text, simply says that he wished 'to remove the taint of sympathy usually found in this place'. *Lear* was too cruel to fit Johnson's world-view, too soft for Mr Brook's. In either case it is distorted into compliance.

There is, it must be admitted, a major difference between our attitudes to the play and those of the eighteenth century. Then there was, in aesthetic judgements as well as in ethical and scientific, a uniformity relatively little disturbed by vagaries of individual taste or theory. This could not, on the longest view, be said of us. In these matters ours is an age of plurality. More, and more various, opinions have been expressed about the play in this century than in the whole period of its life before 1900. We shall come to this matter of plurality of opinion in a moment. But it would be folly to allow it to deflect our attention from what is equally striking – that the play remains what it has been for at least a century and a half, part of our canon of masterpieces, essential to our very notion of literary value. It is thus a testimony of a certain continuity in our culture. Our plural and dissenting opinions have not generally been of a kind that destroys that continuity of valuation; to attempt that would be to attack cultural assumptions far wider than one play can represent.

There have been such assaults. I suppose we nowadays pay as little attention to Tolstoy's strictures on *Lear* as we do to Bradley's systematic exposure of its defects and improbabilities. This is in some ways unfortunate, for Tolstoy's is, as it has to be, an attack not only on Shakespeare but upon the whole culture which receives *King Lear* as a central classic. He understands that the character of a culture, and its choice of central classics, are related, and holds that neither is exempt from the enquiries of the moralist. Most of us think of the late Tolstoy as a crank – it is the culture's judgement on him. But this does not in itself invalidate all his judgements on the culture. For example, the view that our often uncritical veneration of Shakespeare looks like the result of some form of 'mass hypnosis' is one that students have a real duty to consider. Tolstoy is often wrong as to facts, often simply intemperate or silly, but he is nonetheless talking about something important, which is why Orwell thought it worth the trouble to dig out his essay and refute it.

Orwell's essay has always seemed to me a very good one, but it is once more a duty of the reader to reflect that one can be on the right side and yet make some of the mistakes Tolstoy made. Consider, for example, Orwell on the defects of the play: 'One wicked daughter would have been quite enough, and Edgar is a superfluous character.' There are other remarks of the same kind, and Orwell is candid about what he 'sees' when he closes his eyes and thinks about *Lear*. It is a play, evidently, without the great scene in which Goneril and Regan turn upon their father and show him what it means to value love in terms of possessions. It is a play lacking the moment, which others take to be central, where Lear, inspired by Poor Tom, tears off his 'lendings'. There is no scene on the cliff at Dover, none of Edgar's comment on the depth of human suffering (so much more profound, he discovers, than anybody can actually *say*). Edgar is called superfluous. He is not essential to what Orwell thinks *King Lear* should be, or really is, *about*. In other words, Orwell, too, chooses a 'subtext'. And because we can all do that, and have the terms, inherited or invented, to describe and defend our choice, our cultural unanimity on the value of *King Lear* is expressed in a great variety of ways.

This seems to me equally true also of the recent phase of interpretation usually named 'the new historicism', even though it announces itself as a departure from, and a criticism of, the cultural assumptions which I have mentioned. The neo-historicist approach is represented in this collection by Stephen Greenblatt's essay 'Shakespeare and the Exorcists'. Greenblatt gives the tragedy no pre-eminence over the other texts he discusses; he is concerned with the interplay of discourses in the period – what he calls the 'circulation between the social dimension of an aesthetic strategy, and the aesthetic dimension of a social strategy'. In practice this ought to mean that the particular work of Shakespeare under consideration is not in any way 'privileged' over other texts, for example that of Harsnett, which Greenblatt uses so much more extensively than his predecessors. What we are offered seems to be a form of historical sociology rather than literary criticism, and in work of that sort it would be pointless and distorting to behave as if one text had more literary value than another. Yet in Greenblatt's Shakespearian essays, and in the work of his associates, it is always the 'literary' text that binds the others together, is the focus of the investigation, despite the distance from that text at which the investigation usually begins. This is not to deny that much of the interest of the enquiry arises from the intrinsic value and variety of the material newly brought into relation with Shakespeare, and from the skill with which this operation is performed. These are certainly new ways of talking; but in the end it must seem that they are undertaken not on behalf of Harsnett or of Strachey, but of *King Lear* and *The Tempest*.

Thus the new historicism, for all its apparent novelty, joins the cultural consensus, finds new ways of expressing the value of Shakespeare's plays. However, it ought perhaps to be remarked, in this context, that feminist criticism, which has also flourished in the years since the publication of the first edition of this book, is often inimical to that consensus, and sometimes to Shakespeare as well; for both may be labelled 'patriarchal'. Yet even in this predominantly militant chorus there are voices that condone and preserve inherited valuations; and the intensity with which feminist interest has fastened on Shakespeare, whether to praise or to condemn, is itself an involuntary tribute to his cultural centrality, and discovers new and provocative 'subtexts'.

We can agree that our appraisals are necessarily partial and tentative, though we do not always behave as if we were conscious of this truth. We are more likely to think of them, erroneously, as striving or contributing to some ideal wholeness. When editors emend the text, or explain words and allusions previously misunderstood, or when interpreters indicate hidden patterns of theme or image, or illuminate the historical context, we may entertain the fantasy that eventually we shall reach the end of all such work. Yet we can do so only by suppressing what we really know perfectly well – that such work will never end, whether it consists in discovering more about the historical contexts, or bringing out the relevance of the play to our own times and situations – whether in order to achieve these things we must align *King Lear* with a Theatre of Cruelty in the manner of Artaud, or with the conflict of period discourses enjoined, in their different ways, by both neo-historicism and feminism. Whatever is said, the document itself – the text of *King Lear* – remains at the centre, and disallows, is not by us permitted to allow, any definitive comment. There is no final word, on the culture or on the play.

Criticism, whether ancient or modern, is therefore always and only a matter of detecting and illuminating aspects of a presumptive whole. The play itself is simply there, requiring and requiting intimate attention, but never wholly surrendering to it. Its integrity is indeed exactly what the plurality of opinions established. What is said of it may be the product of a more or less systematic study of literature as a whole, or of intense application to the play itself as an aesthetic object, or as a text for theatrical performance, or as a historical document with a significant relation to many other historical documents, or to the social order that prevailed in its day. There are fashions in these things; for the time being, at any rate, the thematic and imagistic approach of Heilman is disfavoured, and so is the generous yet discriminating humanism of Bradley. One could easily multiply this account of opinions, whether fashionable or outmoded; but the point is that they are all, in their variety and plurality, contributions to a continuity, a continuity not of consensus but of – what is the right word? not reverence, for that is also quite out of fashion – but simply of devoted attention.

However, it is not the purpose of this collection to make the play subserve an investigation into the problems and the variety of critical techniques. Here the critics ought to be servants of the play and its readers; their business is to freshen the medium in which the work survives, and to provide us with insights and explanations that will strengthen our own apprehension of it. This is not a function we can be systematic about, since every reader will absorb from the criticism what blends best with his own mind. Nevertheless it may be useful to isolate two aspects of the criticism that follows. In so far as the play has a continuous cultural effect we should expect some continuity of topic in the criticism; and in so far as we test its patience by varying our reading by period and person we should be able to differentiate between types of modern criticism.

As to the first of these, it seems clear that although strictures on the limitations of Bradley's approach are now commonplace we continue to meditate upon some of his central problems – for example, upon the meanings and implications of Lear's last words over Cordelia's body. And these are essentially the crux also of Dr Johnson's difficulties. The problems, then, are perennial; but the solutions vary. It may seem strange, but one characteristically modern solution to the problem of justice in the play is Christian, or as Professor Empson would say neo-Christian. This crops up with many different emphases, including the candidly allegorical. Some critics consider and qualify this interpretation, others throw it out altogether. But the topic continues to seem important, for reasons which doubtless should be sought outside the play, in the texture of our civilisation. Even critics who are fully in the Romantic tradition, and seek in a work of this kind a whole self-sufficient world, with no ethical or religious elements directly derived from the world outside, are nevertheless unable to evade this issue. At least this proves we are still talking about the same play.

To Swinburne there was no justice in *King Lear*, which has so much to say on the subject; there was no 'twilight of atonement', only a night of tragic fatalism. Therefore he made Gloucester's

> As flies to wanton boys are we to the gods,
> They kill us for their sport —

a central text. Bradley dissented, feeling that no work could be called great that was so totally pessimistic, and that the truth lies no more in Gloucester's attitude (which in any case he changes) than in Edgar's 'The gods are just', with its confidence in a rigidly vengeful god; rather we feel pity and terror blend with 'a sense of law and beauty' to form a quasi-religious mystery. Evil exists, and must be renounced, but the soul may be untouched by evil, and in the long run good survives; evil is self-limiting.

The merit of Bradley's approach, though we may sometimes find his terms too vague, is that he persistently treats the play as a very complex whole, containing many apparent contradictions which cannot be resolved on the ethical level. He thought of Lear as in some sense purified and redeemed, as dying in joy, though he allows our pain at knowing the joy to be baseless. Later critics are not content with this formulation; if there is mysterious suffering they want to show that it cannot be without reference to the religion of mysterious suffering. So Lear is a Christ-figure and the play alludes constantly to Christian doctrines of patience and redemption, heaven and hell. Sometimes Cordelia too is a Christ-figure, going about her father's business, harrowing hell.[1]

Clearly there are enormous cultural differences between a critic who reads the play thus, and one who refuses to do so; but they still share a problem. This was originally posed by Shakespeare himself, as we have seen. In his source neither the King nor Cordelia died. There was no Edmund, no madness. The storm was the wrath of a Christian god meting out justice. Shakespeare offers intimations of Christian apocalypse but frustrates them; he makes Lear like Job, but denies him divine compensations; Lear's sufferings seem to end and are then renewed. Job curses the day he was born but Job has a Redeemer; Lear speaks of life as beginning in misery only to continue and end in it. Edgar teaches his father that we have to seek the strength to bear all, and then bear more. Sunk, as he thinks, to the lowest possible point, Edgar is at once confronted by his father blind and miserable [IV i]. In one of the most extraordinary scenes in the whole of Shakespeare [V ii] he leaves his father to go to battle, hoping to return with the comfort of a victory for the right. The

battle proceeds offstage, and we are left with the sightless Gloucester
to guess at its outcome. Then Edgar returns with news of defeat, and
one more rough lesson in patience:

> What, in ill thoughts again? Men must endure
> Their going hence, even as their coming hither:
> Ripeness is all. Come on.
> GLO.   And that's true too.

How often does one hear 'Ripeness is all' without the rest of that
line? Yet the need to carry on, the need to accept, are essential to its
meaning. The eleven lines of this scene prepare us for the dreadful
end. It is wrong to select meanings from them, especially, I think,
Christian meanings.

Perhaps, as J. C. Maxwell suggested – and it is an insight which
Mr Elton does much to confirm in his big book – perhaps Shakespeare was always thinking of a situation in which he would place
his pagan world before the eyes of an audience which would make its
own religious corrections, knowing themselves better instructed
than the ancient men on the stage. Or perhaps we should think of
the whole thing as a fictive experiment in human misery, saying,
'This is what it could, or will, be like, when kings are reduced to
mere mortality, when men's lives are as cheap as beasts; when
reason is reduced to madness, and virtue to destruction.' But having
rejected the partial interpretation we find our own explanations even
more partial and generalised. We return to the basic dilemma.

The present collection includes a thoughtful study of the Christian
interpretation by Barbara Everett, whose view is that the play is a
product of a naturally Christian world-view, but that it lacks
doctrinal and allegorical Christian dimensions. Here, as in Mr
Elton's more historical survey of Renaissance attitudes to providence (not all of them by any means 'Christian'), we have necessary
correctives, and as Mr Elton remarks, 'the obstacles to an orthodox
theological reading of *King Lear*, in which the protagonist moves
from sin and suffering to redemption are ... formidable ...' (*King
Lear and the Gods*, p. 263). In *Hamlet*, a few years earlier, Shakespeare had christianised, to some extent, a pagan story; here he de-
christianises the old *Leir*; and in both plays he is asking for, counting
on, a strong response from the audience to a series of implicit

questions. This is where we have to cope with the plurality of modern interpretations. If the play is of this kind, how should we expect the critics to fare who seek global explanations, or who say, 'This play is a world of its own, and we are trying to find out its physics'?

Some take the physics to be accessible to historical method, as when Mr Elton tells us about Renaissance scepticism, or Miss Welsford about the background of the Fool. But some of it requires new ways of looking, new techniques. 'Holist' approaches, of rather different kinds, are represented by the essays of G. Wilson Knight and R. B. Heilman. Each of these critics has written more about the play than is included here. Knight's famous essay here reprinted is followed, in *The Wheel of Fire*, by an equally impressive study of 'The *Lear* Universe', a work of revolutionary importance which nevertheless finally rejoins the 'redemptive' view of the play; and Heilman wrote a long book, *This Great Stage* (1948), developing the thematic approach of the present essay. Readers of Knight's essay should reflect that it preceded Jan Kott's 'absurdist' approach by a generation, and appeared before Beckett was heard of; and it exposes to our view an authentic dimension of the work which Dr Johnson, say, never suspected. As Heilman observes, 'the unity of *King Lear* lies very little on the surface' – he himself seeks it in 'the ramifications of dramatic and imagistic constructs', and in this brief essay adumbrates a concept of that unity which he required a whole book to work out. Other critics, hostile to Heilman's 'spatial' approach, would reject his insights with his method. The question of what the play *means* – whether it is 'pessimistic' or whatever, is inseparably related to the question of how one apprehends its wholeness, for example whether spatially or sequentially. We see only what is visible from where we stand, and what we have trained our eye to observe.

That criticism, even of a work whose value is unchallenged, should be incorrigibly plural, is a justification for a book of this kind. There are continuities of topic, but the handling must vary with the needs of periods and individuals. The Absurd *Lear* of the Sixties, the feminist *Lear* of the Eighties, the post-structuralist text called *Lear*, are just as selective as the happy-ending *Lear* or the redemptive *Lear*. In our minds as readers these critical propositions dissolve like sugar into some new and also imperfect whole, from which in turn, perhaps, another soluble proposition will derive. Examining some of these propositions as a philosopher and a moralist, Stanley Cavell offers his own mature and original view of the play; unfortunately I have been able to include less than half of his essay.

It may well seem too facile for an editor to take so grandly judicial an attitude to his contributors, himself claiming immunity by venturing nothing; and I agree that I have an obligation, in the last page or two available, to offer a hint of my own partial *Lear*. In this play, not for the first time, Shakespeare concerns himself with the contrast between the two bodies of the king: one lives by ceremony, administers justice in a furred gown, distinguished by regalia which set him above nature. The other is born naked, subject to disease and pain, and protected only by the artifices of ceremony from natural suffering and nakedness. So Lear is stripped, and moves from the ceremonies of the first scene to the company of a naked 'natural', the thing itself. The play deals with what intervenes between our natural and our artificially comfortable conditions: ceremony, justice, love, evil. Since our defences against nature are fallible we need to learn the patience to do without them. On the heath any shelter is a grace, and there too the ceremonious folly of the Court Fool yields to the seemingly authentic natural madness of Poor Tom. Robbed of the contrivances which make life tolerable, we are like men at the end of the world, when no hope can exist except of an end and a divine judgement; but the pain, though terrible, is never at an end, the trial can be protracted beyond our worst imagining.

Lear does not *say* such things, it only presents them. It forces us to contemplate what, day in and day out, we prefer to forget: this is what it can be like, this is what it can mean to be human. Its characters jump, as we do, to their premature conclusions: Gloucester sees men as a game for the gods, but later he calls the gods 'ever gentle'; Albany sees the operation of justice in the death of Cornwall; Cordelia says the gods are 'kind'. As in life there are indications of providence, demands upon fortitude, occasions of despair. The end is woe and nakedness. But the play is not committed; it only shows us humanity at the cliff-edge of its own imaginings. It allows Lear his beautiful delusions of a life with Cordelia. It gives to the encounter of Lear and Gloucester at Dover, which I take to be the highest point in the history of tragedy, the blaze of human imagination, the full power of human speech. And however we may dwell upon the detail – the fusion of such themes as nature, clothing, nothingness, sight – we shall only possess the play by a living submission to it, and by a readiness to accept that each of us, in the course of a lifetime, may well – as if we too were a succession of different persons and different periods – know many different versions of *King Lear*.

NOTE

1. For a summary account of Christian interpretations, see W. R. Elton, *King Lear and the Gods* (1966), ch. 1.

PART ONE

Early Comments
and Critiques

Nahum Tate   (1681)

To my Esteemed Friend *Thomas Boteler*, Esq; Sir, You have a natural Right to this Piece, since by your Advice I attempted the Revival of it with Alterations. Nothing but the Pow'r of your Persuasions, and my Zeal for all the Remains of *Shakespear* cou'd have wrought me to so bold an Undertaking. I found that the New-modelling of this Story wou'd force me sometimes on the difficult Task of making the chiefest Persons speak something like their Character, on Matter whereof I had no Ground in my Author. *Lear's* real and *Edgar's* pretended Madness have so much of *extravagant Nature* (I know not how else to express it), as cou'd never have started but from our *Shakespear's* Creating Fancy. The Images and Language are so odd and surprizing, and yet so agreeable and proper, that whilst we grant that none but *Shakespear* could have form'd such Conceptions; yet we are satisfied that they were the only Things in the World that ought to be said on those Occasions. I found the whole to answer your account of it, a Heap of Jewels, unstrung, and unpolisht; yet so dazling in their Disorder, that I soon perceiv'd I had seiz'd a Treasure. 'Twas my good Fortune to light on one Expedient to rectify what was wanting in the Regularity and Probability of the Tale, which was to run through the whole, as *Love* betwixt *Edgar* and *Cordelia*; that never chang'd a Word with each other in the Original. This renders *Cordelia's* Indifference, and her Father's Passion in the first Scene, probable. It likewise gives Countenance to *Edgar's* Disguise, making that a generous Design that was before a poor Shift to save his Life. The Distress of the Story is evidently heightened by it; and it particularly gave Occasion of a New Scene or Two, of more Success (perhaps) than Merit. This method necessarily threw me on making the Tale conclude in a Success to the innocent distrest Persons: Otherwise I must have incumbred the Stage with dead Bodies, which Conduct makes many Tragedies conclude with unseasonable Jests. Yet was I wract with no small Fears for so bold a Change, till I found it well receiv'd by my Audience; and if this will not satisfy the Reader, I can produce an Authority that questionless will. *Neither is it of so Trivial an Undertaking to make a Tragedy end happily, for 'tis more difficult to save than 'tis to Kill: The Dagger and Cup of Poison are always in*

Readiness; but to bring the Action to the last Extremity, and then by probable means to recover All, will require the Art and Judgment of a Writer, and cost him many a Pang in the Performance.

I have one thing more to apologize for, which is that I have us'd less Quaintness of Expression even in the Newest Parts of this Play. I confess, 'twas Design in me, partly to comply with my Author's Style, to make the Scenes of a Piece, and partly to give it some Resemblance of the Time and Persons here Represented. This, Sir, I submit wholly to you, who are both a Judge and Master of Style. Nature had exempted you before you went Abroad from the Morose Saturnine Humour of our Country, and you brought home the Refinedness of Travel without the Affectation. Many faults I see in the following Pages, and question not but you will discover more; yet I will presume so far on your Friendship as to make the whole a Present to you, and Subscribe myself *Your obliged Friend and humble Servant*, N. TATE.

PROLOGUE

Since by Mistakes your best delights are made
(For e'en your Wives can please in Masquerade),
'Twere worth our while, to have drawn you in this Day
By a new Name to our old honest Play;
But he that did this Evenings Treat prepare ⎫
Bluntly resolv'd before hand to declare ⎬
Your Entertainment should be most old Fare. ⎭
Yet hopes since in rich *Shakespear's* soil it grew ⎫
'Twill relish yet, with those whose tasts are true, ⎬
And his Ambition is to please a Few. ⎭
If then this Heap of Flow'rs shall chance to wear
Fresh beauty in the Order they now bear,
Even this *Shakespear's* Praise; each rustick knows
'Mongst plenteous Flow'rs a Garland to Compose
Which strung by this Course Hand may fairer show
But 'twas a Power Divine first made 'em grow,
Why should these Scenes lie hid, in which we find
What may at once divert and teach the Mind;
Morals were always proper for the stage,
But are ev'n necessary in this Age.
Poets must take the Churches Teaching Trade,
Since Priests their Province of Intrigue invade;
But we the worst in this Exchange have got,
In vain our Poets Preach, whilst Churchmen Plot.

SOURCE: Dedication and Prologue to his version of *King Lear*, 1681.

Samuel Johnson (1765)

To the end of most plays I have added short strictures, containing a general censure of faults or praise of excellence; in which I know not how much I have concurred with the current opinion, but I have not, by any affectation of singularity, deviated from it. Nothing is minutely and particularly examined, and therefore it is to be supposed that in the plays which are condemned there is much to be praised, and in those which are praised much to be condemned.

General Observation. The tragedy of *Lear* is deservedly celebrated among the dramas of Shakespeare. There is perhaps no play which keeps the attention so strongly fixed; which so much agitates our passions and interests our curiosity. The artful involutions of distinct interests, the striking opposition of contrary characters, the sudden changes of fortune, and the quick succession of events, fill the mind with a perpetual tumult of indignation, pity, and hope. There is no scene which does not contribute to the aggravation of the distress or conduct of the action, and scarce a line which does not conduce to the progress of the scene. So powerful is the current of the poet's imagination that the mind which once ventures within it is hurried irresistibly along.

On the seeming improbability of Lear's conduct it may be observed that he is represented according to the histories at that time vulgarly received as true. And perhaps if we turn our thoughts upon the barbarity and ignorance of the age to which this story is referred, it will appear not so unlikely as while we estimate Lear's manners by our own. Such preference of one daughter to another, or resignation of dominion on such conditions, would be yet credible if told of a petty prince of Guinea or Madagascar. Shakespeare, indeed, by the mention of his earls and dukes, has given us the idea of times more civilized and of life regulated by softer manners; and the truth is that though he so nicely discriminates and so minutely describes the characters of men, he commonly neglects and confounds the characters of ages, by mingling customs ancient and modern, English and foreign.

My learned friend Mr Warton, who has in the *Adventurer* very minutely criticized this play, remarks that the instances of cruelty are too savage and shocking, and that the intervention of Edmund destroys the simplicity of the story. These objections may, I think, be answered by repeating that the cruelty of the daughters is an historical fact, to which the poet has added little, having only drawn it into a series by dialogue and action. But I am not able to apologize with equal plausibility for the extrusion of Gloucester's eyes, which seems an act too horrid to be endured in dramatic exhibition, and such as must always compel the mind to relieve its distress by incredulity. Yet let it be remembered that our author well knew what would please the audience for which he wrote.

The injury done by Edmund to the simplicity of the action is abundantly recompensed by the addition of variety, by the art with which he is made to co-operate with the chief design, and the opportunity which he gives the poet of combining perfidy with perfidy and connecting the wicked son with the wicked daughters, to impress this important moral, that villainy is never at a stop, that crimes lead to crimes and at last terminate in ruin.

But though this moral be incidentally enforced, Shakespeare has suffered the virtue of Cordelia to perish in a just cause, contrary to the natural ideas of justice, to the hope of the reader, and, what is yet more strange, to the faith of chronicles. Yet this conduct is justified by the Spectator, who blames Tate for giving Cordelia success and happiness in his alteration and declares that, in his opinion, *the tragedy has lost half its beauty*. Dennis has remarked, whether justly or not, that to secure the favorable reception of *Cato, the town was poisoned with much false and abominable criticism*, and that endeavors had been used to discredit and decry poetical justice. A play in which the wicked prosper and the virtuous miscarry may doubtless be good, because it is a just representation of the common events of human life; but since all reasonable beings naturally love justice, I cannot easily be persuaded that the observation of justice makes a play worse; or that, if other excellencies are equal, the audience will not always rise better pleased from the final triumph of persecuted virtue.

In the present case the public has decided. Cordelia, from the time of Tate, has always retired with victory and felicity. And, if my sensations could add anything to the general suffrage, I might relate, I was many years ago so shocked by Cordelia's death that I know not whether I ever endured to read again the last scenes of the play till I undertook to revise them as an editor.

There is another controversy among the critics concerning this play. It is disputed whether the predominant image in Lear's disordered mind be the loss of his kingdom or the cruelty of his daughters. Mr Murphy, a very judicious critic, has evinced by induction of particular passages that the cruelty of his daughters is the primary source of his distress, and that the loss of royalty affects him only as a secondary and subordinate evil. He observes with great justness that Lear would move our compassion but little, did we not rather consider the injured father than the degraded king.

The story of this play, except the episode of Edmund, which is derived, I think, from Sidney, is taken originally from Geoffrey of Monmouth, whom Holinshed generally copied; but perhaps immediately from an old historical ballad, of which I shall insert the greater part. My reason for believing that the play was posterior to the ballad, rather than the ballad to the play, is that the ballad has nothing of Shakespeare's nocturnal tempest, which is too striking to have been omitted, and that it follows the chronicle; it has the rudiments of the play but none of its amplifications; it first hinted Lear's madness but did not array it in circumstances. The writer of the ballad added something to the history, which is a proof that he would have added more if more had occurred to his mind, and more must have occurred if he had seen Shakespeare.

SOURCE: From the Preface and Notes of his edition, 1765.

A. W. Schlegel   (1811)

As in *Macbeth* terror reaches its utmost height, in *King Lear* the science of compassion is exhausted. The principal characters here are not those who act, but those who suffer. We have not in this, as in most tragedies, the picture of a calamity in which the sudden blows of fate seem still to honour the head which they strike, and where the loss is always accompanied by some flattering consolation in the memory of the former possession; but a fall from the highest elevation into the deepest abyss of misery, where humanity is stripped of all external and internal advantages and given up a prey to naked helplessness. The threefold dignity of a king, an old man, and a father, is dishonoured by the cruel ingratitude of his unnatural daughters; the old Lear, who out of a foolish tenderness has given away every thing, is driven out to the world a wandering beggar; the childish imbecility to which he was fast advancing changes into the wildest insanity, and when he is rescued from the disgraceful destitution to which he was abandoned, it is too late: the kind consolations of filial care and attention and of true friendship are now lost to him; his bodily and mental powers are destroyed beyond all hope of recovery, and all that now remains to him of life is the capability of loving and suffering beyond measure. What a picture we have in the meeting of Lear and Edgar in a tempestuous night and in a wretched hovel! The youthful Edgar has, by the wicked arts of his brother, and through his father's blindness, fallen, as the old Lear, from the rank to which his birth entitled him; and, as the only means of escaping further persecution, is reduced to assume the disguise of a beggar tormented by evil spirits. The King's fool, notwithstanding the voluntary degradation which is implied in his situation, is, after Kent, Lear's most faithful associate, his wisest counsellor. This good-hearted fool clothes reason with the livery of his motley garb; the high-born beggar acts the part of insanity; and both, were they even in reality what they seem, would still be enviable in comparison with the King, who feels that the violence of his grief threatens to overpower his reason. The meeting of Edgar with the blinded Gloster is equally heart-rending; nothing can be more affecting than to see the ejected son become the father's guide, and the good angel, who under the disguise of insanity, saves him by an ingenious and pious fraud from the horror and despair of self-murder. But who can possibly enumerate all the different combinations and situations by which our minds are here as it were stormed by the poet? Respecting the structure of the whole I will only make one observation. The story of Lear and his daughters was left by Shakespeare exactly as he found it in a fabulous tradition, with all the features characteristical of the simplicity of old times. But in that tradition there is not the slightest trace of the story of Gloster and his sons, which was derived by Shakespeare from another source. The incorporation of the two stories has been censured as destructive of the unity of action. But whatever contributes to the intrigue or the *dénouement* must always possess unity. And with what ingenuity and skill are the two main parts of the composition dovetailed into one another! The pity felt by Gloster for the fate of Lear becomes the means which enables his son Edmund to effect his complete destruction, and affords the outcast Edgar an opportunity of being the saviour of his father. On the other hand, Edmund is active in the cause of Regan and Goneril; and the criminal passion which they both entertain for him induces them to execute justice on each other and on themselves. The laws of the drama have therefore been sufficiently complied with; but that is the least: it is the very combination which constitutes the sublime beauty of the work. The two cases resemble each other in the main: an infatuated father is blind towards his well-disposed child, and the unnatural children, whom he prefers, requite him by the ruin of all his happiness. But all the circumstances are so different, that these stories, while they each make a correspondent impression on the heart, form a complete contrast for the imagination. Were Lear alone to suffer from his daughters, the impression would be limited to the powerful compassion felt by us for his private misfortune. But two such unheard-of examples taking place at the same time have the appearance of a great commotion in the moral world: the picture becomes gigantic, and fills us with such alarm as we should entertain at the idea that the heavenly bodies might one day fall from their appointed orbits. To save in some degree the honour of human nature, Shakespeare never wishes his spectators to forget that the story takes place in a dreary and barbarous age: he lays particular stress on the circumstance that the Britons of that day were still heathens, although he has not made all the remaining circumstances to coincide learnedly with the time which he has chosen. From this point of view we must judge of many coarsenesses in expression and manners; for instance, the immodest manner in which Gloster acknowledges his bastard, Kent's quarrel with the Steward, and more especially the cruelty personally inflicted on Gloster by the Duke of Cornwall. Even the virtue of the honest Kent bears the stamp of an iron age, in which the good and the bad display the same uncontrollable energy. Great qualities have not been superfluously assigned to the King; the poet could command our sympathy for his situation, without concealing what he had done to bring himself into it. Lear is choleric, overbearing, and almost childish from age, when he drives out his youngest daughter because she will not join in the hypocritical exaggerations of her sisters. But he has a warm and affectionate heart, which is susceptible of the most fervent gratitude; and even rays of a high and kingly disposition burst forth from the eclipse of his understanding. Of Cordelia's heavenly beauty of soul, painted in so few words, I will not venture to speak; she can only be named in the same breath with Antigone. Her death has been thought too cruel; and in England the piece is in acting so far altered that she remains victorious and happy. I must own, I cannot conceive what ideas of art and dramatic connexion those persons have who suppose that we can at pleasure tack a double conclusion to a tragedy; a melancholy one for hard-hearted spectators, and a happy one for souls of a softer mould. After surviving so many sufferings, Lear can only die; and what more truly tragic end for him than to die from grief for the death of Cordelia? and if he is also to be saved and to pass the remainder of his days in happiness, the whole loses its signification. According to Shakespeare's plan the guilty, it is true, are all punished, for wickedness destroys itself; but the virtues that would bring help and succour are everywhere too late, or over-matched by the cunning activity of malice. The persons of this drama have only such a faint belief in Providence as heathens may be supposed to have; and the poet here wishes to show us that this belief requires a wider range than the dark pilgrimage on earth to be established in full extent.

SOURCE: from *Lectures on Dramatic Art and Literature*, 1811.

S. T. Coleridge   (1811–12)

Of all Shakespeare's plays *Macbeth* is the most rapid, *Hamlet* the slowest, in movement. *Lear* combines length with rapidity – like the hurricane and the whirlpool, absorbing while it advances. It begins as a stormy day in summer, with brightness; but that brightness is lurid, and anticipates the tempest.

I i 1–6
    KENT   I thought the king had more affected the Duke of Albany than
    Cornwall.

GLOU. It did always seem so to us: but now, in the division of the kingdom, it appears not which of the dukes he values most; for equalities are so weighed that curiosity in neither can make choice of either's moiety.

It was not without forethought, and it is not without its due significance, that the triple division is stated here as already determined and in all its particulars, previously to the trial of professions, as the relative rewards of which the daughters were to be made to consider their several portions. The strange, yet by no means unnatural, mixture of selfishness, sensibility, and habit of feeling derived from and fostered by the particular rank and usages of the individual; the intense desire to be intensely beloved, selfish, and yet characteristic of the selfishness of a loving and kindly nature – a feeble selfishness, self-supportless and leaning for all pleasure on another's breast; the selfish craving after a sympathy with a prodigal disinterestedness, contradicted by its own ostentation and the mode and nature of its claims; the anxiety, the distrust, the jealousy, which more or less accompany all selfish affections, and are among the surest contradistinctions of mere fondness from love, and which originate Lear's eager wish to enjoy his daughter's violent professions, while the inveterate habits of sovereignty convert the wish into claim and positive right, and the incompliance with it into crime and treason; these facts, these passions, these moral verities, on which the whole tragedy is founded, are all prepared for, and will to the retrospect be found implied in, these first four or five lines of the play. They let us know that the trial is but a trick; and that the grossness of the old king's rage is in part the natural result of a silly trick suddenly and most unexpectedly baffled and disappointed. This having been provided in the fewest words, in a natural reply to as natural a question, which yet answers a secondary purpose of attracting our attention to the difference or diversity between the characters of Cornwall and Albany; the premises and data, as it were, having been thus afforded for our after-insight into the mind and mood of the person whose character, passions, and sufferings are the main *subject-matter* of the play; from Lear, the *persona patiens* of his drama, Shakespeare passes without delay to the second in importance, to the main *agent* and prime mover – introduces Edmund to our acquaintance, and with the same felicity of judgement, in the same easy, natural way, prepares us for his character in

the seemingly casual communication of its origin and occasion.
From the first drawing up of the curtain he has stood before us in the
united strength and beauty of earliest manhood. Our eyes have been
questioning him. Gifted thus with high advantages of *person*, and
further endowed by nature with a powerful intellect and a strong
energetic will, even without any concurrence of circumstances and
accident, pride will be the sin that most easily besets him. But he is
the known and acknowledged son of the princely Gloster. Edmund,
therefore, has both the germ of pride and the conditions best fitted to
evolve and ripen it into a predominant feeling. Yet hitherto no
reason appears why it should be other than the not unusual pride of
person, talent, and birth, a pride auxiliary if not akin to many
virtues, and the natural ally of honorable impulses. But alas! in his
own presence his own father takes shame to himself for the frank
avowal that he is his father – has 'blushed so often to acknowledge
him that he is now braz'd to it'. He hears his mother and the
circumstances of his birth spoken of with a most degrading and
licentious levity – described as a wanton by her own paramour, and
the remembrance of the animal sting, the low criminal gratifications
connected with her wantonness and prostituted beauty assigned as
the reason why 'the whoreson must be acknowledged'. This, and the
consciousness of its notoriety – the gnawing conviction that every
shew of respect is an effort of courtesy which recalls while it
represses a contrary feeling – this is the ever-trickling flow of
wormwood and gall into the wounds of pride, the corrosive virus
which inoculates pride with a venom not its own, with envy, hatred,
a lust of that power which in its blaze of radiance would hide the
dark spots on his disk, with pangs of shame, personally undeserved
and therefore felt as wrongs, and a blind ferment of vindictive
workings towards the occasions and causes, especially towards a
brother whose stainless birth and lawful honors were the constant
remembrancers of *his* debasement, and were ever in the way to
prevent all chance of its being unknown or overlooked and forgotten.
Add to this that with excellent judgement, and provident for the
claims of the moral sense, for that which relatively to the drama is
called poetic justice; and as the fittest means for reconciling the
feelings of the spectators to the horrors of Gloster's after sufferings –
at least, of rendering them somewhat less unendurable (for I will not
disguise my conviction that in this one point the tragic has been
urged beyond the outermost mark and *ne plus ultra* of the dramatic)

– Shakespeare has precluded all excuse and palliation of the guilt incurred by both the parents of the base-born Edmund by Gloster's confession that he was at the time a married man and already blest with a lawful heir of his fortunes. The mournful alienation of brotherly love occasioned by primogeniture in noble families, or rather by the unnecessary distinctions engrafted thereon, and this in children of the same stock, is still almost proverbial on the continent – especially, as I know from my own observation, in the south of Europe – and appears to have been scarcely less common in our own island before the Revolution of 1688, if we may judge from the characters and sentiments so frequent in our elder comedies – the younger brother, for instance, in Beaumont and Fletcher's *Scornful Lady*, on one side, and the Oliver in Shakespeare's own *As You Like It*, on the other. Need it be said how heavy an aggravation the stain of bastardy must have been, were it only that the younger brother was liable to hear his own dishonor and his mother's infamy related by his father with an excusing shrug of the shoulders, and in a tone betwixt waggery and shame.

By the circumstances here enumerated as so many predisposing causes, Edmund's character might well be deem'd already sufficiently explained and prepared for. But in this tragedy the story or fable constrained Shakespeare to introduce wickedness in an outrageous form, in Regan and Goneril. He had read nature too heedfully not to know that courage, intellect, and strength of character were the most impressive forms of power, and that to power in itself, without reference to any moral end, an inevitable admiration and complacency appertains, whether it be displayed in the conquests of a Napoleon or Tamerlane, or in the foam and thunder of a cataract. But in the display of such a character it was of the highest importance to prevent the guilt from passing into utter *monstrosity* – which again depends on the presence or absence of causes and temptations sufficient to *account* for the wickedness, without the necessity of recurring to a thorough fiendishness of nature for its origination. For such are the appointed relations of intellectual power to truth, and of truth to goodness, that it becomes both morally and poetically unsafe to present what is admirable – what our nature compels us to admire – in the mind, and what is most detestable in the heart, as co-existing in the same individual without any apparent connection, or any modification of the one by the other. That Shakespeare has in one instance, that of Iago, approached to this, and that he has done it successfully, is perhaps the most astonishing proof of his genius, and the opulence of its resources. But in the present tragedy, in which he was compelled to present a Goneril and Regan, it was most carefully to be avoided; and, therefore, the one only conceivable addition to the inauspicious influences on the preformation of Edmund's character is given in the information that all the kindly counteractions to the mischievous feelings of shame that might have been derived from co-domestication with Edgar and their common father, had been cut off by an absence from home and a foreign education from boyhood to the present time, and the prospect of its continuance as if to preclude all risk of his interference with the father's views for the elder and legitimate son:

He hath been out nine years, and away he shall again.

It is well worthy notice, that *Lear* is the only serious performance of Shakespeare the interest and situations of which are derived from the assumption of a gross improbability; whereas Beaumont and Fletcher's tragedies are, almost all, founded on some out-of-the-way accident or exception to the general experience of mankind. But observe the matchless judgement of Shakespeare! First, improbable as the conduct of Lear is, in the first scene, yet it was an old story, rooted in the popular faith – a thing taken for granted already, and consequently without any of the *effects* of improbability. Secondly, it is merely the canvas to the characters and passions, a mere *occasion* – not (as in Beaumont and Fletcher) perpetually recurring, as the cause and *sine qua non* of the incidents and emotions. Let the first scene of *Lear* have been lost, and let it be only understood that a fond father had been duped by the hypocritical professions of love and duty on the part of two daughters to disinherit a third, previously, and deservedly, more dear to him, and all the rest of the tragedy would retain its interest undiminished, and be perfectly intelligible. The *accidental* is nowhere the groundwork of the passions, but the κάθογον, that which in all ages has been and ever will be close and native to the heart of man – parental anguish from filial ingratitude, the genuineness of worth, tho' coffered in bluntness, the vileness of smooth iniquity. Perhaps I ought to have added the *Merchant of Venice*; but here too the same remarks apply. It was an old tale; and substitute any other danger than that of the pound of flesh (the circumstance in which the improbability lies), yet all the situations and the emotions appertaining to them remain equally excellent and appropriate.

ı i 84–92

> LEAR ... what can you say to draw
> A third more opulent than your sisters? Speak.
> COR. Nothing, my Lord.
> LEAR Nothing!
> COR. Nothing.
> LEAR Nothing will come of nothing: speak again.
> COR. Unhappy that I am, I cannot heave
> My heart into my mouth: I love your majesty
> According to my bond; nor more nor less.

Something of disgust at the ruthless hypocrisy of her sisters, some little faulty admixture of pride and sullenness in Cordelia's 'Nothing'. It is well contrived to lessen the glaring absurdity of Lear; but the surest plan is that of forcing away the attention from the nursery-tale the moment it has answered its purpose, that of supplying the canvas to paint on. This is done by Kent — his punishment displaying Lear's *moral* incapability of resigning the sovereign power in the very moment of disposing of it.

Kent is the nearest to perfect goodness of all Shakespeare's characters, and yet the most *individualized*. His passionate affection and fidelity to Lear acts on our feelings in Lear's own favor; virtue itself seems to be in company with him.

ı ii 9–14

> EDM.   ... Why brand they us
> With base? with baseness? bastardy? base, base?
> Who in the lusty stealth of nature take
> More composition and fierce quality
> Than doth, within a dull, stale, tired bed,
> Go to the creating a whole tribe of fops.

In this speech of Edmund you see, as soon as a man cannot reconcile himself to reason, how his conscience flies off by way of appeal to nature, who is sure upon such occasions never to find fault, and also how shame sharpens a predisposition in the heart to evil. For it is a profound moral, that shame will naturally generate guilt; the oppressed will be vindictive, like Shylock, and in the anguish of undeserved ignominy the delusion secretly springs up, of getting over the moral quality of an action by fixing the mind on the mere physical act alone.

I iii 13–22. *Goneril authorizes the Steward to be rude to Lear*

The Steward (as a contrast to Kent) is the only character of utter unredeemable *baseness* in Shakespeare. Observe even in this the judgement and invention. What could the willing tool of a Goneril be? Not a vice but this of baseness was left open for him.

I iv. Old age, like infancy, is itself a character. In Lear the natural imperfections are increased by life-long habits of being promptly obeyed. Any addition of individuality would be unnecessary and painful. The relations of others to him, of wondrous fidelity and frightful ingratitude, sufficiently distinguish him. Thus he is the open and ample play-room of *nature's* passions.

The Fool is no comic buffoon to make the groundlings laugh, no forced condescension of Shakespeare's genius to the taste of his audiences. Accordingly, he is *prepared* for – brought into living connection with the pathos of the play, with the sufferings.

> Since my young lady's going into France, sir, the fool hath much pined away.

The Fool is as wonderful a creation as the Caliban – an inspired idiot.

The monster Goneril prepares what is *necessary*, while the character of Albany renders a still more maddening grievance possible; viz. Regan and Cornwall in perfect sympathy of monstrosity. Not a sentiment, not an image that can give pleasure on its own account is admitted. Pure horror when they are introduced, and they are brought forward as little as possible.

I v 43
LEAR   O, let me not be mad, not mad . . .

The mind's own anticipation of madness.

The deepest tragic notes are often struck by a half sense of an impending blow. The Fool's conclusion of this act by a grotesque prattling seems to indicate the dislocation of feeling that has begun and is to be continued.

II i 66–7
EDM.   . . . he replied,
     'Thou unpossessing bastard . . .'

'*Thou unpossessing bastard*' – the secret poison in Edmund's heart – and then poor Gloster's 'Loyal and *natural* boy', as if praising the *crime* of his birth!

II i 91–2
REG.   What, did my father's godson seek your life?
He whom my father named? Your Edgar?

Incomparable! 'What, did *my father's*', etc., compared with the
unfeminine violence of the 'all vengeance comes too short' – and yet
no reference to the guilt but to the accident.

II ii 90–2
CORN.   This is some fellow,
   Who, having been praised for bluntness, doth affect
   A saucy roughness.

In thus placing these profound general truths in such mouths as
Cornwall's, Edmund's, Iago's, etc., Shakespeare at once gives them
and yet shews how indefinite their application.

II iii. Edgar's false madness taking off part of the shock from the true,
as well as displaying the profound difference. Modern attempts at
representing madness lightheadedness, as Otway's, etc.
   In Edgar's ravings Shakespeare all the while lets you see a fixed
purpose, a practical end in view; in Lear's, there is only the brooding
of the one anguish, an eddy without progression.

III iv. What a world's *convention* of agonies! Surely, never was such a
scene conceived before or since. Take it but as a picture for the eye
only, it is more terrific than any a Michael Angelo inspired by a
Dante could have conceived, and which none but a Michael Angelo
could have executed. Or let it have been uttered to the blind, the
howlings of convulsed nature would seem converted into the voice of
conscious humanity.
   The scene ends with the first symptoms of positive derangement –
here how judiciously interrupted by the fifth scene in order to allow
an interval for Lear in full madness to appear.

III vii. What can I say of this scene? My reluctance to think
Shakespeare wrong, and yet –
   Later. Necessary to harmonise their cruelty to their father.

SOURCE: from Notes on *King Lear*.

.   .   .   .   .   .

If indeed *King Lear* were to be tried by the laws which Aristotle established, and Sophocles obeyed, it must be at once admitted to be outrageously irregular; and supposing the rules regarding the unities to be founded on man and nature, Shakespeare must be condemned for arraying his works in charms with which they ought never to have been decorated. I have no doubt, however, that both were right in their divergent courses, and that they arrived at the same conclusion by a different process.

Without entering into matters which must be generally known to persons of education, respecting the origin of tragedy and comedy among the Greeks, it may be observed, that the unities grew mainly out of the size and construction of the ancient theatres: the plays represented were made to include within a short space of time events which it is impossible should have occurred in that short space. This fact alone establishes, that all dramatic performances were then looked upon merely as ideal. It is the same with us: nobody supposes that a tragedian suffers real pain when he is stabbed or tortured; or that a comedian is in fact transported with delight when successful in pretended love.

If we want to witness mere pain, we can visit the hospitals: if we seek the exhibition of mere pleasure, we can find it in ballrooms. It is the representation of it, not the reality, that we require, the imitation, and not the thing itself; and we pronounce it good or bad in proportion as the representation is an incorrect, or a correct imitation. The true pleasure we derive from theatrical performances arises from the fact that they are unreal and fictitious. If dying agonies were unfeigned, who, in these days of civilisation, could derive gratification from beholding them?

Performances in a large theatre made it necessary that the human voice should be unnaturally and unmusically stretched, and hence the introduction of recitative, for the purpose of rendering pleasantly artificial the distortion of the face, and straining of the voice, occasioned by the magnitude of the building. The fact that the ancient choruses were always on the stage made it impossible that any change of place should be represented, or even supposed.

The origin of the English stage is less boastful than that of the Greek stage: like the constitution under which we live, though more barbarous in its derivation, it gives more genuine and more diffused liberty, than Athens in the zenith of her political glory ever possessed. Our earliest dramatic performances were religious, founded chiefly upon Scripture history; and, although countenanced by the clergy, they were filled with blasphemies and ribaldry, such as the most hardened and desperate of the present day would not dare to utter. In these representations vice and the principle of evil were personified; and hence the introduction of fools and clowns in dramas of a more advanced period.

While Shakespeare accommodated himself to the taste and spirit of the times in which he lived, his genius and his judgment taught him to use these characters with terrible effect, in aggravating the misery and agony of some of his most distressing scenes. This result is especially obvious in *King Lear*: the contrast of the Fool wonderfully heightens the colouring of some of the most painful situations, where the old monarch in the depth and fury of his despair, complains to the warring elements of the ingratitude of his daughters.

> ... Spit, fire! spout, rain!
> Nor rain, wind, thunder, fire, are my daughters:
> I tax not you, you elements, with unkindness,
> I never gave you kingdom, call'd you children;
> You owe me no subscription: then, let fall
> Your horrible pleasure; here I stand, your slave,
> A poor, infirm, weak; and despis'd old man.   [III ii]

Just afterwards, the Fool interposes, to heighten and inflame the passion of the scene.

In other dramas, though perhaps in a less degree, our great poet has evinced the same skill and felicity of treatment; and in no instance can it be justly alleged of him, as it may be of some of the ablest of his contemporaries, that he introduced his fool, or his clown, merely for the sake of exciting the laughter of his audiences. Shakespeare had a loftier and a better purpose, and in this respect availed himself of resources, which, it would almost seem, he alone possessed.

SOURCE: from his second lecture in the series *Shakespeare and Milton*, 1811–12.

Charles Lamb   (1810–11)

To see Lear acted, to see an old man tottering about the stage with a walking-stick, turned out of doors by his daughters in a rainy night, has nothing in it but what is painful and disgusting. We want to take him into shelter and relieve him. That is all the feeling which the acting of Lear ever produced in me. But the Lear of Shakespeare cannot be acted. The contemptible machinery by which they mimic the storm which he goes out in, is not more inadequate to represent the horrors of the real elements, than any actor can be to represent Lear: they might more easily propose to personate the Satan of Milton upon a stage, or one of Michael Angelo's terrible figures. The greatness of Lear is not in corporal dimension, but in intellectual: the explosions of his passion are terrible as a volcano: they are storms turning up and disclosing to the bottom that sea, his mind, with all its vast riches. It is his mind which is laid bare. This case of flesh and blood seems too insignificant to be thought on; even as he himself neglects it. On the stage we see nothing but corporal infirmities and weakness, the impotence of rage; while we read it, we see not Lear, but we are Lear, we are in his mind, we are sustained by a grandeur which baffles the malice of daughters and storms; in the aberrations of his reason, we discover a mighty irregular power of reasoning, immethodized from the ordinary purposes of life, but exerting its powers, as the wind blows where it listeth, at will upon the corruptions and abuses of mankind. What have looks, or tones, to do with that sublime identification of his age with that of the *heavens themselves*, when in his reproaches to them for conniving at the injustice of his children, he reminds them that 'they themselves are old'. What gesture shall we appropriate to this? What has the voice or the eye to do with such things? But the play is beyond all art, as the tamperings with it shew: it is too hard and stony; it must have love-scenes and a happy ending. It is not enough that Cordelia is a daughter, she must shine as a lover too. Tate has put his hook in the nostrils of this Leviathan, for Garrick and his followers, the showmen of the scene, to draw the mighty beast about more easily. A happy ending! as if the living martyrdom that Lear had gone through, the flaying of his feelings alive, did not make a fair dismissal from the stage of life the only decorous thing for him. If he is to live and be happy after, if he could sustain this world's burden after, why all this pudder and preparation, why torment us with all this unnecessary sympathy? As if the childish pleasure of getting his gilt robes and sceptre again could tempt him to act over again his misused station, as if at his years, and with his experience, any thing was left but to die.

Lear is essentially impossible to be represented on a stage.

SOURCE: from 'On the Tragedies of Shakespeare', in *The Reflector*, 1810–11.

John Keats   (1818)

> O golden-tongued Romance, with serene lute!
>   Fair plumed Siren, Queen of far-away!
>   Leave melodizing on this wintry day,
> Shut up thine olden pages, and be mute:
> Adieu! for, once again, the fierce dispute
>   Betwixt damnation and impassioned clay
>   Must I burn through; once more humbly assay
> The bittersweet of this Shakespearian fruit:
> Chief poet! and ye clouds of Albion,
>   Begetters of our deep eternal theme!
> When through the old oak forest I am gone,
>   Let me not wander in a barren dream,
> But, when I am consumèd in the fire
> Give me new phoenix wings to fly at my desire.

SOURCE: 'On Sitting Down to Read *King Lear* Once Again', 1818.

P. B. Shelley (1821)

The Athenians employed language, action, music, painting, the dance, and religious institutions, to produce a common effect in the representation of the highest idealisms of passion and of power; each division in the art was made perfect in its kind by artists of the most consummate skill, and was disciplined into a beautiful proportion and unity one towards the other. On the modern stage a few only of the elements capable of expressing the image of the poet's conception are employed at once. We have tragedy without music and dancing; and music and dancing without the highest impersonations of which they are the fit accompaniment, and both without religion and solemnity. Religious institution has indeed been usually banished from the stage. Our system of divesting the actor's face of a mask, on which the many expressions appropriated to his dramatic character might be moulded into one permanent and unchanging expression, is favourable only to a partial and inharmonious effect; it is fit for nothing but a monologue, where all the attention may be directed to some great master of ideal mimicry. The modern practice of blending comedy with tragedy, though liable to great abuse in point of practice, is undoubtedly an extension of the dramatic circle; but the comedy should be as in *King Lear*, universal, ideal, and sublime. It is perhaps the intervention of this principle which determines the balance in favour of *King Lear* against the *Oedipus Tyrannus* or the *Agamemnon*, or, if you will, the trilogies with which they are connected; unless the intense power of the choral poetry, especially that of the latter, should be considered as restoring the equilibrium. *King Lear*, if it can sustain this comparison, may be judged to be the most perfect specimen of the dramatic art existing in the world; in spite of the narrow conditions to which the poet was subjected by the ignorance of the philosophy of the drama which has prevailed in modern Europe. Calderon, in his religious *Autos*, has attempted to fulfil some of the high conditions of dramatic representation neglected by Shakespeare; such as the establishing a relation between the drama and religion, and the accommodating them to music and dancing; but he omits the observation of conditions still more important, and more is lost than gained by the substitution of the rigidly-defined and ever-repeated idealisms of a distorted superstition for the living impersonations of the truth of human passion.

SOURCE: from *A Defence of Poetry*, 1821.

PART TWO

Twentieth-century Studies

Maynard Mack   Actors and Redactors   (1965)

I

King Lear is a problem. Lamb, as everyone knows, judged the role of the king unactable.[1] Thackeray found the play in performance 'a bore', despite his feeling that 'it is almost blasphemy to say that a play of Shakespear's is bad'.[2] Tolstoy deplored 'the completely false "effects" of Lear running about the heath, his conversation with the Fool and all these impossible disguises, failures to recognize and accumulated deaths'.[3] And Bradley, who regarded the play as Shakespeare's greatest work but 'too huge for the stage', drew up a long list of gross 'improbabilities' that no one has succeeded in arguing away.[4]

Among the grosser improbabilities that Bradley points out are Edgar's and Kent's continuing in disguise well after the purposes of disguise have been served; Gloucester's willingness to believe when Edmund shows him the forged letter, that one son would write to another when both are living in the same house, and specifically would put in writing such patricidal meditations as these; Gloucester's failure to show surprise when suddenly, during the fight with Oswald, his escort drops into peasant dialect; Gloucester's determination to go to Dover to commit suicide, as if there were no other way or place of dying; and finally, Edmund's long delay in telling of his order on the lives of Lear and Cordelia after he himself is mortally wounded and has nothing to gain. One could add considerably to the list. Probably we should add to it at least the unlikely nature of Edgar's disguise, the implausibility that neither his disguise nor Kent's is seen through, the fact that Gloucester is blinded for his treason instead of being killed, and the 'almost babyish' goings on, as one reviewer describes them, of the play's first scenes:

The old man who parcels out his kingdom by the map; the daughters who overdo their thanks with a fulsome excess that any child would see through; the simple, obvious contrast of the daughter who cannot say 'thank you' at all; the absurd wrath of the old man over a situation that any father with any daughter could not fail to understand. Then follow undignified things,

acts of schoolboy rudeness, pushings and kickings and trippings up. . . .
How, you ask, are these primitive, rather absurd, folks going to excite in you
the proper tragic emotions?[5]

It will not do to say that these things go unnoticed in performance. What we notice in performance is whatever we bring with us a
capacity to notice, and this includes all we have learned from
reading and discussion. Moreover, anyone who goes to a performance of *King Lear* with his eyes open will soon be aware that what
he watches onstage deviates markedly from the ordinary Shakespearean norms of probability in tragedy. In this play alone among
the tragedies we are asked to take seriously literal disguises that
deceive. Romeo's appearing masked at the Capulet ball and Iago's
advising Roderigo to 'defeat thy favor with a false beard' in
following Desdemona to Cyprus (a circumstance we never hear of
again) obviously put no similar strain on credulity. This is the only
Shakespearean tragedy, too, in which a number of the characters are
conceived in terms of unmitigated goodness and badness, and the
only one, apart from the early *Titus*, where the plot is made up of
incidents each more incredible – naturalistically – than the last:
from the old king's love test and Kent's return to serve him as Caius,
through Edmund's successful rise, Edgar's implausible disguise,
Lear's mad frolic in the storm with beggar and fool, to Gloucester's
leap and Edmund's duel with a nameless challenger who subse-
quently proves to be his brother. This is the heady brew of romance,
not tragedy. If Polonius had seen a performance of *King Lear*, we
can be sure he would have invented a suitable compound name
for its kind: something like 'tragical-comical-historical-pastoral-
romantical', each of which terms might be defended as suiting one
aspect of the play.

Neither will it do to pretend that the problematic *King Lear* is an
invention of the scholar and literary critic. Quite the reverse. All
that is necessary to appreciate the puzzles the play poses onstage is
to think seriously about producing it. Mr Peter Brook, we are told,
described it, while readying it for his recent production with Paul
Schofield in the title role, as 'a mountain whose summit had never
been reached', the way up strewn with the shattered bodies of earlier
visitors – 'Olivier here, Laughton there: it's frightening.'[6] Miss
Margaret Webster, whose experience in directing Shakespeare for
all sorts of actors and audiences is formidable, has called *King Lear*

'the least actable of the four plays' (i.e. *Hamlet, Othello, King Lear,* and *Macbeth*), adding that '*Macbeth* whatever the spiritual or abstract significance with which it has been variously endowed, has always been played for its tremendous dramatic impact', and that '*Othello* insures a sweep of movement which, in the theatre, over-whelms all theoretical debate as to the motivation of its principal characters' – whereas in *Lear* 'the lack of this fundamental theatre economy' makes difficulty.[7] Reviewers and theatre critics have many times voiced similar reservations. When friendly to the play, they have questioned at the very least whether it is possible to perform the first storm scene [III ii] 'so that it looks and sounds like an intelligible piece of theatre'.[8] When unfriendly, they have been more pungent:

You like Shakespeare?
Maybe this is an unfair question, because there is an awful lot of Shakespeare, and you could be pardoned for liking some but not all.
Frankly, that's the way I feel. I have never liked *King Lear*, the excessively wordy and expensive bijou which opened at the National Theatre last night with Louis Calhern in the lead role ...
Mr Calhern munches on most of the scenery and, at one juncture, nearly gnaws the occupants of the first row center, but that is the requirement of the title part and he plays it to what used to be called the hilt.
If you will harken back to the days of your childhood when somebody made you read it, you will recall that the story concerns the mad convolutions of this King and the deceitful behavior of his three daughters and their separate swains. Things get so tough, as you'll remember, that the monarch flips his skimmer.[9]

Give or take a Broadway cliché or two, this approximates many a theatregoer's impression of *King Lear* today, onstage as well as off, and (if the truth were told) many a student reader's.

If *King Lear* as a work of literature is either Shakespeare's greatest achievement, freely compared by its devotees to the sublimest inventions of the artistic imagination, or else a work of childish absurdity inspiring 'aversion and weariness'[10] in others besides Tolstoy; if as a play it is either unsuited to actual stage performing, or on the contrary is only understood when performance has tied together the 'series of intellectual strands' which compose it[11] and drawn our attention 'away from what otherwise might seem puzzling, distasteful, or foolish',[12] clearly we have a problem. . . .

II

The stage history of *King Lear* has been haunted, possibly from its very beginnings, by practical problems of communication with the audience. We do not know why the mad scene in the 'farmhouse', where Lear stages a mock trial of his hard-hearted elder daughters with joint stools to represent them [III vi], is missing from the folio text, printed seventeen years after the play was first acted. The excision may have been made only to shorten the playing time; but it may also have been made, as Professor Kenneth Muir acknowledges in his Arden edition (Introduction, p. xlviii), because the original audiences laughed. If we may judge from the asides that Edgar utters to guide the spectators' response to Lear's antics whenever he is on the stage with him, this possibility was a matter of real concern to the playwright, who knew, as the creator of Malvolio and Hamlet well might, that for the most part contemporary audiences expected madness to be entertaining. One other complete scene missing from the folio text is that in which Kent and a Gentleman discuss Cordelia's reception of the news of her father's sufferings [IV iii]. Here they wrap Cordelia in a mantle of emblematic speech that is usually lost on a modern audience's ear and difficult for a modern actor to speak with conviction. We cannot assume that the Elizabethan actor and audience had our kinds of difficulty with the scene, but what kind did they have – or was this omission too intended merely to shorten the performance?

During the first seventy-five years of its existence, we can make only guesses like these about the history of *King Lear* onstage. We know that on the reopening of the theatres after the Restoration it continued to be played for a time 'as Mr Shakespeare wrote it, before it was altered by Mr Tate' – so John Downes assures us in his *Roscius Anglicanus* (1708), p. 26 – but we do not know what interpretation it was given or what success it met. There may, however, be an answer to the latter question in the fact that the play was before long wholly rewritten by Nahum Tate, so that between 1681, the date of Tate's redaction, and 1838, the year in which Macready restored almost the whole of Shakespeare's original text in a historic production at Covent Garden, Shakespeare's *King Lear* was never, as far as is known, seen in performance. Tate's *King Lear* occupied the stage and throve.

Tate's *King Lear* invites ridicule and deserves it, but is nonetheless illuminating. A line in its verse prologue may be taken to mean (what would not be at all surprising) that Shakespeare's version had ceased to appeal to Restoration playgoers, whose favored diet, apart from comedy, consisted mainly of heroic plays and other subspecies of epic romance. 'Why should', Tate writes,

> These Scenes lie hid, in which we find
> What may at once divert and teach the Mind?

From his dedicatory letter it is clear that he regards his bringing of Shakespeare's scenes before the Restoration public as a pious tribute. He has been emboldened to it by a persuasive friend (a certain Thomas Boteler) and by his own 'Zeal for all the Remains of Shakespeare'. When we open to the text, we discover that his zeal for these remains has carried him to invent a love affair between Cordelia and Edgar, to omit France and Lear's Fool, to give Cordelia a waiting woman named Arante, to supply a happy ending, and to omit, conflate, and rearrange Shakespeare's scenes while rewriting (and reassigning) a good deal of his blank verse. Tate's own description of these efforts, in his letter to Boteler, suggests that, like 'art' in Aristotelian aesthetics, his function has been to help extravagant 'Nature' – 'a Heap of Jewels, unstrung, and unpolisht . . . dazling in their Disorder' – realize its implicit goals. And in a curious literal-minded way, that is exactly what he has done. He has seized on the romance characteristics of Shakespeare's play and restored it to what must have seemed to him its intended genre.

In his version Cordelia is abducted by ruffians at the command of Edmund, who intends to rape her. The ruffians are driven off by Edgar in his Poor Tom disguise – upon which, he reveals himself and receives avowal of his beloved's affection. They *exeunt* together with a convenient flint and steel ('the Implements Of Wand'ring Lunaticks') to light a fire at which she can dry her 'Storm drench'd Garments'. In similar vein, we have a scene in '*A Grotto*' with 'Edmund *and* Regan *amorously seated, listening to Musick*'; a scene in which Edmund receives and reads a billet-doux from each of Cordelia's sisters; an episode in which Gloucester repines at his incapacity to take part in the battle, comparing himself (in a reminiscence of Job) to a 'disabled Courser' who snuffs the fighting from afar and foams 'with Rage'; and another episode in which King Lear, asleep in prison with his head in Cordelia's lap, rouses as Edmund's soldiers enter to hang Cordelia, and holds them at bay, killing two of them, till Edgar and Albany come to his rescue. Tate had an unerring eye for romantic melodrama, and his handling of his original points up very clearly for all who are willing to see them the melodramatic potentialities of the plot from which Shakespeare began.

The other goal of Tate's changes was to clarify motivations. He notes in his dedicatory letter that the virtue of the love affair he has invented for Edgar and Cordelia lies in rendering 'Cordelia's Indifference, and her Father's Passion in the first Scene, probable', and in giving 'Countenance to Edgar's Disguise, making that a generous Design that was before a poor Shift to save his life'. What this means, in detail, is that Tate's Cordelia consciously tempts her father to leave her dowerless in order that Burgundy may refuse her (Tate's play, as noted, omits the King of France altogether), and that Tate's Edgar, whom after her own rejection Cordelia unexpectedly rejects that she may test his devotion, determines to disguise himself (rather than make away with himself in his lover's despair) on the chance that he may yet be of service to her. With the same end in view, Tate firms up the appearances of plausibility throughout. His play opens with Edmund's soliloquy, in order that Edmund may inform us that he has incensed his father against his brother, with

> A Tale so plausible, so boldly utter'd,
> And heightened by such lucky Accident,
> That now the slightest Circumstance confirms him,
> And base-born *Edmund* spight of Law inherits.

Here Edmund is credited with an initial deception of his father offstage and earlier, details remaining unspecified, in order to render more credible the scene in which Gloucester accepts the forged letter. Lear's scene of folly is also prepared for. Immediately following Edmund's soliloquy, Gloucester and Kent enter to him, and when he has been introduced by Gloucester as the 'generous Boy' whose loyalty he means to reward, both men deplore the forthcoming division of the kingdom, bearing witness in advance to Lear's 'Infirmity' of age, his customary 'wild Starts of Passion', and his 'Temper ... ever ... unfixt, chol'rick and sudden'.

Other difficulties are met with similar expedients. Edmund's deception of his brother takes place while Edgar is in a brown study induced by Cordelia's rejection of his love and hardly follows what his brother says. Cornwall's speech marking Edmund for his own –

'Natures of such deep trust we shall much need' – is given by Tate to Regan and extended by a comment which prepares the audience for their subsquent liaison. Gloucester's incriminating letter 'guessingly set down' and sent by 'one that's of a neutral heart And not from one oppos'd' becomes in Tate some despatches Gloucester has himself addressed to the Duke of Cambrai urging help against the sisters, and thus gives Cornwall a more acceptable motive for his cruelty to the old man. When Edgar is seen with his blind father, he tells us immediately why he does not reveal himself: it is for fear the old man's heart will break with extremes of grief and joy. Such is Tate's method throughout. The upshot of his reworking is that there is no longer question but that the play is indeed tragical-comical-historical-pastoral romance and, in a sad, shriveled way, effective 'theatre'. And so it proved for one hundred and fifty-seven years.

III

I have dwelt on Tate's *King Lear* because its stage history is actually longer than any other continuous stage history the play has yet had, and because it established, I think, for a very long time (even after the text had been restored) the performer's approach to the play. Tate's text was the vehicle for all the actors who tried Lear during Pope's and Johnson's century: Betterton, George Powell, Robert Wilkes, Barton Booth, Anthony Boheme, James Quin, Garrick, Spranger Barry, John Kemble, and several more. We know very little about any of them before Garrick. Lear was widely reputed to be Garrick's finest role. His interpretation of the part, as well as the sensibility of his period, may be seen in Edward Tighe's account of his effect on the Montgomery sisters:

The expression of the eldest was wonderful and such as the mighty master would have smiled to see. She gazed, she panted, she grew pale, then again the blood rose in her cheeks, she was elevated, she almost started out of her seat, and *tears began to flow*.[13]

Garrick played the king as an 'honest, well-meaning, ill-used old man',[14] partly because his own stature was unsuited to a more majestic mien, but largely, one suspects, because that was the one genuine human thing that Tate's *King Lear* had left in it. A contemporary describes him in the role as a 'little old white-haired man . . . with spindle-shanks, a tottering gait, and great shoes upon the little feet';[15] and though this was intended to ridicule him, there is no reason to doubt its substantial accuracy. We know from other sources that great age was emphasized in his make-up, that his performance colored 'all the Passions, with a certain Feebleness suitable to the Age of the King',[16] and that in his own view, expressed in a letter to his friend Tighe, '*Lear* is certainly a *Weak* man, it is part of his Character – violent, old and *weakly* fond of his Daughters'.[17] What Garrick saw in the play as a whole, according to Professor G. W. Stone, who had studied Garrick productions of *King Lear* more carefully than any man alive, was a 'Shakespearean play which could surpass competition from all writers of pathetic tragedy and could command the emotional pleasure of tears more successfully than sentimental comedy'.[18]

Garrick was a very great actor and played the play that he saw in *King Lear* with a kind of absolute distinction, if we may judge from the lyrical responses of his contemporaries. But he was the prisoner of the Tate text and perhaps of his audience's expectations. After toying at one point with the idea of restoring the Fool, he abandoned the idea as too 'bold an attempt',[19] and though urged early in his career to put away Tate and give '*Lear* in the *Original, Fool* and all',[20] he never got further than restoring part of the original Shakespearean verse: the story remained 'Tatefied', including love affair, happy ending, and all. With respect to his audience's expectations, Garrick's caution was well advised. We know how Samuel Johnson felt about the death of Cordelia ('I was many years ago so shocked by Cordelia's death that I know not whether I ever endured to read again the last scenes of the play till I undertook to revise them as an editor'),[21] and when George Colman produced a version of the play in 1768 with the love story omitted and (it would seem) the catastrophe restored, it received short shrift. One review observed: '[Colman having] considerably heightened the distress of the catastrophe, we doubt very much whether humanity will give him her voice in preference to Tate';[22] and another:

We have only to observe here, that Mr *Colman* has made several very judicious alterations, at the same time that we think his having restored the original distressed catastrophe is a circumstance not greatly in favour of humanity or delicacy of feeling, since it is now rather too shocking to be borne; and the rejecting the Episode of the loves of Edgar and Cordelia, so happily conceived by Tate, has beyond all doubt, greatly weakened the Piece, both in the perusal and representation . . .[23]

Even Colman had not ventured so far as to restore the Fool. 'After the most serious consideration,' he tells us in his Advertisement to the published copy, 'I was convinced that such a scene "would sink into burlesque" in the representation and would not be endured on the modern stage.'[24]

For all the talent of the eighteenth-century actors, there was nothing in their representations of Lear to give the lie to Lamb's penetrating summary: 'Tate has put his hook in the nostrils of this Leviathan, for Garrick and his followers, the showmen of the scene, to draw the mighty beast about more easily.'[25]

IV

The qualities in *King Lear* which impressed the eighteenth century, when it confronted Shakespeare's play instead of Tate's, may be gathered from Samuel Johnson:

The tragedy of *Lear* is deservedly celebrated among the dramas of Shakespeare. There is perhaps no play which keeps the attention so strongly fixed; which so much agitates our passions and interests our curiosity. The artful involutions of distinct interests, the striking opposition of contrary characters, the sudden changes of fortune, and the quick succession of events, fill the mind with a perpetual tumult of indignation, pity, and hope. There is no scene which does not contribute to the aggravation of the distress or conduct of the action, and scarce a line which does not conduce to the progress of the scene. So powerful is the current of the poet's imagination that the mind which once ventures within it is hurried irresistibly along.[26]

When we place beside this a passage from Hazlitt's review of Edmund Kean's production of 1820, we realize at once that the critical emphasis has significantly changed:

There is something . . . in the gigantic, outspread sorrows of Lear, that seems to elude his grasp, and baffle his attempts at comprehension. . . . [The passion in Lear is] like a sea, swelling, chafing, raging, without bound, without hope, without beacon, or anchor. Torn from the hold of his affections and fixed purposes, he floats a mighty wreck in the wide world of sorrows. . . . Abandoned of fortune, of nature, of reason, and without any energy of purpose, or power of action left – with the grounds of all hope and comfort failing under it – but sustained, reared to a majestic height out of the yawning abyss . . . [the character of Lear] stands a proud monument, in the gap of nature, over barbarous cruelty and filial ingratitude. . . . There are pieces of ancient granite that turn the edge of any modern chisel: so perhaps the genius of no living actor can be expected to cope with Lear. Mr Kean chipped off a bit of the character here and there: but he did not pierce the solid substance, nor move the entire mass.[27]

'Gigantic, outspread', 'like a sea', 'a mighty wreck', 'reared to a majestic height out of the yawning abyss', 'ancient granite', 'mass' – all this is a new world, and it does not stem exclusively from Hazlitt's characteristic intellectual abandon and hyperbole of style. Lamb's testimony, we recall, is essentially the same: 'they might more easily propose to personate the Satan of Milton upon a stage, or one of Michael Angelo's terrible figures'.[28] And the note continues to be heard right down the century to Bradley, whose lectures bring the Romantic expansionist interpretation of Shakespeare to a noble close:

the immense scope of the work; the mass and variety of intense experience which it contains; the interpenetration of sublime imagination ... the vastness of the convulsion both of nature and of human passion ... the strange atmosphere, cold and dark, [enfolding the play's figures] and magnifying their dim outlines like a winter mist; the half-realized sugges-tions of vast universal powers working in the world of individual fates and passions.[29]

The theatre, however, is more conservative than are literary critics. There is very little evidence to show that any of the great nineteenth-century productions of *King Lear* departed essentially from the lines laid down by Garrick's feeble and downtrodden king. Edmund Kean played for passion rather than pathos, and was scolded by the *Examiner* for doing so: '[Lear's] ebullitions of rage cannot be more freely given than by Mr Kean, but there is something in that gifted Actor, which is at war with a delineation of corporeal and mental weakness; and consequently of the pathos which may spring out of them.'[30] Yet even Kean missed the grandeur of the part sadly, as Hazlitt testifies. His madness was 'imbecility instead of phrenzy';[31] 'he drivelled and looked vacant'.[32]

Macready also played *King Lear* for passion, but not to the exclusion of pathos, especially in his relations with the Fool. In Macready's production of 1838 the part of the Fool was restored to the play for the first time since the seventeenth century, together with a text that was now entirely Shakespearean apart from some cuts and rearrangements.[33] Macready had even graver doubts than Garrick's and Colman's about how the Fool would go down with a contemporary audience, and considered omitting the part till after rehearsals were under way. But on describing to a colleague his notion of 'the sort of fragile, hectic, beautiful-faced, half-idiot-looking boy that he should be', it was observed to him that the part should be played by a woman, and this suggestion won him over.[34] We can see here very clearly that the processes of sentimentalizing set in motion by Tate did not come to a halt when Tate's text was replaced. The Restoration and eighteenth century had excluded the Fool as coarse and grotesque; the Victorian period readmitted him, but not as a cracked brain guarding 'incommunicable secrets' – this is Robert Speaight's fine phrase;[35] rather, as a sort of feverish Peter Pan, or a Burne-Jones rendering of Matthew Arnold on Shelley.

Macready's conception of the role of Lear suggests that possibly he had encountered Lamb's strictures on the usual Lear of the theatre ('an old man tottering about the stage with a walking-stick'), or Hazlitt's on Kean. 'The towering range of thought with which [Lear's] mind dilates, identifying the heavens themselves with his griefs,' Macready noted, 'and the power of conceiving such vast imaginings, would seem incompatible with a tottering trembling frame'.[36] But as with Macready's Fool, so with his King. He was moving in his tragic kingliness and paternity; he spoke the first curse with a terrifying 'still intensity',[37] the second with a 'screaming vehemence' that 'greatly exceeded in power the first',[38] and, like all his predecessors, drew 'sighs and tears which shook the audience' when he woke to recognize Cordelia.[39] But nothing in the reviews suggests that he brought to life, or was in any way aware of, the brooding, mythic, almost apocalyptic hints and intimations that for most of us today lie just beyond the story of domestic pathos and seem already to be glimpsed fitfully in the sentences of Hazlitt and Lamb, quoted earlier, and in Coleridge's superb outburst on III iv:

O what a world's convention of agonies is here! All external nature in a storm, all moral nature convulsed – the real madness of Lear, the feigned madness of Edgar, the babbling of the Fool, the desperate fidelity of Kent. Surely such a scene was never conceived before or since! Take it but as a picture for the eye only, it is more terrific than any which a Michel Angelo, inspired by a Dante, could have conceived, and which none but a Michel Angelo could have executed.[40]

Though Macready was an exceptionally fine actor, like Garrick, and like Garrick one of very few of the older actors who could feel his way to a total conception of a role rather than play a pastiche of electrifying moments in the manner of Kean, he remained the prisoner of conceptions that had got their start with Tate. So did the remainder of the nineteenth century. The role of Lear was altogether sentimentalized by Phelps; played by Booth, according to one review, like 'an angry, conventional Polonius',[41] and according to Tennyson, in a way 'most interesting, most touching and powerful, but not a bit like Lear';[42] and then 'degraded' by Irving ('to the level of a doddering lunatic')[43] in a performance after which one drama critic is reported to have said to his colleagues: 'Now who's going to tell the truth about this?'[44] To sum up with the verdict of a witty student of mine,[45] himself a promising actor, the Lears of the nineteenth century after Macready may 'best be pictured as a halting procession of senile old men, trudging at various rates of speed toward the sacred grove of Bathos'.

V

Two changes by Kean's and Macready's time 'revised' the impression of *King Lear* onstage almost as thoroughly as Tate had done. One was the use of stage machines. Already in Kean's production of 1820 there had been provided for the heath scenes a river overflowing its banks and 'scenic trees . . . composed of distinct boughs which undulated in the wind, each leaf. . . a separate pendant rustling with the expressive sound of nature itself'.[46] When Macready produced his wholly Shakespearean *King Lear* in 1838, such effects were continued and improved. 'From beginning to end', said the reviewer for *John Bull*:

the scenery of the piece . . . corresponds with the period, and with the circumstances of the text. The castles are heavy, sombre, solid; their halls adorned with trophies of the chase and instruments of war; druid circles rise in spectral loneliness out of the heath, and the 'dreadful pother' of the elements is kept up with a verisimilitude which beggars all that we have hitherto seen attempted. Forked lightnings, now vividly illumine the broad horizon, now faintly coruscating in small and serpent folds, play in the distance; the sheeted element sweeps over the foreground, and then leaves it in pitchy darkness; and wind and rain howl and rush in 'tyranny of the open night'.[47]

The persistence of this taste in staging *Lear* through the rest of the century may be best gauged from the comment of G. C. D. Odell, to whose pioneering *Shakespeare from Betterton to Irving* all studies of Shakespeare in performance are necessarily in debt. It was the opinion of Odell, writing as late as 1920, that this passage from *John*

Bull describes an ideal performance – 'a nobly conceived and ably executed revival of a great tragedy; in intention nothing could surpass it even to-day'.[48]

The other theatrical change that shielded nineteenth-century audiences from the savage impact of the play as Shakespeare wrote it was localization in time. Those who have *King Lear* fresh in mind will recall that the primitivism of its atmosphere and the folk tale cast of the 'choosing' episode in the first scene are offset continually by a vivid contemporaneous Elizabethanism, giving the effect, as so often in Shakespeare, of no single time and therefore all time. No member of Shakespeare's original audience, hearing Edgar's chatter on the life of farm communities [III iv] or Lear's on urban knavery [IV vi], or looking at the symbolic hierarchies of state and family in their 'robes and furr'd gowns' [I i], could doubt for a moment that the play was about a world with which he was deeply and centrally engaged. Such engagement by Victoria's time was a commodity not easily to be enjoyed.

We must be careful not to exaggerate the impairments suffered by Shakespearean drama when replacement of the apron stage by curtain and proscenium increased the imaginative distance between spectator and action; or when elaboration of scenery and scene changing and stage machines impinged on the role that Shakespeare had assigned to poetry, sometimes rendering it superfluous, sometimes swallowing it up in noise (as happened invariably with the storm scene in *Lear*), and always so far extending the playing time as to require cutting the poetic text severely. We must not exaggerate the losses, but some loss there certainly was, increased in the case of *Lear* by the sentimentalization which was a legacy from Tate. When to these factors was added the archaeological impulse of the nineteenth-century stage to convert poetry and myth into history, something like a dead end was in sight for all plays like *King Lear* in which poetry and myth contribute most of what rises above the level of *drame bourgeois*.

It made little difference which historical epoch was chosen: Macready played the play with druid circles, Charles Kean as belonging to 'the Anglo-Saxon era of the eighth century',[49] Irving as of 'a time, shortly after the departure of the Romans, when the Britons would naturally inhabit the houses [that the Romans had] left vacant'.[50] The result was to mask the play's archetypal character, distancing its cruelties as the errors of a barbarous age with no compelling relation to oneself. This attitude the abrupt opening scene too easily encourages in any case. It so encouraged it in Samuel Johnson that he temporarily lost his usual sensitivity to what is *semper, ubique, et ab omnibus*:

Perhaps if we turn our thoughts upon the barbarity and ignorance of the age to which this story is referred, it will appear not so unlikely as while we estimate Lear's manners by our own. Such preference of one daughter to another, or resignation of dominion on such conditions, would be yet credible if told of a petty prince of Guinea or Madagascar.[51]

And it continued to encourage opinion of this kind for a century and a half. Here is the reaction of a London theatre critic in 1909:

The people remind you of some simple South Sea Islanders in some 18th century traveller's narrative – peering through the wrong end of a telescope, expressing their emotions by uncouth dances, and filled with delight by the present of some coloured beads.[52]

VI

The eighteenth-century *King Lears* with their benign ending were perhaps the natural product of an age which held that under the appearances of things lay an order of justice which it was the job of literature to imitate, not to hide. Those of the nineteenth century, in which Shakespeare's text had been increasingly restored but was trammeled in stage effects and historical place and time, gave equally natural expression to the principles of a period whose best poet (happily he did not often practice his own preachment) said that poetry was made of the real language of real men, and whose most systematic critic imagined he had engaged what was important about literature when he talked of *race, milieu, moment*.

In a number of ways, our own century seems better qualified to communicate and respond to the full range of experience in *King Lear* than any previous time, save possibly Shakespeare's own. We are familiar with the virtues of the bare unlocalized Elizabethan platform stage, and can recover them at will, with the immense added resource of modern lighting. After two world wars and Auschwitz, our sensibility is significantly more in touch than our grandparents' was with the play's jagged violence, its sadism, madness, and processional of deaths, its wild blends of levity and horror, selfishness and selflessness, and the anguish of its closing scene. We have not the Victorians' difficulty, today, in discerning behind its foreground story of a family quarrel intimations of mortality on a far grander scale: we know that we go to see in Lear one who is as much a portent as a man[53] – 'a great oak struck by lightning',[54] 'a stricken Colossus',[55] a 'broken column at whose feet others bewail their lesser woes',[56] a figure out of 'Blake, with a suggestion of Dürer'[57] – and that the play as a whole, with its kings, beggars, fools, blindness, madness, and storm, casts shadows of unearthly grandeur on any twentieth-century imagination that will submit itself to it. Its fascination for us is plain from the statistics of performance. During the eighteenth century there were nineteen distinct productions on the London stage, five by Garrick; during the nineteenth century, twenty-one, fourteen by 1845, but only six in the sixty-two years from 1858 to 1920. Already (to 1962) in this century there have been twenty-three London (and I include Stratford-on-Avon) productions, nineteen beginning with 1931, or better than one each biennium through the past three decades. As a critic for the London *Times* wrote in reviewing Olivier's performance in 1946, it has been 'a period rich in notable Lears'.[58]

Rich indeed. Without going outside the English stage or the period since 1930, one may name John Gielgud, William Devlin, Randall Ayrton, Donald Wolfit, Laurence Olivier, Stephen Murray, Michael Redgrave, Charles Laughton, Paul Scofield. Some of these have taken the part in as many as four separate productions,[59] and all have played it with gratifying and instructive differences. Interpretations have ranged from Gielgud's monarch of 'Olympian grandeur'[60] in 1940 (from all accounts the greatest performance of our time) – through Olivier's 'Swell-head the Tyrant' of 1946, an interpretation containing, we are told, 'an illuminating remnant of the fussy, feeble, Justice Shallow'[61] – through Redgrave's towering ruin of 1953, who even in the opening scene was 'almost too decrepit to draw his huge sword'[62] – to Laughton's uncompromising repudiation of the 'grand' Lear in 1959, in favor of an intense portrayal of a smaller, more immediately sympathetic figure, less king than father, less father than 'representative of the common man',[63] whose physical appearance is said to have reminded spectators of 'Father Christmas' and 'Old King Cole'.[64]

Interpretations of the play as a whole have also run the gamut. The stress of Byam Shaw's production in 1959 for Laughton was 'modern', 'realistic', 'human' – calculated 'to put the play within the scope and comprehension of a mass Shakespearean audience'.[65] The

Lewis Casson–Granville-Barker production of 1940 for Gielgud appears to have been largely based on Barker's intuition of 'mega-lithic grandeur' in the play as in the monarch.[66] Gielgud's 1955 production, with contributions by the Japanese designer Isamu Noguchi, sought a setting and costumes which 'would be free of historical and decorative conventions, so that the timeless, univer-sal, and mythical quality of the story may be clear'[67] – though the effect proved at odds with the intent and, as Gielgud recalled later, 'little short of disastrous'.[68] In 1962, Peter Brook tried for a 'frame of reference' as 'Beckettian' as possible, and a 'world . . . like Beckett's . . . in a constant state of decomposition', even down to costumes of leather 'textured to suggest long and hard wear' and furniture 'once sturdy, but now decaying back into its hard, brown grain'.[69] A year earlier (to cross abruptly an ocean and a continent) Herbert Blau of the San Francisco Actors' Workshop had mounted the play with a group of Method actors by relating it for them to Beckett and Genet.[70]

All this is healthy, no doubt, and shows the vitality of the play as well as of the twentieth-century theatre. But the question as to whether it is Shakespeare's play that is communicated by these means is not settled by the presence of enthusiastic audiences and rave reviews (even supposing, which is far from the truth, that most of these productions drew such audiences and reviews): Garrick's Tatefied and sentimentalized text also drew them, and so did Macready's coruscating lightning and leaves. If I may consult my own experience during the same three decades, I am obliged to register the suspicion that our stage, for all its advantages, and with a few honorable exceptions, has worked out ways of altering the effect of Shakespeare's text which are quite as misleading as any our ancestors used, and seem to spring, at least in large part, from the same determination to rationalize, or generalize, or unify according to a particular plan what is not regular, not rational, or not really unifiable on that plan.

VII

The siren's rock on which efforts to bring *King Lear* to the stage (as well as, in some quarters, critical efforts to interpret it) oftenest split is the desire to motivate the bizarre actions that Shakespeare's play calls for in some 'reasonable' way. This desire lay behind many of Tate's alterations, as we saw. It helped influence the nineteenth century to rationalize absurdity and barbarity by attributing them (in the manner exemplified by Dr Johnson's allusion to petty princes of Madagascar) to some appropriately remote and barbarous time or place. It prompted Bradley to regard his considerable list of inconsistencies and implausibilities as serious 'dramatic defects'. And it seems to have misled Mr Empson, usually an astute critic, into seeing in Lear's speeches to Gloucester in Dover fields a sex interest that is 'ridiculous and sordid' in so elderly a man[71] – as indeed it may have to be considered if we assume that the relation of Lear to his speeches is the same as that of (say) Hedda Gabler to hers.

Such expectancies have disposed most directors and actors in our period to ignore Shakespeare's clear signposts (informing us that psychological structure is not what we are to look for) in favor of rationalistic expedients of varying absurdity. Laughton's 'funny old Father Christmas in a white nightgown, mild and chubby, looking forward to a party where he is to give away the presents',[72] was, among other things, a way of supplying character-motivation to Lear's perplexing behavior in the opening scene, as was Gielgud's senile mandarin of 1955, 'all mutterings, shakings, graspings, and palsied twitchings'.[73] But these solutions were purchased at high cost to the 'great image of authority' – inviolable, charismatic, a kind of *primum mobile* (as the monarch always is in the Renaissance) of the political and social macrocosm, and properly too its chief stay against anarchy. This is the Lear which Shakespeare's opening scene calls for and without which both the subsequent collapse of the image and the anarchy generated by its removal lose force. Something like a climax in this rationalizing mode was reached in Peter Brook's production for Paul Scofield in 1962. There in I iv, evidently to justify Goneril's complaints about her father's retinue and thus motivate her insolence to him, Lear's knights literally demolished the set, throwing plates and tankards, upending the heavy table on which presumably the king's dinner was soon to be served, and behaving in general like boors[74] – as if the visible courtesy of their spokesman earlier [I iv 54–78], Albany's significant unawareness of what Goneril is complaining about, and Lear's explicit description of his knights:

> My train are men of choice and rarest parts,
> That all particulars of duty know,
> And in the most exact regard support
> The worships of their name –

had no existence in the play.

Lear is not an easy domestic guest: this we know from his conduct in the first scene, and from however much we may choose to believe of the list of grievances his daughter catalogues to Oswald in I iii. But to justify Goneril is to obscure from the audience the relentless movement by which the man who is cynically humored so long as (in the Fool's words) he bears bags is maneuvered into surrender by two daughters whom Kent calls 'dog-hearted', Albany calls 'Tigers, not daughters', and the gentlest voice in the play calls 'Shame of ladies!' This movement begins to take shape in I i ('We must do something and i' th' heat'); is implemented, with Oswald as tool, in I iii ('Put on what weary negligence you please . . . I'd have it come to question'); is reported on and perhaps expanded in the letters Goneril sends Regan, which decide the latter to be absent from her house when Lear arrives there; and is finally revealed, in II iv, as a visible trap, between whose ponderous jaws, whether by studied plan or opportunism, Lear is first squeezed dry of all his remaining dignities and illusions and then spat away.

The destruction of Goneril's dining hall by Lear and his knights was so vivid an act of aggression in the Brook production that it fixed Lear in the mind as not only a vindictive but a powerfully supported figure, who might easily take back his gift of the kingdom at any time and was silly not to. It also obscured the fact that in the play's terms, Lear being her father, nothing can possibly justify Goneril. As Lear feels that Cordelia in scene i 'wrench'd' his 'frame of nature From the fix'd place' – an image which invites us to see beyond it the ruining of a great building or even a rupture in the cosmic frame itself – so Goneril's actions are eventually seen by Albany to be violences striking at the very foundation of the natural order. On the one hand, she is like the flood which 'cannot be border'd certain in itself', and will, given the opportunity, as Ulysses says in *Troilus and Cressida*, 'make a sop of all this solid globe'; on the other hand, she is like the branch that tears itself from the fostering tree. Throughout the play, Shakespeare brilliantly humanizes both Goneril and Regan by the shifting passions and appetites he traces in their speech, but this is a different matter from 'motivation'. The motivation of the sisters lies not in what Lear has done to them, but in what they are. The fact that they are paradigms of evil rather than (or as well as) exasperated spoilt children whose patience has been exhausted gives them their stature and dramatic force.

VIII

The newest and most unpromising form that efforts to rationalize *King Lear* have taken is that of playing what is called in today's theatrical jargon the 'subtext'. A play's subtext, according to the views of those who favor this approach, is the underlying 'reality' to which its verbal text points: 'language is gesture, there is a life to which the words give life, and it is to that life we [are] finally responsible' (see below, p. 68). As a device for training actors, I am willing to believe that this conception has merit. It derives from but extends familiar Stanislavsky techniques which seek to help the actor transform the disjunct speeches and gestures of an acting part as written into some sort of organic and, as it were, psychosomatic continuum. But in the hands of many directors in today's theatre, where the director is a small god, subtext easily becomes a substitute for text and a license for total directorial subjectivity – in ways that may readily be illustrated from the recent productions of Peter Brook and Herbert Blau.

The most obvious result of subtextualizing is that director and (possibly) actor are encouraged to assume the same level of authority as the author. The sound notion that there is a life to which the words give life can with very little stretching be made to mean that the words the author set down are themselves simply a search for the true play, which the director must intuit in, through, and under them. Once he has done so, the words become to a degree expendable. This view of a text probably does no harm when applied to plays whose destiny is to be consumed this season and forgotten next. In these, directors and actors often collaborate throughout rehearsals and trial run, and the resulting 'vehicle', as it is so rightly called, conveys the talents of both.

Directing a classical text might, one supposes, be conducted on more modest principles. And in theory it is. Modern directors of Shakespeare, no less than Garrick, profess to love him. As Blau points out in his interesting and sensitive account of his San Francisco production, 'We have done some plays in which we have thrown a text to the winds of our own psychological behavior – but who is going to feel superior to *King Lear*?'[75] A page earlier, in a description of Blau's management of the heath scene, we meet with this:

Let me say this: we lost words. To do what we tried to do, especially on the heath, and make every word absolutely intelligible is almost impossible. There was an incredible amount of detailed activity, incessant motion – what we were after was the muscular projection of the interior nature of madness. I am not saying that every word shouldn't be intelligible; but I don't think it was the fault of the actors' methodology . . . so much as what was required of them. Nor am I saying that the scenes were unintelligible. Far from that. Whatever they didn't have, one felt the storm as a nightmare; one saw the descent to absolute dispossession on the part of the King; one felt the visceral dominance of lunacy in that lucid trial of the daughters. To the extent that the words are the life of the design, we did everything we could to respect them. Even our improvisations were not improvisations emancipated from the text; but language is gesture, there is a life to which the words give life, and it is to that life we were finally responsible. But let me emphasize again: we relinquished clarity only in those marginal cases where what was being done couldn't be done without relinquishing it – given those circumstances and those actors.

In short, even in *King Lear*, when the chips are down for the subtextualist, rather than relinquish 'what we were after', or 'what was being done' by directorial inspiration, he will relinquish the author's text.

And what *was* being done on this occasion? How marginal were the situations in which clarity had to be relinquished? We may gather an answer from Blau's description of the staging of the storm. It is worth attention because it shows the often very fine creative imagination by which, in the modern directorial theatre, Shakespeare's own imaginative effort, his text, is swallowed up. 'The unifying factor' in the storm scene, says Mr Blau, 'was the music, chaos dazzled by its own coherence'. The phrase alone might give us pause: how will a mere actor make out where chaos itself is dazzled? But we hasten on to discover how the bedazzlement was achieved:

It was an electronic score. . . . The basic sound was a kind of drone of vast amplitude . . . composed . . . of three elements: the sound of Lear's voice saying the word 'I' into an open piano; a single pure pitch; and a cello note – which was a subliminal factor, buried in the storm, but which emerged as the storm progressed as an impulse of healing. That cello note later emerged in the sleep music of Lear, in the reunion with Cordelia. Exquisite, lovely then. But in the storm it was part of the swell of derangement. The three elemental sounds were impacted on tape, improvised upon, made dense until the drone appeared, like the troubled breathing of the earth projected by Lear upon the universe. Over this was imposed another sound track of accidental electronic sounds; during the whole sequence, perhaps about thirty-five minutes, during which the sound never stopped, these occurred at unpredictable moments. Thus, the scene could never be the same. They came whirling or hissing or singing out of the atmosphere, and the actors had to play with them. Then there was still another sequence of sounds, orchestrated explicitly with Lear's 'Blow winds' speech – in which the synchronization of language, sound, and action was meant to establish a perfect harmony of derangement, Lear and the storm locked by sound in a kind of cosmic embrace. Some of the sounds were fierce, indescribably active; and the Fool danced half-witted in their ambience, like an hallucinated lightning bug.

. . . Tom screamed. The Fool screamed. Lear screamed. Adding the unison of their derangement to the sound and fury of the storm. This unison was what we worked for. In the body. They moved like animals, improvising on each other's gestures and sounds, borrowing them from each other, virtually changing identities. A metamorphosis. A sound would screech down from above; Tom would seem to pluck it out of the air; Lear would move as if he had created it. The Fool would slither between them, recovering the cloak which Lear had given Tom, jealous that his function was being preëmpted. Synesthesia. We worked for a precise disorder of sense impressions. . . .[76]

Some of the ideas here are fascinating. They would be superbly at home in *King Lear* rewritten as a tragic ballet. But the homely circumstance that the reader of this hypnotic account must not lose sight of is that, onstage for thirty-five minutes during the heath scenes, three sequences of electronic sounds – some 'fierce, indescribably active', one sequence a complete variable occurring 'at unpredictable moments', all the sequences overlaid by wild screams and accompanied by 'incessant motion . . . the muscular projection of the interior nature of madness' – competed for the spectator's attention with Shakespeare's words. We may safely guess which factor won. But this, I suspect, was not the only or perhaps the chief damage. Shakespeare's words were intended, with the help of a few rumblings of cannon balls in the Elizabethan theatre's upper storey, to produce a storm in the audience's imagination. When instead the storm is produced *for* the audience with such brilliance of detail by nontextual means, Shakespeare's text is left without a function, and so is the audience's imagination. The spectator understands the storm in the sense or senses the director has attached to it; he is not compelled, as he is by Shakespeare's poetry, to grope for meanings and relations and to compound them for himself.

IX

This point becomes clear if we consider a further aspect of the Brook and Blau productions. Mr Blau's subtext was, he tells us, based on Nothing – that is to say on the 'nothing' uttered by Cordelia in her first answer to her father's question, and in his reply: 'Nothing will come of nothing.' Following this lead, the San Francisco production presented in Edgar's disguising an effort to feel 'what it is like *to become nothing*', in Lear's madness the upsurge of 'Nothing', in Goneril's and Regan's stripping away of Lear's knights a 'rhythm of reduction, back to Nothing'; in Cordelia's 'no cause, no cause' the mystery of what issues from Nothing – her *acte gratuit* of I i, and later her gratuitous charity. Even the exit of the three madmen from the heath was contrived on a 'movement ... with a regressive motion, as if Lear were thinking back to that elusive Nothing'.[77]

One is impelled again to pay tribute to the subtlety of the director's imagination. Once more, however, to the extent that any of his intention managed to cross the footlights as meaning, directorial imagination has run away with the play. Shakespeare's text unquestionably includes the arabesque on Nothing that Blau notes, together with many cognate allusions of the same character; but in the play itself all these must struggle for *lebensraum* with other allusions and patterns of widely different colorings and contrasting implications. They are not extrapolated out, as here, to suffuse the whole with one hue. How subjective and simplistic the view of *King Lear* is that finally emerges from this kind of reading may be assessed from Blau's comment on suicide, 'In this world', he writes, 'we are back, as the Bishop says in [Genet's] *The Balcony*, in the sacred clearing where suicide at last becomes possible. In fact, the subtext constantly brings the characters to that question which Gloucester makes explicit and which Camus thought the major philosophical question of our time: why not suicide?'[78]

This is intoxicating stuff – but what resemblance does it bear to the play that Shakespeare wrote? One casts about in vain to name the characters that the play 'constantly brings' to the question of suicide. Gloucester? Yes, but only once. Lear? Not a trace of it. Edgar? Only to thwart his father's intent, and in his mad speeches as the unjust serving-man on the heath. Cordelia, Kent, Albany, the Fool? Unimaginable. Not really imaginable for Edmund or Cornwall either. Only Goneril in the play actually commits suicide, and her act, undertaken to avoid retribution for her poisoning of Regan and her plot on her husband's life, is hardly what Genet and Camus had in mind.

According to Charles Marowitz's 'log' of the Brook production, for which he was assistant director, the search for the subtext of *King Lear* in London yielded equally exhilarating results. 'Everywhere one looks', he notes, summarizing Brook's conception of the play and presumably his own,

one sees only the facade and emblems of a world, and, ironically, as characters acquire sight, it enables them to see only into a void. . . . It is not so much Shakespeare in the style of Beckett as it is Beckett in the style of Shakespeare, for Brook believes that the cue for Beckett's bleakness was given by the merciless *King Lear*.[79]

Merciless, it may be. Yet Marowitz confesses that it took tinkering to give the play the bleakness that Beckett is supposed to have derived from it. 'One problem with *Lear*', he notes, in a sentence that seems to contemplate the problem as the driver of a bulldozer contemplates a tree, 'is that like all great tragedies it produces a catharsis. The audience leaves the play shaken but assured.' Clearly this would not do in a production of *King Lear* describable as 'Beckett in the style of Shakespeare'. Something had to be done, 'and i' th' heat'.

Accordingly, 'to remove the tint of sympathy usually found at the end of the Blinding Scene',

Brook cut Cornwall's servants and their commiseration of Gloucester's fate. Once the second 'vile jelly' had been thumbed out of his head, Gloucester is covered with a tattered rag and shoved off in the direction of Dover. Servants clearing the stage collide with the confused blind man and rudely shove him aside. As he is groping about pathetically, the house-lights come up – the action continuing in full light for several seconds afterwards. If this works, it should jar the audience into a new kind of adjustment to Gloucester and his tragedy. The house-lights remove all possibility of aesthetic shelter, and the act of blinding is seen in a colder light than would be possible otherwise.[80]

At the end of the play, where 'the threat of a reassuring catharsis is even greater', Marowitz suggested that

instead of silence and repose, which follows the last couplet, it might be disturbing to suggest another storm – a greater storm – was on the way. Once the final lines have been spoken, the thunder could clamour greater than ever before, implying that the worst was yet to come. Brook seconded the idea, but instead of an overpowering storm, preferred a faint, dull rumbling which would suggest something more ominous and less explicit.[81]

X

After such knowledge, what forgiveness – for those who would be content to see *King Lear* as Shakespeare wrote it? To censure virtuosity and experiment seems ungenerous: no one good custom must be allowed to corrupt the world. To insist on fidelity to ancient texts may be pedantic: it is the scholar's habit at his least endearing. Yet the question that inevitably arises in the mind after studying either of these recent treatments of *King Lear* (or indeed, most we have been given in my lifetime) is Robert Frost's question: what to make of a diminished thing? However liberating the conception of subtext may be in theory, it is reductive in practice, as has been the directorial theatre generally.[82] Both are likely to persuade to 'nameless somethings' (as Pope calls unformed creative impulses in his great lines on literary distortion in the *Dunciad*) in preference to the author's text; both encourage emphasizing a part of the text in lieu of the whole and amplifying that part so as to unmake the intricacies and overset the balance of the original; even in the most sensitive hands, their effect is to do the work that in poetic drama is properly the work of the audience's imagination, and thus make 'entertainment' of what should be participation in a ritual enactment of one's own deepest experience; and this is to say nothing of the cuttings, rearrangements, and reapportionings which are also justified in their name.

It is true that Shakespeare's play, with a little adjusting, can be made to yield Brook, Blau, and Beckett as it was formerly made to yield Tate and Garrick. Like the spokesman of *Leaves of Grass* it is large, it contains multitudes; and it is inexhaustibly patient of the images of ourselves we thrust upon it . . . What is also true is that our extrapolations from it in order to get a hook into the nostrils of Leviathan do no permanent harm. The mountain remains, as Brook says, long after those who seek to climb it have been decently interred. Does this mean that nothing like the whole play is actable, that the best we can do in the theatre, as so often in our criticism, is to capture one dimension of it at a time? Or does it mean that something like the whole play might be actable and knowable if we

were to come to it with other ends in view than rationalizing the
irrational, regularizing the irregular, and unifying on a particular
plan what cannot be unified on such a plan?

SOURCE: *King Lear in Our Time* (1965).

NOTES

1. 'On the Tragedies of Shakespeare' (1808) in *The Life, Letters, and
Writings of Charles Lamb*, ed. Percy Fitzgerald (n.d.), IV 205.
2. *The Letters and Private Papers of William Makepeace Thackeray*, ed.
Gordon Ray (1945), II 292.
3. L. N. Tolstoy, 'On Shakespeare and the Drama', tr. V. Tchertkoff, in
Fortnightly Review, NS, LXXXVII (1907), 66.
4. A. C. Bradley, *Lectures on Shakespearean Tragedy* (1904), pp. 247,
256 ff.
5. A. B. Walkley in *The Times*, 1909; reprinted in *The English Dramatic
Critics*, ed. James Agate (1932), p. 270.
6. As quoted by Charles Marowitz, Brook's associate in the production,
in '*Lear* Log', in *Encore*, X (1963), 22.
7. *Shakespeare Today* (1957), p. 214.
8. Brooks Atkinson in *New York Times*, 26 Dec 1950, reviewing the Louis
Calhern–John Housman production.
9. John McLain, *New York Journal-American*, 26 Dec 1950.
10. Tolstoy, op. cit. in *Fortnightly Review*, NS, LXXXVI (1906), 981.
11. Brook's opinion, as quoted by Marowitz, op. cit. p. 21.
12. Arnold Szyfman, '*King Lear* on the Stage: a producer's reflections', in
Shakespeare Survey, XIII (1960), 71.
13. *Private Correspondence of David Garrick*, ed. James Boaden (1831), I
157.
14. Thomas Wilkes, *A General View of the Stage* (1759), p. 241.
15. Sir John Hill, *The Actor, or A Treatise on the Art of Playing* (1755),
p. 151.
16. [Samuel Foote], *A Treatise of the Passions* (1747), p. 22.
17. *Letters of David Garrick*, ed. D. M. Little and G. M. Kahrl (1963), II
682.
18. See his 'Garrick's Production of *King Lear*: a study in the temper of
the eighteenth-century mind', in *Studies in Philology*, XLV (1948), 91. See
also A. C. Sprague, *Shakespearean Players and Performances* (1953), pp. 21–
40, and *Shakespeare and the Actors* (1944), pp. 281–97, and K. A. Burnim,
David Garrick, Director (1961), pp. 141–51.
19. Thomas Davies, *Dramatic Miscellanies* (1783), II 267.
20. *An Examen of the New Comedy, Call'd The Suspicious Husband, With
Some Observations upon Our Dramatick Poetry and Authors, To Which Is
Added, a Word of Advice to Mr G-rr-ck* (1747), p. 35.
21. 'General Observations' on *King Lear* in his edition of Shakespeare
(1765), reprinted in *Samuel Johnson on Shakespeare*, ed. W. K. Wimsatt, Jr
(1960), p. 98.

22. *The Theatrical Review, or The New Companion to the Playhouse* (1772), I 213.

23. Ibid. p. 334. In his *Shakespeare from Betterton to Irving* (1920) G. C. D. Odell assigns this quotation – I believe erroneously – to *The Theatrical Register, or A Complete List of Every Performance at the Different Theatres, for the year 1769*, a publication I have not been able to identify.

24. *The History of King Lear, As It Is Performed at the Theatre Royal in Covent Garden* (1768), p. v. This published version retains Tate's ending.

25. Op cit. IV 206.

26. Op. cit. p. 96.

27. *London Magazine*, I (1820), 687.

28. Op. cit. IV 205.

29. Op. cit. 247.

30. *Examiner* (London), 2 Mar 1823.

31. *Courier* (London), 25 Apr 1820.

32. *London Magazine*, I 689.

33. Kean, in 1823, had replaced much of Tate's fifth Act, including the happy ending, and had been criticized by reviewers for not extending his restorations to the whole.

34. *Diaries of William Charles Macready*, ed. William Toynbee (1912), I 438.

35. 'The Actability of *King Lear*: reminiscences of thirty years of performances', in *Drama Survey*, II (1962), 51.

36. *Macready's Reminiscences and Selections from His Diaries and Letters*, ed. Sir Frederick Pollock (1875), I 207.

37. *Examiner*, 4 Feb 1838.

38. William Winter, *Shakespeare on the Stage* (1915), p. 401. See also Lady Juliet Pollock, *Macready as I Knew Him* (1884), p. 104.

39. Winter, op. cit. p. 402.

40. *Lectures and Notes on Shakespeare ... Now First Collected by T. Ashe* (1908), p. 341.

41. *Bell's Life in London, and Sporting Chronicle*, 19 Feb 1881.

42. Reported by Winter, op. cit. p. 449.

43. H. B. Baker, *A History of the London Stage and Its Famous Players, 1576–1903* (1904), p. 305.

44. See Laurence Irving, *Henry Irving, the Actor and His World* (1951), p. 551.

45. Donald D. Knight, formerly of the Yale School of Drama.

46. George Raymond, *Memoirs of Robert William Elliston, Comedian* (Concluding Series, 1845), pp. 232–3.

47. *John Bull*, 28 Jan 1838, XVIII 45.

48. *Shakespeare from Betterton to Irving*, II 211.

49. Charles Kean's preface to his acting edition, quoted by Odell, op. cit. II 352. Garrick had introduced historical costuming – 'Old English Dresses' – in his last production of the play, 21 May 1776 (*London Chronicle*, 21–3 May 1776).

50. *The Times* (London) II Nov 1892.

51. In his 'General Observation', op. cit. p. 96.

52. A. B. Walkley, *The Times*, 4 Sept 1909. (Walkley goes on to show, however, that the play gets 'hold of you' in spite of this.)

53. Granville-Barker's description of the Lear of I i: 'more a magnificent portent than a man'. *Prefaces to Shakespeare* (1952), I 285.

54. Richard Buckle, reviewing John Gielgud's 1955 production of *King Lear* in *Observer*, 31 July 1955.

55. *The Times*, 26 Jan 1943, in a review of a performance by Donald Wolfit.

56. James Agate, reviewing John Gielgud's first production, in *Sunday Times*, 19 Apr 1931.

57. *The Times* in the review above mentioned of Donald Wolfit's performance.

58. Issue of 25 Sept 1946.

59. Gielgud in 1931, 1940, 1950, 1955; Wolfit in 1943, 1944, 1945, and 1953.

60. *The Times*, 16 Apr 1940.

61. Ivor Brown, in *Observer*, 29 Sept 1946.

62. *The Times*, 15 July 1953.

63. *The Times*, 19 Aug 1959.

64. e.g. W. A. Darlington (*New York Times*, 13 Sept 1959) and Muriel St Clare Byrne ('*King Lear* at Stratford-on-Avon, 1959', in *Shakespeare Quarterly*, XI (1960) 191).

65. Ibid. pp. 190, 205.

66. Op. cit. I 271. Gielgud's notes on Barker's hints, set down at the time in his rehearsal copy, may be consulted in his *Stage Directions* (1963), app. I.

67. Program note (quoted in *The Times*, 27 July 1955).

68. 'A Shakespearean Speaks His Mind', in *Theatre Arts*, XLIII (1959), 69–71.

69. Marowitz, op. cit. p. 21.

70. See his 'A Subtext Based on Nothing', in *Tulane Drama Review*, VIII (1963), 122 ff. The quotations below are reprinted by permission.

71. William Empson, *The Structure of Complex Words* (1951), p. 138.

72. Darlington, loc. cit.

73. Richard Buckle, in the *Observer*, 31 July 1955.

74. 'Scofield is a Stalin . . . a guttural upstart whose behavior is so arbitrary and graceless, so jack-booted and ham-fisted, that audiences may begin by sharing the shocked embarrassment of his family and in-laws. . . . This Lear wolfs his food, hammers the table while he cackles at dirty jokes, and overturns the table in fury when crossed. He even belches in the middle of his farewell to his daughter. . . . And so another aspect of Lear is erased. As well as the King, we have lost the High Priest.' Alan Brien, 'Openings: London', in *Theatre Arts* , XLVII (1963), 58. It is fair to add that Brien found the losses compensated by 'the man of flesh and blood'. Many others including myself looked in vain for such a man.

75. Op. cit. p. 131.

76. Ibid. pp. 128–9. Blau's somewhat different account of his production in *Theatre Arts*, XLV (1961), 80, may suggest that certain of the effects described above existed more fully in the producer's retrospective imagina-

tion than in the audience's experience at the time. Several spectators have
assured me that they were quite unaware of these intentions.

77. Ibid. pp. 122–9.
78. Ibid. p. 124.
79. Op. cit. p. 21.
80. Ibid. pp. 28–9.
81. Ibid. p. 29.
82. One of the more spectacular current instances of directorial reduc-
tiveness was Marowitz's *Hamlet*, performed at the Akademie der Künste in
West Berlin on 20 Jan 1965. An hour in length, the play had lost several of
its characters, including Horatio; lines given in the original to one speaker
had been reassigned to another; the part of the prince was played in white
clown-face. My point is not that such experiments are wrong, only that they
diminish Shakespeare along with our opportunities of seeing what Shakespeare actually wrote.

A. C. Bradley (1904)   King Lear

King Lear seems to me Shakespeare's greatest achievement, but it
seems to me *not* his best play. And I find that I tend to consider it
from two rather different points of view. When I regard it strictly as
a drama, it appears to me, though in certain parts overwhelming,
decidedly inferior as a whole to *Hamlet, Othello* and *Macbeth*. When
I am feeling that it is greater than any of these, and the fullest
revelation of Shakespeare's power, I find I am not regarding it
simply as a drama, but am grouping it in my mind with works like
the *Prometheus Vinctus* and the *Divine Comedy*, and even with the
greatest symphonies of Beethoven and the statues in the Medici
Chapel. . . .

The stage is the test of strictly dramatic quality, and *King Lear* is
too huge for the stage. Of course, I am not denying that it is a great
stage-play. It has scenes immensely effective in the theatre; three of
them – the two between Lear and Goneril and between Lear,
Goneril and Regan, and the ineffably beautiful scene in the Fourth
Act between Lear and Cordelia – lose in the theatre very little of the
spell they have for imagination; and the gradual interweaving of the
two plots is almost as masterly as in *Much Ado*. But (not to speak of

defects due to mere carelessness) that which makes the *peculiar* greatness of King Lear – the immense scope of the work; the mass and variety of intense experience which it contains; the interpenetration of sublime imagination, piercing pathos, and humour almost as moving as the pathos; the vastness of the convulsion both of nature and of human passion; the vagueness of the scene where the action takes place, and of the movements of the figures which cross this scene; the strange atmosphere, cold and dark, which strikes on us as we enter this scene, enfolding these figures and magnifying their dim outlines like a winter mist; the half-realised suggestions of vast universal powers working in the world of individual fates and passions – all this interferes with dramatic clearness even when the play is read, and in the theatre not only refuses to reveal itself fully through the senses but seems to be almost in contradiction with their reports. This is not so with the other great tragedies. No doubt, as Lamb declared, theatrical representation gives only a part of what we imagine when we read them; but there is no *conflict* between the representation and the imagination, because these tragedies are, in essentials, perfectly dramatic. But *King Lear*, as a whole, is imperfectly dramatic, and there is something in its very essence which is at war with the senses, and demands a purely imaginative realisation. It is therefore Shakespeare's greatest work, but it is not what Hazlitt called it, the best of his plays; and its comparative unpopularity is due, not merely to the extreme painfulness of the catastrophe, but in part to its dramatic defects, and in part to a failure in many readers to catch the peculiar effects to which I have referred   a failure which is natural because the appeal is made not so much to dramatic perception as to a rarer and more strictly poetic kind of imagination. For this reason, too, even the best attempts at exposition of *King Lear* are disappointing; they remind us of attempts to reduce to prose the impalpable spirit of the *Tempest*.

I propose to develop some of these ideas by considering, first, the dramatic defects of the play, and then some of the causes of its extraordinary imaginative effect.

We may begin, however, by referring to two passages which have often been criticised with injustice. The first is that where the blinded Gloster, believing that he is going to leap down Dover cliff, does in fact fall flat on the ground at his feet, and then is persuaded that he *has* leaped down Dover cliff but has been miraculously preserved. Imagine this incident transferred to *Othello*, and you realise how completely the two tragedies differ in dramatic atmosphere. In *Othello* it would be a shocking or a ludicrous dissonance, but it is in harmony with the spirit of *King Lear*. And not only is this so, but, contrary to expectation, it is not, if properly acted, in the least absurd on the stage. The imagination and the feelings have been worked upon with such effect by the description of the cliff, and by the portrayal of the old man's despair and his son's courageous and loving wisdom, that we are unconscious of the grotesqueness of the incident for common sense.

The second passage is more important, for it deals with the origin of the whole conflict. The oft-repeated judgment that the first scene of *King Lear* is absurdly improbable, and that no sane man would think of dividing his kingdom among his daughters in proportion to the strength of their several protestations of love, is much too harsh and is based upon a strange misunderstanding. This scene acts effectively, and to imagination the story is not at all incredible. It is merely strange, like so many of the stories on which our romantic dramas are based. Shakespeare, besides, has done a good deal to soften the improbability of the legend, and he has done much more than the casual reader perceives. The very first words of the drama, as Coleridge pointed out, tell us that the division of the kingdom is already settled in all its details, so that only the public announcement of it remains. Later we find that the lines of division have already been drawn* on the map of Britain [line 38], and again that Cordelia's share, which is her dowry, is perfectly well known to Burgundy, if not to France [lines 197, 245]. That then which is censured as absurd, the dependence of the division on the speeches of the daughters, was in Lear's intention a mere form, devised as a childish scheme to gratify his love of absolute power and his hunger for assurances of devotion. And this scheme is perfectly in character. We may even say that the main cause of its failure was not that Goneril and Regan were exceptionally hypocritical, but that Cordelia was exceptionally sincere and unbending. And it is essential to observe that its failure, and the consequent necessity of publicly

---

* KENT   I thought the king had more affected the Duke of Albany than Cornwall.
  GLOS.   It did always seem so to us: but now, in the division of the kingdom, it appears not which of the dukes he values most.

For (Gloster goes on to say) their shares are exactly equal in value. And if the shares of the two elder daughters are fixed, obviously that of the third is so too.

reversing his whole well-known intention, is one source of Lear's extreme anger. He loved Cordelia most and knew that she loved him best, and the supreme moment to which he looked forward was that in which she should outdo her sisters in expression of affection, and should be rewarded by that 'third' of the kingdom which was the most 'opulent'. And then – so it naturally seemed to him – she put him to open shame.

There is a further point, which seems to have escaped the attention of Coleridge and others. Part of the absurdity of Lear's plan is taken to be his idea of living with his three daughters in turn. But he never meant to do this. He meant to live with Cordelia, and with her alone.* The scheme of his alternate monthly stay with Goneril and Regan is forced on him at the moment by what he thinks the undutifulness of his favourite child. In fact his whole original plan, though foolish and rash, was not a 'hideous rashness'[1] or incredible folly. If carried out it would have had no such consequences as followed its alteration. It would probably have led quickly to war,[2] but not to the agony which culminated in the storm upon the heath. The first scene, therefore, is not absurd, though it must be pronounced dramatically faulty in so far as it discloses the true position of affairs only to an attention more alert than can be expected in a theatrical audience or has been found in many critics of the play.

Let us turn next to two passages of another kind, the two which are mainly responsible for the accusation of excessive painfulness, and so for the distaste of many readers and the long theatrical eclipse of *King Lear*. The first of these is much the less important; it is the scene of the blinding of Gloster. The blinding of Gloster on the stage has been condemned almost universally; and surely with justice, because the mere physical horror of such a spectacle would in the theatre be a sensation so violent as to overpower the purely tragic emotions, and therefore the spectacle would seem revolting or shocking. But it is otherwise in reading. For mere imagination the physical horror, though lost, is so far deadened that it can do its duty as a stimulus to pity, and to that appalled dismay at the extremity of human cruelty which it is of the essence of the tragedy to excite. Thus the blinding of Gloster belongs rightly to *King Lear*

---

* I loved her most, and thought to set my rest
  On her kind nursery.

in its proper world of imagination; it is a blot upon *King Lear* as a stage-play.

But what are we to say of the second and far more important passage, the conclusion of the tragedy, the 'unhappy ending', as it is called, though the word 'unhappy' sounds almost ironical in its weakness? Is this too a blot upon *King Lear* as a stage-play? The question is not so easily answered as might appear. Doubtless we are right when we turn with disgust from Tate's sentimental alterations, from his marriage of Edgar and Cordelia, and from that cheap moral which every one of Shakespeare's tragedies contradicts, 'that Truth and Virtue shall at last succeed'. But are we so sure that we are right when we unreservedly condemn the feeling which prompted these alterations, or at all events the feeling which beyond question comes naturally to many readers of *King Lear* who would like Tate as little as we? What they wish, though they have not always the courage to confess it even to themselves, is that the deaths of Edmund, Goneril, Regan and Gloster should be followed by the escape of Lear and Cordelia from death, and that we should be allowed to imagine the poor old King passing quietly in the home of his beloved child to the end which cannot be far off. Now, I do not dream of saying that we ought to wish this, so long as we regard *King Lear* simply as a work of poetic imagination. But if *King Lear* is to be considered strictly as a drama, or simply as we consider *Othello*, it is not so clear that the wish is unjustified. In fact I will take my courage in both hands and say boldly that I share it, and also that I believe Shakespeare would have ended his play thus had he taken the subject in hand a few years later, in the days of *Cymbeline* and the *Winter's Tale*. If I read *King Lear* simply as a drama, I find that my feelings call for· this 'happy ending'. I do not mean the human, the philanthropic, feelings, but the dramatic sense. The former wish Hamlet and Othello to escape their doom; the latter does not; but it does wish Lear and Cordelia to be saved. Surely, it says, the tragic emotions have been sufficiently stirred already. Surely the tragic outcome of Lear's error and his daughters' ingratitude has been made clear enough and moving enough. And, still more surely, such a tragic catastrophe as this should seem *inevitable*. But this catastrophe, unlike those of all the other mature tragedies, does not seem at all inevitable. It is not even satisfactorily motived. In fact it seems expressly designed to fall suddenly like a bolt from a sky cleared by the vanished storm. And although from a wider point of view one may fully recognise the value of this effect, and may even reject with horror the wish for a 'happy ending', this wider point of view, I must maintain, is not strictly dramatic or tragic.

Of course this is a heresy and all the best authority is against it. But then the best authority, it seems to me, is either influenced unconsciously by disgust at Tate's sentimentalism or unconsciously takes that wider point of view. When Lamb – there is no higher authority – writes, 'A happy ending! – as if the living martyrdom that Lear had gone through, the flaying of his feelings alive, did not make a fair dismissal from the stage of life the only decorous thing for him', I answer, first, that it is precisely this *fair* dismissal which we desire for him instead of renewed anguish; and, secondly, that what we desire for him during the brief remainder of his days is not 'the childish pleasure of getting his gilt robes and sceptre again', not what Tate gives him, but what Shakespeare himself might have given him – peace and happiness by Cordelia's fireside. And if I am told that he has suffered too much for this, how can I possibly believe it with these words ringing in my ears:

> Come, let's away to prison:
> We two alone will sing like birds i' the cage.
> When thou dost ask me blessing, I'll kneel down,
> And ask of thee forgiveness: so we'll live,
> And pray, and sing, and tell old tales, and laugh
> At gilded butterflies?

And again when Schlegel declares that, if Lear were saved, 'the whole' would 'lose its significance', because it would no longer show us that the belief in Providence 'requires a wider range than the dark pilgrimage on earth to be established in its whole extent', I answer that, if the drama does show us that, it takes us beyond the strictly tragic point of view.

A dramatic mistake in regard to the catastrophe, however, even supposing it to exist, would not seriously affect the whole play. The principal structural weakness of *King Lear* lies elsewhere. It is felt to some extent in the earlier Acts, but still more (as from our study of Shakespeare's technique we have learnt to expect) in the Fourth and the first part of the Fifth. And it arises chiefly from the double action, which is a peculiarity of *King Lear* among the tragedies. By the side of Lear, his daughters, Kent, and the Fool, who are the principal figures in the main plot, stand Gloster and his two sons, the chief persons of the secondary plot. Now by means of this double action Shakespeare secured certain results highly advantageous even from the strictly dramatic point of view, and easy to perceive. But the disadvantages were dramatically greater. The number of essential characters is so large, their actions and movements are so complicated, and events towards the close crowd on one another so thickly, that the reader's attention,[4] rapidly transferred from one centre of interest to another, is overstrained. He becomes, if not intellectually confused, at least emotionally fatigued. The battle, on which everything turns, scarcely affects him. The deaths of Edmund, Goneril, Regan and Gloster seem 'but trifles here'; and anything short of the incomparable pathos of the close would leave him cold. There is something almost ludicrous in the insignificance of this battle, when it is compared with the corresponding battles in *Julius Caesar* and *Macbeth*; and though there may have been further reasons for its insignificance, the main one is simply that there was no room to give it its due effect among such a host of competing interests.[5]

A comparison of the last two Acts of *Othello* with the last two Acts of *King Lear* would show how unfavourable to dramatic clearness is a multiplicity of figures. But that this multiplicity is not in itself a fatal obstacle is evident from the last two Acts of *Hamlet*, and especially from the final scene. This is in all respects one of Shakespeare's triumphs, yet the stage is crowded with characters. Only they are not *leading* characters. The plot is single; Hamlet and the King are the 'mighty opposites'; and Ophelia, the only other person in whom we are obliged to take a vivid interest, has already disappeared. It is therefore natural and right that the deaths of Laertes and the Queen should affect us comparatively little. But in *King Lear*, because the plot is double, we have present in the last scene no less than five persons who are technically of the first import- ance – Lear, his three daughters and Edmund; not to speak of Kent and Edgar, of whom the latter at any rate is technically quite as important as Laertes. And again, owing to the pressure of persons and events, and owing to the concentration of our anxiety on Lear and Cordelia, the combat of Edgar and Edmund, which occupies so con- siderable a space, fails to excite a tithe of the interest of the fencing- match in *Hamlet*. The truth is that all through these Acts Shakespeare has too vast a material to use with complete dramatic effectiveness, however essential this very vastness was for effects of another kind.

Added to these defects there are others, which suggest that in *King Lear* Shakespeare was less concerned than usual with dramatic fitness; improbabilities, inconsistencies, sayings and doings which suggest questions only to be answered by conjecture. The improbabilities in *King Lear* surely far surpass those of the other great tragedies in number and in grossness. And they are particularly noticeable in the secondary plot. For example, no sort of reason is given why Edgar, who lives in the same house with Edmund, should write a letter to him instead of speaking; and this is a letter absolutely damning to his character. Gloster was very foolish, but surely not so foolish as to pass unnoticed this improbability; or, if so foolish, what need for Edmund to forge a letter rather than a conversation, especially as Gloster appears to be unacquainted with his son's handwriting?[6] Is it in character that Edgar should be persuaded without the slightest demur to avoid his father instead of confronting him and asking him the cause of his anger? Why in the world should Gloster, when expelled from his castle, wander painfully all the way to Dover simply in order to destroy himself [IV i 80]? And is it not extraordinary that, after Gloster's attempted suicide, Edgar should first talk to him in the language of a gentleman, then to Oswald in his presence in broad peasant dialect, then again to Gloster in gentle language, and yet that Gloster should not manifest the least surprise?

Again, to take three instances of another kind: (*a*) only a fortnight seems to have elapsed between the first scene and the breach with Goneril; yet already there are rumours not only of war between Goneril and Regan but of the coming of a French army; and this, Kent says, is perhaps connected with the harshness of *both* the sisters to their father, although Regan has apparently had no opportunity of showing any harshness till the day before. (*b*) In the quarrel with Goneril Lear speaks of his having to dismiss fifty of his followers at a clap, yet she has neither mentioned any number nor had any opportunity of mentioning it off the stage. (*c*) Lear and Goneril, intending to hurry to Regan, both send off messengers to her, and both tell the messengers to bring back an answer. But it does not appear either how the messengers *could* return or what answer could be required, as their superiors are following them with the greatest speed.

Once more, (*a*) why does Edgar not reveal himself to his blind father, as he truly says he ought to have done? The answer is left to mere conjecture. (*b*) Why does Kent so carefully preserve his incognito till the last scene? He says he does it for an important purpose, but what the purpose is we have to guess. (*c*) Why Burgundy rather than France should have first choice of Cordelia's hand is a question we cannot help asking, but there is no hint of any answer.[7] (*d*) I have referred already to the strange obscurity regarding Edmund's delay in trying to save his victims, and I will not extend this list of examples. No one of such defects is surprising when considered by itself, but their number is surely significant. Taken in conjunction with other symptoms it means that Shakespeare, set upon the dramatic effect of the great scenes and upon certain effects not wholly dramatic, was exceptionally careless of probability, clearness and consistency in smaller matters, introducing what was convenient or striking for a momentary purpose without troubling himself about anything more than the moment. In presence of these signs it seems doubtful whether his failure to give information about the fate of the Fool was due to anything more than carelessness or an impatient desire to reduce his overloaded material.

Before I turn to the other side of the subject I will refer to one more characteristic of this play which is dramatically disadvantageous. In Shakespeare's dramas, owing to the absence of scenery from the Elizabethan stage, the question, so vexatious to editors, of the exact locality of a particular scene is usually unimportant and often unanswerable; but, as a rule, we know, broadly speaking, where the persons live and what their journeys are. The text makes this plain, for example, almost throughout *Hamlet, Othello* and *Macbeth*; and the imagination is therefore untroubled. But in *King Lear* the indications are so scanty that the reader's mind is left not seldom both vague and bewildered. Nothing enables us to imagine whereabouts in Britain Lear's palace lies, or where the Duke of Albany lives. In referring to the dividing-lines on the map, Lear tells us of shadowy forests and plenteous rivers, but, unlike Hotspur and his companions, he studiously avoids proper names. The Duke of Cornwall, we presume in the absence of information, is likely to live in Cornwall; but we suddenly find, from the introduction of a place-name which all readers take at first for a surname, that he lives at Gloster [I V I]. This seems likely to be also the home of the Earl of Gloster, to whom Cornwall is patron. But no: it is a night's journey

from Cornwall's 'house' to Gloster's, and Gloster's is in the middle
of an uninhabited heath.[8] Here, for the purpose of the crisis, nearly
all the persons assemble, but they do so in a manner which no casual
spectator or reader could follow. Afterwards they all drift towards
Dover for the purpose of the catastrophe; but again the localities and
movements are unusually indefinite. And this indefiniteness is found
in smaller matters. One cannot help asking, for example, and yet
one feels one had better not ask, where that 'lodging' of Edmund's
can be, in which he hides Edgar from his father, and whether Edgar
is mad that he should return from his hollow tree (in a district where
'for many miles about there's scarce a bush') to his father's castle in
order to soliloquise [II iii] – for the favourite stage-direction, 'a
wood' (which is more than 'a bush'), however convenient to
imagination, is scarcely compatible with the presence of Kent asleep
in the stocks. Something of the confusion which bewilders the
reader's mind in *King Lear* recurs in *Antony and Cleopatra*, the most
faultily constructed of all the tragedies; but there it is due not so
much to the absence or vagueness of the indications as to the
necessity of taking frequent and fatiguing journeys over thousands of
miles. Shakespeare could not help himself in the Roman play; in
King Lear he did not choose to help himself, perhaps deliberately
chose to be vague.

From these defects, or from some of them, follows one result
which must be familiar to many readers of *King Lear*. It is far more
difficult to retrace in memory the steps of the action in this tragedy
than in *Hamlet, Othello,* or *Macbeth*. The outline is of course quite
clear; anyone could write an 'argument' of the play. But when an
attempt is made to fill in the detail, it issues sooner or later in
confusion even with readers whose dramatic memory is unusually
strong.

The position of the hero in this tragedy is in one important respect
peculiar. The reader of *Hamlet, Othello,* or *Macbeth,* is in no danger
of forgetting, when the catastrophe is reached, the part played by the
hero in bringing it on. His fatal weakness, error, wrong-doing,
continues almost to the end. It is otherwise with *King Lear*. When
the conclusion arrives, the old King has for a long while been
passive. We have long regarded him not only as 'a man more sinned
against than sinning', but almost wholly as a sufferer, hardly at all

as an agent. His sufferings too have been so cruel, and our indignation against those who inflicted them has been so intense, that recollection of the wrong he did to Cordelia, to Kent, and to his realm, has been well-nigh effaced. Lastly, for nearly four Acts he has inspired in us, together with this pity, much admiration and affection. The force of his passion has made us feel that his nature was great; and his frankness and generosity, his heroic efforts to be patient, the depth of his shame and repentance, and the ecstasy of his reunion with Cordelia, have melted our very hearts. Naturally, therefore, at the close we are in some danger of forgetting that the storm which has overwhelmed him was liberated by his own deed.

Yet it is essential that Lear's contribution to the action of the drama should be remembered; not at all in order that we may feel that he 'deserved' what he suffered, but because otherwise his fate would appear to us at best pathetic, at worst shocking, but certainly not tragic. And when we were reading the earlier scenes of the play we recognised this contribution clearly enough. At the very beginning, it is true, we are inclined to feel merely pity and misgivings. The first lines tell us that Lear's mind is beginning to fail with age.[9] Formerly he had perceived how different were the characters of Albany and Cornwall, but now he seems either to have lost this perception or to be unwisely ignoring it. The rashness of his division of the kingdom troubles us, and we cannot but see with concern that its motive is mainly selfish. The absurdity of the pretence of making the division depend on protestations of love from his daughters, his complete blindness to the hypocrisy which is patent to us at a glance, his piteous delight in these protestations, the openness of his expressions of preference for his youngest daughter – all make us smile, but all pain us. But pity begins to give way to another feeling when we witness the precipitance, the despotism, the uncontrolled anger of his injustice to Cordelia and Kent, and the 'hideous rashness' of his persistence in dividing the kingdom after the rejection of his one dutiful child. We feel now the presence of force as well as weakness, but we feel also the presence of the tragic ὕβρις. Lear, we see, is generous and unsuspicious, of an open and free nature, like Hamlet and Othello, and indeed most of Shakespeare's heroes, who in this, according to Ben Jonson, resemble the poet who made them. Lear, we see, is also choleric by temperament – the first of Shakespeare's heroes who is so. And a long life of absolute power, in which he has been flattered to the top of his bent, has produced in him that blindness to human limitations, and that presumptuous self-will, which in Greek tragedy we have so often seen stumbling against the altar of Nemesis. Our consciousness that the decay of old age contributes to this condition deepens our pity and our sense of human infirmity, but certainly does not lead us to regard the old King as irresponsible, and so to sever the tragic *nexus* which binds together his error and his calamities.

The magnitude of this first error is generally fully recognised by the reader owing to his sympathy with Cordelia, though, as we have seen, he often loses the memory of it as the play advances. But this is not so, I think, with the repetition of this error, in the quarrel with Goneril. Here the daughter excites so much detestation, and the father so much sympathy, that we often fail to receive the due impression of his violence. There is not here, of course, the *injustice* of his rejection of Cordelia, but there is precisely the same ὕβρις. This had been shown most strikingly in the first scene when, *immediately* upon the apparently cold words of Cordelia, 'So young, my lord, and true', there comes this dreadful answer:

> Let it be so; thy truth then be thy dower.
> For, by the sacred radiance of the sun,
> The mysteries of Hecate and the night;
> By all the operation of the orbs
> From whom we do exist and cease to be;
> Here I disclaim all my paternal care,
> Propinquity and property of blood,
> And as a stranger to my heart and me
> Hold thee from this for ever. The barbarous Scythian,
> Or he that makes his generation messes
> To gorge his appetite, shall to my bosom
> Be as well neighbour'd, pitied and relieved,
> As thou my sometime daughter.

Now the dramatic effect of this passage is exactly, and doubtless intentionally, repeated in the curse pronounced against Goneril. This does not come after the daughters have openly and wholly turned against their father. Up to the moment of its utterance Goneril has done no more than to require him 'a little to disquantity' and reform his train of knights. Certainly her manner and spirit in making this demand are hateful, and probably her accusations against the knights are false; and we should expect from any father in Lear's position passionate distress and indignation. But surely the famous words which form Lear's immediate reply were meant to be nothing short of frightful:

> Hear, nature, hear; dear goddess, hear!
> Suspend thy purpose, if thou didst intend
> To make this creature fruitful!
> Into her womb convey sterility!
> Dry up in her the organs of increase;
> And from her derogate body never spring
> A babe to honour her! If she must teem,
> Create her child of spleen; that it may live,
> And be a thwart disnatured torment to her!
> Let it stamp wrinkles in her brow of youth;
> With cadent tears fret channels in her cheeks;
> Turn all her mother's pains and benefits
> To laughter and contempt; that she may feel
> How sharper than a serpent's tooth it is
> To have a thankless child!

The question is not whether Goneril deserves these appalling imprecations, but what they tell us about Lear. They show that, although he has already recognised his injustice towards Cordelia, is secretly blaming himself, and is endeavouring to do better, the disposition from which his first error sprang is still unchanged. And it is precisely the disposition to give rise, in evil surroundings, to calamities dreadful but at the same time tragic, because due in some measure to the person who endures them.

The perception of this connection, if it is not lost as the play advances, does not at all diminish our pity for Lear, but it makes it impossible for us permanently to regard the world displayed in this tragedy as subject to a mere arbitrary or malicious power. It makes us feel that this world is so far at least a rational and a moral order, that there holds in it the law, not of proportionate requital, but of strict connection between act and consequence. It is, so far, the world of all Shakespeare's tragedies.

But there is another aspect of Lear's story, the influence of which modifies, in a way quite different and more peculiar to this tragedy, the impressions called pessimistic and even this impression of law. There is nothing more noble and beautiful in literature than Shakespeare's exposition of the effect of suffering in reviving the greatness and eliciting the sweetness of Lear's nature. The occasional recurrence, during his madness, of autocratic impatience, or of desire for revenge serves only to heighten this effect, and the moments when his insanity becomes merely infinitely piteous do not weaken it. The old King who in pleading with his daughters feels so intensely his own humiliation and their horrible ingratitude, and who yet, at fourscore and upward, constrains himself to practise a self-control and patience so many years disused; who out of old affection for his Fool, and in repentance for his injustice to the Fool's beloved mistress, tolerates incessant and cutting reminders of his own folly and wrong; in whom the rage of the storm awakes a power and a poetic grandeur surpassing even that of Othello's anguish; who comes in his affliction to think of others first, and to seek, in tender solicitude for his poor boy, the shelter he scorns for his own bare head; who learns to feel and to pray for the miserable and houseless poor, to discern the falseness of flattery and the brutality of authority, and to pierce below the differences of rank and raiment to the common humanity beneath; whose sight is so purged by scalding tears that it sees at last how power and place and all things in the world are vanity except love; who tastes in his last hours the extremes both of love's rapture and of its agony, but could never, if he lived on or lived again, care a joy for aught beside – there is no figure, surely, in the world of poetry at once so grand, so pathetic, and so beautiful as his. Well, but Lear owes the whole of this to those sufferings which made us doubt whether life were not simply evil, and men like the flies which wanton boys torture for their sport. Should we not be at least as near the truth if we called this poem *The Redemption of King Lear*, and declared that the business of 'the gods' with him was neither to torment him, nor to teach him a 'noble anger', but to lead him to attain through apparently hopeless failure the very end and aim of life? One can believe that Shakespeare had been tempted at times to feel misanthropy and despair, but it is quite impossible that he can have been mastered by such feelings at the time when he produced this conception.

To dwell on the stages of this process of purification (the word is Professor Dowden's) is impossible here; and there are scenes, such as that of the meeting of Lear and Cordelia, which it seems almost a profanity to touch.[10] But I will refer to two scenes which may remind us more in detail of some of the points just mentioned. The third and fourth scenes of Act III present one of those contrasts which speak as eloquently even as Shakespeare's words, and which were made possible in his theatre by the absence of scenery and the consequent absence of intervals between the scenes. First, in a scene

of twenty-three lines, mostly in prose, Gloster is shown, telling his
son Edmund how Goneril and Regan have forbidden him on pain of
death to succour the houseless King; how a secret letter has reached
him, announcing the arrival of a French force; and how, whatever
the consequences may be, he is determined to relieve his old master.
Edmund, left alone, soliloquises in words which seem to freeze one's
blood:

> This courtesy, forbid thee, shall the duke
> Instantly know; and of that letter too:
> This seems a fair deserving, and must draw me
> That which my father loses; no less than all:
> The younger rises when the old doth fall.

He goes out; and the next moment, as the fourth scene opens, we
find ourselves in the icy storm with Lear, Kent and the Fool, and yet
in the inmost shrine of love. I am not speaking of the devotion of the
others to Lear, but of Lear himself. He had consented, merely for the
Fool's sake, to seek shelter in the hovel:

> Come, your hovel.
> Poor fool and knave, I have one part in my heart
> That's sorry yet for thee.

But on the way he has broken down and has been weeping [III iv 17],
and now he resists Kent's efforts to persuade him to enter. He does
not feel the storm:

> when the mind's free
> The body's delicate: the tempest in my mind
> Doth from my senses take all feeling else
> Save what beats there:

and the thoughts that will drive him mad are burning in his brain:

> Filial ingratitude!
> Is it not as this mouth should tear this hand
> For lifting food to't? But I will punish home.
> No, I will weep no more. In such a night
> To shut me out! Pour on; I will endure.
> In such a night as this! O Regan, Goneril!
> Your old kind father, whose frank heart gave all, –
> O, that way madness lies; let me shun that;
> No more of that.

And then suddenly, as he controls himself, the blessed spirit of kindness breathes on him 'like a meadow gale of spring', and he turns gently to Kent:

> Prithee, go in thyself; seek thine own ease:
> This tempest will not give me leave to ponder
> On things would hurt me more. But I'll go in.
> In, boy; go first. You houseless poverty –
> Nay, get thee in. I'll pray, and then I'll sleep.

But his prayer is not for himself.

> Poor naked wretches, whereso'er you are,

it begins, and I need not quote more. This is one of those passages which make one worship Shakespeare.[11]

Much has been written on the representation of insanity in *King Lear*, and I will confine myself to one or two points which may have escaped notice. The most obvious symptom of Lear's insanity, especially in its first stages, is of course the domination of a fixed idea. Whatever presents itself to his senses, is seized on by this idea and compelled to express it; as for example in those words, already quoted, which first show that his mind has actually given way:

> Hast thou given all
> To thy two daughters? And art thou come to this?[12]

But it is remarkable that what we have here is only, in an exaggerated and perverted form, the very same action of imagination that, just before the breakdown of reason, produced those sublime appeals:

> O heavens,
> If you do love old men, if your sweet sway
> Allow obedience, if yourselves are old,
> Make it your cause;

and:

> Rumble thy bellyful! Spit, fire! spout, rain!
> Nor rain, wind, thunder, fire, are my daughters:
> I tax not you, you elements, with unkindness;

> I never gave you kingdom, call'd you children,
> You owe me no subscription: then let fall
> Your horrible pleasure; here I stand, your slave,
> A poor, infirm, weak, and despised old man:
> But yet I call you servile ministers,
> That have with two pernicious daughters join'd
> Your high engender'd battles 'gainst a head
> So old and white as this. O! O! 'tis foul!

Shakespeare, long before this, in the *Midsummer Night's Dream*, had noticed the resemblance between the lunatic, the lover, and the poet; and the partial truth that genius is allied to insanity was quite familiar to him. But he presents here the supplementary half-truth that insanity is allied to genius.

He does not, however, put into the mouth of the insane Lear any such sublime passages as those just quoted. Lear's insanity, which destroys the coherence, also reduces the poetry of his imagination. What it stimulates is that power of moral perception and reflection which had already been quickened by his sufferings. This, however partial and however disconnectedly used, first appears, quite soon after the insanity has declared itself, in the idea that the naked beggar represents truth and reality, in contrast with those conventions, flatteries, and corruptions of the great world, by which Lear has so long been deceived and will never be deceived again:

> Is man no more than this? Consider him well. Thou owest the worm no silk, the beast no hide, the sheep no wool, the cat no perfume. Ha! here's three on's are sophisticated: thou art the thing itself.

Lear regards the beggar therefore with reverence and delight, as a person who is in the secret of things, and he longs to question him about their causes. It is this same strain of thought which much later [IV vi], gaining far greater force, though the insanity has otherwise advanced, issues in those famous Timon-like speeches which make us realise the original strength of the old King's mind. And when this strain, on his recovery, unites with the streams of repentance and love, it produces that serene renunciation of the world, with its power and glory and resentments and revenges, which is expressed in the speech [V iii]:

> No, no, no, no! Come, let's away to prison:
> We two alone will sing like birds i' the cage:
> When thou dost ask me blessing, I'll kneel down,

> And ask of thee forgiveness: so we'll live,
> And pray, and sing, and tell old tales, and laugh
> At gilded butterflies, and hear poor rogues
> Talk of court news; and we'll talk with them too.
> Who loses, and who wins; who's in, who's out;
> And take upon's the mystery of things,
> As if we were God's spies: and we'll wear out,
> In a wall'd prison, packs and sets of great ones,
> That ebb and flow by the moon.

This is that renunciation which is at the same time a sacrifice offered to the gods, and on which the gods themselves throw incense; and, it may be, it would never have been offered but for the knowledge that came to Lear in his madness.

I spoke of Lear's 'recovery', but the word is too strong. The Lear of the Fifth Act is not indeed insane, but his mind is greatly enfeebled. The speech just quoted is followed by a sudden flash of the old passionate nature, reminding us most pathetically of Lear's efforts, just before his madness, to restrain his tears:

> Wipe thine eyes:
> The good-years shall devour them, flesh and fell,
> Ere they shall make us weep: we'll see 'em starve first.

And this weakness is still more pathetically shown in the blindness of the old King to his position now that he and Cordelia are made prisoners. It is evident that Cordelia knows well what mercy her father is likely to receive from her sisters; that is the reason of her weeping. But he does not understand her tears; it never crosses his mind that they have anything more than imprisonment to fear. And what is that to them? They have made that sacrifice, and all is well:

> Have I caught thee?
> He that parts us shall bring a brand from heaven,
> And fire us hence like foxes.

This blindness is most affecting to us, who know in what manner they will be parted; but it is also comforting. And we find the same mingling of effects in the overwhelming conclusion of the story. If to the reader, as to the bystanders, that scene brings one unbroken pain, it is not so with Lear himself. His shattered mind passes from the first transports of hope and despair, as he bends over Cordelia's body and holds the feather to her lips, into an absolute forgetfulness of the cause of these transports. This continues so long as he can converse with Kent; becomes an almost complete vacancy; and is disturbed only to yield, as his eyes suddenly fall again on his child's corpse, to an agony which at once breaks his heart. And, finally, though he is killed by an agony of pain, the agony in which he actually dies is one not of pain but of ecstasy. Suddenly, with a cry represented in the oldest text by a four-times repeated 'O', he exclaims:

> Do you see this? Look on her, look, her lips,
> Look there, look there!

These are the last words of Lear. He is sure, at last, that she *lives*: and what had he said when he was still in doubt?

> She lives! if it be so,
> It is a chance which does redeem all sorrows
> That ever I have felt!

To us, perhaps, the knowledge that he is deceived may bring a culmination of pain: but, if it brings *only* that, I believe we are false to Shakespeare, and it seems almost beyond question that any actor is false to the text who does not attempt to express, in Lear's last accents and gestures and look, an unbearable *joy*. [13]

To dwell on the pathos of Lear's last speech would be an impertinence, but I may add a remark on the speech from the literary point of view. In the simplicity of its language, which consists almost wholly of monosyllables of native origin, composed in very brief sentences of the plainest structure, it presents an extraordinary contrast to the dying speech of Hamlet and the last words of Othello to the bystanders. The fact that Lear speaks in passion is one cause of the difference, but not the sole cause. The language is more than simple, it is familiar. And this familiarity is characteristic of Lear (except at certain moments, already referred to) from the time of his madness onwards, and is the source of the peculiarly poignant effect of some of his sentences (such as 'The little dogs and all . . .'). We feel in them the loss of power to sustain his royal dignity; we feel also that everything external has become nothingness to him, and that what remains is 'the thing itself', the soul in its bare greatness. Hence also it is that two lines in this last speech show, better perhaps than any other passage of poetry, one of the qualities we have in mind when we distinguish poetry as 'romantic'. Nothing like Hamlet's mysterious sigh, 'The rest is silence', nothing like Othello's memories of his life of marvel and achievement, was possible to Lear. Those last thoughts are romantic in their strangeness: Lear's five-times repeated 'Never', in which the simplest and most unanswerable cry of anguish rises note by note till the heart breaks, is romantic in its naturalism; and to make a verse out of this one word required the boldness as well as the inspiration which came infallibly to Shakespeare at the greatest moments. But the familiarity, boldness and inspiration are surpassed (if that can be) by the next line, which shows the bodily oppression asking for bodily relief. The imagination that produced Lear's curse or his defiance of the storm may be paralleled in its kind, but where else are we to seek the imagination that could venture to follow that cry of 'Never' with such a phrase as 'undo this button', and yet could leave us on the topmost peaks of poetry?[14]

The character of Cordelia is not a masterpiece of invention or subtlety like that of Cleopatra; yet in its own way it is a creation as wonderful. Cordelia appears in only four of the twenty-six scenes of *King Lear*; she speaks – it is hard to believe it – scarcely more than a hundred lines; and yet no character in Shakespeare is more absolutely individual or more ineffaceably stamped on the memory of his readers. There is a harmony, strange but perhaps the result of intention, between the character itself and this reserved or parsimonious method of depicting it. An expressiveness almost inexhaustible gained through paucity of expression; the suggestion of infinite wealth and beauty conveyed by the very refusal to reveal this beauty in expansive speech – this is at once the nature of Cordelia herself and the chief characteristic of Shakespeare's art in representing it. Perhaps it is not fanciful to find a parallel in his drawing of a person very different, Hamlet. It was natural to Hamlet to examine himself minutely, to discuss himself at large, and yet to remain a mystery to himself; and Shakespeare's method of drawing the character answers to it; it is extremely detailed and searching, and yet its effect is to enhance the sense of mystery. The results in the two cases differ correspondingly. No one hesitates to enlarge upon Hamlet, who speaks of himself so much; but to use many words about Cordelia seems to be a kind of impiety.

I am obliged to speak of her chiefly because the devotion she inspires almost inevitably obscures her part in the tragedy. This devotion is composed, so to speak, of two contrary elements, reverence and pity. The first, because Cordelia's is a higher nature than that of most even of Shakespeare's heroines. With the tenderness of Viola or Desdemona she unites something of the resolution, power, and dignity of Hermione, and reminds us sometimes of Helena, sometimes of Isabella, though she has none of the traits which prevent Isabella from winning our hearts. Her assertion of truth and right, her allegiance to them, even the touch of severity that accompanies it, instead of compelling mere respect or admiration, become adorable in a nature so loving as Cordelia's. She is a thing enskyed and sainted, and yet we feel no incongruity in the love of the King of France for her as we do in the love of the Duke for Isabella.

But with this reverence or worship is combined in the reader's mind a passion of championship, of pity, even of protecting pity. She is so deeply wronged, and she appears, for all her strength, so defenceless. We think of her as unable to speak for herself. We think of her as quite young, and as slight and small.[15] 'Her voice was ever soft, gentle, and low'; ever so, whether the tone was that of resolution, or rebuke, or love.[16] Of all Shakespeare's heroines she knew least of joy. She grew up with Goneril and Regan for sisters. Even her love for her father must have been mingled with pain and anxiety. She must early have learned to school and repress emotion. She never knew the bliss of young love: there is no trace of such love for the King of France. She had knowingly to wound most deeply the being dearest to her. He cast her off; and, after suffering an agony for him, and before she could see him safe in death, she was brutally murdered. We have to thank the poet for passing lightly over the circumstances of her death. We do not think of them. Her image comes before us calm and bright and still.

The memory of Cordelia thus becomes detached in a manner from the action of the drama. The reader refuses to admit into it any idea of imperfection, and is outraged when any share in her father's sufferings is attributed to the part she plays in the opening scene. Because she was deeply wronged he is ready to insist that she was wholly right. He refuses, that is, to take the tragic point of view, and, when it is taken, he imagines that Cordelia is being attacked, or is being declared to have 'deserved' all that befell her. But Shake-

speare's was the tragic point of view. He exhibits in the opening
scene a situation tragic for Cordelia as well as for Lear. At a moment
where terrible issues join, Fate makes on her the one demand which
she is unable to meet. . . . it was a demand which other heroines of
Shakespeare could have met. Without loss of self-respect, and
refusing even to appear to compete for a reward, they could have
made the unreasonable old King feel that he was fondly loved.
Cordelia cannot, because she is Cordelia. And so she is not merely
rejected and banished, but her father is left to the mercies of her
sisters. And the cause of her failure – a failure a thousand-fold
redeemed – is a compound in which imperfection appears so
intimately mingled with the noblest qualities that – if we are true to
Shakespeare – we do not think either of justifying her or of blaming
her: we feel simply the tragic emotions of fear and pity.

In this failure a large part is played by that obvious characteristic
to which I have already referred. Cordelia is not, indeed, always
tongue-tied, as several passages in the drama, and even in this scene,
clearly show. But tender emotion, and especially a tender love for
the person to whom she has to speak, makes her dumb. Her love, as
she says, is more ponderous than her tongue.[17]

> Unhappy that I am, I cannot heave
> My heart into my mouth.

This expressive word 'heave' is repeated in the passage which
describes her reception of Kent's letter:

> Faith, once or twice she heaved the name of 'Father'
> Pantingly forth, as if it press'd her heart:

two or three broken ejaculations escape her lips, and she 'starts'
away 'to deal with grief alone'. The same trait reappears with an
ineffable beauty in the stifled repetitions with which she attempts to
answer her father in the moment of his restoration:

LEAR   Do not laugh at me;
   For, as I am a man, I think this lady
   To be my child Cordelia.
COR.   And so I am, I am.
LEAR   Be your tears wet? yes, faith. I pray, weep not;
   If you have poison for me, I will drink it.

> I know you do not love me; for your sisters
> Have, as I so remember, done me wrong:
> You have some cause, they have not.
> COR.   No cause, no cause.

We see this trait, for the last time marked by Shakespeare with a decision clearly intentional, in her inability to answer one syllable to the last words we hear her father speak to her:

> No, no, no, no! Come, let's away to prison:
> We two alone will sing like birds i' the cage:
> When thou dost ask me blessing, I'll kneel down,
> And ask of thee forgiveness: so we'll live,
> And pray, and sing, and tell old tales, and laugh
> At gilded butterflies. . . .

She stands and weeps, and goes out with him silent. And we see her alive no more.

But (I am forced to dwell on the point, because I am sure to slur it over is to be false to Shakespeare) this dumbness of love was not the sole source of misunderstanding. If this had been all, even Lear could have seen the love in Cordelia's eyes when, to his question 'What can you say to draw a third more opulent than your sisters?' she answered 'Nothing'. But it did not shine there. She is not merely silent, nor does she merely answer 'Nothing'. She tells him that she loves him 'according to her bond, nor more nor less'; and his answer,

> How now, Cordelia! mend your speech a little,
> Lest it may mar your fortunes,

so intensifies her horror at the hypocrisy of her sisters that she replies,

>   Good my lord,
> You have begot me, bred me, loved me: I
> Return those duties back as are right fit,
> Obey you, love you, and most honour you.
> Why have my sisters husbands, if they say
> They love you all? Haply, when I shall wed,
> That lord whose hand must take my plight shall carry
> Half my love with him, half my care and duty:
> Sure, I shall never marry like my sisters,
> To love my father all.

What words for the ear of an old father, unreasonable, despotic, but fondly loving, indecent in his own expressions of preference, and blind to the indecency of his appeal for protestations of fondness! Blank astonishment, anger, wounded love, contend within him; but for the moment he restrains himself and asks,

> But goes thy heart with this?

Imagine Imogen's reply! But Cordelia answers,

>   Ay, good my lord.
> LEAR   So young, and so untender?
> COR.   So young, my lord, and true.

Yes, 'heavenly true'. But truth is not the only good in the world, nor is the obligation to tell truth the only obligation. The matter here was to keep it inviolate, but also to preserve a father. And even if truth *were* the one and only obligation, to tell much less than truth is not to tell it. And Cordelia's speech not only tells much less than truth about her love, it actually perverts the truth when it implies that to give love to a husband is to take it from a father. There surely never was a more unhappy speech.

When Isabella goes to plead with Angelo for her brother's life, her horror of her brother's sin is so intense, and her perception of the justice of Angelo's reasons for refusing her is so clear and keen, that she is ready to abandon her appeal before it is well begun; she would actually do so but that the warm-hearted profligate Lucio reproaches her for her coldness and urges her on. Cordelia's hatred of hypocrisy and of the faintest appearance of mercenary professions reminds us of Isabella's hatred of impurity; but Cordelia's position is infinitely more difficult, and on the other hand there is mingled with her hatred a touch of personal antagonism and of pride. Lear's words,

> Let pride, which she calls plainness, marry her![18]

are monstrously unjust, but they contain one grain of truth; and indeed it was scarcely possible that a nature so strong as Cordelia's, and with so keen a sense of dignity, should feel here nothing whatever of pride and resentment. This side of her character is emphatically shown in her language to her sisters in the first scene –

language perfectly just, but little adapted to soften their hearts towards their father – and again in the very last words we hear her speak. She and her father are brought in, prisoners, to the enemy's camp; but she sees only Edmund, not those 'greater' ones on whose pleasure hangs her father's fate and her own. For her own she is little concerned; she knows how to meet adversity:

> For thee, oppressed king, am I cast down;
> Myself could else out-frown false fortune's frown.

Yes, that is how she would meet fortune, frowning it down, even as Goneril would have met it; nor, if her father had been already dead, would there have been any great improbability in the false story that was to be told of her death, that, like Goneril, she 'fordid herself'. Then, after those austere words about fortune, she suddenly asks,

> Shall we not see these daughters and these sisters?

Strange last words for us to hear from a being so worshipped and beloved; but how characteristic! Their tone is unmistakable. I doubt if she could have brought herself to plead with her sisters for her father's life; and if she had attempted· the task, she would have performed it but ill. Nor is our feeling towards her altered one whit by that. But what is true of Kent and the fool (who, like Kent, hastens on the quarrel with Goneril) is, in its measure, true of her. Any one of them would gladly have died a hundred deaths to help King Lear; and they do help his soul; but they harm his cause. They are all involved in tragedy.

Why does Cordelia die? I suppose no reader ever failed to ask that question, and to ask it with something more than pain – to ask it, if only for a moment, in bewilderment or dismay, and even perhaps in tones of protest. These feelings are probably evoked more strongly here than at the death of any other notable character in Shakespeare; and it may sound a wilful paradox to assert that the slightest element of reconciliation is mingled with them or succeeds them. Yet it seems to me indubitable that such an element is present, though difficult to make out with certainty what it is or whence it proceeds. And I will try to make this out, and to state it methodically.

(a) It is not due in any perceptible degree to the fact, which we have just been examining, that Cordelia through her tragic imperfection contributes something to the conflict and catastrophe; and I drew attention to that imperfection without any view to our present problem. The critics who emphasise it at this point in the drama are surely untrue to Shakespeare's mind; and still more completely astray are those who lay stress on the idea that Cordelia in bringing a foreign army to help her father was guilty of treason to her country When she dies we regard her, practically speaking, simply as we regard Ophelia or Desdemona, as an innocent victim swept away in the convulsion caused by the error or guilt of others.

(*b*) Now this destruction of the good through the evil of others is one of the tragic facts of life, and no one can object to the use of it, within certain limits, in tragic art. And, further, those who because of it declaim against the nature of things, declaim without thinking. It is obviously the other side of the fact that the effects of good spread far and wide beyond the doer of good; and we should ask ourselves whether we really could wish (supposing it conceivable) to see this double-sided fact abolished. Nevertheless the touch of reconciliation that we feel in contemplating the death of Cordelia is not due, or is due only in some slight degree, to a perception that the event is true to life, admissible in tragedy, and a case of a law which we cannot seriously desire to see abrogated.

(*c*) What then is this feeling, and whence does it come? I believe that we shall find that it is a feeling not confined to *King Lear*, but present at the close of other tragedies; and that the reason why it has an exceptional tone or force at the close of *King Lear*, lies in that very peculiarity of the close which also – at least for the moment – excites bewilderment, dismay, or protest. The feeling I mean is the impression that the heroic being, though in one sense and outwardly he has failed, is yet in another sense superior to the world in which he appears; is, in some way which we do not seek to define, untouched by the doom that overtakes him; and is rather set free from life than deprived of it. Some such feeling as this – some feeling which, from this description of it, may be recognised as their own even by those who would dissent from the description – we surely have in various degrees at the deaths of Hamlet and Othello and Lear, and of Antony and Cleopatra and Coriolanus. It accompanies the more prominent tragic impressions, and, regarded alone, could hardly be called tragic. For it seems to imply (though we are probably quite unconscious of the implication) an idea which, if developed, would transform the tragic view of things. It implies that the tragic world, if taken as it is presented, with all its error, guilt, failure, woe and waste, is no final reality, but only a part of reality taken for the whole, and, when so taken, illusive; and that if we could see the whole, and the tragic facts in their true place in it, we should find them, not abolished, of course, but so transmuted that they had ceased to be strictly tragic – find, perhaps, the suffering and death counting for little or nothing, the greatness of the soul for much or all, and the heroic spirit, in spite of failure, nearer to the heart of things than the smaller, more circumspect, and perhaps even 'better' beings who survived the catastrophe. The feeling which I have tried to describe, as accompanying the more obvious tragic emotions at the deaths of heroes, corresponds with some such idea as this.[19]

Now this feeling is evoked with a quite exceptional strength by the death of Cordelia.[20] It is not due to the perception that she, like Lear, has attained through suffering; we know that she had suffered and attained in his days of prosperity. It is simply the feeling that what happens to such a being does not matter; all that matters is what she is. How this can be when, for anything the tragedy tells us, she has ceased to exist, we do not ask; but the tragedy itself makes us feel that somehow it is so. And the force with which this impression is conveyed depends largely on the very fact which excites our bewilderment and protest, that her death, following on the deaths of all the evil characters, and brought about by an unexplained delay in Edmund's effort to save her, comes on us, not as an inevitable conclusion to the sequence of events, but as the sudden stroke of mere fate or chance. The force of the impression, that is to say, depends on the very violence of the contrast between the outward and the inward, Cordelia's death and Cordelia's soul. The more unmotived, unmerited, senseless, monstrous, her fate, the more do we feel that it does not concern her. The extremity of the disproportion between prosperity and goodness first shocks us, and then flashes on us the conviction that our whole attitude in asking or expecting that goodness should be prosperous is wrong; that, if only we could see things as they are, we should see that the outward is nothing and the inward is all.

And some such thought as this (which, to bring it clearly out, I have stated, and still state, in a form both exaggerated and much too explicit) is really present through the whole play. Whether Shakespeare knew it or not, it is present. I might almost say that the 'moral' of *King Lear* is presented in the irony of this collocation:

ALBANY   The gods defend her!
    (*Enter LEAR with Cordelia dead in his arms.*)

The 'gods', it seems, do *not* show their approval by 'defending' their own from adversity or death, or by giving them power and prosperity. These, on the contrary, are worthless, or worse; it is not on them, but on the renunciation of them, that the gods throw incense. They breed lust, pride, hardness of heart, the insolence of office, cruelty, scorn, hypocrisy, contention, war, murder, self-destruction. The whole story beats this indictment of prosperity into the brain. Lear's great speeches in his madness proclaim it like the curses of Timon on life and man. But here, as in *Timon*, the poor and humble are, almost without exception, sound and sweet at heart, faithful and pitiful. And here adversity, to the blessed in spirit, is blessed. It wins fragrance from the crushed flower. It melts in aged hearts sympathies which prosperity had frozen. It purges the soul's sight by blinding that of the eyes. Throughout that stupendous Third Act the good are seen growing better through suffering, and the bad worse through success. The warm castle is a room in hell, the stormswept heath a sanctuary. The judgment of this world is a lie; its goods, which we covet, corrupt us; its ills, which break our bodies, set our souls free:

> Our means secure us, and our mere defects
> Prove our commodities.

Let us renounce the world, hate it, and lose it gladly. The only real thing in it is the soul, with its courage, patience, devotion. And nothing outward can touch that.

SOURCE: *Shakespearean Tragedy* (1904).

NOTES

1. It is to Lear's altered plan that Kent applies these words.

2. There is talk of a war between Goneril and Regan within a fortnight of the division of the kingdom [II i 11–12].

3. I mean that no sufficiently clear reason is supplied for Edmund's delay in attempting to save Cordelia and Lear. The matter stands thus. Edmund, after the defeat of the opposing army, sends Lear and Cordelia to prison. Then, in accordance with a plan agreed on between himself and Goneril, he despatches a captain with secret orders to put them both to death *instantly* [v iii 26–37, 244, 252]. He then has to fight with the disguised Edgar. He is

mortally wounded, and, as he lies dying, he says to Edgar (at line 162, *more than a hundred lines* after he gave that commission to the captain):

> What you have charged me with, that have I done;
> And more, much more; the time will bring it out;
> 'Tis past, and so am I.

In 'more, much more' he seems to be thinking of the order for the deaths of Lear and Cordelia (what else remained undisclosed?); yet he says nothing about it. A few lines later he recognises the justice of his fate, yet still says nothing. Then he hears the story of his father's death, says it has moved him and 'shall perchance do good' (what good except saving his victims?); yet he still says nothing. Even when he hears that Goneril is dead and Regan poisoned, he *still* says nothing. It is only when directly questioned about Lear and Cordelia that he tries to save the victims who were to be killed 'instantly' [242]. How can we explain his delay? Perhaps, thinking the deaths of Lear and Cordelia would be of use to Goneril and Regan, he will not speak till he is sure that both the sisters are dead. Or perhaps, though he can recognise the justice of his fate and can be touched by the account of his father's death, he is still too self-absorbed to rise to the active effort to 'do some good, despite of his own nature'. But, while either of these conjectures is possible, it is surely far from satisfactory that we should be left to mere conjecture as to the cause of the delay which permits the catastrophe to take place. The *real* cause lies outside the dramatic *nexus*. It is Shakespeare's wish to deliver a sudden and crushing blow to the hopes which he has excited.

4. I say 'the reader's', because on the stage, whenever I have seen *King Lear*, the 'cuts' necessitated by modern scenery would have made this part of the play absolutely unintelligible to me if I had not been familiar with it. It is significant that Lamb in his *Tale of King Lear* almost omits the sub-plot.

5. Even if Cordelia had won the battle, Shakespeare would probably have hesitated to concentrate interest on it, for her victory would have been a British defeat.

6. It is vain to suggest that Edmund has only just come home, and that the letter is supposed to have been sent to him when he was 'out'. See I ii 38–40, 65–6.

7. The idea in scene i, perhaps, is that Cordelia's marriage, like the division of the kingdom, has really been pre-arranged, and that the ceremony of choosing between France and Burgundy [I i 46–7] is a mere fiction. Burgundy is to be her husband, and that is why, when Lear has cast her off, he offers her to Burgundy first [line 192 ff]. It might seem from 211 ff that Lear's reason for doing so is that he prefers France, or thinks him the greater man, and therefore will not offer him first what is worthless: but the language of France [240 ff] seems to show that he recognises a prior right in Burgundy.

8. The word 'heath' in the stage-directions of the storm-scenes is, I may remark, Rowe's, not Shakespeare's, who never used the word till he wrote *Macbeth*.

9. Of course I do not mean that he is beginning to be insane, and still less that he *is* insane (as some medical critics suggest).

10. I must however point out that the modern stage-directions are most unfortunate in concealing the fact that here Cordelia sees her father again *for the first time.*

11. What immediately follows is as striking an illustration of quite another quality, and of the effects which make us think of Lear as pursued by a relentless fate. If he could go in and sleep after his prayer, as he intends, his mind, one feels, might be saved: so far there has been only the menace of madness. But from within the hovel Edgar – the last man who would willingly have injured Lear – cries, 'Fathom and half, fathom and half! Poor Tom'; the Fool runs out terrified; Edgar, summoned by Kent, follows him; and, at sight of Edgar, in a moment something gives way in Lear's brain, and he exclaims:

> Hast thou given all
> To thy two daughters? And art thou come to this?

Henceforth he is mad. And they remain out in the storm.

I have not seen it noticed that this stroke of fate is repeated – surely intentionally – in the sixth scene. Gloster has succeeded in persuading Lear to come into the 'house'; he then leaves, and Kent after much difficulty induces Lear to lie down and rest upon the cushions. Sleep begins to come to him again, and he murmurs,

> 'Make no noise, make no noise; draw the curtains; so, so, so. We'll go to supper i' the morning. So, so, so.'

At that moment Gloster enters with the news that he has discovered a plot to kill the King; the rest that 'might yet have balm'd his broken senses' is again interrupted; and he is hurried away on a litter towards Dover. (His recovery, it will be remembered, is due to a long sleep artificially induced.)

12. III iv 49. This is [1904] printed as prose in the Globe edition, but is surely verse. Lear has not yet spoken prose in this scene, and his next three speeches are in verse. The next is in prose, and, ending in his tearing off his clothes, shows the advance of insanity.

13. [Lear's death is thus, I am reminded, like *père* Goriot's.] This interpretation may be condemned as fantastic, but the text, it appears to me, will bear no other. This is the whole speech (in the Globe text):

> And my poor fool is hang'd! No, no, no life!
> Why should a dog, a horse, a rat, have life,
> And thou no breath at all? Thou'lt come no more,
> Never, never, never, never, never!
> Pray you, undo this button: thank you, sir.
> Do you see this? Look on her, look, her lips,
> Look. there, look there!

The transition at 'Do you see this?' from despair to something more than hope is exactly the same as in the preceding passage at the word 'Ha!':

> A plague upon you, murderers, traitors all!
> I might have saved her; now she's gone for ever!
> Cordelia, Cordelia, stay a little.
> Ha!
> What is't thou say'st? Her voice was ever soft,
> Gentle, and low, an excellent thing in woman.

As to any other remarks, I will ask the reader to notice that the passage from Lear's entrance with the body of Cordelia to the stage-direction *He dies* (which probably comes a few lines too soon) is 54 lines in length, and that 30 of them represent the interval during which he has absolutely forgotten Cordelia. (It begins when he looks up at the Captain's words, line 275). To make Lear during this interval turn continually in anguish to the corpse, is to act the passage in a manner irreconcilable with the text, and insufferable in its effect. I speak from experience. I have seen the passage acted thus, and my sympathies were so exhausted long before Lear's death that his last speech, the most pathetic speech ever written, left me disappointed and weary.

14. The Quartos give the 'Never' only thrice (surely wrongly), and all the actors I have heard have preferred this easier task. I ought perhaps to add that the Quartos give the words 'Break, heart; I prithee, break!' to Lear, not Kent.

15. 'Our last and least' (according to the Folio reading). Lear speaks again of 'this little seeming substance'. He can carry her dead body in his arms.

16. Perhaps then the 'low sound' is not merely metaphorical in Kent's speech in ɪ i 153 ff:

>   answer my life my judgment,
> Thy youngest daughter does not love thee least;
> Nor are those empty-hearted whose low sound
> Reverbs no hollowness.

17. ɪ i 80. 'More ponderous' is the reading of the Folios, 'more richer' that of the Quartos. The latter is usually preferred, and Mr Aldis Wright says 'more ponderous' has the appearance of being a player's correction to avoid a piece of imaginary bad grammar. Does it not sound more like the author's improvement of a phrase that he thought a little flat? And, apart from that, is it not significant that it expresses the same idea of weight that appears in the phrase 'I cannot heave my heart into my mouth'?

18. Cf. Cornwall's satirical remarks on Kent's 'plainness' in ɪɪ ii 101 ff – a plainness which did no service to Kent's master. (As a matter of fact, Cordelia had said nothing about 'plainness'.)

19. It follows from the above that, if this idea were made explicit and accompanied our reading of a tragedy throughout, it would confuse or even

destroy the tragic impression. So would the constant presence of Christian beliefs. The reader most attached to these beliefs holds them in temporary suspension while he is immersed in a Shakespearean tragedy. Such tragedy assumes that the world, as it is presented, is the truth, though it also provokes feelings which imply that this world is not the whole truth, and therefore not the truth.

20. Though Cordelia, of course, does not occupy the position of the hero.

G. Wilson Knight King Lear and the Comedy of the Grotesque (1930)

It may appear strange to search for any sort of comedy as a primary theme in a play whose abiding gloom is so heavy, whose reading of human destiny and human actions so starkly tragic. Yet it is an error of aesthetic judgement to regard humour as essentially trivial. Though its impact usually appears vastly different from that of tragedy, yet there is a humour that treads the brink of tears, and tragedy which needs but an infinitesimal shift of perspective to disclose the varied riches of comedy. Humour is an evanescent thing, even more difficult of analysis and intellectual location than tragedy. To the coarse mind lacking sympathy an incident may seem comic which to the richer understanding is pitiful and tragic. So, too, one series of facts can be treated by the artist as either comic or tragic, lending itself equivalently to both. Sometimes a great artist may achieve significant effects by a criss-cross of tears and laughter. Tchehov does this, especially in his plays. A shifting flash of comedy across the pain of the purely tragic both increases the tension and suggests, vaguely, a resolution and a purification. The comic and the tragic rest both on the idea of incompatibilities, and are also, themselves, mutually exclusive; therefore to mingle them is to add to the meaning of each; for the result is then but a new sublime incongruity.

King Lear is roughly analogous to Tchehov where *Macbeth* is analogous to Dostoievsky. The wonder of Shakespearian tragedy is ever a mystery – a vague, yet powerful, tangible, presence; an

interlocking of the mind with a profound meaning, a disclosure to
the inward eye of vistas undreamed, and but fitfully understood.
King Lear is great in the abundance and richness of human
delineation, in the level focus of creation that builds a massive
oneness, in fact, a universe, of single quality from a multiplicity of
differentiated units; and in a positive and purposeful working out of
a purgatorial philosophy. But it is still greater in the perfect fusion of
psychological realism with the daring flights of a fantastic imagination. The heart of a Shakespearian tragedy is centred in the imaginative, in the unknown; and in *King Lear*, where we touch the
unknown, we touch the fantastic. The peculiar dualism at the root of
this play which wrenches and splits the mind by a sight of
incongruities displays in turn realities absurd, hideous, pitiful. This
incongruity is Lear's madness; it is also the demonic laughter that
echoes in the *Lear* universe. In pure tragedy the dualism of
experience is continually being dissolved in the masterful beauty of
passion, merged in the sunset of emotion. But in comedy it is not so
softly resolved – incompatibilities stand out till the sudden relief of
laughter or its equivalent of humour: therefore incongruity is the
especial mark of comedy. Now in *King Lear* there is a dualism
continually crying in vain to be resolved either by tragedy or
comedy. Thence arises its peculiar tension of pain: and the course of
the action often comes as near to the resolution of comedy as to that
of tragedy. So I shall notice here the imaginative core of the play,
and, excluding much of the logic of the plot from immediate
attention, analyse the fantastic comedy of *King Lear*.

From the start, the situation has a comic aspect. It has been
observed that Lear has, so to speak, staged an interlude, with
himself as chief actor, in which he grasps expressions of love to his
heart, and resigns his sceptre to a chorus of acclamations. It is
childish, foolish – but very human. So, too, is the result. Sincerity
forbids play-acting, and Cordelia cannot subdue her instinct to any
judgement advising tact rather than truth. The incident is profoundly
comic and profoundly pathetic. It is, indeed, curious that so storm-
furious a play as *King Lear* should have so trivial a domestic basis: it
is the first of our many incongruities to be noticed. The absurdity of
the old King's anger is clearly indicated by Kent:

> Kill thy physician, and the fee bestow
> Upon the foul disease.   [I i 166]

The result is absurd. Lear's loving daughter Cordelia is struck from his heart's register, and he is shortly, old and grey-haired and a king, cutting a cruelly ridiculous figure before the cold sanity of his unloving elder daughters. Lear is selfish, self-centred. The images he creates of his three daughters' love are quite false, sentimentalized: he understands the nature of none of his children, and demanding an unreal and impossible love from all three, is disillusioned by each in turn. But, though sentimental, this love is not weak. It is powerful and firm-planted in his mind as a mountain rock embedded in earth. The tearing out of it is hideous, cataclysmic. A tremendous soul is, as it were, incongruously geared to a puerile intellect. Lear's senses prove his idealized love-figments false, his intellect snaps, and, as the loosened drive flings limp, the disconnected engine of madness spins free, and the ungeared revolutions of it are terrible, fantastic. This, then, is the basis of the play: greatness linked to puerility. Lear's instincts are themselves grand, heroic – noble even. His judgement is nothing. He understands neither himself nor his daughters:

> REGAN   'Tis the infirmity of his age: yet he hath ever but slenderly known himself.
> GONERIL.   The best and soundest of his time hath been but rash . . .
> [I i 296]

Lear starts his own tragedy by a foolish misjudgement. Lear's fault is a fault of the mind, a mind unwarrantably, because selfishly, foolish. And he knows it:

> O Lear, Lear, Lear!
> Beat at this gate that let thy folly in,
> And thy dear judgement out!   [I iv 294]

His purgatory is to be a purgatory of the mind, of madness. Lear has trained himself to think he cannot be wrong: he finds he is wrong. He has fed his heart on sentimental knowledge of his children's love: he finds their love is not sentimental. There is now a gaping dualism in his mind, thus drawn asunder by incongruities, and he endures madness. Thus the theme of the play is bodied continually into a fantastic incongruity, which is implicit in the beginning – in the very act of Lear's renunciation, retaining the 'title and addition' of King, yet giving over a king's authority to his children. As he becomes torturingly aware of the truth, incongruity masters his mind, and fantastic madness ensues; and this peculiar fact of the Lear-theme is reflected in the *Lear* universe:

> GLOUCESTER   These late eclipses in the sun and moon portend no good to us: though the wisdom of nature can reason it thus and thus, yet nature finds itself scourged by the sequent effects: love cools, friendship falls off, brothers divide: in cities, mutinies; in countries, discord; in palaces, treason; and the bond cracked 'twixt son and father. This villain of mine comes under the prediction; there's son against father: the King falls from bias of nature; there's father against child. We have seen the best of our time: machinations, hollowness, treachery, and all ruinous disorders, follow us disquietly to our graves.   [I ii 115]

Gloucester's words hint a universal incongruity here: the fantastic incongruity of parent and child opposed. And it will be most helpful later to notice the Gloucester-theme in relation to that of Lear.

From the first signs of Goneril's cruelty, the Fool is used as a chorus, pointing us to the absurdity of the situation. He is indeed an admirable chorus, increasing our pain by his emphasis on a humour which yet will not serve to merge the incompatible in a unity of laughter. He is not all wrong when he treats the situation as matter for a joke. Much here that is always regarded as essentially pathetic is not far from comedy. For instance, consider Lear's words:

> I will have such revenges on you both
> That all the world shall – I will do such things –
> What they are, yet I know not; but they shall be
> The terrors of the earth.   [II iv 282]

What could be more painfully incongruous, spoken, as it is, by an old man, a king, to his daughter? It is not far from the ridiculous. The very thought seems a sacrilegious cruelty, I know: but ridicule is generally cruel. The speeches of Lear often come near comedy. Again, notice the abrupt contrast in his words:

> But yet thou art my flesh, my blood, my daughter;
> Or rather a disease that's in my flesh,
> Which I must needs call mine: thou art a boil,
> A plague-sore, an embossed carbuncle,
> In my corrupted blood. But I'll not chide thee . . .   [II iv 224]

This is not comedy, nor humour. But it is exactly the stuff of which humour is made. Lear is mentally a child; in passion a titan. The absurdity of his every act at the beginning of his tragedy is contrasted with the dynamic fury which intermittently bursts out, flickers – then flames and finally gives us those grand apostrophes lifted from man's stage of earth to heaven's rain and fire and thunder:

> Blow, winds, and crack your cheeks! rage! blow!
> You cataracts and hurricanoes, spout
> Till you have drench'd our steeples, drown'd the cocks!
>
> [iii ii 1]

Two speeches of this passionate and unrestrained volume of Promethean curses are followed by:

> No, I will be the pattern of all patience;
> I will say nothing.   [iii ii 37]

Again we are in touch with potential comedy: a slight shift of perspective, and the incident is rich with humour. A sense of self-directed humour would, indeed, have saved Lear. It is a quality he absolutely lacks.

Herein lies the profound insight of the Fool: he sees the potentialities of comedy in Lear's behaviour. This old man, recently a king, and, if his speeches are fair samples, more than a little of a tyrant, now goes from daughter to daughter, furious because Goneril dares criticize his pet knights, kneeling down before Regan, performing, as she says, 'unsightly tricks' (ii iv 159) – the situation is excruciatingly painful, and its painfulness is exactly of that quality which embarrasses in some forms of comedy. In the theatre, one is terrified lest some one laugh: yet, if Lear could laugh – if the Lears of the world could laugh at themselves – there would be no such tragedy. In the early scenes old age and dignity suffer, and seem to deserve, the punishments of childhood:

> Now, by my life
> Old fools are babes again; and must be used
> With checks as flatteries.   [i iii 19]

The situation is summed up by the Fool:

LEAR   When were you wont to be so full of songs, sirrah?
FOOL.   I have used it, nuncle, ever since thou madest thy daughters thy mother: for when thou gavest them the rod, and put'st down thine own breeches . . . [i iv 186]

The height of indecency in suggestion, the height of incongruity. Lear is spiritually put to the ludicrous shame endured bodily by Kent in the stocks; and the absurd rant of Kent, and the unreasonable childish temper of Lear, both merit in some measure what they receive. Painful as it may sound, that is, provisionally, a truth we should realize. The Fool realizes it. He is, too, necessary. Here, where the plot turns on the diverging tugs of two assurances in the mind, it is natural that the action be accompanied by some symbol of humour, that mode which is built of unresolved incompatibilities. Lear's torment is a torment of this dualistic kind, since he scarcely believes his senses when his daughters resist him. He repeats the history of Troilus, who cannot understand the faithlessness of Cressid. In *Othello* and *Timon of Athens* the transition is swift from extreme love to revenge or hate. The movement of Lear's mind is less direct: like Troilus, he is suspended between two separate assurances. Therefore Pandarus, in the latter acts of *Troilus and Cressida*, plays a part similar to the Fool in *King Lear*: both attempt to heal the gaping wound of the mind's incongruous knowledge by the unifying, healing release of laughter. They make no attempt to divert, but rather to direct the hero's mind to the present incongruity. The Fool sees, or tries to see, the humorous potentialities in the most heart-wrenching of incidents:

LEAR   O me, my heart, my rising heart! but, down!
FOOL   Cry to it, nuncle, as the cockney did to the eels when she put 'em
i' the paste alive; she knapped 'em o' the coxcombs with a stick, and
cried 'Down, wantons, down!' 'Twas her brother that, in pure kindness
to his horse, buttered his hay.   [II iv 122]

Except for the last delightful touch – the antithesis of the other – that is a cruel, ugly sense of humour. It is the sinister humour at the heart of this play: we are continually aware of the humour of cruelty and the cruelty of humour. But the Fool's use of it is not aimless. If Lear could laugh he might yet save his reason.

But there is no relief. Outside, in the wild country, the storm grows more terrible:

KENT   ... Since I was man
Such sheets of fire, such bursts of horrid thunder,
Such groans of roaring wind and rain, I never
Remember to have heard ...   [III ii 45]

Lear's mind keeps returning to the unreality, the impossibility of what has happened:

> Your old kind father, whose frank heart gave all –
> O, that way madness lies; let me shun that;
> No more of that.   [III iv 20]

He is still self-centred; cannot understand that he has been anything but a perfect father; cannot understand his daughters' behaviour. It is

> as this mouth should tear this hand
> For lifting food to't . . .   [III iv 15]

It is incongruous, impossible. There is no longer any 'rule in unity itself'.[1] Just as Lear's mind begins to fail, the Fool finds Edgar disguised as 'poor Tom'. Edgar now succeeds the Fool as the counterpart to the breaking sanity of Lear; and where the humour of the Fool made no contact with Lear's mind, the fantastic appearance and incoherent words of Edgar are immediately assimilated, as glasses correctly focused to the sight of oncoming madness. Edgar turns the balance of Lear's wavering mentality. His fantastic appearance and lunatic irrelevancies, with the storm outside, and the Fool still for occasional chorus, create a scene of wraith-like unreason, a vision of a world gone mad:

> . . . Bless thy five wits! Tom's a-cold – O, do de, do de, do de. Bless thee from whirlwinds, star blasting, and taking! Do poor Tom some charity, whom the foul fiend vexes: there could I have him now – and there – and there again, and there.   [III iv 57]

To Lear his words are easily explained. His daughters 'have brought him to this pass'. He cries:

> LEAR   Is it the fashion that discarded fathers
>   Should have thus little mercy on their flesh?
>   Judicious punishment! 'twas this flesh begot
>   Those pelican daughters.
> EDGAR   Pillicock sat on Pillicock-hill:
>   Halloo, halloo, loo, loo!
> FOOL   This cold night will turn us all to fools and madmen.
>   [III iv 71]

What shall we say of this exquisite movement? Is it comedy? Lear's profound unreason is capped by the blatant irrelevance of Edgar's couplet suggested by the word 'pelican'; then the two are swiftly all but unified, for us if not for Lear, in the healing balm of the Fool's conclusion. It is the process of humour, where two incompatibles are resolved in laughter. The Fool does this again. Lear again speaks a profound truth as the wild night and Edgar's fantastic impersonation grip his mind and dethrone his conventional sanity:

> LEAR   Is man no more than this? Consider him well. Thou owest the worm no silk, the beast no hide, the sheep no wool, the cat no perfume. Ha! Here's three on's are sophisticated! Thou art the thing itself: unaccommodated man is no more but such a poor, bare, forked animal as thou art. Off, off, you lendings! Come, unbutton here. (*Tearing off his clothes.*)
> FOOL.   Prithee, nuncle, be contented; 'tis a naughty night to swim in.
> [III iv 105]

This is the furthest flight, not of tragedy, but of philosophic comedy. The autocratic and fiery-fierce old king, symbol of dignity, is confronted with the meanest of men; a naked lunatic beggar. In a flash of vision he attempts to become his opposite, to be naked, 'unsophisticated'. And then the opposing forces which struck the lightning-flash of vision tail off, resolved into a perfect unity by the Fool's laughter, reverberating, trickling, potent to heal in sanity the hideous unreason of this tempest-shaken night: "'tis a naughty night to swim in'. Again this is the process of humour: its flash of vision first bridges the positive and negative poles of the mind, unifying them, and then expresses itself in laughter.

This scene grows still more grotesque, fantastical, sinister. Gloucester enters, his torch flickering in the beating wind:

> FOOL   ... Look, here comes a walking fire.
> (*Enter GLOUCESTER, with a torch*)
> EDGAR   This is the foul fiend Flibbertigibbet: he begins at curfew and walks till the first cock ...   [II iv 116]

Lear welcomes Edgar as his 'philosopher', since he embodies that philosophy of incongruity and the fantastically-absurd which is Lear's vision in madness. 'Noble philosopher', he says [III iv 176], and 'I will still keep with my philosopher' [III iv 180]. The unresolved dualism that tormented Troilus and was given metaphysical expression by him [*Troilus and Cressida*, V ii 134–57] is here more

perfectly bodied into the poetic symbol of poor Tom: and since Lear
cannot hear the resolving laugh of foolery, his mind is focused only
to the 'philosopher' mumbling of the foul fiend. Edgar thus serves to
lure Lear on: we forget that he is dissimulating. Lear is the centre of
our attention, and as the world shakes with tempest and unreason,
we endure something of the shaking and the tempest of his mind.
The absurd and fantastic reign supreme. Lear does not compass for
more than a few speeches the 'noble anger' [II iv 279] for which he
prayed, the anger of Timon. From the start he wavered between
affection and disillusionment, love and hate. The heavens in truth
'fool' [II iv 278] him. He is the 'natural fool of fortune' [IV vi 196].
Now his anger begins to be a lunatic thing, and when it rises to any
sort of magnificent fury or power it is toppled over by the ridiculous
capping of Edgar's irrelevancies:

> LEAR To have a thousand with red burning spits
>   Come hissing in upon 'em –
> EDGAR The foul fiend bites my back.   [III vi 17]

The mock trial is instituted. Lear's curses were for a short space
terrible, majestic, less controlled and purposeful than Timon's but
passionate and grand in their tempestuous fury. Now, in madness,
he flashes on us the ridiculous basis of his tragedy in words which
emphasize the indignity and incongruity of it, and make his madness
something nearer the ridiculous than the terrible, something which
moves our pity, but does not strike awe:

> Arraign her first; 'tis Goneril. I here take my oath before this honourable
> assembly, she kicked the poor king her father.   [III vi 49]

This stroke of the absurd – so vastly different from the awe we
experience in face of Timon's hate – is yet fundamental here. The
core of the play is an absurdity, an indignity, an incongruity. In no
tragedy of Shakespeare do incident and dialogue so recklessly and
miraculously walk the tight-rope of our pity over the depths of
bathos and absurdity.

  This particular region of the terrible bordering on the fantastic
and absurd is exactly the playground of madness. Thus the setting of
Lear's madness includes a sub-plot where these same elements are
presented with stark nakedness, and no veiling subtleties. The
Gloucester-theme is a certain indication of our vision and helps us to

understand, and feel, the enduring agony of Lear. As usual, the first scene of this play strikes the dominant note. Gloucester jests at the bastardy of his son Edmund, remarking that, though he is ashamed to acknowledge him, 'there was good sport at his making' [I i 23]. That is, we start with humour in bad taste. The whole tragedy witnesses a sense of humour in 'the gods' which is in similar bad taste. Now all the Lear effects are exaggerated in the Gloucester-theme. Edmund's plot is a more Iago-like, devilish, intentional thing than Goneril's and Regan's icy callousness. Edgar's supposed letter is crude and absurd:

> ... I begin to find an idle and fond bondage in the oppression of aged
> tyranny ...   [I ii 53]

But then Edmund, wittiest and most attractive of villains, composed it. One can almost picture his grin as he penned those lines, commending them mentally to the limited intellect of his father. Yes – the Gloucester-theme has a beginning even more fantastic than that of Lear's tragedy. And not only are the Lear effects here exaggerated in the directions of villainy and humour: they are even more clearly exaggerated in that of horror. The gouging out of Gloucester's eyes is a thing unnecessary, crude, disgusting: it is meant to be. It helps to provide an accompanying exaggeration of one element – that of cruelty – in the horror that makes Lear's madness. And not only horror: there is even again something satanically comic bedded deep in it. The sight of physical torment, to the uneducated, brings laughter. Shakespeare's England delighted in watching both physical torment and the comic ravings of actual lunacy. The dance of madmen in Webster's *Duchess of Malfi* is of the same ghoulish humour as Regan's plucking Gloucester by the beard: the groundlings will laugh at both. Moreover, the sacrilege of the human body in torture must be, to a human mind, incongruous, absurd. This hideous mockery is consummated in Regan's final witticism after Gloucester's eyes are out:

> Go, thrust him out at gates, and let him smell
> His way to Dover   [III vii 93]

The macabre humoresque of this is nauseating: but it is there, and integral to the play. These ghoulish horrors, so popular in Eliza-bethan drama, and the very stuff of the *Lear* of Shakespeare's youth,

Titus Andronicus, find an exquisitely appropriate place in the tragedy of Shakespeare's maturity which takes as its especial province this territory of the grotesque and the fantastic which is Lear's madness. We are clearly pointed to this grim fun, this hideous sense of humour, at the back of tragedy:

> As flies to wanton boys are we to the gods;
> They kill us for their sport.   [IV i 36]

This illustrates the exact quality I wish to emphasize: the humour a boy – even a kind boy – may see in the wriggles of an impaled insect. So, too, Gloucester is bound, and tortured, physically; and so the mind of Lear is impaled, crucified on the cross-beams of love and disillusion.

There follows the grim pilgrimage of Edgar and Gloucester towards Dover Cliff: an incident typical enough of *King Lear* –

> 'Tis the times' plague when madmen lead the blind.
>   [IV i 46]

They stumble on, madman and blind man, Edgar mumbling:

... five fiends have been in poor Tom at once; of lust, as Obidicut; Hobbididance, prince of dumbness; Mahu, of stealing; Modo, of murder, Flibbertigibbet, of mopping and mowing, who since possesses chamber-maids and waiting-women . . .   [IV i 59]

They are near Dover. Edgar persuades his father that they are climbing steep ground, though they are on a level field, that the sea can be heard beneath:

> GLOUCESTER   Methinks the ground is even.
> EDGAR   Horrible steep.
>   Hark, do you hear the sea?
> GLOUCESTER   No, truly.
> EDGAR   Why, then your other senses grow imperfect
>   By your eyes' anguish.   [IV vi 3]

Gloucester notices the changed sanity of Edgar's speech, and remarks thereon. Edgar hurries his father to the supposed brink, and vividly describes the dizzy precipice over which Gloucester thinks they stand:

                                        How fearful
And dizzy 'tis to cast one's eyes so low!
The crows and choughs that wing the midway air
Show scarce so gross as beetles: half way down
Hangs one that gathers samphire, dreadful trade! . . .
                                                    [IV vi 12]

Gloucester thanks him, and rewards him; bids him move off; then
kneels, and speaks a prayer of noble resignation, breathing that
stoicism which permeates the suffering philosophy of this play:

                                     O you mighty gods!
        This world I do renounce, and, in your sights,
        Shake patiently my great affliction off:
        If I could bear it longer, and not fall
        To quarrel with your great opposeless wills,
        My snuff and loathed part of nature should
        Burn itself out.   [IV vi 35]

Gloucester has planned a spectacular end for himself. We are given
these noble descriptive and philosophical speeches to tune our
minds to a noble, tragic sacrifice. And what happens? The old man
falls from his kneeling posture a few inches, flat, face foremost.
Instead of the dizzy circling to crash and spill his life on the rocks
below – just this. The grotesque merged into the ridiculous reaches a
consummation in this bathos of tragedy: it is the furthest, most
exaggerated, reach of the poet's towering fantastically. We have a
sublimely daring stroke of technique, unjustifiable, like Edgar's
emphasized and vigorous madness throughout, on the plane of plot-
logic, and even to a superficial view somewhat out of place imaginatively in so dire and stark a limning of human destiny as is *King
Lear*; yet this scene is in reality a consummate stroke of art. The
Gloucester-theme throughout reflects and emphasizes and exagger-
ates all the percurrent qualities of the Lear-theme. Here the
incongruous and fantastic element of the Lear-theme is boldly
reflected into the tragically-absurd. The stroke is audacious, un-
ashamed, and magical of effect. Edgar keeps up the deceit; persuades his father that he has really fallen; points to the empty sky, as
to a cliff:

                    . . . the shrill-gorged lark
            Cannot be heard so far . . .   [IV vi 59]

and finally paints a fantastic picture of a ridiculously grotesque devil that stood with Gloucester on the edge:

> As I stood here below, methought his eyes
> Were two full moons; he had a thousand noses,
> Horns whelk'd and waved like the enridged sea;
> It was some fiend . . .   [IV vi 70]

Some fiend, indeed.

There is masterful artistry in all this. The Gloucester-theme has throughout run separate from that of Lear, yet parallel, and continually giving us direct villainy where the other shows cold callousness; horrors of physical torment where the other has a subtle mental torment; culminating in this towering stroke of the grotesque and absurd to balance the fantastic incidents and speeches that immediately follow. At this point we suddenly have our first sight of Lear in the full ecstasy of his later madness. Now, when our imaginations are most powerfully quickened to the grotesque and incongruous, the whole surge of the Gloucester-theme, which has just reached its climax, floods as a tributary the main stream of our sympathy with Lear. Our vision has thus been uniquely focused to understand that vision of the grotesque, the incongruous, the fantastically-horrible, which is the agony of Lear's mind:

> *Enter* LEAR, *fantastically dressed with wild flowers.*
>   [IV vi 81]

So runs Capell's direction. Lear, late 'every inch a king', the supreme pathetic figure of literature, now utters the wild and whirling language of furthest madness. Sometimes his words hold profound meaning. Often they are tuned to the orthodox Shakespearian hate and loathing, especially sex-loathing, of the hate-theme. Or again, they are purely ludicrous, or would be, were it not a Lear who speaks them:

> . . . Look, look, a mouse! Peace, peace; this piece of toasted cheese will do't . . .   [IV vi 90]

It is, indeed, well that we are, as it were, prepared by now for the grotesque. Laughter is forbidden us. Consummate art has so forged plot and incident that we may watch with tears rather than laughter the cruelly comic actions of Lear:

> LEAR   I will die bravely, like a bridegroom.² What!
>   I will be jovial: come, come; I am a king,
>   My masters, know you that?
> GENTLEMAN   You are a royal one, and we obey you.
> LEAR   Then there's life in't. Nay, if you get it, you shall get it with
>   running. Sa, sa, sa, sa.   [IV vi 203]

Lear is a child again in his madness. We are in touch with the exquisitely pathetic, safeguarded only by Shakespeare's masterful technique from the bathos of comedy.

But indeed this recurrent stress on the incongruous and the fantastic is not a subsidiary element in *King Lear*: it is the very heart of the play. We watch humanity grotesquely tormented, cruelly and with mockery impaled: nearly all the persons suffer some form of crude indignity in the course of the play. I have noticed the major themes of Lear and Gloucester: there are others. Kent is banished, undergoes the disguise of a servant, is put to shame in the stocks; Cornwall is killed by his own servant resisting the dastardly mutilation of Gloucester; Oswald, the prim courtier, is done to death by Edgar in the role of an illiterate country yokel –

> . . . keep out, che vor ye, or ise try whether your costard or my ballow be
> the harder . . .   [IV vi 247]

Edgar himself endures the utmost degradation of his disguise as 'poor Tom', begrimed and naked, and condemned to speak nothing but idiocy. Edmund alone steers something of an unswerving tragic course, brought to a fitting, deserved, but spectacular end, slain by his wronged brother, nobly repentant at the last:

> EDMUND   What you have charged me with, that have I done;
>   And more, much more; the time will bring it out:
>   'Tis past, and so am I. But what art thou
>   That hast this fortune on me? If thou'rt noble,
>   I do forgive thee.
> EDGAR   Let's exchange charity.
>   I am no less in blood than thou art, Edmund;
>   If more, the more thou hast wrong'd me.
>   My name is Edgar . . .   [V iii 164]

The note of forgiving chivalry reminds us of the deaths of Hamlet and Laertes. Edmund's fate is nobly tragic: 'the wheel has come full circle; I am here' [V iii 176]. And Edmund is the most villainous of all. Again, we have incongruity; and again, the Gloucester-theme reflects the Lear-theme. Edmund is given a noble, an essentially tragic end, and Goneril and Regan, too, meet their ends with something of tragic fineness in pursuit of their evil desires. Regan dies by her sister's poison; Goneril with a knife. They die, at least, in the cause of love – love of Edmund. Compared with these deaths, the end of Cordelia is horrible, cruel, unnecessarily cruel – the final grotesque horror in the play. Her villainous sisters are already dead. Edmund is nearly dead, repentant. It is a matter of seconds – and rescue comes too late. She is hanged by a common soldier. The death which Dostoievsky's Stavrogin singled out as of all the least heroic and picturesque, or rather, shall we say, the most hideous and degrading: this is the fate that grips the white innocence and resplendent love-strength of Cordelia. To be hanged, after the death of her enemies, in the midst of friends. It is the last hideous joke of destiny: this – and the fact that Lear is still alive, has recovered his sanity for this. The death of Cordelia is the last and most horrible of all the horrible incongruities I have noticed:

> Why should a dog, a horse, a rat have life,
> And thou no breath at all?   [V iii 308]

We remember: 'Upon such sacrifices, my Cordelia, the gods themselves throw incense' [IV iii 20]. Or do they laugh, and is the *Lear* universe one ghastly piece of fun?

We do not feel that. The tragedy is most poignant in that it is purposeless, unreasonable. It is the most fearless artistic facing of the ultimate cruelty of things in our literature. That cruelty would be less were there not this element of comedy which I have emphasized, the insistent incongruities, which create and accompany the madness of Lear, which leap to vivid shape in the mockery of Gloucester's suicide, which are intrinsic in the texture of the whole play. Mankind is, as it were, deliberately and comically tormented by the 'gods'. He is not even allowed to die tragically. Lear is 'bound upon a wheel of fire' and only death will end the victim's agony:

> Vex not his ghost: O, let him pass! he hates him
> That would upon the rack of this tough world
> Stretch him out longer.   [V iii 315]

King Lear is supreme in that, in this main theme, it faces the very absence of tragic purpose: wherein it is profoundly different from *Timon of Athens*. Yet, as we close the sheets of this play, there is no horror, nor resentment. The tragic purification of the essentially untragic is yet complete.

Now in this essay it will, perhaps, appear that I have unduly emphasized one single element of the play, magnifying it, and leaving the whole distorted. It has been my purpose to emphasize. I have not exaggerated. The pathos has not been minimized: it is redoubled. Nor does the use of the words 'comic' and 'humour' here imply disrespect to the poet's purpose: rather I have used these words, crudely no doubt, to cut out for analysis the very heart of the play – the thing that man dares scarcely face: the demonic grin of the incongruous and absurd in the most pitiful of human struggles with an iron fate. It is this that wrenches, splits, gashes the mind till it utters the whirling vapourings of lunacy. And, though love and music – twin sisters of salvation – temporarily may heal the racked consciousness of Lear, yet, so deeply planted in the facts of our life is this unknowing ridicule of destiny, that the uttermost tragedy of the incongruous ensues, and there is no hope save in the broken heart and limp body of death. This is of all the most agonizing of tragedies to endure: and if we are to feel more than a fraction of this agony, we must have sense of this quality of grimmest humour. We must beware of sentimentalizing the cosmic mockery of the play.

And is there, perhaps, even a deeper, and less heart-searing, significance in its humour? Smiles and tears are indeed most curiously interwoven here. Gloucester was saved from his violent and tragic suicide that he might recover his wronged son's love, and that his heart might

> 'Twixt two extremes of passion, joy and grief,
> Burst smilingly.   [v iii 200]

Lear dies with the words

> Do you see this? Look on her, look, her lips,
> Look there, look here!   [v iii 312]

What smiling destiny is this he sees at the last instant of racked mortality? Why have we that strangely beautiful account of Cordelia's first hearing of her father's pain:

> ... patience and sorrow strove
> Who should express her goodliest. You have seen
> Sunshine and rain at once: her smiles and tears
> Were like a better way: those happy smilets,
> That play'd on her ripe lip, seem'd not to know
> What guests were in her eyes; which parted thence,
> As pearls from diamonds dropp'd. In brief,
> Sorrow would be a rarity most beloved,
> If all could so become it.   [v iii 18]

What do we touch in these passages? Sometimes we know that all human pain holds beauty, that no tear falls but it dews some flower we cannot see. Perhaps humour, too, is inwoven in the universal pain, and the enigmatic silence holds not only an unutterable sympathy, but also the ripples of an impossible laughter whose flight is not for the wing of human understanding; and perhaps it is this that casts its darting shadow of the grotesque across the furrowed pages of *King Lear*.

Source: *The Wheel of Fire* (1930).

NOTES

1. *Troilus and Cressida* , v ii 138.
2. This is to be related to *Antony and Cleopatra*, iv xii 100, and *Measure for Measure*, iii i 82; also *Hamlet*, iv iv 62.

Enid Welsford   The Fool in *King Lear*   (1935)

Like others of his profession he is very ready to proffer his coxcomb to his betters, but in doing so he does not merely raise a laugh or score a point, he sets a problem. 'What am I? What is madness?' he seems to ask, 'the world being what it is, do I necessarily insult a man by investing him with motley?'

With this apparently comic question the Fool strikes the keynote of the tragedy of Lear. It is a critical, a crucial question which effects a startling division among the dramatis personae – it being for instance obvious that Goneril, Regan and Edmund are not candidates for the cap and bells. It is also a central question which at once resolves itself into a question about the nature of the universe. For the full understanding of its import it is necessary to leave for awhile our meditation on the meaning of the words of the Fool, and to consider instead their reverberation in the play as a whole: examining firstly the disposition of the characters, and secondly the movement of events.

It is a critical commonplace that in *King Lear* Shakespeare deals with the tragic aspect of human life in its most universal form. The conflict of good with evil, of wisdom with folly, the hopeless cry to the deaf Heavens for justice, are presented with something of the simplicity of a morality play. For just as in that type of drama the central figure was the soul of man competed for by the conflicting forces of good and ill; so in *King Lear* the two heroes are erring men, warm-hearted, but self-willed, whose ruin or salvation depends on the issue of a conflict between two sharply opposed groups of people painted far more uncompromisingly in black and white than is customary in Shakespearian tragedy. But if *Lear* has something of the structural simplicity of the morality play it has none of its moral triteness. Where the medieval playwright furnishes answers, Shakespeare provokes questions and reveals ambiguities. Whether he ever suggests a solution is disputable; but there can be little doubt as to the urgency with which he sets the problem of the nature and destiny of goodness.

In *King Lear* all the 'good' characters have one striking quality in common, they have the capacity for 'fellow-feeling' highly developed. At first, it is true, the imperfect heroes demand rather than give sympathy, but the disinterestedness of their adherents is unlimited. The banished Kent

> Followed his enemy King, and did him service
> Improper for a slave.

Perfect and imperfect alike take it for granted that the capacity for sympathetic love is a very valuable but quite normal attribute of human nature. This attribute makes the good characters peculiarly vulnerable and sometimes almost stupidly helpless. In the first place they instinctively trust their fellows, and this trustfulness does not sharpen their powers of discrimination. The imperfect who crave for affection are particularly liable to make silly mistakes, and their suffering and anger when they think themselves deceived make them still more unable to distinguish friend from foe. The perfectly sympathetic are foolish in a different way. They are blind to their own interests. They save others but themselves they cannot save.

The 'bad' characters are the exact opposite of the good in that they are abnormally devoid of 'fellow-feeling'. They may be hardly more egoistic than some of their opponents, but they differ from them in that they are no more anxious to receive sympathy than they are to give it. They seek only to gratify their physical lust and their will-to-power. A slight personal inconvenience seems to them more important than the agony of their closest kinsman, simply because the sense of sympathy and of human relatedness lies wholly outside their experience. For Goneril, Regan and Edmund the world is the world of Hobbes, a world where every man's hand is against every man's, and the only human ties are contracts which reason and self-interest prompt people to make as the only alternative to mutual annihilation, and which no moral scruple need hinder them from breaking when by doing so they defend their own interests. Up to a point the evil are invulnerable. Their activities are never hampered by a distaste for other people's sufferings, trustfulness never dims their powers of observation, and above all they never put themselves into anyone else's power by a desire for his affection.

The distinction between the good and the bad is clear, there is little ambiguity about the word *knave*. It is the meaning of the word *fool* which is obscure, and its obscurity increases with increasing knowledge of the attitude of the good and evil to one another.

On the whole, and this is true of other plays besides *King Lear*, Shakespeare tends to give more intellectual ability to his sinners than to his saints. Edmund, for instance, is so shrewd and witty that he almost wins our sympathy for his unabashed cruelty. To such an one goodness is simply stupidity:

> A credulous father! and a brother noble,
> Whose nature is so far from doing harms,
> That he suspects none: on whose foolish honesty
> My practices ride easy!

But this is trite; Shakespeare penetrates more profoundly than this into the nature of evil. Sympathy and trustfulness make men easily gullible, and consistently egoistic utilitarians ought to value gulls.

But strangely enough they find them most distasteful. 'Well you may fear too far', says Albany, when Goneril suggests that it would be prudent to dismiss her father's train. 'Safer than trust too far', is his wife's characteristic reply. This difference of outlook soon ripens into a real antipathy:

GONERIL   My most dear Gloster!   [Exit EDMUND
   O, the difference of man and man! To thee
   A woman's services are due: *my fool*
   Usurps my body.
OSWALD   Madam, here comes my lord.   [Exit
Enter ALBANY
GONERIL   I have been worth the whistle.
ALBANY   O Goneril!
   You are not worth the dust which the rude wind
   Blows in your face . . .
   She that herself will sliver and disbranch
   From her material sap, perforce must wither,
   And come to deadly use.
GONERIL   No more; the text is *foolish* .
ALBANY   Wisdom and goodness to the vile seem vile:
   Filths savour but themselves. What have you done? . . .
GONERIL   Milk-liver'd man!
   That bear'st a cheek for blows, a head for wrongs . . .
   With plumed helm thy slayer begins threats;
   Whiles thou, *a moral fool*, sitt'st still, and criest
   'Alack, why does he so?'
ALBANY   See thyself, devil!
   Proper deformity seems not in the fiend
   So horrid as in woman.
GONERIL   O vain *fool*!
ALBANY   Thou changed and self-cover'd thing, for shame,
   Be-monster not thy feature.

Goneril's attitude reminds us of the wise advice which the Fool ironically offered to Kent. To Goneril it is the only conceivable kind of wisdom, to Albany it is just plain knavery, to the Fool it is either wisdom or folly according to your point of view. For the puzzle about evil is not that men do not live up to their principles; it is that men can reverse values and say: 'Evil, be thou my good', and that by reason alone it is not possible to prove them wrong. The bad characters in *Lear* have no fellow-feeling, and therefore act consistently from motives of self-interest. The analytic intellect cannot prove that 'fellow-feeling' is a possibility, still less that it is a duty. Respectable philosophers have founded their systems (though not their practice) on the notion that altruism can always be resolved into egoism. Are not Edmund and Goneril, then, justified in seeing the world as they do see it and acting in accordance with their insight? What have the good to say on this subject? Well, they have no intellectual arguments to offer, but two intuitions or convictions, on which they are prepared to act even at the cost of their own lives. Firstly, if love is lunacy so much the worse for sanity: the good will merely in their turn reverse values and say, 'Folly, be thou my wisdom.' Secondly, love or 'fellow-feeling' is a normal attribute of humanity, and as such it does not need proof, for it is its absence, not its presence, that requires explanation. 'Let them anatomize Regan, see what breeds about her heart. Is there any cause in nature that makes these hard hearts?' Recurrent throughout the play is the sense that the breaking of human ties, especially ties of close blood or plighted loyalty, is so abnormal and unnatural that it must be a symptom of some dread convulsion in the frame of things that must bring about the end of the world unless some Divine Power intervenes to redress the balance before it is too late. And more than that, it is so fundamentally abnormal and inhuman that the mere contemplation of it upsets the mental balance of a normal man. As Lear looks into Goneril's heart his wits begin to turn. To Edmund, on the other hand, it is the most natural thing in the world that he should pursue his own interests, whatever the expense to other people.

Which of these parties sees the truth, or rather, to speak more accurately, which point of view does Shakespeare mean us to adopt as we experience his tragedy? Or is this an instance of his notorious impartiality? Is he giving us a tragic illustration of moral relativity? Do Goneril and Cordelia separate good from evil, wisdom from folly, with very different results, only because they have different but equally valid frames of reference for their measurements? If we join the good characters in the play in asking Heaven to decide, that would seem to be the inescapable conclusion, for both Cordelia and Goneril die prematurely. And if it is a fact that some of the good survive, whereas the evil are shown to be by their nature mutually destructive; yet we may set against this the fact that the good suffer more than the evil, that love and suffering, in this play, are almost interchangeable terms and the driving force of the action is derived from the power of the evil to inflict mental agony upon the good. This is particularly important, because the physical death of the hero is not really the tragic climax of this play. Lear, after all, is an old man, and the poignant question about him is not: 'Will he survive?' but rather 'What will happen to his mind?' The real horror lies not in the fact that Goneril and Regan can cause the death of their father, but that they can apparently destroy his human integrity. I say 'apparently', because the whirling ambiguities of the Fool are reflected in the sequence of events as well as in the opinions of the dramatis personae, and it is only after a study of the arrangement of the action that we can rightly decide whether the Heavens are shown as just or wanton, deaf and dumb or most ironically vocal. For, as Aristotle taught us long ago, plot is the soul of tragedy.

It has often been pointed out that Lear has a more passive rôle than most of Shakespeare's tragic characters. Nevertheless he is involved in an event, and his relationship with the Fool is no mere static pictorial contrast, but part of the tragic movement of the play; the movement downwards towards that ultimate exposure and defeat when the King is degraded to the status of the meanest of his servants. We watch the royal sufferer being progressively stripped, first of extraordinary worldly power, then of ordinary human dignity, then of the very necessities of life, deprived of which he is more helpless and abject than any animal. But there is a more dreadful consummation than this reduction to physical nakedness. Lear hardly feels the storm because he is struggling to retain his mental integrity, his 'knowledge and reason', which are not only, as he himself calls them, 'marks of sovereignty', but the essential marks of humanity itself:

> O, let me not be mad, not mad, sweet heaven!
> Keep me in temper, I would not be mad!
>
> O fool, I shall go mad!

Lear's dread is justified, 'sweet heaven' rejects his prayer, and the central scenes on the heath are peopled by a blind, half-crazy nobleman, guided by a naked beggar supposed to be mad, and by an actually mad King served by a half-witted court-jester – an amazingly daring version of the culminating moment of the sottie: the great reversal when the highest dignitaries appear as fools, and the World or even Holy Church herself is revealed in cap and bells.

Do we then find at the heart of this greatest of tragedies the satire of the sottie transmuted into despair? That depends on what happens when we test the quality of Lear's unreason, and on how we answer the question already suggested by his brother in folly: 'Do I insult a man by investing him with motley?'

From the time when Lear's agony begins and he feels his sanity threatened he becomes gradually aware of the sufferings of other people:

> My wits begin to turn. . . .
> Poor fool and knave, I've one part in my heart
> That's sorry yet for thee.

And not only are Lear's sympathies aroused, they are broadened. Goneril and Regan break the closest, most fundamental of human ties, they cannot feel even that kind of parental-filial relationship that the animals feel; whereas in his agony, Lear, who had himself been unnatural to Cordelia, suddenly realizes that all men are one in pain:

> . . . Take physic, pomp:
> Expose thyself to feel what wretches feel,
> That thou may'st shake the superflux to them,
> And show the heavens more just.

As Lear's brain reels, his agony increases and his sympathies expand. The same thing happens to Gloucester, whose blindness parallels Lear's madness:

> . . . heavens, deal so still!
> Let the superfluous and lust-dieted man
> That slaves your ordinance, that will not see
> Because he doth not feel, feel your power quickly;
> So distribution should undo excess,
> And each man have enough.

In several passages *seeing* and *feeling* are compared and contrasted with one another. It is feeling that gives the true sight. 'I stumbled when I saw.' Again we are confronted with the paradoxical reversal of wisdom and folly. At the beginning of the play both Lear and Gloucester are blind fools:

> O, Lear, Lear, Lear!
> Beat at the gate that let thy folly in
> And thy dear judgment out.

Both the good and the evil would agree that Lear had reason for self-reproach, but they would disagree as to the nature of the folly he deplores. To the bad his folly was the folly of trustfulness and affection, to the good it was the folly of distrustfulness and unkindness. But now that the worst has happened, now that Lear has lost his sanity, he has enlarged his vision. As his wits begin to leave him, he begins to see the truth about himself; when they are wholly gone he begins to have spasmodic flashes of insight in which, during momentary lulls in the storm of vengeful personal resentment, he sees the inner truth about the world. 'Thou wouldst make a good fool', said the Fool to his master at the beginning of his misfortunes, and he spoke as a prophet. In his amazing encounter with the *blind* Gloucester, the *mad* Lear has something of the wit, the penetration, the quick repartee of the court-jester. From the realistic point of view it is no doubt a dramatic flaw that Shakespeare does not account more clearly for the fate of the real man in motley; but his disappearance was a poetic necessity, for the King having lost everything, including his wits, has now himself become the Fool. He has touched bottom, he is an outcast from society, he has no longer any private axe to grind, so he now sees and speaks the truth.

And what is the truth? What does the mad Lear see in his flashes of lucidity? Does he see that Goneril was more sensible than Cordelia? Is Mr Wyndham Lewis right in suggesting that it is only the swelling blank verse that differentiates his voice from the disgusted snarling of Thersites? Certainly his vision is a grim one. He sees not one particular event but the whole of human life as a vast sottie:

> LEAR   What, art mad? A man may see how this world goes, with no eyes. Look with thine ears: see how yond justice rails upon yond simple thief. Hark, in thine ear: change places; and, handy-dandy, which is the justice, which is the thief? Thou hast seen a farmer's dog bark at a beggar?
> GLOUCESTER   Ay sir.
> LEAR   And the creature run from the cur? There thou mightest behold the great image of authority: a dog's obeyed in office. . . .
>   . . . Plate sin with gold,
> And the strong lance of justice hurtless-breaks;
> Arm it in rags, a pigmy's straw does pierce it.
> None does offend, none – I say, none; I'll able 'em:

Take that of me, my friend, who have the power
To seal th' accuser's lips. Get thee glass eyes;
And, like a scurvy politician, seem
To see the things thou dost not.

Already we have watched king and noblemen turned into fools
and beggars, now the great reversal of the Saturnalia is transferred
from the action of the tragedy into the mind of the tragic hero, who
discovers in his dotage, what the evil have known from their cradles,
that *in this world there is no poetic justice*:

When we are born, we cry that we are come
To this great stage of fools.

This is the favourite common-place of the Enfants-sans-souci
transposed into the minor key and made matter not for laughter but
for tears.

But it is the falling of these tears (which of course can only be
heard through the blank verse or prose rhythm) which differentiates
Lear the fool from Thersites the cynic. Thersites gloats over the
universality of evil; he never, like Lear, recoils from his vision of sin
with a passionate horror which breaks out into broken cries reeling
between verse and prose, he never begs for 'civet to sweeten his
imagination', still less does he include all under sin that he may have
mercy upon all:

None does offend, none – I say, none; I'll able 'em:
Take that of me, my friend, who have the power
To seal th' accuser's lips.

The statement that Shakespeare tends to give more intellectual
ability to the evil than to the good needs modification. In this play,
at least, the loving characters when they are perfectly disinterested
or when they have lost everything see equally clearly and more
profoundly than do the cold-hearted. But the good and evil react
very differently to the same facts seen with equal clearness, and it
must not be forgotten that the blind Gloucester and mad Lear have
come to know that to see truly 'how the world goes' is to 'see it
feelingly'. And when the world is seen feelingly, what then? Why
then we must be patient. That is all.

'Patience', like 'wisdom', 'folly', 'knavery', 'nature', is one of the key words of this tragedy. As soon as Lear begins to realize the nature of his misfortune, he begins to make pathetic attempts to acquire it, and when his mental overthrow is complete he recommends it as the appropriate response to the misery of life:

> If thou wilt weep my fortunes, take my eyes.
> I know thee well enough; thy name is Gloucester:
> Thou must be patient; we came crying hither:
> Thou know'st, the first time that we smell the air,
> We wawl and cry.

Edgar takes the same point of view:

> What! In ill-thoughts again? Men must endure
> Their going hence, even as their coming hither:
> Ripeness is all.

What is meant? Something different from tame submissiveness or cold stoicism, but completely opposed to that restless activity in pursuit of our own ends which Edmund thinks so preferable to passive obedience to fortune or custom. Patience, here, seems to imply an unflinching, clear-sighted recognition of the fact of pain, and the complete abandonment of any claim to justice or gratitude either from Gods or men; it is the power to choose love when love is synonymous with suffering, and to abide by the choice knowing there will be no Divine Salvation from its consequences.

And here, I think, is the solution of the problem set by the Fool; the problem of apparent moral relativity, 'Wisdom and goodness to the vile seem vile, filths savour but themselves', so that Albany and Goneril have not even sufficient common ground to make a real argument possible. Nevertheless, Shakespeare does not allow us to remain neutral spectators of their debate, he insists that although Goneril's case is as complete and consistent as that of Albany it is *not* equally valid, *not* equally true. In the first place Shakespeare's poetry persuades and compels us to accept the values of the friends rather than of the enemies of Lear. Secondly, Shakespeare makes the fullest possible use of the accepted convention that it is the Fool who speaks the truth, which he knows not by ratiocination but by inspired intuition. The mere appearance of the familiar figure in cap and bells would at once indicate to the audience where the 'punctum indifferens', the impartial critic, the mouthpiece of real sanity, was to be found.

Now the Fool sees that when the match between the good and the evil is played by the intellect alone it must end in a stalemate, but when the heart joins in the game then the decision is immediate and final. 'I will tarry, the Fool will stay – And let the wise man fly.' That is the unambiguous wisdom of the madman who sees the truth. That is decisive. It is decisive because, so far from being an abnormal freakish judgment, it is the instinctive judgment of normal humanity raised to heroic stature; and therefore no amount of intellectual argument can prevent normal human beings from receiving and accepting it, just as, when all the psychologists and philosophers have said their say, normal human beings continue to receive and accept the external world as given to them through sense perception. 'They that seek a reason for all things do destroy reason', notes the judicious Hooker; our data, our premises, we must simply receive, and receive not only through our heads but also through our senses and our hearts. To see truly is to 'see feelingly'.

It would seem, then, that there is nothing contemptible in a motley coat. The Fool is justified, but we have not yet a complete answer to his original query: 'What is folly?' Which is the wise man, which is the fool? To be foolish is to mistake the nature of things, or to mistake the proper method of attaining to our desires, or to do both at once. Even Edmund and Edgar, even Goneril and Albany, could agree to that proposition. But have the perfectly disinterested made either of these mistakes and have not the self-interested made them both? The evil desire pleasure and power, and they lose both, for the evil are mutually destructive. The good desire to sympathize and to save, and their desires are partially fulfilled, although as a result they have to die. Nor have the good mistaken the nature or 'mystery of things' which, after all, unlike Edmund, they have never professed either to dismiss or to understand. It is, indeed, as we have seen, the good who are normal. Lear, in his folly, is not reduced, as he fears, to the level of the beasts, but to essential naked humanity, 'unaccommodated man', 'the thing itself'. It is the evil who 'be-monster' themselves, it is the sight of Goneril which makes Albany fear that

> It will come,
> Humanity must perforce prey on itself,
> Like monsters of the deep.

In this connection it is not without interest that the Elizabethan playwrights made conventional use of the inherited belief in thunder as the voice of the Divine Judge, and that the Divine inspiration of madmen has always been a widespread and deeply rooted popular superstition.

Not that I would suggest that this great tragedy should be regarded as a morality play full of naïve spiritual consolation. That Shakespeare's ethics were the ethics of the New Testament, that in this play his mightiest poetry is dedicated to the reiteration of the wilder paradoxes of the Gospels and of St Paul, that seems to me quite certain. But it is no less certain that the metaphysical comfort of the Scriptures is deliberately omitted, though not therefore necessarily denied. The perfectly disinterested choose lovingkindness because they know it to be intrinsically desirable and worth the cost, not because they hope that the full price will not be exacted. It is Kent's readiness to be unendingly patient which makes him other than a shrewder and more far-calculating Edmund. If the thunder had ceased at Lear's bidding, then Lear would not have become a sage-fool. What the thunder says remains enigmatic, but it is this Divine ambiguity which gives such force to the testimony of the human heart. Had the speech of the gods been clearer, the apparently simple utterances of the Fool would have been less profound:

> FOOL   He that has a little tiny wit,
>   With hey, ho, the wind and the rain,
>   Must make content with his fortune's fit,
>   For the rain it raineth every day.
> LEAR   True, my good boy.

And so we reach the final reversal of values. 'Ay every inch a king', says Lear in his madness, and we do not wholly disagree with him. The medieval clergy inaugurated the Saturnalia by parodying the Magnificat: Shakespeare reverses the process. Lear's tragedy is the investing of the King with motley: it is also the crowning and apotheosis of the Fool.

SOURCE: *The Fool* (1935). Reprinted in Kermode, *Four Centuries of Shakespearian Criticism* (1965).

George Orwell   Lear, Tolstoy and the Fool   (1950)

Tolstoy's pamphlets are the least known part of his work, and his attack on Shakespeare[1] is not even an easy document to get hold of, at any rate in an English translation. Perhaps, therefore, it will be useful if I give a summary of the pamphlet before trying to discuss it.

Tolstoy begins by saying that throughout life Shakespeare has aroused in him 'an irresistible repulsion and tedium'. Conscious that the opinion of the civilized world is against him, he has made one attempt after another on Shakespeare's works, reading and re-reading them in Russian, English and German; but 'I invariably underwent the same feelings; repulsion, weariness and bewilderment'. Now, at the age of seventy-five, he has once again re-read the entire works of Shakespeare, including the historical plays, and

I have felt with an even greater force, the same feelings – this time, however, not of bewilderment, but of firm, indubitable conviction that the unquestionable glory of a great genius which Shakespeare enjoys, and which compels writers of our time to imitate him and readers and spectators to discover in him non-existent merits – thereby distorting their aesthetic and ethical understanding – is a great evil, as is every untruth.

Shakespeare, Tolstoy adds, is not merely no genius, but is not even 'an average author', and in order to demonstrate this fact he will examine *King Lear*, which, as he is able to show by quotations from Hazlitt, Brandes and others, has been extravagantly praised and can be taken as an example of Shakespeare's best work.

Tolstoy then makes a sort of exposition of the plot of *King Lear*, finding it at every step to be stupid, verbose, unnatural, unintelligible, bombastic, vulgar, tedious and full of incredible events, 'wild ravings', 'mirthless jokes', anachronisms, irrelevancies, obscenities, worn-out stage conventions, and other faults both moral and aesthetic. *Lear* is, in any case, a plagiarism of an earlier and much better play, *King Leir*, by an unknown author, which Shakespeare stole and then ruined. It is worth quoting a specimen paragraph to illustrate the manner in which Tolstoy goes to work. Act III, scene ii (in which Lear, Kent and the Fool are together in the storm) is summarized thus:

Lear walks about the heath and says words which are meant to express his despair: he desires that the winds should blow so hard that they (the winds) should crack their cheeks and that the rain should flood everything, that lightning should singe his white head, and the thunder flatten the world and destroy all germs 'that make ungrateful man'! The fool keeps uttering still more senseless words. Enter Kent: Lear says that for some reason during this storm all criminals shall be found out and convicted. Kent, still unrecognized by Lear, endeavours to persuade him to take refuge in a hovel. At this point the fool utters a prophecy in no wise related to the situation and they all depart.

Tolstoy's final verdict on *Lear* is that no unhypnotized observer, if such an observer existed, could read it to the end with any feeling except 'aversion and weariness'. And exactly the same is true of 'all the other extolled dramas of Shakespeare, not to mention the senseless dramatized tales, *Pericles, Twelfth Night, The Tempest, Cymbeline, Troilus and Cressida*'.

Having dealt with *Lear* Tolstoy draws up a more general indictment against Shakespeare. He finds that Shakespeare has a certain technical skill which is partly traceable to his having been an actor, but otherwise no merits whatever. He has no power of delineating character or of making words and actions spring naturally out of situations, his language is uniformly exaggerated and ridiculous, he constantly thrusts his own random thoughts into the mouth of any character who happens to be handy, he displays a 'complete absence of aesthetic feeling', and his words 'have nothing whatever in common with art and poetry'.

'Shakespeare might have been whatever you like,' Tolstoy concludes, 'but he was not an artist.' Moreover, his opinions are not original or interesting, and his tendency is 'of the lowest and most immoral'. Curiously enough, Tolstoy does not base this last judgement on Shakespeare's own utterances, but on the statements of two critics, Gervinus and Brandes. According to Gervinus (or at any rate Tolstoy's reading of Gervinus) 'Shakespeare taught . . . that one *may be too good*', while according to Brandes: 'Shakespeare's fundamental principle . . . is that *the end justifies the means*.' Tolstoy adds on his own account that Shakespeare was a jingo patriot of the worst type, but apart from this he considers that Gervinus and Brandes have given a true and adequate description of Shakespeare's view of life.

Tolstoy then recapitulates in a few paragraphs the theory of art which he had expressed at greater length elsewhere. Put still more shortly, it amounts to a demand for dignity of subject matter, sincerity, and good craftsmanship. A great work of art must deal with some subject which is 'important to the life of mankind', it must express something which the author genuinely feels, and it must use such technical methods as will produce the desired effect. As Shakespeare is debased in outlook, slipshod in execution and incapable of being sincere even for a moment, he obviously stands condemned.

But here there arises a difficult question. If Shakespeare is all that Tolstoy has shown him to be, how did he ever come to be so generally admired? Evidently the answer can only lie in a sort of mass hypnosis, or 'epidemic suggestion'. The whole civilized world has somehow been deluded into thinking Shakespeare a good writer, and even the plainest demonstration to the contrary makes no impression, because one is not dealing with a reasoned opinion but with something akin to religious faith. Throughout history, says Tolstoy, there has been an endless series of these 'epidemic suggestions' – for example, the Crusades, the search for the Philosopher's Stone, the craze for tulip growing which once swept over Holland, and so on and so forth. As a contemporary instance, he cites, rather significantly, the Dreyfus case, over which the whole world grew violently excited for no sufficient reason. There are also sudden short-lived crazes for new political and philosophical theories, or for this or that writer, artist or scientist – for example, Darwin who (in 1903) is 'beginning to be forgotten'. And in some cases a quite worthless popular idol may remain in favour for centuries, for 'it also happens that such crazes, having arisen in consequence of special reasons accidentally favouring their establishment correspond in such a degree to the views of life spread in society, and especially in literary circles, that they are maintained for a long time'. Shakespeare's plays have continued to be admired over a long period because 'they corresponded to the irreligious and immoral frame of mind of the upper classes of his time and ours'.

As to the manner in which Shakespeare's fame *started*, Tolstoy explains it as having been 'got up' by German professors towards the end of the eighteenth century. His reputation 'originated in Germany, and thence was transferred to England'. The Germans chose to elevate Shakespeare because, at a time when there was no German drama worth speaking about and French classical literature was beginning to seem frigid and artificial, they were captivated by

Shakespeare's 'clever development of scenes' and also found in him a good expression of their own attitude towards life. Goethe pronounced Shakespeare a great poet, whereupon all the other critics flocked after him like a troop of parrots, and the general infatuation has lasted ever since. The result has been a further debasement of the drama – Tolstoy is careful to include his own plays when condemning the contemporary stage – and a further corruption of the prevailing moral outlook. It follows that 'the false glorification of Shakespeare' is an important evil which Tolstoy feels it his duty to combat.

This, then, is the substance of Tolstoy's pamphlet. One's first feeling is that in describing Shakespeare as a bad writer he is saying something demonstrably untrue. But this is not the case. In reality there is no kind of evidence or argument by which one can show that Shakespeare, or any other writer, is 'good'. Nor is there any way of definitely proving that – for instance – Warwick Deeping is 'bad'. Ultimately there is no test of literary merit except survival, which is itself an index to majority opinion. Artistic theories such as Tolstoy's are quite worthless, because they not only start out with arbitrary assumptions, but depend on vague terms ('sincere', 'important' and so forth) which can be interpreted in any way one chooses. Properly speaking one cannot *answer* Tolstoy's attack. The interesting question is: why did he make it? But it should be noticed in passing that he uses many weak or dishonest arguments. Some of these are worth pointing out, not because they invalidate his main charge but because they are, so to speak, evidence of malice.

To begin with, his examination of *King Lear* is not 'impartial', as he twice claims. On the contrary, it is a prolonged exercise in misrepresentation. It is obvious that when you are summarizing *King Lear* for the benefit of someone who has not read it, you are not really being impartial if you introduce an important speech (Lear's speech when Cordelia is dead in his arms) in this manner: 'Again begin Lear's awful ravings, at which one feels ashamed, as at unsuccessful jokes.' And in a long series of instances Tolstoy slightly alters or colours the passages he is criticizing, always in such a way as to make the plot appear a little more complicated and improbable, or the language a little more exaggerated. For example, we are told that Lear 'has no necessity or motive for his abdication', although his reason for abdicating (that he is old and wishes to retire from the cares of state) has been clearly indicated in the first scene.

It will be seen that even in the passage which I quoted earlier, Tolstoy has wilfully misunderstood one phrase and slightly changed the meaning of another, making nonsense of a remark which is reasonable enough in its context. None of these misreadings is very gross in itself, but their cumulative effect is to exaggerate the psychological incoherence of the play. Again, Tolstoy is not able to explain why Shakespeare's plays were still in print, and still on the stage, two hundred years after his death (*before* the 'epidemic suggestion' started, that is); and his whole account of Shakespeare's rise to fame is guesswork punctuated by outright misstatements. And again, various of his accusations contradict one another: for example, Shakespeare is a mere entertainer and 'not in earnest', but on the other hand he is constantly putting his own thoughts into the mouths of his characters. On the whole it is difficult to feel that Tolstoy's criticisms are uttered in good faith. In any case it is impossible that he should fully have believed in his main thesis – believed, that is to say, that for a century or more the entire civilized world had been taken in by a huge and palpable lie which he alone was able to see through. Certainly his dislike of Shakespeare is real enough, but the reasons for it may be different, or partly different, from what he avows; and therein lies the interest of his pamphlet.

At this point one is obliged to start guessing. However, there is one possible clue, or at least there is a question which may point the way to a clue. It is: why did Tolstoy, with thirty or more plays to choose from, pick out *King Lear* as his especial target? True, *Lear* is so well known and has been so much praised that it could justly be taken as representative of Shakespeare's best work; still, for the purpose of a hostile analysis Tolstoy would probably choose the play he disliked most. Is it not possible that he bore an especial enmity towards this particular play because he was aware, consciously or unconsciously, of the resemblance between Lear's story and his own? But it is better to approach this clue from the opposite direction – that is, by examining *Lear* itself, and the qualities in it that Tolstoy fails to mention.

One of the first things an English reader would notice in Tolstoy's pamphlet is that it hardly deals with Shakespeare as a poet. Shakespeare is treated as a dramatist, and in so far as his popularity is not spurious, it is held to be due to tricks of stage-craft which give good opportunities to clever actors. Now, so far as the English-speaking countries go, this is not true. Several of the plays which are most valued by lovers of Shakespeare (for instance, *Timon of Athens*) are seldom or never acted, while some of the most actable, such as *A Midsummer Night's Dream*, are the least admired. Those who care most for Shakespeare value him in the first place for his use of language, the 'verbal music' which even Bernard Shaw, another hostile critic, admits to be 'irresistible'. Tolstoy ignores this, and does not seem to realize that a poem may have a special value for those who speak the language in which it was written. However, even if one puts oneself in Tolstoy's place and tries to think of Shakespeare as a foreign poet it is still clear that there is something that Tolstoy has left out. Poetry, it seems, is *not* solely a matter of sound and association, and valueless outside its own language-group: otherwise how is it that some poems, including poems written in dead languages, succeed in crossing frontiers? Clearly a lyric like 'To-morrow is Saint Valentine's Day' could not be satisfactorily translated, but in Shakespeare's major work there is something describable as poetry that can be separated from the words. Tolstoy is right in saying that *Lear* is not a very good play, as a play. It is too drawn-out and has too many characters and sub-plots. One wicked daughter would have been quite enough, and Edgar is a superfluous character: indeed it would probably be a better play if Gloucester and both his sons were eliminated. Nevertheless, something, a kind of pattern, or perhaps only an atmosphere, survives the complications and the *longueurs*. *Lear* can be imagined as a puppet show, a mime, a ballet, a series of pictures. Part of its poetry, perhaps the most essential part, is inherent in the story and is dependent neither on any particular set of words, nor on flesh-and-blood presentation.

Shut your eyes and think of *King Lear*, if possible without calling to mind any of the dialogue. What do you see? Here at any rate is what I see; a majestic old man in a long black robe, with flowing white hair and beard, a figure out of Blake's drawings (but also, curiously enough, rather like Tolstoy), wandering through a storm and cursing the heavens, in company with a Fool and a lunatic. Presently the scene shifts and the old man, still cursing, still understanding nothing, is holding a dead girl in his arms while the Fool dangles on a gallows somewhere in the background. This is the bare skeleton of the play, and even here Tolstoy wants to cut out most of what is essential. He objects to the storm, as being unnecessary, to the Fool, who in his eyes is simply a tedious nuisance and an excuse for making bad jokes, and to the death of

Cordelia, which, as he sees it, robs the play of its moral. According to Tolstoy, the earlier play, *King Leir*, which Shakespeare adapted

terminates more naturally and more in accordance with the moral demands of the spectator than does Shakespeare's: namely, by the King of the Gauls conquering the husbands of the elder sisters, and by Cordelia, instead of being killed, restoring Leir to his former position.

In other words the tragedy ought to have been a comedy, or perhaps a melodrama. It is doubtful whether the sense of tragedy is compatible with belief in God: at any rate, it is not compatible with disbelief in human dignity and with the kind of 'moral demand' which feels cheated when virtue fails to triumph. A tragic situation exists precisely when virtue does *not* triumph but when it is still felt that man is nobler than the forces which destroy him. It is perhaps more significant that Tolstoy sees no justification for the presence of the Fool. The Fool is integral to the play. He acts not only a sort of chorus, making the central situation clearer by commenting on it more intelligently than the other characters, but as a foil to Lear's frenzies. His jokes, riddles and scraps of rhyme, and his endless digs at Lear's high-minded folly, ranging from mere derision to a sort of melancholy poetry ('All thy other titles thou hast given away; that thou wast born with'), are like a trickle of sanity running through the play, a reminder that somewhere or other in spite of the injustices, cruelties, intrigues, deceptions and misunderstandings that are being enacted here, life is going on much as usual. In Tolstoy's impatience with the Fool one gets a glimpse of his deeper quarrel with Shakespeare. He objects, with some justification, to the raggedness of Shakespeare's plays, the irrelevancies, the incredible plots, the exaggerated language: but what at bottom he probably most dislikes is a sort of exuberance, a tendency to take – not so much a pleasure as simply an interest in the actual process of life. It is a mistake to write Tolstoy off as a moralist attacking an artist. He never said that art, as such, is wicked or meaningless, nor did he even say that technical virtuosity is unimportant. But his main aim, in his later years, was to narrow the range of human consciousness. One's interests, one's points of attachment to the physical world and the day-to-day struggle, must be as few and not as many as possible. Literature must consist of parables, stripped of detail and almost independent of language. The parables – this is where Tolstoy differs from the average vulgar puritan – must themselves be works of art, but pleasure and curiosity must be excluded from them. Science, also, must be divorced from curiosity. The business of science, he says, is not to discover what happens but to teach men how they ought to live. So also with history and politics. Many problems (for example, the Dreyfus case) are simply not worth solving, and he is willing to leave them as loose ends. Indeed his whole theory of 'crazes' or 'epidemic suggestions', in which he lumps together such things as the Crusades and the Dutch passion of tulip growing, shows a willingness to regard many human activities as mere ant-like rushings to and fro, inexplicable and uninteresting. Clearly he could have no patience with a chaotic, detailed, discursive writer like Shakespeare. His reaction is that of an irritable old man who is being pestered by a noisy child. 'Why do you keep jumping up and down like that? Why can't you sit still like I do? In a way the old man is in the right, but the trouble is that the child has a feeling in its limbs which the old man has lost. And if the old man knows of the existence of this feeling, the effect is merely to increase his irritation: he would make children senile, if he could. Tolstoy does not know, perhaps, just *what* he misses in Shakespeare, but he is aware that he misses something, and he is determined that others shall be deprived of it as well. By nature he was imperious as well as egotistical. Well after he was grown up he would still occasionally strike his servant in moments of anger, and somewhat later, according to his English biographer, Derrick Leon, he felt 'a frequent desire upon the slenderest provocation to slap the faces of those with whom he disagreed'. One does not necessarily get rid of that kind of temperament by undergoing religious conversion, and indeed it is obvious that the illusion of having been reborn may allow one's native vices to flourish more freely than ever, though perhaps in subtler forms. Tolstoy was capable of abjuring physical violence and of seeing what this implies, but he was not capable of tolerance or humility, and even if one knew nothing of his other writings, one could deduce his tendency towards spiritual bullying from this single pamphlet.

However, Tolstoy is not simply trying to rob others of a pleasure he does not share. He is doing that, but his quarrel with Shakespeare goes further. It is the quarrel between the religious and the humanist attitudes towards life. Here one comes back to the central theme of *King Lear* which Tolstoy does not mention although he sets forth the plot in some detail.

Lear is one of the minority of Shakespeare's plays that are unmistakably *about* something. As Tolstoy justly complains, much rubbish has been written about Shakespeare as a philosopher, as a psychologist, as a 'great moral teacher', and whatnot. Shakespeare was not a systematic thinker, his most serious thoughts are uttered irrelevantly or indirectly, and we do not know to what extent he wrote with a 'purpose' or even how much of the work attributed to him was actually written by him. In the sonnets he never even refers to the plays as part of his achievement, though he does make what seems to be a half-ashamed allusion to his career as an actor. It is perfectly possible that he looked on at least half of his plays as mere pot-boilers and hardly bothered about purpose or probability so long as he could patch up something, usually from stolen material, which would more or less hang together on the stage. However, that is not the whole story. To begin with, as Tolstoy himself points out, Shakespeare has a habit of thrusting uncalled-for general reflections into the mouths of his characters. This is a serious fault in a dramatist, but it does not fit in with Tolstoy's picture of Shakespeare as a vulgar hack who has no opinions of his own and merely wishes to produce the greatest effect with the least trouble. And more than this, about a dozen of his plays, written for the most part later than 1600, do unquestionably have a meaning and even a moral. They revolve round a central subject which in some cases can be reduced to a single word. For example, *Macbeth* is about ambition, *Othello* is about jealousy, and *Timon of Athens* is about money. The subject of *Lear* is renunciation, and it is only by being wilfully blind that one can fail to understand what Shakespeare is saying.

Lear renounces his throne but expects everyone to continue treating him as a king. He does not see that if he surrenders power, other people will take advantage of his weakness: also that those who flatter him the most grossly, i.e. Regan and Goneril, are exactly the ones who will turn against him. The moment he finds that he can no longer make people obey him as he did before, he falls into a rage which Tolstoy describes as 'strange and unnatural', but which in fact is perfectly in character. In his madness and despair, he passes through two moods which again are natural enough in his circumstances, though in one of them it is probable that he is being used partly as a mouthpiece for Shakespeare's own opinions. One is the mood of disgust in which Lear repents, as it were, for having been a

king, and grasps for the first time the rottenness of formal justice and
vulgar morality. The other is a mood of impotent fury in which he
wreaks imaginary revenges upon those who have wronged him. 'To
have a thousand with red burning spits come hissing in upon 'em!',
and:

> It were a delicate stratagem to shoe
> A troop of horse with felt: I'll put't in proof;
> And when I have stol'n upon these sons-in-law,
> Then kill, kill, kill, kill, kill, kill!

Only at the end does he realize, as a sane man, that power, revenge
and victory are not worth while:

> No, no, no, no! Come, let's away to prison . . .
> . . . and we'll wear out
> In a wall'd prison, packs and sects of great ones
> That ebb and flow by th' moon.

But by the time he makes this discovery it is too late, for his death
and Cordelia's are already decided on. That is the story, and,
allowing for some clumsiness in the telling, it is a very good story.

But is it not also curiously similar to the history of Tolstoy
himself? There is a general resemblance which one can hardly avoid
seeing, because the most impressive event in Tolstoy's life, as in
Lear's, was a huge and gratuitous act of renunciation. In his old age,
he renounced his estate, his title and his copyrights, and made an
attempt – a sincere attempt, though it was not successful – to escape
from his privileged position and live the life of a peasant. But the
deeper resemblance lies in the fact that Tolstoy, like Lear, acted on
mistaken motives and failed to get results he had hoped for.
According to Tolstoy, the aim of every human being is happiness,
and happiness can only be attained by doing the will of God. But
doing the will of God means casting off all earthly pleasures and
ambitions, and living only for others. Ultimately, therefore, Tolstoy
renounced the world under the expectation that this would make
him happier. But if there is one thing certain about his later years, it
is that he was *not* happy. On the contrary, he was driven almost to
the edge of madness by the behaviour of the people about him, who
persecuted him precisely *because* of his renunciation. Like Lear,
Tolstoy was not humble and not a good judge of character. He was
inclined at moments to revert to the attitudes of an aristocrat, in

spite of his peasant's blouse, and he even had two children whom he had believed in and who ultimately turned against him – though, of course, in a less sensational manner than Regan and Goneril. His exaggerated revulsion from sexuality was also distinctly similar to Lear's. Tolstoy's remark that marriage is 'slavery, satiety, repulsion' and means putting up with the proximity of 'ugliness, dirtiness, smell, sores', is matched by Lear's well-known outburst:

> But to the girdle do the gods inherit,
> Beneath is all the fiends';
> There's hell, there's darkness, there's the sulphurous pit,
> Burning, scalding, stench, consumption, etc., etc.

And though Tolstoy could not foresee it when he wrote his essay on Shakespeare, even the ending of his life – the sudden unplanned flight across country, accompanied only by a faithful daughter, the death in a cottage in a strange village – seems to have in it a sort of phantom reminiscence of *Lear*.

Of course, one cannot assume that Tolstoy was aware of this resemblance, or would have admitted it if it had been pointed out to him. But his attitude towards the play must have been influenced by its theme. Renouncing power, giving away your lands, was a subject on which he had reason to feel deeply. Probably, therefore, he would be more angered and disturbed by the moral that Shakespeare draws than he would be in the case of some other play – *Macbeth*, for example – which did not touch so closely on his own life. But what exactly *is* the moral of *Lear*? Evidently there are two morals, one explicit, the other implied in the story.

Shakespeare starts by assuming that to make yourself powerless is to invite an attack. This does not mean that *everyone* will turn against you (Kent and the Fool stand by Lear from first to last), but in all probability *someone* will. If you throw away your weapons, some less scrupulous person will pick them up. If you turn the other cheek, you will get a harder blow on it than you got on the first one. This does not always happen, but it is to be expected, and you ought not to complain if it does happen. The second blow is, so to speak, part of the act of turning the other cheek. First of all, therefore, there is the vulgar commonsense moral drawn by the Fool: 'Don't relinquish power, don't give away your lands.' But there is also another moral. Shakespeare never utters it in so many words, and it does not very much matter whether he was fully aware of it. It is contained in the story, which, after all, he made up, or altered to suit his purposes. It is: 'Give away your lands if you want to, but don't expect to gain happiness by doing so. Probably you won't gain happiness. If you live for others, you must live *for others*, and not as a roundabout way of getting an advantage for yourself'.

Obviously neither of these conclusions could have been pleasing to Tolstoy. The first of them expresses the ordinary, belly-to-earth selfishness from which he was genuinely trying to escape. The other conflicts with his desire to eat his cake and have it – that is, to destroy his own egoism and by so doing to gain eternal life. Of course, *Lear* is not a sermon in favour of altruism. It merely points out the results of practising self-denial for selfish reasons. Shakespeare had a considerable streak of worldliness in him, and if he had been forced to take sides in his own play, his sympathies would probably have lain with the Fool. But at least he could see the whole issue and treat it at the level of tragedy. Vice is punished, but virtue is not rewarded. The morality of Shakespeare's later tragedies is not religious in the ordinary sense, and certainly is not Christian. Only two of them, *Hamlet* and *Othello*, are supposedly occurring inside the Christian era, and even in those, apart from the antics of the ghost in *Hamlet*, there is no indication of a 'next world' where everything is to be put right. All of these tragedies start out with the humanist assumption that life, although full of sorrow, is worth living, and that Man is a noble animal – a belief which Tolstoy in his old age did not share.

Tolstoy was not a saint, but he tried very hard to make himself into a saint, and the standards he applied to literature were other-worldly ones. It is important to realize that the difference between a saint and an ordinary human being is a difference of kind and not of degree. That is, the one is not to be regarded as an imperfect form of the other. The saint, at any rate Tolstoy's kind of saint, is not trying to work an improvement in earthly life: he is trying to bring it to an end and put something different in its place. One obvious expression of this is the claim that celibacy is 'higher' than marriage. If only, Tolstoy says in effect, we would stop breeding, fighting, struggling and enjoying, if we could get rid not only of our sins but of everything else that binds us to the surface of the earth – including love, then the whole painful process would be over and the Kingdom of Heaven would arrive. But a normal human being does not want the Kingdom of Heaven: he wants life on earth to continue. This is not solely because he is 'weak', 'sinful' and anxious for a 'good time'. Most people get a fair amount of fun out of their lives, but on balance life is suffering, and only the very young or the very foolish imagine otherwise. Ultimately it is the Christian attitude which is self-interested and hedonistic, since the aim is always to get away from the painful struggle of earthly life and find eternal peace in some kind of Heaven or Nirvana. The humanist attitude is that the struggle must continue and that death is the price of life. 'Men must endure their going hence, even as their coming hither: Ripeness is all' – which is an un-Christian sentiment. Often there is a seeming truce between the humanist and the religious believer, but in fact their attitudes cannot be reconciled: one must choose between this world and the next. And the enormous majority of human beings, if they understood the issue, would choose this world. They do make that choice when they continue working, breeding and dying instead of crippling their faculties in the hope of obtaining a new lease of existence elsewhere.

We do not know a great deal about Shakespeare's religious beliefs, and from the evidence of his writings it would be difficult to prove that he had any. But at any rate he was not a saint or a would-be-saint: he was a human being, and in some ways not a very good one. It is clear, for instance, that he liked to stand well with the rich and powerful, and was capable of flattering them in the most servile way. He is also noticeably cautious, not to say cowardly, in his manner of uttering unpopular opinions. Almost never does he put a subversive or sceptical remark into the mouth of a character likely to be identified with himself. Throughout his plays the acute social critics, the people who are not taken in by accepted fallacies, are buffoons, villains, lunatics or persons who are shamming insanity or are in a state of violent hysteria. *Lear* is a play which this tendency is particularly well marked. It contains a great deal of veiled social criticism – a point Tolstoy misses – but it is all uttered either by the Fool, by Edgar when he is pretending to be mad, or by Lear during his bouts of madness. In his sane moments Lear hardly ever makes an intelligent remark. And yet the very fact that Shakespeare had to use these subterfuges shows how widely his thoughts ranged. He could not restrain himself from commenting on almost everything, although he put on a series of masks in order to do so. If one has once read Shakespeare with attention, it is not easy to go a day without quoting him, because there are not many subjects of major importance that he does not discuss or at least mention somewhere or other, in his unsystematic but illuminating way. Even the irrelevancies that litter every one of his plays – the puns and riddles, the lists of names, the scraps of 'reportage' like the conversation of the carriers in *Henry IV*, the bawdy jokes, the rescued fragments of forgotten ballads – are merely the products of excessive vitality. Shakespeare was not a philosopher or a scientist, but he did have curiosity, he loved the surface of the earth and the process of life – which, it should be repeated, is *not* the same thing as wanting to have a good time and stay alive as long as possible. Of course, it is not because of the quality of his thought that Shakespeare has survived, and he might not even be remembered as a dramatist if he had not also been a poet. His main hold on us is through language. How deeply Shakespeare himself was fascinated by the music of words can probably be inferred from the speeches of Pistol. What Pistol says is largely meaningless, but if one considers his lines singly they are magnificent rhetorical verse. Evidently, pieces of resounding nonsense ('Let floods o'erswell, and fiends for food howl on', etc.) were constantly appearing in Shakespeare's mind of their own accord, and a half-lunatic character had to be invented to use them up.

Tolstoy's native tongue was not English, and one cannot blame him for being unmoved by Shakespeare's verse, nor even, perhaps, for refusing to believe that Shakespeare's skill with words was something out of the ordinary. But he would also have rejected the whole notion of valuing poetry for its texture – valuing it, that is to say, as a kind of music. If it could somehow have been proved to him that his whole explanation of Shakespeare's rise to fame is mistaken, that inside the English-speaking world, at any rate, Shakespeare's popularity is genuine, that his mere skill in placing one syllable beside another has given acute pleasure to generation after generation of English-speaking people – all this would not have been counted as a merit to Shakespeare, but rather the contrary. It would simply have been one more proof of the irreligious, earthbound nature of Shakespeare and his admirers. Tolstoy would have said that poetry is to be judged by its meaning, and that seductive sounds merely cause false meanings to go unnoticed. At every level it is the same issue – this world against the next: and certainly the music of words is something that belongs to this world.

A sort of doubt has always hung around the character of Tolstoy, as round the character of Gandhi. He was not a vulgar hypocrite, as some people declared him to be, and he would probably have imposed even greater sacrifices on himself than he did, if he had not been interfered with at every step by the people surrounding him, especially his wife. But on the other hand it is dangerous to take such men as Tolstoy at their disciples' valuation. There is always the possibility – the probability, indeed – that they have done no more than exchange one form of egoism for another. Tolstoy renounced wealth, fame and privilege; he abjured violence in all its forms and was ready to suffer for doing so; but it is not easy to believe that he abjured the principle of coercion, or at least the *desire* to coerce others. There are families in which the father will say to his child, 'You'll get a thick ear if you do that again', while the mother, her eyes brimming over with tears, will take the child in her arms and murmur lovingly, 'Now, darling, *is* it kind to Mummy to do that?' And who would maintain that the second method is less tyrannous than the first? The distinction that really matters is not between violence and non-violence, but between having and not having the appetite for power. There are people who are convinced of the wickedness both of armies and of police forces, but who are nevertheless much more intolerant and inquisitorial in outlook than the normal person who believes that it is necessary to use violence in certain circumstances. They will not say to somebody else, 'Do this, that and the other or you will go to prison', but they will, if they can, get inside his brain and dictate his thoughts for him in the minutest particulars. Creeds like pacifism and anarchism, which seem on the surface to imply a complete renunciation of power, rather encourage this habit of mind. For if you have embraced a creed which appears to be free from the ordinary dirtiness of politics – a creed from which you yourself cannot expect to draw any material advantage – surely that proves that you are in the right? And the more you are in the right, the more natural that everyone else should be bullied into thinking likewise.

If we are to believe what he says in his pamphlet, Tolstoy has never been able to see any merit in Shakespeare, and was always astonished to find that his fellow-writers, Turgenev, Fet and others thought differently. We may be sure that in his unregenerate days Tolstoy's conclusion would have been: 'You like Shakespeare – I don't. Let's leave it at that'. Later, when his perception that it takes all sorts to make a world had deserted him, he came to think of

Shakespeare's writings as something dangerous to himself. The more pleasure people took in Shakespeare, the less they would listen to Tolstoy. Therefore nobody must be *allowed* to enjoy Shakespeare, just as nobody must be allowed to drink alcohol or smoke tobacco. True, Tolstoy would not prevent them by force. He is not demanding that the police shall impound every copy of Shakespeare's works. But he will do dirt on Shakespeare, if he can. He will try to get inside the mind of every lover of Shakespeare and kill his enjoyment by every trick he can think of, including – as I have shown in my summary of his pamphlet – arguments which are self-contradictory or even doubtfully honest.

But finally the most striking thing is how little difference it all makes. As I said earlier, one cannot *answer* Tolstoy's pamphlet, at least on its main counts. There is no argument by which one can defend a poem. It defends itself by surviving, or it is indefensible. And if this test is valid, I think the verdict in Shakespeare's case must be 'not guilty'. Like every other writer, Shakespeare will be forgotten sooner or later, but it is unlikely that a heavier indictment will ever be brought against him. Tolstoy was perhaps the most admired literary man of his age, and he was certainly not its least able pamphleteer. He turned all his powers of denunciation against Shakespeare, like all the guns of a battleship roaring simultaneously. And with what result? Forty years later Shakespeare is still there completely unaffected, and of the attempt to demolish him nothing remains except the yellowing pages of a pamphlet which hardly anyone has read, and which would be forgotten altogether if Tolstoy had not also been the author of *War and Peace* and *Anna Karenina*.

SOURCE: *Shooting an Elephant* (1950).

NOTE

1. *Shakespeare and the Drama.* Written about 1903 as an introduction to another pamphlet, *Shakespeare and the Working Classes*, by Ernest Crosby.

Robert B. Heilman   The Unity of
King Lear   (1948)

Mark Van Doren prescribes, as one of the duties laid upon the students in a great-books college of which he has written a brief account, the ability to state precisely the unity of *King Lear*. It may be added that when the students are able to pass this test, their understanding of at least one drama ought to satisfy a quite exacting preceptor. For the unity of *King Lear* lies very little on the surface; it can be described only partially in terms of plot relationships; indeed, as in all high art, it is a question of theme; and theme extends itself subtly into the ramifications of dramatic and imagistic constructs. This unity is not much discussed by the professorial gentlemen to whom Mr Van Doren's young men might turn for dramaturgic clues; the various editors of the play, in fact, are intently and innocently questing for sources, and dates, and stage history; and in their busyness they have not much time left, as one of them candidly – and undisturbedly – puts it, for aesthetic criticism. But some of them do desire to show that the master, being the master, has not erred in his duplicity of plot; so Gloucester's family situation and experiences, we are told, heighten the effect produced by Lear's family situation and experiences; and again, the two plots come together in the dealings between Lear and Gloucester, and between Edmund and the two sisters who desire him; and again, in these interrelationships inhere some remarkable ironies which otherwise the play would be without. These points are soundly made, and they are necessary preliminaries. To them we might add, also, that the Gloucester plot is initiated after the Lear plot is firmly under way, and effectually ended while Lear has still much left to do – a kind of chronological discipline of the materials which betokens the author's tact. And in IV vi, in which Lear's madness brings him to a climax of disillusioned insight, so that the gnomic Edgar can distill from this scene the paradox 'Reason in madness', Lear weaves Gloucester into his brilliant synthesis of the world and of the play: '. . . Your eyes are in a heavy case, your purse in a light. You see how the world goes. . . . A man may see how the world goes with no eyes.' Insofar as the subject of the play is Lear's mind, Gloucester has become a part of that subject.

But these considerations are relatively peripheral, and we still need to inquire in what way it is that the two stories of youth-and-age, of father-and-child, are not mere replicas, and what advantage in their coexistence transcends the rhetorical. What, in other words, is the meaning of the Lear plot, and the meaning of the Gloucester plot, and how are the meanings related? To define this fundamental kinship we must first examine the tragic flaws of the protagonists. The flaws may be described, I think, as errors of understanding, and *King Lear* may be read as a play about the ways of perceiving truth: it has a good deal to say about the ways in which the human reason may function, and about the imagination. Our problem then is to discover how this thematic substance receives necessarily different, rather than arbitrarily repetitious, formulations in the Lear plot and in the Gloucester plot.

Lear does not have the pride in reason of, say, Oedipus or Faustus, but he does undertake to reason about certain phenomena, and by reasoning faultily he inaugurates a series of tragic consequences. His very first error is typically rationalistic: the introduction of a mensurational standard where it is not applicable. He insists upon the untenable proposition that love can be measured, as if it were a material quantum of a certain size or shape. In his intellectual confusion he forgets that deeds rather than words are the symbols of love. The confusion may be described quite literally as a failure of imagination: love must be apprehended by images, and the images are richly available to him – not in verbal shortcuts and formulae, but in the lives of daughters whom he has observed from infancy. Now this kind of evidence, when it is not abstracted by literary art from the full and resistant texture of experience, is vast and inchoate and difficult; Lear shirks a demanding task – the imaginative apprehension of symbols, we all know, is not easy – and seeks an easy rationalistic way out. His failure of understanding here is analogous to his failure to perceive that a king cannot be a king without a crown and cannot maintain his perquisites by a kind of oral recipe or contract, that is, a purely rationalized formulation of a status which involves responsibilities as well as rights. From his endeavour to bound a value by irrelevant standards of measurement, Lear goes on to still another error: his misinterpretation of those verbal measurements of love which his demands have brought forth: he is wholly taken in by the meaningless abstractions and hyperboles of Goneril and Regan and – in another striking failure of

imagination – completely misses the import of Cordelia's precise
metaphor, 'I love your Majesty/According to my bond; no more nor
less.' Lear, then, invites tragedy by three errors of understanding –
errors with regard to the nature of kingship, the nature of love, and
the nature of language (the value of certain statements about love).
Then: these errors are not the negligible slips of a mere observer who
has time to check and prove and correct; they are the terrible
mistakes of a man of action, of a man whose action is a public action.
Lear *imposes* on his world his erroneous conclusions about children
and court.

Gloucester accepts rather than imposes: his trouble is inaugurated
by Edmund's spontaneously undertaking, without being offered
such an opening as Lear gives to Goneril and Regan, to deceive his
father. Both fathers, of course, are muddled; even while, ironically,
they feel astute, they reason wrongly from the evidence. Like Lear,
Gloucester might have consulted his nonrational, experiential
awareness of his child's quality. Yet Gloucester is the object of
manipulation; his error of understanding is that he too easily falls
under the influence exerted upon him. We have other evidence,
however, of the nature of his flaw. Edmund's illegitimacy we are
never allowed to forget, and near the end Edgar specifically connects
Gloucester's suffering with his adultery; he tells Edmund, 'The dark
and vicious place where thee he got/Cost him his eyes.' Then there is
the even more obvious evidence of Gloucester's attitude to the new
Goneril–Regan regime: Gloucester plainly has doubts about the
way things are going, but that a principle is involved, a principle
which insists that he make a stand, simply does not occur to him. He
regrets Cornwall's stocking Lear's follower, Kent; but he himself
contributes to the infuriation of Lear by his efforts to 'fix it up'
between him and Cornwall. 'You know the fiery quality of the
Duke', he tells Lear, and, more maddeningly for Lear, 'I would have
all well betwixt you.' Gloucester has hopes that he can 'do business
with' Cornwall: despite his genuine discomfort, he is inclined to
accept the status quo. Now, what a glance at his whole career tells us
is that his conduct is all of a piece: Goucester is the passive man who
is too ready to fall in with whatever influences are brought to bear
upon him. He is the man who falls into step with the world, especially
when to be out of step would mean a stern quarrel both with the
world and with a part of himself. In the liaison of which Edmund is
the fruit he fell in with the worldliness that took sexual morality

lightly; years later – even in Edmund's hearing, it seems – he refers jauntily to Edmund's origin. Then he falls in with Edmund's suggestions about the evil purposes of Edgar: he becomes the man of the world who knows a plot when he sees one and knows what to do about it, and who is incapable of opposing the immediate pressure by drawing, painstakingly, upon the knowledge which transcends the circumstances of the moment. Finally, as we have seen, he falls in with, does his best to get on with, the Goneril–Regan tyranny. A fine stroke in the management of this part of the play is the ambiguity of the lines in which Gloucester tells Edmund that he intends to aid Lear. His sympathies are unquestionably aroused; that is one part of the picture. But it is also true that he says, 'These injuries the King now bears will be revenged home; there's part of a power already footed; we must incline to the King.' He does pity Lear, but it is equally true that to be pro-Lear may be a good thing; and Gloucester is at least in part maneuvering toward the comfortable stream of things. Not until he suffers for it is his new commitment morally in the clear. His whole tendency toward conformity – toward 'adjustment', as we say in these high times – has already been admirably summarized by his astrological habit of mind, which, we should observe, is shared by no one else in the play. It exactly suits Gloucester. If 'These late eclipses in the sun and moon portend no good to us', what can he do about it? It is Gloucester's flaw never wholly to understand what is implied in the situations in which he finds himself, even though he feels wordlywise enough. Not that he voluntarily seeks what is evil: it is simply that he too easily yields to that in which he should see evil.

Lear, without questioning his own rightness, imposes his will upon others; Gloucester accepts the will of others without effectually questioning their rightness. Thus Lear and Gloucester are, in terms of structure, not duplicates, but complements: this is one key to the unity of *King Lear*. The completeness of the play, its cosmic inclusiveness, which we sense without being able to put our finger upon it, is in part attributable to this double-focused presentation of the tragic error of understanding. We see its basic forms, action and inaction; one tragic character imposes error, the other accepts it. The roles continue consistently throughout the play – Lear as active, Gloucester as passive. Gloucester, it is clear, does at times *act* – enough to become more than an allegorical figure, than a worldlier Griselda. But things keep happening *to* him: whereas Lear combats his daughters furiously and dashes of his own will out into the night, Gloucester is betrayed, is captured, and is tortured. The master touch in the depiction of his career is that his giving in finally becomes giving up: he yields to despair (the Christian anachronisms are familiar to all commentators), suicide is to be his final adjustment. It is wholly right, for the worldly man is one who, by accepting the custom of the time, despairs of the good. But Lear is always a vigorous, aggressive figure; he fights his daughters to the bitter end; even in his madness he imposes his personality upon the others. At the time of his recovery he is contrastingly quiet for a brief while, but again at the end he becomes a commanding, dominating figure beside whom the others seem small. He kills 'the slave that was a hanging thee' (V iii 274) and dies trying to establish that Cordelia is alive.

Lear and Gloucester are tragic heroes: they are essentially good men. We have seen the complementary errors of understanding to which the good man is liable, and thus two kinds of genesis of evil in the world. Now a part of the remarkable fullness of the play is that it shows us not only the release of evil but the subsequent course of evil. In Goneril and Regan, and in Edmund, we see the evil which originates in Lear and Gloucester set free in the world. The old men themselves come to insight through suffering, but they have loosed forces that do terrible damage before they destroy themselves. Yet other children of Lear and Gloucester not only combat the evil forces but also, by their very existence and by positive aid to their unjust parents, contribute to whatever of recovery the old men achieve. The children as a group, that is to say, represent the different elements which are in conflict in the fathers; hence, in a play with an unusually large number of main characters and a great complexity of actions, there is the tightest integration of their component elements. We see good and evil in conflict in the world, but by the structure of the play we are reminded that the conflict is an emanation of that in the individual soul. By the fact of relationship the outer and the inner evil become one, the two struggles are united. The children are not children for nothing; to be the father of Goneril is to create a symbol of the evil brought forth from oneself. The discerning reader of the play will hardly feel that he has done all his duty by hating Goneril.

Edmund's worldliness is an amplification and a positivizing of Gloucester's. Gloucester wants to do as the world does and be comfortable; Edmund wants to have what the world has – 'have lands by wit', as he puts it – and 'grow' and 'prosper' in it. The shallow foxiness which Gloucester exhibits in his imagined detection of Edgar ripens into an effective wiliness in Edmund. Gloucester forgets morality; Edmund flouts it. Edmund is half of Gloucester, liberated from the other half, and matured in its own terms. Gloucester's gullibility – the ironic failure of his self-conscious worldliness – becomes the whole of Edgar as Edgar is seen at the beginning of the play; the emergent moral mastery of Gloucester is paralleled in the development of personal force in Edgar; the kindliness of Gloucester to Lear is the same love and loyalty which come to Gloucester himself from Edgar. Edgar's final defeat of Edmund, Edgar's reunion with his father, and his conquest of his father's despair may all be read as a symbolic version of the gaining of the upper hand, in Gloucester, of the portion of his moral being which had long been in eclipse. But this extension of inner conflicts into conflicting characters who in part objectify the warring subjective elements is most marked in Lear's family. From the start, of course, we discern in Cordelia the sharp insight into people and values of which Lear is capable and to which he is restored by the eventual, tardy revival of his imagination; in her is Lear's submerged tenderness, just as his tempestuousness is echoed in Kent; in the aid which both of them give him we see Lear's better side struggling for the mastery. Yet Cordelia is more complex than some critics have been willing to admit, for there is in her some admixture of what Coleridge called sullenness – of a recusancy, a stubborn antipathy to the disciplining, restricting action which involvement in the world makes inevitable. The unfettered personality may in some contexts be the right moral goal; but it may lead to a narrow protection of self; it is not a moral absolute. Lear will not rule, and he will not understand the terms in which experience speaks; Cordelia will not accept the terms of speech imposed by experience. There is a clash of wills, each combatant bent on self-protection. Lear's withdrawal ironically evokes Cordelia's withdrawal; the daughter springs from the father. In this reading Cordelia becomes a part of the tragic substance rather than a mere innocent and pathetic victim of the forces clashing in the world.

The symbolism of kinship is subtlest and most important in the link between Lear and his elder daughters: here we find the central irony of the play and a fundamental statement of theme. Lear's tragic flaw is the whole being of Goneril and Regan. Lear makes a fatal error of understanding: then his essential method of thought is picked up by his daughters and made their way of life. In dividing the land, Lear introduces a principle which Goneril and Regan carry on to a logical extreme; they show what happens when an element in him is freed from the restraint imposed by the rest of the personality. In this play, personality is the equilibrium of conflicting forces; evil is ready at all times to break loose from the spiritual whole; autonomy is its end, and any disturbance of tensions may set it on its way. Lear, we have seen, forces the use of the principle of measurement where it is not applicable; he introduces a spirit of calculation; and he is ruthless in punishing what does not contribute to his proposed advantage. Thus Goneril and Regan come to power. And what comes to power with them is the spirit of calculation: in fact, throughout the rest of the play we see Shakespeare tracing the history of three people – Edmund's alliance with the sisters is morally right – in whom the cold calculation of advantage has almost totally excluded adherence to other values. Shelley said of his world that it had substituted calculation for imagination. That is precisely what has happened in the world of the play: Lear's imagination has failed – the value-preserving faculty – and so there have come into control the imagination-less calculators. One by one they dispose of, or plan to dispose of, their enemies. In the final irony they turn on and dispose of each other – a magnificent symbol of the self-destructiveness of their kind of world.

The play, of course, is full of ironic reversals. Of those relevant to the question of unity, the most remarkable is the coming to understanding of Gloucester and Lear. Gloucester gains full insight just as he is blinded; the man who accepts too easily is punished at his one moment of high affirmation – the assertion of the values of the old order against the up-to-date world. Lear's new insight is initially pounded into him in I iv and II iv, the scenes in which he is all but incredulous of the blows poured upon him by Goneril and Regan. These scenes demand our notice because it is they which establish the moral link between Lear and his elder daughters. For in these scenes the main business is the quarrel over the number of retainers Lear is to have: the quarrel takes the form of bargaining, even haggling. But this is not the first haggling in the play: the first dispute over amounts and prices, so to speak, is that brought about in I i by Lear's demanding that his daughters measure their love for him. There, he insisted on an inappropriate calculation; here, he is the victim of an inappropriate calculation by the very daughters who had profited from his own misapplied arithmetic. The daughters' love required a different kind of estimate from that which Lear proposed; likewise his demand for a hundred retainers needs to be estimated by another standard than the rational one of necessity. The daughters apply Lear's own error – the seeking of a rationalistic shortcut through a difficult area of meaning which has to be traversed, in the long run, by extrarational means. Love must be felt through its proper symbols; the retainers must be imaginatively understood as symbols of position. The utilitarian standard is absolutely irrelevant. So the whole issue is brilliantly summarized in the first line of Lear's last speech before the storm: 'O, reason not the need' [II iv 267]. But the reasoning of need in these scenes is a symptom of the new way of life that is to dominate Lear's kingdom. That way of life was prepared for by Lear himself. His daughters might have said to Lear, 'We cannot reason our love'. In effect Cordelia did say it: by using a metaphor rather than the neat logical statement Lear wanted.

King Lear suggests the reasons why it is right for tragedy to use characters 'in high place' and intra-family complications – as it regularly did in Greek and Elizabethan practice. Rulers were public figures; their tragedies became representative; ennoblement through suffering was a general and meaningful, not a shut-off private experience by which many suffered but few were ennobled. Yet in the public plot melodrama is just around the corner: our view of public life always inclines to the melodramatic, for we look for heroes and villains whom we can understand simply. We tend to identify evil with certain figures or groups, and if we can injure or destroy them, we cause the good to triumph. We look for Gonerils and Regans and Edmunds and turn all our wrath upon them; we forget the Goneril and Regan and Edmund that are within us all. The public event may obscure the private reality, the private reality in terms of which the experience is universal. But the ultimate identity of public and private is exactly figured forth in the symbolism of kinship: the family mediates between the soul of man and the community to which he belongs. It is at once a public fact and a projection of the soul; through it the representatively public and the representatively private are seen to be one. By being the father of Goneril and of Cordelia, Lear includes both of them within himself;

we cannot then idly hate Goneril as evil but we must recognize the genesis of evil and hence modify our sympthetic identification with Lear so that it includes a sensitiveness to the spiritual trouble within him. Thus we move from melodrama, which represents the external- ized conflict as reality, to tragedy, in which the externalized conflict exactly corresponds to the war within the soul – whether the begetting is an affirmation and an imposition of error or a Gloucester-like acquiescence in worldly imperfections. Some such understanding of tragedy, and of the mode of its universality, follows from an examination of the remarkable unity of *King Lear*.

SOURCE: *Sewanee Review* (1948).

Barbara Everett The New *King Lear* (1960)

It is generally acknowledged that *King Lear* is not only a much better play than its principal source, *King Leir and his three daughters*, but also a quite different one. It is not a pious chronicle- history, but a tragedy in a pagan setting. Yet the orthodox approach to *King Lear* has, in recent years, so much stressed the 'Christian' content and method of the play, that it is sometimes a little difficult to know which of the two plays is in question. It seems, at any rate, a very far cry from the days when Johnson could object that 'Shake- speare has suffered the virtue of Cordelia to perish in a just cause, contrary to the natural ideas of justice, to the hope of the reader, and what is yet more strange, to the faith of chronicles . . .'[1] Though the pressure of human feeling, and a particular belief in the moral responsibility of the arts, could make Johnson accept with relief the public's decision to allow Cordelia to retire 'with victory and felicity', his own 'sensations' allowed him no doubt as to the real ending of Shakespeare's play: 'I was many years ago so shocked by Cordelia's death, that I know not whether I ever endured to read again the last scenes of the play till I undertook to revise them as an editor.' And it must, surely, be principally of this play that Johnson was thinking when he made the grave charge against Shakespeare that 'he sacrifices virtue to convenience, and is so much more careful to please than instruct, that he seems to write without any moral purpose . . . he makes no just distribution of good and evil . . .'

Johnson is making here a firm judgement on Shakespeare as an artist: that, despite all his great gifts, he failed to satisfy the moral sense in any but the most elementary way ('he that thinks reasonably must think morally'). If one compares this with, for instance, the Introduction to the New Arden *King Lear*, then it is clear that an equally firm judgement is being made, which is precisely opposite to Johnson in its conclusions: 'the symbolic significance of the trial of the two daughters by a mad beggar, a dying Fool, and a serving-man is perfectly clear. *He hath put down the mighty from their seats, and hath exalted the humble and meek* . . . The old Lear died in the storm. The new Lear is born in the scene in which he is reunited with Cordelia. His madness marked the end of the wilful, egotistical monarch. He is resurrected as a fully human being. We can tell from his protest –

> You do me wrong to take me out of the grave

that the awakening into life is a painful·process. After the reconciliation, Lear makes only two more appearances. In the scene in which he is being led off to prison he has apparently overcome his desire for vengeance; he has left behind him all those attributes of kingship which had prevented him from attaining his full stature as a man; he has even passed beyond his own pride. At the beginning of the play he is incapable of disinterested love, for he uses the love of others to minister to his own egotism. His prolonged agony and his utter loss of everything free his heart from the bondage of the selfhood. He unlearns hatred, and learns love and humility. He loses the world and gains his own soul. . . . The play is not, as some of our grandfathers believed, pessimistic and pagan; it is rather an attempt to provide an answer to the undermining of traditional ideas by the new philosophy that called all in doubt.' Even so long a quotation as this cannot do justice to Professor Muir's fullness and variety of approach in the Introduction; but it can suggest his ideas on what he calls Shakespeare's 'religious attitude' and on the nature of the work of art he is discussing. Shakespeare, for him, is obviously *not* merely content with 'the real state of sublunary nature', but has imposed upon it something approaching a transcendental design, didactic in intention; and this is (so, I think, the stress of such criticism suggests) the greatest of his great gifts. That a work of art can carry such widely divergent interpretations is a sign of its vitality. But when two such interpretations can seem to be mutually exclusive, it is perhaps worth while to wonder on what bases the propositions rest; so that, if they cannot be reconciled, they may, at least, be clarified.

To suggest that Johnson was not taking the play 'seriously', or was not 'responding' to it fully, would of course be quite misleading. He feels 'a perpetual tumult of indignation, pity, and hope ... So powerful is the current of the poet's imagination, that the mind, which once ventures within it, is hurried irresistibly along.' He is, rather, disturbed by that very intensity with which he feels a piece in which 'the virtuous miscarry'. The quality in the play which seems to dominate his mind and impress him so deeply is its logic of action and character, whereby 'villainy is never at a stop ... crimes lead to crimes, and at last terminate in ruin'. In his discussion of the play, the words which recur are 'events ... story ... action'; his reactions are caused by the 'plot', which presents a spectacle of motivated actions culminating in almost intolerable suffering.

Those critics who find in the play either a partial, or a total Christian allegory, are alike in one thing, however different their respective approaches may be: this is an interest in such parts of the play as seem to make a statement which is differentiated from the 'plot' (that is, the story as it would stand as a prose tale). They are interested in the kind of 'poetic' statements which the play seems to make, in contradistinction from what actually happens. Thus Professor Muir quotes the famous lines beginning 'We two alone will sing like birds i' th' cage ...' and quotes approvingly from another critic: 'A life of sins forgiven, of reciprocal charity, of clear vision, and of joyous song – what is this but the traditional heaven transferred to earth?' And Professor Knight, stressing the 'purgatorial' aspect of *King Lear*, finds much of the play's meaning in the lines uttered by Lear on his awakening – 'Thou art a soul in bliss ...': 'The naturalism of King Lear pales before this blinding shaft of transcendent light. This is the justification of the agony, the sufferance, the gloom'.[2] Curiously, in the word 'justification', we come close not only to the world of distinctively Christian experience, but to the world of 'poetic justice', which Johnson looked for in the play, and could not find.

Such a stress on the 'poetry' of the play is of course a Romantic one, in the sense that one finds the beginnings of such criticism – the 'plot' being poetry, rather than what happens to characters-in-action – in the great Romantic critics. The sense that Shakespeare is creating a great spiritual adventure, to which the outer world – whether of 'what actually happens', or of stage representation – merely offers expendable symbols, is first found in Lamb's famous attack on stage performances of *King Lear*: 'The greatness of Lear is not in corporal dimension, but in intellectual . . . On the stage we see nothing but corporal infirmities and weakness, the impotence of rage; while we read it, we see not Lear, but we are Lear; we are in his mind. . .'.[3] Hazlitt quotes this passage in writing on *King Lear*, and supports Lamb's contention that the poet's work is to 'personate passion, and the turns of passion' with his own: 'the greatest strength of genius is shown in describing the strongest passions . . . our sympathy with actual suffering is lost in the strong impulse given to our natural affections, and carried away with the swelling tide of passion, that gushes from and relieves the heart'.[4] Coleridge, a greater and subtler critic than either Lamb or Hazlitt, stresses, like them, the 'independence of the interest on the story as the ground work of the plot'.[5] It is Lear's 'character, passions, and suffering' which are 'the main subject-matter of the play'. '*Lear* is the most tremendous effort of Shakespeare as a *poet*.' *King Lear* has become King Lear: the play moves us by sympathy for Lear: and that sympathy is created by poetry. We enter, as it were, the poetic element which is Lear's world, and whatever happens is dominated by what is felt (which is principally what Lear feels) and what is felt is found in the poetry. Since 'poetry' used in the Romantic sense is, I think, plot-less – Being, so to speak, rather than Becoming – the stress on the 'unhappy ending' of *Lear*, that Johnson could scarcely 'endure', grows less and less: what is valuable in the play has no 'ending'.

Though these critics stress 'feeling' in *King Lear*, their treatment of the play could scarcely be called transcendental. The first critic of whom the word might be used is, of course, Bradley; though he himself acknowledges his debt to Dowden, who stresses the sovereignty of the 'moral world' in the play. Bradley's profound study of the play is remarkable, both for the way in which he feels a Romantic sympathy for, or participation in, the central character, to an extreme degree, and also for the way in which he soberly refuses to take it any further. If he directs the reader to a more 'transcendental' interpretation of the play, he does so hesitantly, hedging his observations round with careful reservations. Thus when he suggests that we should call 'this poem *The Redemption of King Lear*'[6] (what happens to Lear's soul outweighing what happens to his body) he does so only in answer to such criticism as Swinburne's, that stresses the 'pessimism' of the play, and himself affirms the power and partial verity of such criticism; and the narrowing reference, too, to the play as 'this poem', is counteracted by the constant analysis of character and dramatic effect. Again, he closes his essay on the play with the affirmation that at least a part of its beauty, and at least a part of its meaning, depend on the feelings aroused by the death of Cordelia: 'If only we could see things as they are, we should see that the outward is nothing and the inward is all . . . Let us renounce the world, hate it, and lose it gladly. The only real thing in it is the soul, with its courage, patience, and devotion. And nothing outward can touch that.' But this very affirmation he balances by saying that 'this strain of thought . . . pursued further and allowed to dominate . . . would destroy the tragedy; for it is necessary to tragedy that we should feel that suffering and death do matter greatly, and that happiness and life are not to be renounced as worthless.' Cordelia's death may arouse a sense of unworldly values, but Cordelia herself is far from perfect, and fully involved in the tragedy: 'At the moment where terrible issues join, fate makes on her the one demand which she is unable to meet.'

Thus, though Bradley is the first to make an impressive appeal for a more 'mystical' interpretation of *King Lear*, he insists again and again that it is a 'mystery we cannot fathom', and that no explicitly religious interpretation will serve: 'Any theological interpretation of the world on the author's part is excluded from [the tragedies], and their effect would be disordered or destroyed equally by the ideas of righteous or unrighteous omnipotence . . . If we ask why the world should generate that which convulses and wastes it, the tragedy gives no answer, and we are trying to go beyond tragedy in seeking one.' His feeling for the intense actuality of Shakespearian characterisation (and the ability to see a dramatic character as a cluster of images is not, perhaps, one that comes without some peculiar habituation) makes him resist any theoretical design overriding such characterisation: 'Perhaps, in view of some interpretation of Shakespeare's plays, it may be as well to add that I do not dream of suggesting that in any of his dramas Shakespeare imagined two abstract principles or passions conflicting, and incorporated them in persons.' For him, the plays stand rather at the point where intensity of experience becomes religious potentiality: but that potentiality finds no fit expression in the world that is the necessary stage for tragedy, and becomes rather aspiration, suffering, moral responsibility. It might perhaps be said that this sense of unfulfilled potentiality is a part of his vision of Shakespearian tragedy.

To turn from Bradley to the criticism of *King Lear* that has appeared over the last twenty or thirty years is to realise to what a startling extent it is indebted to him – startling, in that he has hardly been popular among critics for a very long time. Obviously the 'new' approach to *King Lear* cannot wholly be explained by Bradley's influence. A greater knowledge, both of Elizabethan rhetoric and poetic technique, and of what has been called 'the Elizabethan world picture' in its debt to mediaeval thought, has made readers see the play as a poetic work, whose imagery has as great an effect on the mind as the plot and characters, and also as a work that has a strong strain of the allegorical and even of the didactic. But it is interesting to see so many of Bradley's cautious hints and suggestions purified of their accompanying reservations and now seen as dominating the play. The famous suggestion, for instance, that Lear dies 'in an agony of ecstasy' is now accepted almost universally: what is interesting is its appearance in critics as different as Professor Empson ('He dies of a passion of joy at the false belief that Cordelia has recovered'[7]), Professor Wilson Knight ('what smiling destiny is this he sees at the last instant of racked mortality?'[8]) and Professor Muir ('His actual death-blow is not his bereavement but his joy when he imagines that Cordelia is not dead after all. That joy was based on an illusion. The earlier joy of reconciliation, however shortlived, was not an illusion: it was the goal of Lear's pilgrimage. His actual death was comparatively unimportant'). The mere borrowing of what is certainly a fine, and may be a true, interpretation of Lear's last words is less important than the hypothesis, or suggestion, that accompanies this reading in two of the three: the 'smiling destiny' ('their effect would be disordered or destroyed equally by the ideas of righteous or unrighteous omnipotence') and 'his actual death was comparatively unimportant' ('suffering and death do matter greatly').

What is most remarkable is the predominance of the idea of the feeling of 'reconciliation' at the end of the tragedy, which is Bradley's attempt to answer the question of 'tragic pleasure': since one finds this quite as strong in those who would probably deny keenly any affiliation to Bradley, or even any desire to see the play as a Christian allegory; the sense of a 'happy ending' takes the form of what is called variously the Restoration of Order, or of the Family Bond, or of Reason. In reading such studies, one is impressed by their inner coherence and their cogent force; yet one remembers, perhaps, Bradley's own introduction of such a thesis of 'moral order', and his doubtful conclusion: 'Nor does the idea of a moral order asserting itself against attack or want of conformity answer in full to our feelings regarding the tragic character . . . When, to save its life and regain peace from this intestinal struggle, it casts [the tragic heroes] out, it has lost a part of its own substance – a part more dangerous and unquiet, but far more valuable and nearer to its heart, than that which remains . . . That this idea, though very different from the idea of a blank fate, is no solution to the riddle of life is obvious; but why should we expect it to be such a solution? Shakespeare was not attempting to justify the ways of God to men, or to show the universe as a Divine Comedy.'

Bradley's *Redemption of King Lear* is tempered by such considerations. The modern King Lear is certainly redeemed: what has disappeared is Bradley's 'honest doubt'. 'Shakespeare makes [*King Lear*] end, not in the final victory of evil, but in the final victory of good . . . *King Lear* is, like the *Paradiso*, a vast poem on the victory of true love.'[9] '[*King Lear*] is at least as Christian as the Divine Comedy.'[10] If *King Lear* is to be a Christian allegory, then search must be made for a Christ-figure; Lear, in that he is the *persona patiens*, is given some such characteristics, but he is too completely individualised to serve. Thus stress falls on Cordelia, as both the most beautiful, and the most lightly sketched-in of the characters. 'Divine love, symbolised by Cordelia, enters a kingdom already divided against itself, which is the Christian definition of hell . . . If Bradley be right, it is not the chance, but the certainty that she does indeed so live [in resurrection] which causes Lear's hitherto indomitable heart to break, and the great sufferer dies at last, not of sorrow, but in an ecstasy of joy.'[11] Perhaps one ought to remember precisely what Bradley *did* say: 'To us, perhaps, the knowledge that he is deceived may bring a culmination of pain: but if it brings *only* that, I believe we are false to Shakespeare . . . All that matters is what she is. How this can be when, for anything the tragedy tells us, she has ceased to exist, we do not ask; but the tragedy itself makes us feel that somehow it is so.' A similar statement of Cordelia's allegorical function can be found elsewhere: 'Cordelia, in that she represents the principle of love, is idealised . . .'[12] 'Cordelia cannot stand for individual sanity without at the same time standing for rightness in the relation of man to man – social sanity . . . Cordelia for Shakespeare is virtue . . . [she] stands for wholeness . . . Cordelia is Shakespeare's version of singleness and integration . . . She constitutes the apex of the pyramid . . . She is the norm itself. . .'[13] Again, one returns by contrast to Bradley's patient attempts to trace *all* the strands of characterisation he finds in Cordelia, however much less simple this may make the final effect: 'Yes, "heavenly true". But truth is not the only good in the world, nor is the obligation to tell truth the only obligation. The matter here was to keep it inviolate, but also to preserve a father. And even if truth *were* the one and only obligation, to tell much less than truth is not to tell it.'

Such recent studies have enriched the reading of *King Lear* to such a degree, by illuminating the strange blend of feelings and attitudes, of theology and philosophy that the play contains, that one would be far from wishing to 'prove', in any way, their inferiority to Bradley, or to Coleridge, or to Johnson. A study of the genealogy, or growth, of such an interpretation may simply help to show how a play that must still seem, to the naïf consciousness, appalling in its content and terrible in its conclusions, can be described as almost a Divine Comedy: 'He unlearns hatred, and learns love and humility. He loses the world and gains his own soul.' It is a truism that every age of criticism finds in Shakespeare precisely what it is looking for: and perhaps what it looks for is really there, in a potential form. An image, or a human character, are both potentials, and may be interpreted *ad infinitum*. And yet, for all the pleasures of eclecticism in criticism, it is always possible to have reservations about any theory, or attitude, that is both extreme and exclusive; and criticism that sees a Shakespearian tragedy as at least tending toward didactic allegory of a peculiar kind, is surely even more doctrinal in its assertions than is a 'judging' critic like Johnson, who has a resourceful habit of giving back with one hand, so to speak, what he has taken away with the other. Johnson's conclusions on *King Lear* bear out his contention that 'there is always an appeal open from criticism to nature', and throw open the argument to the reason of the common reader: 'A play in which the wicked prosper, and the virtuous miscarry, may doubtless be good, because it is a just representation of the common events of human life: but since all reasonable beings naturally love justice, I cannot easily be persuaded, that the observation of justice makes a play worse . . .' These words are rather hesitant and perplexed, than bombastic; whereas the reader is, perhaps, a little provoked to dissent by the very doctrinaire quality evinced in such phrases as 'the *certainty* that she does indeed so live . . .', 'the symbolic significance of the trial of the two daughters . . . is *perfectly clear*'.

It is obviously impossible to decide, simply, whether or not *King Lear* is a 'Christian' play. To set it beside a play that uses even so great a degree of Christian context, as *Dr Faustus*, is to realise what one means by the phrase 'a mind naturally Christian'; *King Lear* is not only profoundly concerned with the moral repercussions of desires and actions, nor does it simply present an area of imaginative experience that constantly moves from philosophical into moral and metaphysical speculation, but it also presents these words, 'moral' and 'metaphysical', in a peculiarly Christian way. The splendours of pride, passion, aspiration, are constantly mutating, as it were, into the virtues of humility, gentleness, and endurance. Yet, when all this is said, there remains the fact that there are many kinds of art, and many kinds of statement, that a 'mind naturally Christian' might make. Montaigne also seems, from his writing, to have loved gentleness and courage; yet it would be difficult to make a case for him as a Christian allegorist. The question is not open to solution either way, nor is it, strictly speaking, the critic's business to answer it. All that might be argued is rather the *kind* of statement which Shakespeare is making in *King Lear*; whether or not it is as doctrinal, and as didactic, as it seems in, for instance, Professor Muir's version of the play.

Much of the poetry in the play that is quoted as evidence of Lear's apprehension of 'Heavenly' things – such as, for instance, the two passages mentioned above: 'We two alone will sing like birds i' th' cage . . .' and 'Thou art a soul in bliss . . .' seems to me to be peculiarly conditioned by the way it is used in the play. These passages are of such great beauty that one realises the degree of imaginative potency that they have. And yet Shakespeare often reserves his most 'beautiful' passages, in the tragedies, for a peculiar purpose: to suggest, that is, an imaginative state in ironical opposition to the actual, or to create an atmosphere or a scene that is in some ways irrelevant to the central issues, and heightens them by contrast. One may quote the lyrical phantasies of the mad Ophelia, or the exquisite pastoral of her death, occurring in a play of darkness, corruption, and sophistication; or the elaborate splendour of Othello's 'It is the cause, it is the cause, my soul' – surely the most 'beautiful' speech in the play – which is based on the completely unfounded assumption that Desdemona is unfaithful; or Duncan's and Banquo's praise of the serene calm of the castle that is to hold the blood of one, and the ghost of the other. In both the *King Lear* passages, imagination is 'still, still far wide'. The beautiful and curiously civilised vision of a purgatorial wheel, or the dream of a shared life in a hermit's cell, are both, with their exquisite rhythm and lucid images, in some way apart from what one thinks of as the 'poetic language' of the play, and – to one reader at least – less impressive and moving than this language at its height, as in Lear's and the other characters' speeches in the storm, and Lear's at Cordelia's death. Nor is the poetic vision embodied in such speeches as 'We two alone . . .' of such a power as to outweigh, so to speak, the truth of the action in which they occur. The issue at hand is the battle which, being lost, must result eventually in the death of both Lear and Cordelia. In relation to that issue, Lear's speeches have the nature of decorative art, integral perhaps only in the sense that they contribute to the tragedy of a man in love with 'our lives' sweetness' in a world that refuses to be sweet. The deliberately child-like tone that enters the second of these speeches especially ('And pray, and sing, and tell old tales, and laugh') certainly can be said to have a divine innocence, but it can also be said to reduce the world of the play to something like a child's playground; to be 'God's spies' and to see the flux of human life turn to a game of cards ('wear out packs' may perhaps stand this interpretation) may be a true vision of the 'little world of man', but it is very little indeed, compared to the rest of the play.

The scenes which are most full of explicitly 'Christian' phrasing, or suggestion, or feeling, are confined, on the whole, to one particular part of the play; that is, to the period between the storm-scenes and the last long scene that contains the meeting of Edgar and Edmund and Lear's entry with Cordelia dead in his arms. It is, perhaps, possible that the mood and tone of these scenes may be caused as much by artistic reasons as by moral design. The storm-scenes form the first climax of the play, to which the whole of the first part proceeds with a speed, violence, and – despite the sense of confusion of time and place – an emotional logic that brings a feeling of complete inevitability: one action of violence generates another with compulsive force. In the storm-scenes Lear is at his most powerful and, despite moral considerations, at his noblest; the image of a man hopelessly confronting a hostile universe and withstanding it only by his inherent powers of rage, endurance, and perpetual questioning, is perhaps the most purely 'tragic' in Shakespeare. The last scene of all returns to this mood, and forms a second climax, but the tragic mood is altered by the addition of understanding to Lear's character. The presence of purely tragic pain – the desire to 'crack heaven's vault' and deny inevitability by a powerful outcry of feeling – is rarefied, as it were, by a more precise knowledge of the source of that pain: the universal issues are intensified and clarified to the form of a single dead body. It is these parts of the play that provide the dominant tragic effect. The quieter scenes on Dover cliff (with the intellectualised memory or echo of violence in Gloster's 'suicide'), the moment of Lear's awakening and first meeting with Cordelia, and the scene in which they are taken away to prison, form a necessary bridge between the more tragic scenes, designed both to rest and to prepare the mind, and to accumulate a sense of the knowledge or understanding necessary to the second climax of the play – that of Lear's death. Hence they will stress not so much what happens, what is seen and felt, but rather what is intellectually understood, and their tone will become necessarily more contemplative and philosophical. The characters, too, of both Lear and Gloster will suffer a diminishment, absorbed, as it were, into the 'background' –

> As mad as the vex'd sea, singing aloud,
> Crown'd with rank fumiter and furrow weeds . . .

It remains possible that even if one does not lay stress on these particular scenes, and concentrates, rather, on the scenes which show Lear suffering from intense evil, one might make, out of his history, the kind of Christian morality that shows a man 'losing the world and gaining his own soul'; and this remains a permanent possibility, in that any picture of good and evil actions must contain suggestions of Christian experience, especially where the good suffer. One can, perhaps, merely remember the strength of Bradley's argument –

that in the world of Shakespearian tragedy, one single 'nature' generates both good and evil. *King Lear* surely begins, at least, on an assumption that the world of 'life' itself – the world, perhaps, of *Twelfth Night* and *Henry IV* – is rich, powerful, beautiful, and important. That the faculties of the mind and body, and the strength and significance of the individual, should be impaired and lost in the course of a play, remains in itself *a* tragedy, if not *the* tragedy. A concept that can include the suggestion that a hero's death is 'comparatively unimportant', is at least a little dangerous – however 'metaphysically' it is taken – in that one of the vital functions of tragedy is, surely, to ennoble and illuminate the moment of death. Whatever the structural climax of a Shakespearian tragedy may be, its emotional climax must remain the moment of its hero's death. And the lesser forms of death in a tragedy come with only a slightly smaller impact – loss of profession, loss of love, loss of friends. The worst performance of *King Lear* – and those seen by Lamb were presumably far from good – can at any rate present 'an old man tottering about the stage with a walking-stick', and, with this, at least a part of the tragedy. That Lear should be forced, by the evil of two of his daughters, to kneel and plead ironically

> Dear daughter, I confess that I am old:
> Age is unnecessary: on my knees I beg
> That you'll vouchsafe me raiment, bed, and food . . .

is terrible, and the moral impact of the moment is great; but that Lear should choose, because of the goodness of his third daughter, to kneel and confess seriously

> I am a very foolish fond old man
> Fourscore and upward, not an hour more nor less;
> And, to deal plainly,
> I fear I am not in my perfect mind . . .

has also something of the terrible in it, and the impact is not, perhaps, what could be called precisely a 'moral' one. Shakespearian tragedy often acts, so to speak, under the level of moral responsibility. Lear's 'compensation' is said to be that at least he learns from his sufferings: he 'loses the world, and gains his soul'. But *what* he learns is that he is 'not ague-proof', that he is 'old and foolish'; and this in itself contains further ranges of common suffering. No moralistic outline that blurs this can be fully satisfying. Such an outline must also, to some degree, blur the character of Lear. A phrase like 'he loses the world' suggests a context of peculiarly Christian experience; that is, it suggests a man (like, for instance, Polyeucte) who makes a conscious and responsible choice, and is aware of at least some of the unhappiness he is willing to suffer. Lear's character is surely scarcely comparable. His greatness lies not in the choice of 'the good', but in the transformation, into something vital and strong, of the suffering that is forced upon him, partly as a result of his own foolishness; and this transformation is a part of that love of the 'pride of life' that is involved in his first mistake, and that never leaves him up to his death. He fights passionately, at his noblest, against the form of death that the Lear of Professor Muir's revised version of the play would accept willingly – the death of self; his last speeches are as much devoted to an infinitely pathetic threnody for his own waning powers, as they are to the dead Cordelia.

That Lear is represented as a character making perpetual discoveries is certainly true, even if it is hard to accept that the moral weight of these discoveries presents some kind of counterpoint to the sufferings he undergoes; since, if he merely 'learns humility', then humility is represented in such a physical way that it contains in itself further active suffering. But perhaps Lear in fact 'learns' something rather different from this, or in a rather different way. That society may be corrupt, that justice may become meaningless in the light of this corruption, that both private and public loyalties may be broken and an old order turned into chaos, that humanity is 'not ague-proof' – none of these is a particularly new or exciting statement. The interest lies, rather, in the light in which these discoveries show themselves to a certain peculiar character. Lear is divested of that degree of civilised intelligence, subtlety and rationality that Hamlet and Macbeth, and perhaps even Othello, possess: that he shows, often, the consciousness of a child, with immense power and will, is a truism of criticism. The one gift that he possesses is a colossal power of life itself: 'We that are young Shall never see so much, nor live so long.' He is represented as feeling – and not only feeling, but living through, enduring, and becoming consciously and responsibly aware of – actions of profound evil; he feels, with a child's intensity, a range of suffering that a child could never meet. All these forms of evil – the weakness of age, the denial of power, the cruelty of his servants and subjects, social corruption and injustice – present themselves to him as a denial of life, at its profoundest and most simply physical; not, as with the other heroes, as a denial of purity, or of honour, or of imagination, or of the spirit. One recalls Berenson's insistence on the quality of what he calls 'life enhancement' by stimulating the sense of 'tactile values' to creativity, in Italian Renaissance painting; similarly Lear commands attention continually by the degree to which the simplest discoveries become, through him, a matter of immediate physical experience, felt both intensely and comprehensively.

This faculty to be found in the play, of an imaginative recreation of a physical awareness both intense and wide-ranging, from 'I feel this pin prick' to 'this great world shall so wear out to nought', is accompanied by something that is in one sense its diametric opposite, and in one sense an extension of itself: which is an apprehension of nothingness. There is a sense in which this apprehension of absolute cessation of being, appearing whenever the word 'nothing' drops into the dialogue, is a worse evil than any of the forms of moral evil that Lear meets. Ironically, the Midas touch of the poet converts even what appals the moral sense into something, if not beautiful, at least intensely interesting, and intensely alive; it is surely not possible to argue that Goneril, who is, in one of Albany's few magnificent phrases

> not worth the dust
> That the rude wind blows in your face –

is less *interesting* than the just and dull Albany himself. The only way, perhaps, in which Renaissance art can convey a sense of evil, or death, is by an antithesis of itself. Thus Lear, whose one heroic quality is a habit of totality of experience, demanding absolutes of love, of power and of truth itself ('who is it who can tell me who I am?' . . . 'Thou art the thing itself . . .') is 'rewarded' by an apprehension of the one absolute that the tragic world can offer – the absolute of silence and cessation; and even this apprehension is hedged about by a paradoxical and painful vitality: 'Why should a dog, a rat, a horse have life And thou no life at all?' The silence of the dead Cordelia is a final summary of the presence of what Donne calls 'absence, darkness, death; things which are not', throughout the play, wherever a question is asked and not answered, or a command is not obeyed. That this silence *may* contain, strangely enough, as much potentiality of good as of evil, is suggested by the degree of intense life generated by Cordelia's first 'Nothing'; but one thing, at least, it finishes – the idea of the overriding power of heroic and individual experience. The hero is only a hero insofar as he is able to envisage the limits of the heroic world.

It is perhaps in this way that one could make out a case for a 'metaphysical' *King Lear*; that it shows a world of extreme power and vitality embracing its antithesis. This sense of startling disparities contained within one imaginative world is much more reminiscent of a mind like Pascal's than of the symbolic clarity of a Morality or the simplicity of a mystery play. Intellectual reflection on the play is more likely to need to quote, as it were, phrase after phrase of Pascal's, than to refine from the play itself a pious summary. 'On n'est pas misérable sans sentiment. Une maison ruinée ne l'est pas. Il n'y a que l'homme de misérable. *Ego vir videns* . . . La grandeur de l'homme est grande en ce qu'il se connaît misérable. Un arbre ne se connaît pas misérable. C'est donc être misérable que de se connaître misérable; mais c'est être grand que de connaître qu'on est misérable . . . Toutes ces misères-là prouvent sa grandeur. Ce sont misères de grand seigneur, misères d'un roi dépossédé.' 'Quand l'univers l'écraserait, l'homme serait encore plus noble que ce qui le tue, parce qu'il sait qu'il meurt; et l'avantage que l'univers a sur lui, l'univers n'en sait rien.'[14] One feels a sense of recognition in such phrases because, though Pascal was a man almost certainly wholly unlike Shakespeare in mind, temperament and way of life, his writing postulates a world in which it is still possible to think both seriously and ironically of 'La grandeur de l'homme', and to see that the conditions on which such grandeur is based are close to those of tragic experience. One of these conditions is a profound doubt – 'une impuissance de prouver' – which perpetually accompanies 'une idée de la vérité'; the only entire certainty is death: 'Le dernier acte est sanglant, quelque belle que soit la comédie en tout le reste'. Pascal's image of man – perhaps one learned from Montaigne – is of a creature bewilderingly made 'un milieu entre rien et tout', perpetually conditioned and limited by his senses, and yet able to comprehend 'all and nothing'.

It is such an image that Lear presents in the closing scene of the play. Whether or not Lear's 'Look there' does, as Bradley interprets it, suggest a belief that Cordelia is still alive, the last half-dozen lines as a whole condense the poetic experience of the play, whereby the physical and the non-physical are shown in their mysterious relationship.

> Thou'll come no more,
> Never, never, never, never, never!
> Pray you, undo this button. Thank you sir.
> Do you see that? Look on her, look, her lips,
> Look there, look there!

It is natural enough that the central character of a poetic tragedy should finish by directing the attention, as it were, finally to the closed mouth of a dead human being, an image which presents most of what can be said about the physical limitations to an aspiring mind. Each of the great tragedies ends similarly with a momentary directing of the attention to the full effect of the tragic action:

> What is it you would see?
> If aught of woe or wonder, cease your search . . .
> give order that these bodies
> High on a stage be placed to the view . . .
>
> Look on the tragic loading of this bed.
> This is thy work.
>
> Behold where stands
> Th' usurper's cursed head . . .

That Lear should himself turn chorus – ('Look on her, look . . .)' and himself endure 'the new acquist Of true experience from this great event' even while still alive, is consonant with his rôle throughout the play: his own death is the one thing that cannot be presented through the heroic consciousness.

Perhaps the chief reason, then, why one feels doubt about an extremely allegorical interpretation of the play is not that such an interpretation can be said to be 'wrong', but simply that the play succeeds so well in another way. Rather than setting up an absolute dichotomy between the 'world' and 'the soul', between concretes and abstracts, it shows a continual relation between the two that strengthens and enriches both; so that a sense of extreme evil can be conveyed in a phrase of casual malice – ('What need one?' 'And all night, too') and a sense of extreme good in the commonest expression of a woman's kindness:

Mine enemy's dog,
Though he had bit me, should have stood that night
Against the fire; and wast thou fain, poor father,
To hovel thee with swine and rogues forlorn
In short and musty straw? Alack, alack!

It also fulfils that function by which tragedy makes the unendurable endurable by bringing it within an artistic design, while retaining its essential truth; the forms of suffering in the play are transformed not so much by being seen '*sub specie aeternitatis*', but rather by being seen as forms of intense life. If the play exhilarates, it is less because 'Cordelia, from the time of Tate, has always retired with victory and felicity', whether temporal or spiritual, than because it exhibits a poetic power in the writing of the play itself, in the consciousness given to its central character, and in the responsive awareness of audience or reader, that can understand and endure imaginatively actions of great suffering, and by understanding can master them: '. . . L'homme serait encore plus noble que ce qui le tue, parce qu'il sait qu'il meurt.' If 'Hamlet and Lear are gay', and if tragedy does exist to 'give a great kick at human misery', then this is perhaps more because of the gaiety of mastery inherent in the creative act than because of any cheerful propositions made by tragedy itself. The more terrible the propositions, the greater is the mastery; the greater the degree of the 'un-tragic', the 'un-sublime', contained – the ugly, the humiliating, the petty, the chaotic, the ridiculous, the mad, the gross, the casual and the carnal – then the greater is the act that can turn these into 'the good, the beautiful, and the true', and yet retain the nature of the things themselves. Whether this is, in itself, a highly moral act is a question too difficult to answer; but it is, perhaps, not best answered by turning *King Lear* into a morality play.

SOURCE: *Critical Quarterly* (Winter, 1960).

NOTES

1. Johnson, *Preface and Notes to Shakespeare* (1765).
2. G. Wilson Knight, *The Wheel of Fire* (1949).
3. Lamb, 'On the Tragedies of Shakespeare', in *The Reflector* (1810–1811).
4. Hazlitt, *Characters of Shakespeare's Plays* (1817–18).
5. Coleridge, *Shakespearian Criticism*, ed. T. M. Raysor (1936).
6. Bradley, *Shakespearean Tragedy* (1957).

7. Empson, *The Structure of Complex Words* (1951).
8. G. Wilson Knight, op. cit.
9. R. W. Chambers, *King Lear* (1939).
10. J. F. Danby, *Shakespeare's Doctrine of Nature* (1949).
11. G. Bickersteth, *The Golden World of King Lear*, B. A. Lecture, 1936.
12. G. Wilson Knight, op. cit.
13. J. F. Danby, op. cit.
14. Pascal, *Pensées*.

John Holloway   King Lear   (1961)

King Lear, a play set (unlike *Macbeth*) in the legendary prehistory of Britain, depicts a world which is remote and primaeval. This is not to deny that it has life and meaning for all times: its permanent relevance is what follows from having the quality of legend, and the primaeval as subject. Nor is it a merely trite observation about the play. To apprehend this fact is to be led to a decisive truth. The action of *King Lear* comprises an event which today has largely lost its meaning; though one, indeed, which points back to men's original and deepest fears and convictions, and seems to have been part of their consciousness from primitive times.

This by now largely archaic idea is present elsewhere in the tragedies. It is brought before the mind in the guards' words at the death of Antony:

SECOND GUARD   The star is fall'n.
FIRST GUARD   *And time is at his period.*   [IV xiv 106]

It is in Macduff's words at Duncan's murder:

> Shake off this downy sleep, Death's counterfeit,
> And look on death itself. Up, up, and see
> *The great doom's image*! Malcolm! Banquo!
> *As from your graves rise up* and walk like sprites
> To countenance this horror!   [II iii 74]

The point here is that the king's end is like the end of the world: not the Day of Judgement, but the universal cataclysm which was to precede it. Twice, in *Lear*, the idea is mentioned explicitly. Kent, when he sees Lear enter with Cordelia dead in his arms, says:

> Is this the promis'd end?

and Edgar replies:

> Or image of that horror?   [v iii 263]

The mad Lear and the blinded Gloucester meet:

> GLOU. O, let me kiss that hand!
> LEAR   Let me wipe it first, it smells of mortality.
> GLOU. O ruin'd piece of nature! *This great world*
> *Shall so wear out to nought.*   [IV vi 132]

The idea of a universal deflection of Nature towards evil and disaster (as prelude to final salvation) seems to call forth an echo elsewhere in the play. Gloucester's well-known reference to 'these late eclipses of the sun and moon' [I ii 99] re-echoes the words of St Luke on the end of the world:

And there shalbe signes in the Sunne, and in the Moone, & in the starres; and upon the earth trouble among the nations, with perplexitie, the sea and the water roring: And mens hartes fayling them for feare, and for looking after those thinges which are comming on the worlde: for the powers of heaven shalbe shaken.   [21: 25–6]

The storm on the heath recalls what the book of Revelation says of Armageddon:

And there folowed voyces, thundringes, and lightnynges: and there was a great earthquake, such as was not since men were upon the earth . . .
                      [16: 18]

For the Elizabethans, the End of the World was a living conviction and even something of a current fear. We touch here on one of the oldest of traditions: that notion of the world's turning upside down which Archilochus already employs when, having unexpectedly seen an eclipse of the sun, he says that the fish might as well now come and feed on land, or wolves feed in the sea. Repeated incessantly, by Shakespeare's time this was a long-established commonplace; but when Hooker (though merely adapting Arno-bius) finds his imagination kindled by this thought, and turns from detailed analysis to write with the full range of his eloquence, the idea is present in all its power and solemnity:

> Now if nature should intermit her course . . . if those principal and mother elements of the world . . . should lose the qualities which they now have; if the frame of that heavenly arch erected over our heads should loosen and dissolve itself; if celestial spheres should forget their wonted motions . . . if the moon should wander from her beaten way, the times and seasons of the year blend themselves by disordered and confused mixture, the winds breathe out their last gasp, the clouds yield no rain, the earth be defeated of heavenly influence, the fruits of the earth pine away as children at the withered breasts of their mother no longer able to yield them relief; what then would become of man himself?

The reader of Shakespeare has thus to recognize that the 'Eliza-bethan World Picture' pictured an order quite different from anything which would now come to mind as order. Coherent and providential system as it was, it included within itself a standing potentiality for progressive transformation into chaos. Paradoxically, the more that the world is conceived in religious terms, the easier is it for a potentiality of deflection into chaos to stand as no radical infringement, but a genuine ingredient of order. Further than this, for Shakespeare's time collapse into universal chaos was not merely a permanent possibility in a fallen (though divinely created) Nature: it was a foreordained part of created Nature's route to salvation; and to envisage it, to dwell on it, to comprehend what it could be like, was part of what went to make up a comprehension of God's governance of the world.

How *Lear* is in part a rehearsal of this terrible potentiality of Nature becomes plainer, if one bears in mind that what the descent into chaos would be like was delineated by tradition. It already had its familiar contours and features. There is no need here to do more than hint briefly at the length and strength of this tradition. If we go back, for example, to Mark 13, which is the chapter in that gospel corresponding to Luke 21 (the account of the final calamity of the world which was briefly quoted above) we see the major concerns of *Lear* emerge one by one: 'There shal nation rise against nation, & kingdome against kingdome: and there shalbe earthquakes . . . the brother shall betray the brother to death, and the father the sonne: and the children shal rise against their fathers and mothers, and shal put them to death. From this one might turn to Wulfstan's *Sermon to the English People*, composed in response to the chaos overtaking England when the Danish invasion was at its height: '. . . the father did not stand by his child, nor the child by the father, nor one brother by another . . .' and – sign of the traditional combination of ideas from which Lear itself emerged – Wulfstan goes on immediately to speak of how treachery, unlawfulness and infidelity to one's lord have spread everywhere throughout the land.

What must have been a passage familiar to all of Shakespeare's audience, the Homily of 1574 *Against Disobedient and Wilful Rebellion*, also clearly sees dissension between parents and children as the predictable counterpart of dissension in the body politic: 'when the subjects unnaturally do rebel against their prince . . . countrymen to disturb the public peace and quietness of their country, for defence of whose quietness they should spend their lives: the brother to seek, and often to work the death of his brother; the son of the father, the father to seek or procure the death of his sons, being at man's age, and by their faults to disinherit their innocent children. . . .' Donne's well-known reference to how 'new philosophy calls all in doubt' in the First Anniversary belongs to the same train of thought. These words, so often quoted in bleak and misleading isolation, easily misrepresent the main weight of Donne's argument. This by no means expresses a new-found disquiet resulting from new astronomy or anything like it. All that such things do for Donne is provide mere topical confirmation of that fallen condition which is established on other grounds and by the longest of traditions.

> Then, as mankinde, so is the worlds whole frame
> Quite out of joynt, *almost created lame*:
> For, before God had made up all the rest,
> Corruption entred, and deprav'd the best:
> It seis'd the Angels . . .
> The noblest part, man, felt it first; and then
> Both beasts and plants, curst in the curse of man.
> *So did the world from the first houre decay . . .*

Here is the beginning of Donne's discussion. The reference to 'new philosophy' has a subordinate place in the middle of it. The poet goes straight on to rehearse the traditional counterparts of chaos in Nature (counterparts, needless to say, having nothing to do with 'new philosophy'), and these take us straight back to *Lear*:

'Tis all in peeces, all cohaerence gone;
All just supply, and all Relation:
Prince, Subject, Father, Sonne are things forgot,
For every man alone thinkes he hath got
To be a Phoenix, and that then can bee
None of that kinde, of which he is, but hee . . .

Finally, a passage from Burton's *Anatomy of Melancholy*, resuming the same point, also relates it directly to the twin threads of action which run through the movement of the play: 'Great affinity is there betwixt a political and an economic body [i.e. a house or family]; they differ only in magnitude; *as they have both likely the same period* . . . six or seven hundred years, so many times they have the same means of their vexation and overthrow; as namely riot, a common ruin of both.'

Disruption in the kingdom, disruption in the family, linked by tradition, were facets of that universal disruption of Nature, that Descent into Chaos, which for millennia had been a standing dread of mankind and at the same time one of mankind's convictions about providential history in the future.

King Lear is an exploration of this potentiality to quite a different degree from, say, *Macbeth*. The nadir of that play, the point at which Macbeth's own evil nature seems to diffuse evil throughout his whole country, falls short of what happens even at the very start of *Lear*. In *Macbeth* the evil emanates from one man (or one couple) quite alone. In *Lear* it seems, from the first, like an infection spreading everywhere, affecting a general change in human nature, even in all nature. Those, like Kent and Cordelia, who stand out against its progress, manifest its influence even in doing so: as if Burton's 'riot' could be countered (which may be true, indeed) only by riot of another kind. The disease is general; antidotes are helpless or non-existent; the course must be run.

In its details, the play sometimes displays an extraordinary realism. Lear's hesitation before he demands to see the supposedly sick Duke of Cornwall and his inability to believe that his messenger has been set in the stocks, Edgar's impersonation of the peasant, the whole dialogue in Act V scene iii between Albany, Edmund, Goneril and Regan, are all instances of unforgettable rightness and richness in catching the complex and individualized movements of minds vehemently working and intently engaged. Yet for a sense of the play as a whole this has less weight than what is almost its opposite: an action deliberately stylized so that its generic quality and its decisive movement should stand out more than its human detail. This is true, notably, of the division of the kingdom with which the play opens. We must see this as stylized not merely in its quality as it takes place on the stage, but in how it points forward. Time and again this kind of event occurs in contemporary drama (*Gorboduc, The Misfortunes of Arthur, Selimus, Woodstock, Locrine* are examples). Its status as decisively misguided or evil is not in doubt; and it is the established sign or first step in a movement which threatens chaos or actually brings it. The direction and nature of what is to happen in *Lear* need not be inferred by the spectator through his detailed response to the behaviour and dialogue of the actors. Richly as it may be confirmed and elaborated in these things, its essence stands starkly before him in the stylization of a known kind of opening event. The intricate complication of the story, the detailed characterization, do nothing to obscure what is clear in the almost folk-tale quality of how the play begins. '*We have seen* the best of our time.'

Those words of Gloucester are essentially dynamic words, and this movement and dynamic ought to be seen in an aspect of *King Lear* which has been so much discussed that here it need not be discussed in full: its imagery. That the characters in the play are repeatedly likened to the lower orders of creation, for example, gives no mere general or pervasive tinge to the work, and embodies no merely general idea about humanity at large. It cannot be found in the opening scene. It arrives as the action begins to move, and becomes dominant as the quality of life which it embodies becomes dominant in the play. Just as it is not enough for Professor Muir to say that the plot of *Lear* 'expressed the theme of the parent–child relationship' – for it expressed no mere problem or issue, because it depicts a particular movement which begins when that relationship fails in a definite way – so it is not enough for him to refer to 'the prevalence of animal imagery' and to add merely: 'This imagery is partly designed to show man's place in the Chain of Being, and to bring out the subhuman nature of the evil characters, partly to show man's weakness compared with the animals, and partly to compare human life to the life of the jungle.' The hedge-sparrow that fed the cuckoo, the sea-monster that is less hideous than ingratitude in a child, ingratitude itself sharper than a serpent's tooth, the wolfish visage of Goneril, are not scattered through the play as mere figurative embodiments of those discursive or philosophical

interests. They burst upon the audience altogether, at the close of
Act I. If they throw out some general and discursive suggestion
about 'human life', that is far less prominent than how they qualify
the phase of the action which comes at that point, crowding the
audience's imagination, surrounding the human characters with the
subhuman creatures whose appearance they are fast and eagerly
assuming.

Likewise, when Kent [II ii 67–89] speaks of the rats 'that bite the
holy cords atwain', and the men who follow their masters like
ignorant dogs or are no different from cackling geese, we are offered
no general comment upon human life, but a context in imagery for
the conduct of Oswald which preoccupies here and now. The society
of the play, in its descent into animality, had reached this point.
Edgar, shortly after, underlines the change going on before our eyes:

> I will preserve myself; and am bethought
> To take the basest and most poorest shape
> That ever penury in contempt of man
> *Brought near to beast.*   [II iii 6]

The descent continues; Regan, Cornwall, Gloucester and Edgar are
all drawn in as its ministers or its victims; and now the images gain a
new quality. They do indeed become general, for the disease they
reflect and stress has become general. The play is indeed coming to
depict, in Hooker's phrase, an earth 'defeated of heavenly influence';
and the Fool's

Horses are tied by the heads, dogs and bears by th' neck, monkeys by th'
loins, and *men* by the legs . . .   [II iv 7]

underlines this. 'Man's life is cheap as beast's', Lear adds a moment
later [II iv 266].

All this is enforced by the progressive transformation, as Act II
advances, of the settled society of men, with their fixed abodes, into
a confusion of people constantly leaving their homes, constantly on
horseback and riding recklessly from place to place. Lear's own
words, towards the close of this movement, make the point of it:

> They have travelled all the night! Mere fetches!
> *The images of revolt and flying off.*   [II iv 87]

Yet Lear himself, quitting Goneril, is the first to break with the
settled order:

> ... Darkness and devils!
> Saddle my horse; call my train together.
>
> ... Prepare my horses.
>
> ... Go, go, my people,.
>
> ... way, away!   [ɪ iv 251–2, 258, 272, 289]

Goneril, in the person of her messengers, is quick to follow his example:

> Take you some company, and away to horse ...
>   [ɪ iv 337]

Next, it is Cornwall of whom Edmund, at his father's castle, says:

> He's coming hither now, *i' th' night, i' th' haste,*
> And Regan with him.   [ɪɪ i 24]

And Kent explains that this hurried journey was the immediate result, like the spreading of an infection, of a letter from Goneril:

> ... Which presently they read; on whose contents
> They summoned up their meiny, straight took horse,
> Commanded me to follow ...   [ɪɪ iv 33]

Regan has already set the tone of her journey more fully than she intended:

> CORNWALL   You know not why we came to visit you.
> REGAN   Thus *out of season, threading dark-eyed night,*
>   [ɪɪ ii 118]

The last appearance of this motif of the horse and the homeless rider comes once again from Lear himself:

> GLO.   The king is in high rage.
> CORN.   Whither is he going?
> GLO.   He calls to horse; but will I know not whither ...
>   Alack, the night comes on, and the high winds
>   Do sorely ruffle; for many miles about
>   There's scarce a bush.

Nothing could lead on more clearly to the idea that the society of men is becoming the chaotic world of the outlaw.

This descent from humanity, however, is something which cannot be envisaged fully through the idea of the brute and its animal life alone. It is a descent, embodied in the action, enriched by imagery, and confirmed by what is said as comment, far below brutality. Lear does not only 'choose . . . To be a comrade with the wolf and owl' [II iv 207]. He sinks lower still: recreant against Nature and outcast among its creatures:

> This night, wherein the cub-drawn bear would crouch,
> The lion, and the belly-pinched wolf
> Keep their fur dry, unbonneted he runs,
> And *bids what will* take all.   [II i 12]

Edgar joins him ['What art thou that dost grumble there i' th' straw?' asks Kent, III iv 43]. The spectacle is of man below the animals, since he combines the vices of all of them in his single self:

Hog in sloth, fox in stealth, wolf in greediness, dog in madness, lion in prey . . .   [III iv 91]

It is only now, when all left of humanity seems to be a madman, a beggar and a jester surrounded by the storm, that the extreme is reached, and the thought of it put forward at last:

> LEAR   Why, thou wert better in a grave than to answer with thy uncover'd body this extremity of the skies. Is man no more than this? Consider him well.

[this 'him' means Edgar as much as man in general]

> Thou ow'st the worm no silk, the beast no hide, the sheep no wool, the cat no perfume. Here's three on us are sophisticated! Thou art the thing itself: unaccommodated man is no more but such a poor, bare, forked animal as thou art. Come, off, you lendings! Come, unbutton here.   [III iv 100]

Regan and Goneril also seem to pass down through, and out of, the whole order of Nature; though they are its monsters not its remnants. The word itself, already recurrent in the present discussion, is explicitly used of each of them [III vii 101; IV ii 62–3]; and Albany, in two of the comments which he makes about his wife, draws attention not only to the kind of movement which the play has displayed so far, but also – and it is an important new point – to that

further movement with which it will close. He asserts that what has
happened so far is bringing his society (again the stress is upon the
movement, upon its being *brought*) to the condition of the sea, with
its universal war, unlimited in savagery, of all against all:

> If that the heavens do not their visible spirits
> Send quickly down to tame these vile offences,
> *It will come*
> Humanity must perforce prey on itself,
> Like monsters of the deep.   [IV ii 46]

Besides this, he indicates what may be expected to ensue:

> That nature which condemns its origin
> Cannot be border'd certain in itself;
> She that herself will sliver and disbranch
> From her material sap, perforce must wither
> And come to deadly use . . .   [IV ii 32]

The thought is near to that of Cornwall's servants:

> SECOND SERV.   I'll never care what wickedness I do
>   If this man come to good.
> THIRD SERV.   If she live long,
> And in the end meet the old course of death,
> Women will all turn monsters.   [III vii 98]

Lear's part in this change is a special one. He is not only the
'slave' of the elements; he is also the man to whom Kent said '... you
have that in your countenance that I would fain call master ...
authority' [I iv 27]. But his special part is best understood by
dwelling upon something which has seldom received much attention: the clear parallel (though it is also a clearly limited one)
between the condition of Lear, and that in the Old Testament of
Job. This follows on naturally from how the play brings men down
to animals, because Gloucester's 'I' th' last night's storm I such a
fellow saw / Which made me think a man a worm' [IV i 33], recalls
Job's 'I sayde . . . to the wormes, You are my mother, and my syster'
[17: 14]. Again, Albany's 'O Goneril! / You are not worth the dust
which the rude wind / Blows in your face' sees Goneril as less than
the dust, and thus echoes a thought constant in Job: 'nowe must I
sleepe in the dust'; 'Thou madest me as the mould of the earth, and
shalt bring me into dust agayne'; 'our rest together is in the dust';

'one dyeth in his ful strength . . . another dyeth in the bitternesse of
his soule . . . they shal sleepe both alike in the earth and the wormes
shal cover them'; 'all fleshe shall come to nought at once, and al men
shal turne agayne unto dust' [7: 21; 10: 9; 21: 23–6; 34: 15].

Yet these two points are merely the beginning of a much wider
resemblance. Job's patience is something that Lear early claims for
himself (II iv 229; cf 'I will be the pattern of all patience' [II ii 37]),
and that Gloucester ultimately acquires:

> henceforth I'll bear
> Affliction till it do cry out itself
> 'Enough, enough,' and die.   [IV vi 75]

There are many other links in matters, comparatively speaking, of
detail. 'Thou puttest my fete also in the stockes' [13: 27]; 'for the
vehemencie of sorowe is my garment changed, which compasseth
me about as the coller of my coat' (30: 18; cf 'come, unbutton here',
III iv 106; and 'pray you undo this button', V iii 309); 'Wherefore do
wycked men liue, come to theyr olde age, and encrese in ryches'
(21: 7; cf 'Is there any cause in nature that makes these hard hearts',
III vi 76, and the servant's '. . . if she live long, / And in the end meet
the old course of death . . .', III vii 99).

Besides these sharp if local resemblances, there are passages in
Job that seem to resume whole sections of the play: 'They cause the
poore to turne out of the way . . . they cause the naked to lodge
wythout garment and wythout coveryng in the colde. They are wet
wyth the showres of the mountaynes, and embrace the rocks for
want of a covering' [24: 4–8]. 'Heare then the sound of his voice, &
the noyse that goeth out of his mouth. He directeth it under the
whole heaven, and his lyght [= lightning] unto the endes of yᵉ
world. A roryng voyce foloweth . . . thundreth marveylously wyth
his voyce . . . He commandeth the snow, and it falleth upon earth: he
geueth the rayne a charge, & the shouers have their strength and fal
downe' (37: 2–6). Finally (though it still remains, to discuss exactly
what light these parallels throw) in one passage Lear's whole
situation is summed up: 'Myne owne kinsfolkes haue forsaken me
and my best acquaynted haue forgotten me. The seruantes and
maydes of myne owne house tooke me for a stranger, and I am
become as an aliant [= alien] in theyr sight. I called my seruant,
and he gaue me no answere . . . Al my most familiers abhorred me:
and they whome I loued best are turned agaynst me' [19: 14–18].

A resemblance, even a massive resemblance such as exists here, is one thing; light thrown on the exact contour of *King Lear* is another. Yet light is certainly thrown, and abundantly. How this is so may perhaps best be seen through taking note of something both plain and remarkable about the action of the play: what might be called not its *action*, but its *protraction*. In one sense, *Lear* is a much longer play than it need have been – need have been, that is, to have been less ambitiously tragic. By the middle of Act IV (or even the end of Act III) something of an ordinary tragic action has been completed. Lear has fallen from being the minion of Fortune (when the play opens he is presented as in one sense a king of kings) to being its chief victim. Through the ordeal of this fall, his eyes have been opened. From being one who 'hath ever but slenderly known himself' [I i 292], he has come to say 'Here I stand your slave, / A poor infirm, weak and despised old man' [III ii 19]. He has learnt, moreover, or re-learnt, the central and traditional lessons that good kings must know:

> Poor naked wretches, wheresoe'er you are,
> That bide the pelting of this pitiless storm,
> How shall your houseless heads and unfed sides,
> Your loop'd and window'd raggedness, defend you
> From seasons such as these? O, I have ta'en
> Too little care of this! Take physic, pomp;
> Expose thyself to feel what wretches feel. . . .
>
> [III iv 28]

The lines express something of what Piers Plowman learns from Hunger, and the facts to which they point are those explicit in the Wakefield *Second Shepherds' Play*, and implicit indeed in the *Magnificat*. The twin passages which begin:

> Tremble, thou wretch
> That hast within thee undivulged crimes
> Unwhipped of justice . . .   [III ii 51]

and

> Thou rascal beadle, hold thy bloody hand.
> Why dost thou lash that whore? Strip thy own back;
> Thou hotly lusts to use her in that kind
> For which thou whip'st her . . .   [IV vi 160]

are not well seen as philosophical passages about appearance and reality. Their import is moral. They are conventional and traditional, their power lying in this very embodiment of the familiar facts of human hypocrisy in all their brutal force and immediacy; and their point of origin is St Paul: '. . . Thou therfore which teaches another, teachest thou not thy selfe? thou that preachest, A man should not steale, doest thou steale? Thou that sayest, A man should not commit adulterie, doest thou commit adultery? thou that abhorrest idoles, committest thou sacriledge? Thou that gloriest in the Lawe, through breaking the Law dishonourest thou God . . .?' [Romans 2: 21–3]. Moreover, Lear had learned to repent: '. . . these things sting / His mind so venomously that burning shame / Detains him from Cordelia' [IV iv 45]; and by the end of Act IV it partly seems that his madness has ceased: 'Be comforted, good madam. The great rage, / You see, is killed in him' [IV iv 78].

The completeness of this change must not be insisted on beyond a certain point (though that there is something of the same kind in Gloucester's situation seems clear enough). A transition from blindness and injustice, through suffering, to self- knowledge, responsibility and repentance, is not the final import even of this long central section of the play. Nevertheless, it is there plainly enough. The materials exist for a more conventional and less protracted tragedy which could have ended well before the beginning of Act V. If we ask what extends the play further, the Book of Job reveals the answer.

What makes the situation of Job unique may be brought out by starting from the position of Job's comforters: Eliphaz's 'Who ever perished being an innocent? or where were the upright destroyed' [4: 7], and Bildad's 'if thou be pure and upright, then surely he wil awake up unto thee' [8: 6]. The comforters are orthodox. The men God punishes are sinners. Those who live piously under affliction, he restores; and so far as they are concerned, the sinister implications in Job's case are plain enough. But Job's protracted afflictions are a challenge to this orderly and consoling doctrine. When, despite his miseries, he 'holdeth fast to his integrity' ('In all this Job sinned not') his miseries are simply redoubled. This is the extraordinary event, the terrifying paradox indeed, which begins and demands the discussion that occupies the rest of the work. If there is any order of Nature at all, good must now replace evil; instead, evil returns twofold and is prolonged far beyond its proper span.

The action of *Lear* is also prolonged by this same conception.

Repeatedly, we are made to think that since Nature is an order
(though doubtless a stern one) release from suffering is at hand; but
instead, the suffering is renewed. Act IV, the Act in which the play
takes on its second and more remarkable lease of life, conspicuously
begins with this very turn of thought and situation. Edgar, seeing
himself at the very bottom of Fortune's wheel, finds cause for hope
(living as he thinks in a world of order) in that fact alone:

> To be worst,
> The lowest and most dejected thing of fortune,
> Stands still in esperance, lives not in fear.
> The lamentable change is from the best;
> The worst returns to laughter. Welcome, then,
> Thou unsubstantial air that I embrace! [IV i 2]

At this very moment, he encounters his father and sees that he has
been blinded; and his response is to recognize the very potentiality of
life which was embodied in the story of Job:

> O gods! Who is't can say 'I am at the worst'?
> I am worse than e'er I was . . .
> And worse I may be yet. The worst is not
> So long as we can say 'This is the worst'. [IV i 26]

The bitter reversal of events comes again and again. It is less than
the full truth to say (as was suggested on p. 187) that Lear recovers
from his madness during Act IV. The 'great rage' may be killed in
him, but among his first words to Cordelia, when he is awakened out
of sleep and we hope momentarily for his recovery, are:

> If you have poison for me, I will drink it. [IV vii 72]

Cordelia's army, coming to rescue her father, succeeds only in
putting her as well as him into the hands of their worst enemies.
Later it seems as if Lear and Cordelia are to find a kind of private
happiness in prison together. Yet even as this vision forms in our
minds, we recall Edmund's threat, and realize that

> The good years shall devour them, flesh and fell,
> Ere they shall make us weep . . . [v iii 24]

is hopeless fantasy on Lear's part, and only too soon to be proved so.

Later still, the threat appears to be removed; for as he is dying Edmund confesses to his plot, and the Captain is sent hurrying to save Cordelia from death. But again, we are worse than e'er we were: the only result, the immediate result, is Lear's entry with Cordelia in his arms.

Perhaps this ironic turn in events, this constant intensifying of disaster at the moment when disaster seems to be over, is represented yet once again in the play: in the very moment of Lear's death. Conceivably, Lear is meant to think for a moment that Cordelia is alive; and dies before he realizes his mistake. Certainly, our hopes for Lear himself are, in a limited sense, raised once more by the words of Albany which immediately precede Lear's last speech. On either or both these counts, it seems as if some kind of remission is at hand; but at this moment Lear suffers the last infliction of all. Nor is it possible to accept, as true in anything but an incomplete and strained sense, R. R. Chambers' opinion that both Lear and Gloucester 'die of joy'. Edgar has already given the audience the exact truth of Gloucester's death:

> But his flaw'd heart –
> Alack, too weak the conflict to support! –
> 'Twixt two extremes of passion, joy and grief,
> Burst smilingly.   [v iii 196]

The last two words confirm a paradoxical combination of joy and grief, they do not convert it to a state of bliss; and it is a somewhat bold interpretation of the moment of Lear's death, one which without the parallel to Gloucester (and perhaps with it) would be over-bold, to assert that there, joy lies even in equal balance with grief. That Lear's heart breaks is clear from the words of Kent ('Break heart, I prithee break'); and that this is the culmination of an ordeal of torment renewed almost beyond belief, is what we are instructed to see by what this reliable authority says next:

> Vex not his ghost. O, let him pass! He hates him
> That would *upon the rack* of this rough world
> Stretch him out longer.   [v iii 312]

This in fact is the note sounded throughout the closing scenes. The world can be to mankind, and has been to Lear, a rack: a scene of suffering reiterated past all probability or reason. It can be a place of which Edgar was able to say, at the beginning of Act IV:

World, world, O world!
But that thy strange mutations make us hate thee,
Life would not yield to age.   [IV i 10]

Later, only a few moments before the play closes, he goes on from
the account of his father's death to hint plainly at the coming death
of Kent:

EDMUND   . . . but speak you on;
   You look as you had something more to say.
ALBANY   If there be more, more woeful, hold it in;
   For I am almost ready to dissolve,
   Hearing of this.
EDGAR   This would have seem'd a period
   To such as love not sorrow; but another,
   To amplify too much, would make much more,
   And *top extremity.*
   While I was big in clamour, came there in a man . . .
   . . . His grief grew puissant, and the strings of life
   Began to crack.

This is to underline once more the idiom of the play's later
movement, its reiteration of suffering, to 'top extremity', when it
seems that suffering must surely be over.

At this stage in the discussion, one must try to record the note
upon which *King Lear* is resolved. It is not easy to do so, and it is less
easy than more than one distinguished critic has allowed. One
interpretation, certainly, has attracted many readers. We may frame
it, with Professor Chambers, as 'the victory of Cordelia and of Love';
or with Professor Knights, as the 'complete endorsement of love as a
quality of being', or with Professor Wilson Knight, as 'the primary
persons, good and bad, die into love'. It is better to see the play thus,
than to regard its close as the embodiment only of cynicism, chaos
and despair. But one should remind oneself at this point of what,
surely, is familiar knowledge: that love (unless that word is taken, as
I fear it is often taken, to mean every good thing) is a value with a
great but finite place in human life; and that if it is a full description
of the affirmation on which the play closes, that affirmation is a
limited one; is indeed, curiously inadequate, curiously out of scale
with the range, power and variety of the issues of life on which this
incomparable work has touched. Those for whom the word 'love' is
a talisman will find this suggestion objectionable. That may be an
argument in its favour.

With these considerations in mind, one may incline to see the close of *Lear* in another light. The survivors of Cleopatra, say, and of Brutus and Coriolanus, indeed speak as though these characters enjoyed a kind of victory or triumph even in death. When, at the close of *Lear*, Shakespeare characteristically gives those who survive the protagonist lines which suggest what the audience is to see in his end, it is not to any victory or triumph, through love or anything else, that he makes them direct our attention. He causes them to agree that there has never been such a case of a man stretched out on the rack of the world, and released at last. At the close of *Macbeth* there is much emphasis on a movement of regeneration, a restoration of good at the level of the body politic. Lear ends more sombrely. 'Our present business ... is general woe', says Albany, appealing to Kent and Edgar for nothing more optimistic than to help him rule and 'the *gor'd* state *sustain*' – the modest ambition of that last word should not be missed. The last speech of all, that of Edgar, seems peculiarly significant, for all its bald rhyming:

> The weight of this sad time we must obey:
> *Speak what we feel, not what we ought to say,*
> The oldest hath borne most; *we that are young*
> Shall never see so much nor live so long.

The ordeal has been unique in its protraction of torment, and the note is surely one of refusal to hide that from oneself, refusal to allow the terrible potentialities of life which the action has revealed to be concealed once more behind the veil of orthodoxy and the order of Nature. If there is such an order, it is an order which can accommodate seemingly limitless chaos and evil. The play is a confrontation of that, a refusal to avert one's gaze from that. Its affirmation is as exalted, humane and life-affirming as affirmation can be, for it lies in a noble and unflinching steadiness, where flinching seems inevitable, in the insight of its creator.

To turn to a more intimate awareness of the personal bonds on which the play closes is to extend and amplify this, and still to see something other than what deserves the name of 'love' *tout court*. Perhaps there is a clue in the fact that it is Edmund ['Yet Edmund was beloved', V iii 239] and only Edmund, who speaks of love by itself. We are meant, of course, to see it as embodied always in what Cordelia does; but in her sole reference to this in the later scenes of the play, what she at once goes on to speak of is not her love but, in effect, her duty:

> No blown ambition does both our arms incite,
> But love, dear love, *and our ag'd father's right.*
>
> [IV iv 26]

This stress, not on loving alone, but on doing and being what it falls to one to do and be, is so insistent that its having been left unregarded is surprising. Cordelia's first speech of any substance to the re-awakened Lear confirms its relevance for both her and him:

> O look upon me, sir,
> And hold your hands in benediction o'er me.
> No, sir, you must not kneel. [IV vii 57]

What she wants is for him to do what it is a father's duty to do: not what it is *her* duty to do in return. The same kind of thought is prominent in Lear's first speech after capture:

> When thou dost ask me blessing, I'll kneel down,
> And ask of thee forgiveness. [V iii 10]

Each of them is to do what (paradoxically, in Lear's case) it is appropriate for them to do: the idea is of service and duteousness, not love in any simple or emotional sense. In just this light, too, are we invited to see Edgar's bond with his father:

> ALBANY How have you known the miseries of your father?
> EDGAR By nursing them, my Lord . . .
>   . . . became his guide,
> Led him, begg'd for him, sav'd him from despair;
> Never – O fault! – reveal'd myself unto him
> Until some half-hour past, when I was arm'd;
> Not sure, though hoping, of this good success,
> I asked his blessing, and from first to last
> Told him my pilgrimage. [V iii 180–96]

Kent's devotion to Lear is of course one in which feeling means service:

> I am the very man . . .
> That from your first of difference and decay
> Have followed your sad steps. [V iii 285]

> I have a journey, sir, shortly to go.
> My master calls me; I must not say no.   [v iii 321]

The bond which remains, at the play's close, among the other (or perhaps only) survivors, is of the same kind:

> ALBANY   ... Friends of my soul, you twain
> Rule in this realm, and the gor'd state sustain.   [v vii 319]

With these many pointers in mind, perhaps the final import of the reconciliation of Lear to Cordelia, or Gloucester to Edgar, may also be seen as meaning more than the word 'love' can easily mean, at least in our own time; and as being, in the end, one with the whole of what happens at the close of the drama. That the closing phase is one in which the evil in the play proves self-destructive, is well known. Evil has come, it has taken possession of the world of the play, it has brought men below the level of the beasts, it has destroyed itself, and it has passed. Good (I have argued) is far from enjoying a triumphant restoration: we are left with the spectacle of how suffering can renew itself unremittingly until the very moment of death.

If, at the close, some note less despairing than this may be heard, it comes through our apprehending that in an austere and minimal sense, Edmund's words 'the wheel has come full circle' extend, despite everything, beyond himself. Below the spectacle of suffering everywhere in possession, is another, inconspicuous but genuine: that the forces of life have been persistently terrible and cruel, but have also brought men back to do the things it is their part to do. Union with Cordelia barely proves Lear's salvation: his salvation is what Kent says, release from a life of torment. But that union is the thing to which he rightly belongs. He deviated from it, and life itself brought him back. So with Gloucester. To follow the master, to sustain the state, to bless one's child, to succour the aged and one's parents – this idea of being brought back to rectitude is what the play ends with. These are the things which it falls to living men to do; and if the play advances a 'positive', I think it is that when men turn away from how they should live, there are forces in life which constrain them to return. In this play, love is not a 'victory'; it is not that which stands at 'the centre of the action', and without which 'life is meaningless'; it does not rule creation. If anything rules creation, it is (though only, as it were, by a hairsbreadth) simply rule itself. What order restores, is order. Men tangle their lives; life, at a price, is self-untangling at last.

In view of these things, how fantastic it would be to call *King Lear* a play of intrigue! Yet this idea, immediate though its rejection must be, does indeed suggest the many things going on, and being intricately fitted together, which mark the closing scenes of the play. This very fact is what leads back from the attitudes of the play to what is more intimate with its substance, and with the experience which it offers to us in its sequence. The war with France, the intrigue between Edmund and the sisters, the emergence of Albany, Edmund's plot with the captain and his duel with Edgar, densen into a medium of something like quotidian life, through which and beyond which Lear's own situation stands out in isolation. It is the very variety in the strands of life which brings out how, at the end, life as it were stands back from Lear; and affords him a remoteness, a separation from his fellows, in which his ordeal is completed.

This is the culmination, moreover, of how he begins. As in the tragedies which have been discussed already, at the outset the protagonist is at the focal point of all men's regard. But Lear's progressive isolation does not steal upon him, or his audience, unawares. Relinquishing the kingdom, repudiating Cordelia, banishing Kent, cursing Goneril [I iv 275–89], departing wrathfully from Regan:

> He calls to horse, and will I know not whither
>
> [II iv 296]

– all these actions set Lear, of his own free will, apart from his fellows; and are the prelude to how he sets himself apart, first from human contact of any kind whatsoever:

> No, rather I abjure all roofs, and choose
> To wage against the enmity o' th' air . . .   [II iv 207]

and then from the whole of Nature:

> This night, wherein the cub-drawn bear would crouch,
> The lion, and the belly-pinched wolf
> Keep their fur dry, unbonneted he runs,
> And *bids what will take all*.   [III i 12]

Yet Lear's position is ambiguous. In his first speech on the heath he is not only the almost satanic enemy of Nature, cursing it in its entirety; but also its victim.

> Strike flat the thick rotundity o' th' world
> Crack nature's moulds, all germens spill at once,
> That make ingrateful man. . . .   [III ii 7]

is followed almost at once by:

> . . . Here I stand, your slave,
> A poor, infirm, weak and despis'd old man.

If the tenor of the first passage is unmistakably like that of Macbeth's giant defiance ('though the treasure / Of nature's germens tumble all together / Even till destruction sicken – answer me / To what I ask you . . .)', the second has its counterpart in *Macbeth* as well. Macbeth's 'They have tied me to a stake; I cannot fly' has its closest parallel, indeed, in Gloucester's 'I am tied to the stake, and I must stand the course' (III vii 53]; but if Gloucester is like Macbeth in that his fate is more of an execution than anything else, so is Lear. Kent's thought of him on the rack is a variant of his own

> I am bound
> Upon a wheel of fire; that mine own tears
> Do scald like molten lead.   [IV vii 46]

The parallel with Macbeth is a strange and clear one; and the full currency in Shakespeare's own mind of the image through which we see the king in the later part of the play must be brought to attention and life. Today, the direction 'enter Lear, fantastically dressed with weeds' can easily seem mere fantasy without a background, or have merely some kind of enrichment in generalized associations with fertility and its converse. For Shakespeare, Lear's status in this scene must have been much more exact and significant. The figure

> Crown'd with rank fumiter and furrow weeds,
> With hardocks, hemlock, nettles, cuckoo-flow'rs,
> Darnel and all the idle weeds that grow
> In our sustaining corn . . .   [IV iv 3]

whose first words are 'I am the King himself', who jests and preaches [IV vi 181], who is filled with a conviction that he is soon to be killed ('I will die bravely, like a smug bridegroom', IV vi 200; 'If you have poison for me, I will drink it', IV vii 72), who can say: 'Nay, an you get it, you shall get it by running', and run away dressed in his flowers and pursued by the attendants – this figure is easily recognizable. He is a Jack-a-Green, at once hero and victim of a popular ceremony. For a moment, he is a hunted man literally, as he is in spirit throughout the play. Nor is such a level of interest in any way out of place for Lear. There is much of the quality of folk thinking or acting, of the folk-tale, about his whole career. This shows in the stylized opening scene, in the formality and symmetry of his break with the three sisters, in his mock court in the outhouse and in this Jack-a-Green spectacle, right through to his final entry – which cannot but call up the legendary 'Come not between the dragon and his wrath' of the opening tableau, and in which Lear and Cordelia must appear not as king and princess, but, beyond normal life, as emblems of the extremes of what is possible in life.

Over the four plays which have been discussed so far there seems by now to emerge, with increasing clarity, a repeated and recognizable pattern. In *Lear* it is surely inescapable. Despite the rich detail and realism of this play, the action and the staging are stylized largely throughout. The protagonist (followed, less fully but in some ways more plainly, by Gloucester) pursues a well-marked rôle. He is the man who begins as centre of his whole world, but who is progressively set, both by the other characters and by himself, apart from it and against it. 'Against' means above, in solitary defiance, and below, in an ordeal of protracted suffering which takes on the quality of a hunt. His response to this may indeed be a growing awareness and comprehension of where he stands; but if this makes the onward movement of the action profounder and more impressive, it in no way retards or redirects it; and its end is a death which, though realistically the outcome of the human situation of the play, has at the same time the quality of stylized and ritual execution. All is foreseen, nothing can be delayed or hastened or mitigated. We are led, in fact, to envisage a new metaphor for the status of the tragic rôle in these plays; to see running through the work, besides its other interests, its detailed representation of life, its flow of ideas, its sense of good and evil, something which might be called the vertebrate structure of its intrinsic design; the developing line, unabridged, of a human sacrifice.

SOURCE: *The Story of the Night: Shakespeare's Major Tragedies* (1961).

W. R. Elton   Double Plot in
King Lear   (1966)*

According to Bradley, the double plot chiefly contributes to Lear's 'structural weakness', 'the secondary plot fills out a story which would by itself have been somewhat thin', and 'the sub-plot simply repeats the theme of the main story'.[1] Although the double action is thus held to be fatally defective and to be filling which is 'simply' repetitive, some critics have excused it on the grounds that it universalizes ingratitude and intensifies the tragic effect. Since Shakespeare succeeded, however, in the neighboring tragedies of *Othello* and *Macbeth*, in achieving intensity and universality without recourse to such devices, a further attempt to account for its unique and apparently uneconomic occurrence may be appropriate.

Among other explanations for the double plot is that which identifies in Lear and Gloucester traditional aspects of the sensitive soul: the irascible and the concupiscible matching the protagonists' anger and lechery. This traditional dualism could, because of its medieval and Renaissance conventionality, tend to dramatic recognition.

Following Plato's conventional division,[2] Erasmus' Folly believes Jupiter has set up against our diminutive reason 'two . . . masterless tyrants'. These are 'anger, that possesses the region of the heart, and consequently the very fountain of life, the heart itself; and lust, that stretches its empire everywhere'.[3] King James's teacher, George Buchanan, in *De jure regni apud Scotos* points out that

two most loathsome monsters, anger and lust, are clearly apparent in mankind. And what else do laws strive for or accomplish than that these monsters be made obedient to reason? . . . He, therefore, who releases a king, or anyone else, from these bonds does not merely release a man, but sets up two exceedingly cruel monsters in opposition to reason. . . .[4]

In addition, the second book of the *Faerie Queene* presents the familiar opposition of wrath and lust, the irascible in cantos i–vi, the

---

* Quotations from *King Lear* are from the Arden edition, ed. Kenneth Muir (1952). Quotations from other Shakespearean plays are from the Globe edition of the *Works*, ed. William George Clark and William Aldis Wright (1952).

concupiscible in cantos vii–xii. Guillaume Du Vair's *The Moral Philosophie of the Stoicks*, translated by Thomas James (1598), speaks of the senses as disturbing 'that part of the soule where concupiscence and anger dooth lodge' and raising a 'tumult ... in the mind, that reason during this furie can not bee heard'.[5] Huarte de San Juan's *The Examination of Mens Wits* (1594) notes, regarding their ability to repress inferior powers, that 'our first parents ... lost this qualitie, and the irascible and concupiscible remained ...' [p. 250]. Montaigne's influential disciple, Pierre Charron, in *De la sagesse* (1601) distinguishes between '*Concupiscible*, and *Irascible* Faculties'.[6] Lodowick Bryskett's *A Discourse of Civill Life* (1606) identifies 'the two principall appetites, the irascible and the concupiscible' [p. 48].[7]

Because in Renaissance drama differences in rank may imply other personal distinctions, the royal Lear represents the higher portion of the human creature, his reason being closer to the divine; while the more lowly Earl of Gloucester represents its nether portion. Rank also has its afflictions. Tommaso Buoni's *Problemes of Beautie and All Humane Affections*, whose translation appeared in 1606, attempts to explain an accepted fact: 'Why are great Princes commonly afflicted with the griefes of the mind, and men of baser condition with those of the body' [p. 235].[8] Since passions, as Du Vair's *The Moral Philosophie of the Stoicks* remarks, 'darken and obscure the eye of reason' [p. 62], anger and madness assail the king, who suffers most in the mind, putting out his reason's light; while the 'dark place' of physical lust and 'nether crimes', as well as the physical darkness of blinding, attend his fellow *persona patiens*. Mankind's upper half, closer to the angels, and the nether half, bestial, are symbolized, for example, in Lear's centaur speech [IV vi 126–34].[9]

Before the end of the fourth Act the protagonists, in this last of meeting places, grope together, minds dim and eye sockets empty, like creatures out of Bruegel's 'Parable of the Blind'.[10] Lacking even the compensatory vision of the mad Cassandra or the blind Tiresias, they enact a parable of the limitations of human knowledge. Yet, if Lear and Gloucester cannot, in a sense, 'know' or 'see', they can feel; but the irony is that their hard-earned gift of feeling only makes them suffer more. The limit of their knowledge, like Edgar's, is the suffering it brings. As do Montaigne[11] and Sidney's *Arcadia* [I 227], Webster's *The Duchess of Malfi* [III v 81–4], for example, expresses the Sophoclean position:

> Thou art happy, that thou hast not understanding
> To know thy misery: For all our wit
> And reading, brings us to a truer sence
> Of sorrow. . . .

According to the traditional irascible-concupiscible distinction, Lear's intellectual error of anger receives the conventional punishment of madness (*ira furor brevis*), and Gloucester's physical sin of lechery the conventional retribution of blindness. Yet it is evident that Gloucester, in addition to such irascible passions as fear and despair, also participates in Lear's angry propensities; the earl's rash and premature fury at Edgar parallels Lear's outburst at Cordelia. 'I am almost mad myself' [III iv 170], Gloucester confesses to Kent. On the other hand, Lear, at least figuratively, shares Gloucester's blindness. Blind from the start, dim of sight at the end ('Mine eyes are not o' th' best', V iii 279), he anticipates both Gloucester and the darkening of his own mind's eye: 'Old fond eyes,/Beweep this cause again, I'll pluck ye out' [I iv 310–11].

A further iterated parallel is that between joy and sorrow, both of which were usually ascribed to the concupiscent faculty. Renaissance psychology recognized the perverse and convulsive effects of such extremes. For example, Nashe speaks of 'many whom extreame joy & extreame griefe hath forced to runne mad' [II 114–15], and Timothy Bright in *A Treatise of Melancholie* (1586), which Shakespeare probably knew, remarks, 'What marvell . . . if contraries in passions bring forth like effects; as to weepe & laugh, both for joy & sorrow? For as it is oft seene that a man weepeth for joy, so is [it] not straunge to see one laugh for griefe' [pp. 148–9].[12]

In this regard, the similarity between the deaths of Gloucester and Lear accentuates their difference: Gloucester perishes between extremes of grief and of joy at the knowledge that his son was 'miraculously' preserved [V iii 196–9]; Lear dies between extremes of a kind of joy in his desperate illusion of her lips' movement and of grief in his emphatic knowledge that his daughter was needlessly butchered. While such emotional extremities were divisive, immoderateness of joy alone could cause death. 'Sudden Joy', says the Renaissance proverb (Tilley J86), 'kills sooner than excessive grief.' 'For it is not possible', declares Mabbe's 1623 translation of Alemán's *Guzman de Alfarache*, 'that any mans heart should dissemble a sudden joy. Though it sometimes so hapneth, that excesse of joy, doth suffocate the naturall heat, and deprive it of it's life.'[13] Especially in an old or enfeebled man, the extremes themselves could wrenchingly cause violence. Apropos, the *Celestina* in Mabbe's translation (1631) remarks:

> on the one side he is oppressed with sadness and melancholy ... on the other side transported with that gladsome delight and singular great pleasure.... And thou knowest that, where two such strong and contrary passions meet, in whomsoever they shall house themselves with what forcible violence they will work upon a weak and feeble subject.[14]

Analogous to the above, as well as to the microcosmic weather analogy of Lear [cf III i, ii], is Cordelia's own joy and grief as described by the Gentleman [IV iii 18–20]:

> You have seen
> Sunshine and rain at once; her smile and tears
> Were like, a better way....[15]

Proberbially reflected in the *Arcadia* and in other parallels, the contrast is echoed also in S.S.'s *The Honest Lawyer*: 'So I have seene (me thinkes) Sun-shine in raine' (1616, sig. B).[16] Finally, as in Bright, cited earlier, it is anticipated in the perversity of the Fool:

> *Then they for sudden joy did weep,*
> *And I for sorrow sung.*   [I iv 182–3][17]

Progressively skeptical and Epicurean with regard to the gods, Lear is set up against the superstitious and eventually 'Stoic' Gloucester, their differences, like their similarities, being great. In crediting the ominousness of eclipses, Gloucester, although Epicurean on a sensual level, assumes an un-Epicurean position, for followers of Epicurus rejected such prognostication. On the other hand, Gloucester's belief in omens could, like his later tenuous acceptance of 'ripeness', associate him with a Stoic view, which also vigorously defended both intuitive and inductive divination.[18]

Further, in an earlier tragedy Shakespeare had already employed the classical distinction as a measure of a character's shifting viewpoint; the scornful and Epicurean Cassius, at a moment of defeat, partially repudiates his previous rejection of omens:

> You know that I held Epicurus strong
> And his opinion: now I change my mind,
> And partly credit things that do presage.   [v i 77–9][19]

As it does with regard to attitudes toward thunder and the stars, *Julius Caesar*'s opposition of the Epicurean Cassius and the Stoic Brutus foreshadows a similar antithesis in *King Lear*. Still earlier, the *Taming of the Shrew* [I i 27–40] had philosophically posed Epicurean delights against Stoic repressions. In Jacobean, Caroline, and Restoration comedy, moreover, the opposition between Stoic and Epicurean continues, and that duality, as a recent study of Etherege reminds us,[20] underlies works of such dramatists as Chapman, Jonson, Thomas Nabbes, and Fletcher.

As superstitious 'over-believer' and skeptical 'under-believer', Gloucester and Lear tend to two of the best-known pagan philosophical attitudes in the Renaissance. In 1604 Andrew Willet's *Thesaurus ecclesiæ* juxtaposes those points of view:

First, both the Stoickes and Epicures (which were two of the most famous sects of Philosophers amongst the Gentiles, as we may reade Act. 17.18.) are confuted: The first whereof did bring in a fatall necessitie, making all things to depend, not upon the will and providence of God, but upon a certain connexion of causes, to the which the divine power it selfe should be subject: like as vaine Astrologers and star-gazers do attribute all to their constellations and aspects of starres. But the Scripture teacheth us, *that the Lord doth in heaven and earth whatsoever it pleaseth him, Psal.* 135–6: he is not forced by, or tyed to any such fatall conjunction of causes.

Having piously derogated the fatalistic, astrological, and Stoic pattern, Willet turns next to its equally contemned Epicurean counterpart, which removes God's providence from earthly cares:

The Epicures ... [like] many carnall men ... cannot look into Gods providence, as the Preacher speaketh in the person of such, Eccle. 9.10. *Time and chance cometh to all.* Ambrose hereof writeth well.... *The Epicures thinke, that God taketh no care of us: and Aristotle, that Gods providence descendeth no lower then the Moone: but what workeman doth cast off the care of his worke?*[21]

Of the four ancient schools most esteemed by the humanists – Platonism, Aristotelianism, Stoicism, and Epicureanism – the last is espoused by More's Utopians, who regard the Stoics as their particular adversaries.[22] 'I wil no Stoickes of my Jury', pronounces

Sir John Harington in *An Apologie* (1596, sig. Cc 1ᵛ); 'of the twoo extreames, I would rather have Epicures'. Yet in a chapter on 'the opposite opinions of the Stoicks and Epicures' Thomas Jackson's *A Treatise of the Divine Essence and Attributes*, part II (1629), notes that 'The Stoicks did well in contradicting the Epicures, which held *fortune* and *Chance* to rule all things . . .' [p. 179].

Moreover, cosmic Epicureanism and Stoicism had personal corollaries, which are attacked, for instance, in Miles Mosse's *Scotlands Welcome* (1603), assailing contemporary atheists: '*Epicures* they are, for they hunt after pleasure as after their chiefest good. . . . *Stoickes* they are: for though they love to dispute of Action and Practise, yet themselves covet to sit in ease and quietnesse' [p. 76]. In addition, William Fulbeck's *A Booke of Christian Ethicks or Moral Philosophie* (1587) describes the alternatives facing his contemporaries, who may seem, according to their actions, 'fooles to the Stoikes, blockes to the Epicures' (sig. E). It is such want of feeling that evokes Marullus's outcry in *Julius Caesar*, 'You blocks, you stones, you worse than senseless things!' [I i 40], as well as Montaigne's repeated attacks upon 'Stoicall impassibility'; compare the commonplace jest in *Taming of the Shrew* on 'stoics' and 'stocks' [I i 31]. Speaking of a philosopher, Montaigne says, 'Hee would not make himselfe a stone or a blocke, but a living, discoursing and reasoning man . . .', and the essayist admits himself not 'begotten of a blocke or stone'.[23] Sidney's *Arcadia*, too, following the tale of the 'Paphlagonian' king, observes,

> Griefe is the stone which finest judgement proves:
> For who grieves not hath but a blockish braine.
> [I 227][24]

As Edgar has been shown above to provide indications contrary to Stoicism, so Lear, whom he parallels, repudiates such unfeeling impassiveness. 'Howl, howl, howl! O! you are men of stones . . .' [V iii 257].

Indeed, anger marks both Lear's opening scene, when he rages at Cordelia, and his closing scene, when at her death he storms at the heavens. Although anger was associated with the irascibility of old age, the emotion was not always discredited. On the one hand, 'in age', notes *The Pilgrimage of Man* (1606), 'man is wonderfully changed, he is prompt to wrath . . .' (sig. D2), as the evil daughters agree, 'You see how full of changes his age is . . . the unruly waywardness that infirm and choleric years bring with them' [I i 287, 298–9]. Yet, on the other hand, in Kent's reply to Cornwall, 'but anger hath a privilege' [II ii 71; cf *King John*, IV iii 32], and in Lear's prayer for 'noble anger' [II iv 278] may be heard an attitude antithetical to the Stoic injunction. As King James himself confesses, 'I love not one that will never bee Angry: For as hee that is without *Sorrow*, is without *Gladnesse*: so hee that is without *Anger*, is without *Love*',[25] while Bacon points out, 'To seek to extinguish Anger utterly is but a bravery of the Stoics.'[26] Similarly, William Sclater's *An Exposition . . . upon the First Epistle to the Thessalonians* (1619) argues against Stoic repression of such emotions and, like Lear, indicts 'men of stones':

The opinion of Stoickes, not allowing to their Wise man any use of Affections, not to sigh or change countenance at any crosse accident, sorts neither with Religion nor Reason. . . . Another sort of men wee have, in practice more than Stoicall; whom no crosse from God or men can affect to sorrow . . . their patience is it, or rather their blockish senselesnesse?

[p. 317]

Indeed, a Renaissance point of view, like Lear's, exalted a virtuous anger. Ficino and the Florentine humanists, for example, helped effect a change with regard to the traditional sin of *ira*, transforming it partly to a 'noble rage',[27] as in Lear's desired 'noble anger', which, instead of bursting forth, comes deliberately called.

Similar in their deaths, the protagonists provide a basis for comparison also in their lives. Although both are, as Lamb said, on the 'verge of life', for Gloucester the verge is symbolized by a physical cliff, while for Lear it is the more terrible Dover of the mind, as in Gerard Manley Hopkins's

> O the mind, mind has mountains; cliffs of fall
> Frightful, sheer, no-man-fathomed.

Yet the common language of their reununciation-resolves, Lear's 'To shake all cares and business from our age' [I i 39] and Gloucester's presuicidal

> This world I do renounce, and in your sights
> Shake patiently my great affliction off   [IV vi 35–6]

in light of the consequence of such attempts, may suggest that human suffering is unshakable; the attempt to escape leads only to further suffering. Whereas the abject Gloucester falls undignifiedly, Lear stands erect as he challenges the elements to 'Singe my white head!' [III ii 6]. The latter's attitude to life as well as to death seems summed up in several lines of *Choice, Chance, and Change* (1606), regarding one who, being 'moulded of a noble mind', has 'steele unto the backe' and 'Cries not with feare, to heare a thunder cracke.' Such a person

> Stoupes not to death untill the heart do crack:
> Lives like himselfe, and at his latest breath
> Dies like himselfe. . . . (sig. [K3])

If *Hamlet* shows the mature Shakespeare deliberately exploiting parallel ideas for dramatic effect – for example, the various attitudes toward the ghost of the sentinels, Hamlet, and Horatio in Act I – the more complex *Lear* reveals him employing such ideas to provide the very structure of the play itself. Moreover, Renaissance conventions may adequately account for Shakespeare's unprecedented duplication; and I suggest that there may be no real loss of economy, since Lear and Gloucester stand for recognizably antithetical religious positions in this tragedy of man's relation to the heavens.

Conventionally paired, superstition and skepticism (or atheism) assumed a relation of polarity as well as, inevitably, of similarity: extremes to the mean of faith, they were both irreligious. Suggested by Plutarch in 'Of Superstition',[28] the concept of true faith as the *via media* between superstition and skepticism was restated, in terms favorable to itself, by Renaissance Calvinism, which conveniently consigned Catholicism to a superstitious or atheistic limbo. Marking the distinction, Hooker, after castigating atheists, turns his ire on practicers of superstition: 'Wherefore to let go this execrable crew [of atheists and Machiavellians], and to come to extremities on the contrary hand.'[29] James's *Basilicon Doron* (Edinburgh, 1603), advises his son, regarding his conscience, 'especially . . . to keepe it free from two diseases, wherewith it useth oft to be infected; to wit, Leaprosie, & superstition: the former is the mother of Atheisme, the other of Heresies' [p. 15]. Elsewhere James utters the aphorism, 'The Devill alwaies avoydes the meane, and waites upon extremities; So hath he sought to devide the world betwixt *Atheisme*, and *Superstition*.'[30] That superstition was the counterpart of atheism, that both were irreligious, is, typically, the conviction of Joseph Hall, who, in his *Characters of Vertues and Vices* (1608), observes:

'The Superstitious hath too manie Gods, the Prophane man hath none at all . . .' [p. 93].

Between reason, the soul's left hand, and faith, her right, true religion walked; any deviation to the left led to atheism, any excess to the right led to superstition. Among numerous texts illustrative of the dichotomy, Burton may be cited: 'For methods sake I will reduce them [the fallacious doctrines] to a twofold division, according to those two extreames of *Excesse* and *Defect*, impiety and Superstition, idolatry and Athisme.'[31] A mock prognostication of 1608, *The Penniles Parliament of Thread-bare Poets* [sig. B3], announces, 'Athistes, by the Law, shall be as Odious, as they are Carles: and those that depend on Destiny, and not on God, may chaunce looke through a narrow Lattice at Footemans Inne', meaning prison. As Bacon observes in his essay 'Of Superstition', the one, atheism, 'is unbelief', while 'the other', superstition, 'is contumely: and certainly superstition is the reproach of the Deity'. Just as atheism, he supposes, is related to wariness, so superstition is totally unreasonable and therefore the greater threat to political stability; it 'bringeth in a new *primum mobile*, that ravisheth all the spheres of government'.[32] By virtue of their superstition, especially, pagans were led to atheism, polytheism tending to break down men's faith. Fitzherbert's *Second Part of a Treatise*, cited above, alludes to the pagan inclination to both atheism and superstition. In like fashion, what has been termed the first sixteenth-century English pantheon of the heathens' gods, Stephen Batman's *The Golden Booke of the Leaden Goddes* (1577) in its dedication claims to show 'into what . . . Atheisme . . . Idolatrye, and Heresie, they have . . . affiaunced their beleeves'.

Finally, while the superstitious-concupiscible character might be seen as passively accepting, the skeptical-irascible might be regarded as a dynamically rejecting type. Contemporary ideas of belief and unbelief, of the passive and the active, could also in this manner be assimilated to antithetical structural elements. Ironically, while at the start Lear is caught by belief in his evil daughters and disbelief in his good daughter, he is throughout the middle portion of the play torn between his previous belief and disbelief in his daughters as well as in his gods. For Lear, belief is sanity, and its loss becomes insanity. Having 'caught' Cordelia [v iii 21] and having again lost her, Lear in his last words composes a tension of nihilistic unbelief and the tenuously supported illusion that Cordelia still breathes.

Whether the double plot is, in fact, uneconomic is, of course, relative to interpretative criteria and dimensions, as well as to the type of play it is judged to embody. It is conceivable, for instance, that Bradley's recognition of the work's moral symmetry, its almost equal division into powers of good and evil, might legitimately be extended to structure as to sense. In this drama of duplicity and betrayal the doubleness of man's nature and the irresolution of his mysterious sojourn on earth are mirrored in the two protagonists. Since Shakespearean openings customarily provide clues to the action, it is significant that the initial lines [I i 1–7] deal in dualities: the Albany–Cornwall antithesis, the division of the kingdom, and the observation that 'equalities are so weigh'd that curiosity in neither can make choice of either's moiety'. Similarly, the legitimate Edgar is, to Gloucester, 'no dearer in my account' than the illegitimate Edmund [I i 20–1]. Further, while near the beginning the state, the family, as well as the protagonists' hearts are split (Gloucester's 'old heart is crack'd, it's crack'd' II i 90), at the end, with the family severed and the state still 'gor'd' [V iii 320], Lear's voice would 'crack' the heavens, and both old men die, their hearts cleft in twain. The duality of Hamlet,[33] as reflected, for instance, in his dictional iterations, develops in *Lear* into a structural principle.

In addition, while facilitating an expanding multiplicity, the double plot helps sustain unity and maintain interests by its alternation of diverse characters and events reflecting the focal problems. Hence, in one sense Edgar's succession of quick-change roles may be allied to the general dramatic strategy. Further, through his proxy relationship, as during Lear's madness, Gloucester also assumes a larger expository and choral burden, thereby freeing the main character for more central utterances. From one point of view, therefore, the Gloucester plot may be said to frame the main plot, producing an effect analogous to that obtained by the contrast between prose and verse usual in Shakespeare. Finally, the Gloucester contrast might, in part, 'purge' Lear of some possible theatrical disadvantage of old age and heighten the audience empathy frequently reserved for the *virtù* of a younger hero. For Gloucester's 'We have seen the best of our time' [I ii 117–18] may be, in one sense, an admission somewhat less applicable to Lear.

Indeed, it may be possible to regard the double plot as a developing metaphor, opening up the principal action into two parts that mirror each other. Such a device would be appropriate to a play in which the protagonist expresses a dissociation between his name and his identity (e.g. 'This is not Lear:/Does Lear walk thus?' [I iv 234–5]), so that his person dissolves into a dual personage, a character in search of himself. Paralleled by Edgar's quest for identity, Lear demands his own identity of his daughters, his retainers, his Fool, and himself [I i, iv; II iv], his sane and insane pursuit of his 'name' being, in effect, an image of the dramatic action. In the dissolution of identity which marks the opening, Lear and Edgar lose theirs, Cordelia disappears, and Kent and Edgar assume disguises. While the villains hypocritically ply their new roles, and Albany is 'ignorant' [I iv 282] and confused, Edmund provides the nominalistic rationale which dissolves names, as he displaces their possessors.

From one point of view, indeed, Lear may be said sequentially to dissociate into his children, Goneril and Regan (selfish willfulness) and Cordelia (courageous adamancy), as Gloucester may be seen successively to dissolve into his components, Edmund (lust) and Edgar (pathos). Here, fatherhood, as in Dostoievsky's Karamazov family, involves not only the problem of identity but also that of identity in multiplicity. Thus, through self-alienation and division, characters generate proxies for themselves, as well as analogues of each other. As the play moves, therefore, Lear's problem is seen revolving from different angles, above and below, through the continual presence onstage of proxy characters, as well as of the gods who are in their 'heavens' while all is not right with the world.

Further, if *Hamlet*'s play-within-the-play holds 'the mirror up to nature', *Lear*'s double plot holds the mirror up to the heavens themselves. Just as Cordelia reflects the aspect of steadfast love, Edgar that of unchanging pity, and Kent of virile loyalty, Gloucester generally mirrors, centaur-fashion, Lear's all-too-human side, as the heavens mirror Lear's royal demigod or Promethean side. In addition, while *Hamlet*'s play-within-the-play centripetally reflects its hero in relation to his corrupt courtly audience, *Lear*'s play-within-the-cosmos, with the gods as spectators, more centrifugally throws the image of mankind against the questionable heavens. After a certain point in *Lear*, for example, human actions are invoked to 'show the Heavens more just' [III iv 36].

Lending the central situation sharper reality, Gloucester's physical suffering intensifies Lear's mental anguish, the passion of the blinding [III vii] preceding the height of Lear's mad frenzy [IV vi]. In addition to its perspective on pain, Gloucester's role fills out the dimensions of Lear's; the latter's function is identified not only through his own words and actions but also through those of the figures who stand proxy for him. When, for example, Gloucester warns against the 'purpos'd low correction' [II ii 142] in putting Kent in the stocks, both earls act partly as anticipatory Lear symbols. Called 'shame' by Lear [II iv 6] and by Kent [II iv 45], the villains' offense against Kent, the latter observes, is 'Against the grace and person of my master' [II ii 132]. Again, as Cornwall and Regan punish both these royal followers, the king's vacated place on the throne descends to Kent's seat in the stocks [II ii iv] and to Gloucester's chair during the old earl's blinding [III vii].

Enriching and underscoring the play's significances, the double plot facilitates its elaborate contrapuntal movements. In I i the king is actively involved in his own duping; while in I ii, II i, and III iii Gloucester is the more passive victim of a protracted deception. In contrast to Lear's dynamic behavior, the proxy role of the slower-witted Gloucester reveals in less rapid detail how an analogous deception might come about. Similarly, the implicit first-Act debate between Gloucester and Edmund [I ii] is contrapuntal to the Gloucester–Lear antithesis; Edmund's attitude toward Gloucester's credulity in part foreshadows Lear's mounting skepticism of his own previous belief. While the old earl continues to be gulled, Lear in I iv and V is educated in his folly by the Fool.

In the proxy scene of II ii the king is shown abused. In II iv the two protagonists are brought together onstage for comparison, as they are again during the heath scene of III iv and in IV vi While Gloucester continues, in III iii, to be deceived by Edmund, Lear, in III ii, has already challenged the supernal deceivers, or at least their elemental messengers. Thus Lear is able, earlier than Gloucester [III iv versus IV i], to invoke, through ironically reversed prayers, human examples for heavenly justification. Gloucester's customarily de-layed counterpoint reaches his passion of the body [III vii] after Lear has already begun his passion of the mind [III ii 67: 'My wits begin to turn', and III iv, vi]. While Lear's eyes have been opened, Glouces-ter's 'vile jellies' are being extinguished. Indeed, Lear's mad 'trial' of the villains [III vi] ironically introduces the villains' 'trial' [III vii] of Gloucester; madness and 'justice' are juxtaposed. Whereas mental suffering serves to animate Lear, Gloucester's blinding produces a deeper passivity and an implicit presuicidal renunciation of the world of action [IV i 20–1]. Gloucester's attempt at self-destruction

[IV vi] contrasts, in its futile indignity, with Lear's heroic challenge to the elements [III ii 6], as the latter's fearless jeopardy of life is suggested by Cordelia at IV vii 31–6. In IV vi, by a masterly irony, madman and blind man are brought together and confronted.

Although Gloucester for most of the play lags behind and echoes Lear, the last scenes reverse the order, as the antihero foreshadows the hero's concluding lines. Gloucester's 'suicide' and 'restoration' [IV vi] prepare for Lear's moving 'rebirth' scene [IV vii]. The earl's quiescent acceptance of 'ripeness' [V ii 11] sets the stage for his king's frenzied rejection of Cordelia's most 'unripe' extinction [V iii]. And Gloucester's death offstage (described by Edgar, V iii 196–9) anticipates, without distracting from, the intensified pathos of Lear's last earthly moment [V iii 310–11].

While Bradley ascribes confusion to the double plot, it is evident that confusion might only have been compounded by compressing *Lear*'s conceptual elaboration within narrower limits. Indeed, the device may rather be an agent of clarity, assimilating to drama's limited economy the intellectual freight of this cosmic tragedy. For in one respect the double action is related to the fashion in which the play may be said to 'think', the work being, in its own terms, a developed and dialectical argument. Examining the total conspectus of human existence under the heavens and delving also into 'hell', the drama is structurally consonant with Shakespeare's most epic or total play.

Ironically, the structural mode employed depends partly upon the traditional device of analogy in a drama which suggests, through its dissolution of natural law and hierarchy, the incipient breakdown of analogy. In a final sense, however, as the religious poles become assimilated to the dramatic ones, *King Lear* is not 'about' ideas at all but acts out rather its essential tragedy of human experience. Ultimately, then, the double plot is an instrument of complexity, the assurance of a multifaceted ambivalence which, contrary to the salvation hypothesis, probes and tests, without finally resolving, its argument of mysterious human suffering.

SOURCE: *King Lear and the Gods* (1966).

NOTES

1. *Shakespearean Tragedy* (New York, 1955), pp. 205, 210, 211. C. Harley Granville-Barker, *Prefaces to Shakespeare* (1958), 1 270, who charges that *Lear* 'suffers somewhat under the burden' of the double plot.

2. *The Dialogues of Plato*, tr. Benjamin Jowett (Oxford, 1953) e.g. 1 451

(*Phaedo*, 94d); II 293–4 (*Republic*, 439e); III 143–4 (*Phaedrus*, 237d–238b).
Cf '. . . Account of the Allegory of the Poem', in Torquato Tasso, *Jerusalem Delivered*, tr. Edward Fairfax, ed. Henry Morley (1890) pp. 441–2.

3. Erasmus, *The Praise of Folly*, tr. John Wilson (1668: Ann Arbor, 1958).

4. *The Powers of the Crown in Scotland*, tr. Charles F. Arrowood (Austin, Texas, 1949), p. 128.

5. Ed. Rudolf Kirk (New Brunswick, N.J., 1951), p. 64.

6. *Of Wisdom*, tr. George Stanhope (1697), I 174.

7. See also Nicolas Coeffeteau, *A Table of Humane Passions* (1621), pp. 5–6, 61–3. See 'La Luxure et la Colère. Chapiteau roman à Vézelay', in Raimond van Marle, *Iconographie de l'art profane* (La Haye, 1931–2) II 73, fig. 85. William Blandie's *The Castle . . .* (1581), fo. 13, finds the amatory and the choleric implanted in us. On the connection of the irascible passions with the heart and the concupiscible with the liver, see Sir Thomas Browne, *Pseudodoxia epidemica* (1646), p. 110. Such writers as Du Vair and Charron lead to Descartes; and since Descartes believed he was the first to demonstrate the untenability of the traditional irascible-concupiscible distinction, it may be supposed that, with few exceptions, the difference was recognized through the Renaissance. See Descartes, *Les Passions de l'âme*, ed. Pierre Mesnard (Paris, 1937), pp. 45–6, 111–19.

8. See Buoni's work for other mind–body parallels; e.g. cf. Lear's 'Nature, being oppress'd', which 'commands the mind/To suffer with the body' [II iv 108–9]; cf also III iv 11–12 with Buoni's 'Why are griefes of the body communicated unto the minde, and those of the minde unto the body?' [p. 227]. Yet Buoni suggests that the 'griefes of the minde' are 'farre greater than those of the Body' (pp. 232–5). On the mind–body relationship, see also Chapman's *Sir Giles Goosecap* (1601–3), v ii 1–50.

9. Cf. Lear's description [IV vi 126–9] and Anthony Copley's *A Fig for Fortune* (1596) sig. B. Cf M. P. Tilley, *A Dictionary of the Proverbs in England in the Sixteenth and Seventeenth Centuries* (Ann Arbor, 1950), W 520. See Montaigne's citation from Jerome, 'Diaboli virtus in lumbis est', in *Essays*, tr. John Florio, 3 vols (Everyman's Library, 1946), III 86. The distinction is, of course, Platonic. See also Horace, *De arte poetica*, line 4 (tr. H. Rushton Fairclough, Loeb Classical Lib. (1926) p. 450). From the name of Sidney's Arcadian villainess, Cecropia, Shakespeare could have recalled the notion of bodily division, for Cecrops, mythical first king of Athens, had a serpent's form below the waist. On the 'woman-serpent' convention see John M. Steadman, 'Tradition and Innovation in Milton's "Sin": the problem of literary indebtedness', in *Philological Quarterly*, XXXIX (1960), 93–103. Analogously, Richard Linche's *The Fountaine of Ancient Fiction*, (1599), sig. Kii, presents an image of Jupiter, the upper parts naked, suggesting divine light, the lower parts clothed, suggesting darkness and the 'illecebrous blandishments' of the world's delights. Benjamin Rudyerd's *Le Prince d'amour* (1660), p. 33, observes, regarding woman, 'The Equinoctial maketh even the day and the night at the girdle; the upper Hemisphere hath day, and the lower night.' To Chapman, centaurs are a symbol of what man has become. Cf. Jonson's Lady Centaure in *Epicoene*; Dekker, *The Seven*

Deadly Sinnes of London (1606), in *The Non-Dramatic Works of Thomas Dekker*, ed. Alexander B. Grosart, II (1885), 79.

10. If Coleridge correctly compares the heath scene of III iv to Michelangelo, the protagonists' Brueghelesque decline one Act later may suggest a significant commentary.

11. Pierre Villey-Desmeserets, 'Montaigne et les poètes dramatiques anglais du temps de Shakespeare', in *Revue d'histoire littéraire de la France*, XXIV (1917), 380–1. Cf. Ecclesiastes, passim; Tilley S141 ('Much Science much sorrow') and K188. Cf *The Defence of Contraries*, tr. Anthony Munday (1593), pp. 23–32: 'That ignorance is better than knowledge'. See *The Tragedie of Cræsus* (1604), *The Poetical Works of Sir William Alexander*, ed. L. E. Kastner and H. B. Charlton, I (Manchester, 1921), 82, lines 2083–4. See also Webster's *The White Devil*, V vi 259–60, on the unhappiness of confounding 'knowledges'. In addition, compare Lear's name and the current sense of 'lere' as learning (cited in *Oxford English Dictionary* s.v. 'lear', from Spenser, *The Shepheardes Calender* [1579] May, line 262; John Ferne, *The Blazon of Gentrie* [1586] p. 22; Lyly, *Mother Bombie* [1594] II v). Lear, who 'hath ever but slenderly known himself' [I i 293–4], invokes 'marks of ... knowledge' [I iv 240–1], as he presses further, 'Who is it that can tell me who I am?' [I iv 238]. Cf E. R. Curtius's 'Etymology as a Category of Thought', in *European Literature and the Latin Middle Ages*, tr. Willard R. Trask (New York, 1953), pp. 495–500; the tradition of *nomen atque omen*, and the literary practice of symbolic naming in virtually all ages. The heroic eponym, like 'Oedipus' (suggesting both knowledge and pride), functions here as ironical leitmotiv, emphasizing not only self-identity and the means of the work's unfolding but also the irony of the dramatic quest.

12. Cf Pedro Mcxía's opposition between grief and joy, *The Treasurie of Auncient and Moderne Times*, tr. Thomas Milles (1613), p. 716; and the table in Nannus Mirabellius, *Polyanthea* (Venice, 1592), p. 76. See also Thomas Nashe, 'A ... Prognostication', in *Works*, ed. Ronald B. McKerrow, rev. ed. F. P. Wilson, 5 vols (Oxford, 1958), III 390; *Venus and Adonis*, lines 413–14.

13. III 167. Death through joy is also mentioned in *The Problemes of Aristotle* (1597), sig. [F7ᵛ]; John Marston, *Antonios Revenge*, I v, in *Plays*, ed. H. Harvey Wood, 3 vols (Edinburgh, 1934–9), I 81; Buoni, *Problemes*, pp. 242–4; Scipion Dupleix, *The Resolver: or Curiosities of Nature* (1635), pp. 250–2. James Hart in ... *The Diet of the Diseased* (1633), p. 400 cites Galen in support of the view that 'some might die of too great joy'.

14. Ed. H. Warner Allen (New York [1923]), p. 210. See John Davies of Hereford's *Microcosmos* (1603), pp. 45, 75, on the destructive or fatal effect of extremes of joy and grief. The emotions were familiar subjects in the grammar-school study of Cicero's *Tusculanae disputationes*. Gregory of Nyssa's *De hominis opificio* explains joy, grief, and tears as connected with the expansion or contraction of the blood vessels; and Melanchthon considers joy and sorrow to be the explosion and contraction ultimately related to the heart and blood.

15. Cf Webster, *The Devil's Law-Case*, I ii 130–1; Joseph Hall, *Epistles*, I (1608), 143.

16. Tilley L92a. On the *Arcadia* see Muir [at IV iii 18–25] and Henry

Wotton cited by George Steevens (New Variorum *Lear*, p. 252). Samuel C. Chew, *The Pilgrimage of Life* (New Haven, 1962), pp. 120–1, relates smiling and grief together to a Renaissance depiction of patience.

17. Robert Armin, who probably played Lear's Fool, speaks in *A Nest of Ninnies* (1608) of one whose manner was 'ever to weepe in kindnesse, and laugh in extreames' (*Fools and Jesters: With a Reprint of Robert Armin's Nest of Ninnies*, Shakespeare Soc. (1842), p. 38). The Fool's song echoes a popular one; see Peter J. Seng, 'An Early Tune for the Fool's Song in *King Lear*', in *Shakespeare Quarterly* IX (1958), 583–5; and Hyder E. Rollins, '*King Lear* and the Ballad of "John Careless"', in *Modern Language Review*, xv (1920), 87–9.

18. Cicero's *De divinatione* distinguishes the two. See bk I, ch. xi; bk II, ch. xxvi.

19. Cf Cassius's earlier view [I iii 46–52]. Shakespeare's recollection could have been strengthened by Plutarch's references to Cassius's Epicureanism: before Caesar's murder, again at Sardis, where Cassius reasons with Brutus against the fanciful vision of spirits, and finally before Philippi (*Lives* of Caesar and Brutus). As Cassius later retreats from Epicureanism, so Brutus later seems to debate some notions of Stoicism [v i 101–19]. In addition, Macbeth's self-proclaimed endurance [e.g. v iii 9–10] may suggest an analogous dualism in his obdurate scorn of 'English' epicures' [line 8].

20. Dale Underwood, *Etherege and the Seventeenth-Century Comedy of Manners* (New Haven, 1957). Stoic virtue and Epicurean pleasure form antithetical choices in the famous temptation of Hercules; see Erwin Panofsky, *Hercules am Scheidewege* (Leipzig, 1930), and Hallett Smith, *Elizabethan Poetry: a study in conventions, meaning and expression* (Cambridge, Mass., 1952), pp. 290–303.

21. Cambridge, pp. 24–5. In his *De natura deorum*, Cicero singled out the two schools; see Introduction, *De natura deorum. Liber primus*, ed. A. S. Pease (Cambridge, Mass., 1955), pp. 13–14. Cf Cicero's refutation of Epicurean ethics in *De finibus*, bk II; reply in Seneca, *Moral Essays*, tr. John W. Basore, II (Cambridge, Mass., 1935), 121, 123, and Lucian's Epicurean attack on Stoicism. See Ficino on Stoicism and Epicureanism in 'De quatuor sectis philosophorum', in *Supplementum Ficinianum*, ed. Paul O. Kristeller (Florence, 1937), II 7–11; Montaigne repeatedly juxtaposes the two sects; e.g. II 108–9; II 203.

22. More's Utopians share the Epicurean opposition to superstitious fear and dread of death, while they reject Epicurean ethics. The Stoic-Epicurean antithesis is expressed, e.g. in the section headed 'Antonius pro Epicureis & pro natura contra stoicos' in Lorenzo Valla's *De voluptate*, tr. Vincenzo Grillo as *Il piacere* (Naples, 1948), p. 33; and in Erasmus's 'The Epicurean', in *The Colloquies*, tr. N. Bailey (1878), II 326–45, where the serious Spudæus debates with the Epicurean Hedonius.

23. III 272; II 207; III 309; cf III 189.

24. Cf Tilley M172.

25. J. L. S., ed. *Flores Regii ... Spoken by ... James* (1627), no. 2.

26. *Works*, ed. James Spedding *et al.* 14 vols (1857–74), VI 510.

27. See Edgar Wind, *Pagan Mysteries in the Renaissance* (New Haven,

1958), p. 69 and n. Cf John Serranus, *A Godlie and Learned Commentarie upon . . . Ecclesiastes*, tr. John Stockwood (1585), p. 321. Eugene M. Waith, *The Herculean Hero in Marlowe, Chapman, Shakespeare, and Dryden*, (1962) pp. 44–5, cites other views favoring righteous anger, including St Thomas Aquinas's *ira per zelum*. Luther's defense of just anger is well known; see Ewald M. Plass, *What Luther Says, an Anthology* (St Louis, Mo., 1959), I 28–9; II 847, 985. See also Frances A. Yates, *The French Academies of the Sixteenth Century* (1947), pp. 116–20, 143.

28. See also Clement of Alexandria, *The Exhortation to the Greeks*, tr. G. W. Butterworth, Loeb Classical Lib. (1919), p. 51, condemning both atheism and 'daemon-worship' as extremes to be guarded against; and Aquinas, *Summa Theologica*, pt II, qu. XCII, art. I, on religion as a moral virtue containing a mean opposed both to excess (superstition) and deficiency.

29. *Ecclesiastical Polity*, in *Works*, ed. John Keble, 3 vols (Oxford, 1888), II 23.

30. *Flores Regii*, no. 20.

31. *The Anatomy of Melancholy* (Oxford, 1628), p. 579. See also Howard Schultz, *Milton and Forbidden Knowledge* (New York, 1955), p. 265, for numerous other references. See John Weemes, *A Treatise of the Foure Degenerate Sonnes* (1636), p. 36; Weemes's religion-between-two-thieves analogy recurs, e.g. in Alexander Ross's *Gods House, or the House of Prayer* (1642), p. 9. Cf Sidney's allusion to 'the *Philosophers*, who shaking off superstition, brought in *Atheisme*' (*The Defence of Poesie*, in *Complete Works*, ed. Albert Feuillerat, 4 vols (Cambridge, 1922–6), III 34). Richard Bernard's *Contemplative Pictures* (1610), sig. E3ʳ⁻ᵛ, lists 'carnall Atheistes' along with the 'foolishly superstitious'. See further Hobbes, *English Works*, ed. Sir William Molesworth, 11 vols (1839–45), II 277; IV 293; Tilley D234 ('The Devil divides the world between atheism and superstition').

32. *Works*, VI 415–16.

33. See Harry Levin, *The Question of Hamlet* (New York, 1959).

Stanley Cavell   The Avoidance of Love: A Reading of King Lear   (1987)

A common way to remember the history of writing about Shakespeare is to say that until Bradley's *Shakespearean Tragedy* appeared in 1904, and culminating there, its main tradition had concentrated on Shakespeare's characters, whereas in recent generations emphasis has fallen on general patterns of meaning, systems of image or metaphor or symbol now taking the brunt of significance. Like most intellectual maps, this one is not only crude but fails worst in locating the figures one would like best to reach: Can Coleridge or Bradley really be understood as interested in characters *rather than* in the words of the play; or are the writings of Empson or G. Wilson Knight well used in saying that they are interested in what is happening in the words *rather than* what is happening in the speakers of the words? It is, however, equally easy and unhelpful to say that both ends of the tradition have been interested *both* in characters *and* in their words, first because this suggests that there are two things each end is interested in, whereas both would or should insist that they are interested only in one thing, the plays themselves; second, because there is clearly a shift in emphasis within that tradition, and a way of remarking that shift is to say that it moves away from studies of character into studies of words, and because such a shift raises problems of history and of criticism that ought not to be muffled in handy accommodations.

A full description, let alone explanation, of the history of Shakespearean criticism would be part of a full description of Western cultural history since the Renaissance. Failing that, one can still notice that the simply described shift from character to words is implicated in various more or less primitive theories whose hold on contemporary scholars is yet to be traced. For suppose we ask *why* such a shift has occurred. Immediately this becomes two questions: What has discouraged attention from investigations of character? What, apart from this, has specifically motivated an absorbing attention to words? I think that one reason a critic may shun direct contact with characters is that he or she has been made to believe or assume, by some philosophy or other, that characters are not people, that what can be known about people cannot be known about characters, and in particular that psychology is either not appropriate to the study of these fictional beings or that psychology is the province of psychologists and not to be ventured from the armchairs of literary studies. But is any of this more than the merest assumption; unexamined principles which are part of current academic fashion? For what is the relevant psychology? Of course, to account for the behavior of characters one is going to apply to them predicates like 'is in pain,' 'is ironic,' 'is jealous,' 'is thinking of . . .' But does that require psychological expertise? No more than to apply these predicates to one's acquaintances. One reason a critic is drawn to words is, immediately, that attention to characters has often in fact been given apart from attention to the specific words granted them, so it looks as if attention to character is a distraction from the only, or the final, evidence there is for a reading of a literary work, namely the words themselves. But it is then unclear what the words are to be used as evidence for. For a correct interpretation? But what would an interpretation then be of? It often emerges that the evidence provided by the words is to support something called the symbolic structure or the pattern of something or other in the piece. But such concepts are bits of further theories which escape any support the mere presence of words can provide. Moreover, there is more than one procedure which could count as 'attending to words themselves.' (Just as there is more than one way of expressing 'faithfulness to a text.') The New Critics encouraged attention to the ambiguities, patternings, tensions of words; the picture is of a (more or less hidden) structure of which the individual words are parts. Another mode of attention to the particular words themselves is directed to the voice which says them, and through that to the phenomenology of the straits of mind in which only those words said in that order will suffice; here the picture is of a spiritual instant or passage for which only these words discover release, in which they mean deeply not because they mean many things but because they mean one thing completely. This is not necessarily a matter of better or worse but of different modes or needs of poetry.

It seems reasonable to suppose that the success of the New Criticism in the academic study of literature is a function of the way it is *teachable*: You can train someone to read complete poems with sufficient complexity; there is always something to say about them. But it is not clear what would count as training someone to read a lyric. You will have to demonstrate how it rests in the voice, or hauls at it, and you perhaps will not be able to do that without undergoing the spiritual instant or passage for which it discovers release (that is, unable to say what it means without meaning it then and there); and you may or may not be able to do that during a given morning's class, and either eventuality is likely to be inopportune in that place.

The most curious feature of the shift and conflict between character criticism and verbal analysis is that it should have taken place at all. How could any serious critic ever have forgotten that to care about specific characters is to care about the utterly specific words they say when and as they say them; or that we care about the utterly specific words of a play because certain men and women are having to give voice to them? Yet apparently both frequently happen. Evidently what is to be remembered here is difficult to remember, or difficult to do – like attending with utter specificity to the person now before you, or to yourself. It has been common enough to complain of the overinterpretation a critic may be led to, or may have recourse to; the problem, however, is to show us where and why and how to bring an interpretation to a close. (This is no easier than, perhaps no different from, discovering when and how to stop philosophizing. Wittgenstein congratulated himself for having made this possible, saying that in this discovery philosophy is given peace [*Investigations*, §133].)

My purpose here is not to urge that in reading Shakespeare's plays one put words back into the characters speaking them, and replace characters from our possession back into their words. The point is rather to learn something about what prevents these commendable activities from taking place. It is a matter of learning what it is one uses as data for one's assertions about such works, what kinds of appeal one in fact finds convincing. I should like to add that identical problems arise in considering the phenomenon of ordinary language philosophy: There the problem is also raised of determining the data from which philosophy proceeds and to which it appeals, and specifically the issue is one of placing the words and experiences with which philosophers have always begun in alignment with human beings in particular circumstances who can be imagined to be having those experiences and saying and meaning those words. This is all that 'ordinary' in the phrase 'ordinary language philosophy' means, or ought to mean. It does not refer to particular words of wide use, not to particular sorts of people. It reminds us that whatever words are said and meant are said and meant by particular people, and that to understand what they (the words) mean you must understand what they (whoever is using them) mean, and that sometimes people do not see what they mean, that usually they cannot say what they mean, that for various reasons they may not know what they mean, and that when they are forced to recognize this they feel they do not, and perhaps cannot, mean anything, and they are struck dumb. (Here it is worth investigating the fact that the formula 'He said . . .' can introduce either indirect discourse or direct quotation. One might feel: Indirect discourse doesn't literally report what someone *said*, it says what someone *meant*. Then why do we say 'He said . . .' rather than 'He meant . . .', an equally common formula, but used for other purposes? Perhaps the reason is that what is said *is* normally what is meant – if there is to be language. Not more than normally, however, because there are any number of [specific] ways in which and occasions on which one's words do not say what one means. Because the connection between using a word and meaning what it says is not inevitable or automatic, one may wish to call it a matter of convention. But then one must not suppose that it is a convention we would know how to forgo. It is not a matter of convenience or ritual, unless having language is a convenience or unless thinking and speaking are rituals.) If philosophy sometimes looks as if it wishes nothing more than to strike us dumb, then it should not be overlooked that philosophy also claims to know only what an ordinary human being can know, and that we are liable to silence so produced only because we have already spoken, hence thought, hence justified and excused, hence philosophized, and are hence always liable not merely to say more than we know (a favorite worry of modern philosophy) but to speak above the conscience at the back of our words, deaf to our meaning. A philosopher like Austin, it is true, concentrates on examples whose meaning can be brought out by appealing to widely shared, or easily imaginable, circumstances (once he has given directions for imagining them) – circumstances, roughly, that Wittgenstein refers to as one of 'our language games.' But Wittgenstein is also concerned with forms of words whose meaning cannot be elicited in this way – words we sometimes have it at heart to say but whose meaning is not secured by appealing to the way they are ordinarily (commonly) used, because there is no ordinary use of them, in that sense. It is not, therefore, that I mean something *other* than those words would ordinarily mean, but rather that what they mean, and whether they mean anything, depends solely upon whether I am using them so as to make my meaning. (An instance cited by Wittgenstein is Luther's remark that 'faith resides under the left nipple.') In general, Part II of the *Philosophical Investigations* moves into this region of meaning. It is a region habitually occupied by poetry.

King Lear is particularly useful as a source for investigating the question of critical data and for assessing some causes of critical disagreement because there are a number of traditional cruxes in this play for which any critic is likely to feel compelled to provide a solution. Some important ones are these: How are we to understand Lear's motivation in his opening scene? How Cordelia's? Is Gloucester's blinding dramatically justified? What is the relation between the Lear plot and the Gloucester subplot? What happens to the Fool? Why does Edgar delay before revealing himself to his father? Why does Gloucester set out for Dover? Why does France not return with Cordelia? Why must Cordelia die?

In the first half of this essay I offer a reading of the play sticking as continuously to the text as I can – that is, avoiding theorizing about the data I provide for my assertions, appealing to any considerations which, in conscience, convince me of their correctness – in the course of which the traditional cruxes are either answered or altered. Then, in the second half, I ask why it is, if what I say is correct, that critics have failed to see it. This precipitates somewhat extended speculations about the difficulties in the perception of such drama as *King Lear* presents, and I do not expect, even if my reading were accepted, that these speculations will find very immediate assent, nor even very readily be found relevant. But since whatever critical discoveries I can claim to have made hardly result from unheard-of information, full conviction in them awaits a convincing account of what has kept them covered.

I

In a fine paper published a few years ago, Professor Paul Alpers notes the tendency of modern critics to treat metaphors or symbols rather than the characters and actions of Shakespeare's plays as primary data in understanding them, and undertakes to disconfirm a leading interpretation of the symbolic sort which exactly depends upon a neglect, even a denial, of the humanness of the play's characters.[1] If I begin by finding fault with his reading, I put him first to acknowledge my indebtedness to his work. His animus is polemical and in the end this animus betrays him. For he fails to account for the truth to which that leading interpretation is responding, and in his concern to insist that the characters of the play are human beings confronting one another, he fails to characterize them as specific persons. He begins by assembling quotations from several commentators which together compose the view he wishes to correct – the view of the 'sight pattern':

In *King Lear* an unusual amount of imagery drawn from vision and the eyes prompts us to apprehend a symbolism of sight and blindness having its culmination in Gloucester's tragedy. . . . The blinding of Gloucester might well be gratuitous melodrama but for its being imbedded in a field of meanings centered in the concept of *seeing*. This sight pattern relentlessly brings into the play the problem of seeing and what is always implied is that the problem is one of insight. . . . It is commonly recognized that just as Lear finds 'reason in madness' so Gloucester learns to 'see' in his blindness. . . . The whole play is built on this double paradox.[2]

But when Alpers looks to the text for evidence for this theory he discovers that there is none. Acts of vision and references to eyes are notably present, but their function is not to symbolize moral insight; rather, they insist upon the ordinary, literal use of eyes: to express feeling, to weep, and to recognize others. Unquestionably there is truth in this. But the evidence for Alpers's view is not perfectly clear and his concepts are not accurately explored in terms of the events of the play. The acts of vision named in the lines he cites are those of giving *looks* and of *staring*, and the function of these acts is exactly *not* to express feeling, or else to express cruel feeling. Why? Because the power of the eyes to see is being used in isolation from their capacity to weep, which seems the most literal use of them to express feeling.

Alpers's dominant insistence upon the third ordinary use of the eyes, their role in recognizing others, counters common readings of the two moments of recognition central to the 'sight pattern': Gloucester's recognition of Edgar's innocence and Lear's recognition of Cordelia. 'The crucial issue is not insight, but recognition' [Alpers, p. 149]: Gloucester is not enabled to 'see' because he is blinded, the truth is heaped upon him from Regan's luxuriant cruelty; Cordelia need not be viewed symbolically, the infinite poignance of her reconciliation with Lear is sufficiently accounted for by his literal recognition of her. – But then it becomes incomprehensible why or how these children have *not* been recognized by these parents; they had not become literally invisible. They are in each case banished, disowned, sent out of sight. And the question remains: What makes it possible for them to be *received* again?

In each case, there is a condition necessary in order that the recognition take place: Gloucester and Lear must each first recognize himself, and allow himself to be recognized, revealed to another. In Gloucester, the recognition comes at once, on hearing Regan's news:

> O my follies! Then Edgar was abused.
> Kind Gods, forgive me that, and prosper him!
> [II vii 90–1]

In each of these two lines he puts his recognition of himself first. Lear's self-revelation comes harder, but when it comes it has the same form:

> Do not laugh at me;
> For, as I am a man, I think this lady
> To be my child Cordelia.   [IV vii 68–70]

He refers to himself three times, then 'my child' recognizes her simultaneously with revealing himself (as her father). Self-recognition is, phenomenologically, a form of insight; and it is because of its necessity in recognizing others that critics have felt its presence here.[3]

Lear does not attain his insight until the end of the fourth act, and when he does it is climactic. This suggests that Lear's dominating motivation to this point, from the time things go wrong in the opening scene, is to *avoid being recognized*. The isolation and avoidance of eyes is what the obsessive sight imagery of the play underlines. This is the clue I want to follow first in reading out the play.

If the blinding is unnecessary for Gloucester's true seeing of Edgar, why is Gloucester blinded? Alpers's suggestion, in line with his emphasis on the literal presence of eyes, is that because the eyes are physically the most precious and most vulnerable of human organs, the physical assault on them best dramatizes the human capacity for cruelty. But if the symbolic interpretation seems hysterical, this explanation seems overcasual, and in any case does not follow the words. Critics who have looked for a *meaning* in the blinding have been looking for the right thing. But they have been looking for an aesthetic meaning or justification; looking too high, as it were. It is aesthetically justified (it is 'not an irrelevant horror' [Muir, p. lx]) just because it is morally, spiritually justified, in a way which directly relates the eyes to their power to see.

> GLOU.   .... but I shall see
>   The winged vengeance overtake such
>   children.
> CORN. See't shalt thou never.   [III vii 64–6]

And then Cornwall puts out one of Gloucester's eyes. A servant interposes, wounding Cornwall; then Regan stabs the servant from behind, and his dying words, meant to console or establish connection with Gloucester, ironically recall Cornwall to his interrupted work:

> FIRST SERV.   O! I am slain. My lord, you have one eye left
>   To see some mischief on him. Oh!   *Dies*
> CORN.   Lest it see more, prevent it. Out, vile jelly!
>   [III vii 80–2]

Of course the idea of punishment by plucking out eyes has been implanted earlier, by Lear and by Goneril and most recently by Gloucester himself, and their suggestions implicate all of them spiritually in Cornwall's deed. But Cornwall himself twice gives the immediate cause of his deed, once for each eye: to prevent Gloucester from seeing, and in particular to prevent him from seeing *him*. That this scene embodies the most open expression of cruelty is true enough; and true that it suggests the limitlessness of cruelty, once it is given its way – that it will find its way to the most precious objects. It is also true that the scene is symbolic, but what it symbolizes is a function of what it means. The physical cruelty symbolizes (or instances) the psychic cruelty which pervades the play; but what this particular act of cruelty means is that cruelty cannot bear to be seen. It literalizes evil's ancient love of darkness.

This relates the blinding to Cornwall's needs; but it is also related to necessities of Gloucester's character. It has an aptness which takes on symbolic value, the horrible aptness of retribution. (It is not merely literary critics who look for meaning in suffering, attempting to rationalize it. Civilizations have always done it, in their myths and laws; we do it in our dreams and fears of vengeance. They learned to do it from gods.) For Gloucester has a fault, not particularly egregious, in fact common as dirt, but in a tragic accumulation in which society disgorges itself upon itself, it shows clearly enough; and I cannot understand his immediate and complete acquiescence in the fate which has befallen him (his acknowledgment of his folly, his acceptance of Edgar's innocence, and his wish for forgiveness all take just twenty syllables) without supposing that it strikes him as a retribution, forcing him to an insight about his life as a whole. Not, however, necessarily a true insight. He has revealed his fault in the opening speeches of the play, in which he tells Kent of his *shame*.

(That shame is the subject of those speeches is emphasized by Coleridge; but he concentrates, appropriately enough, on *Edmund's* shame.) He says that now he is 'braz'd to it,' that is, used to admitting that he has fathered a bastard, and also perhaps carrying the original sense of soldered fast to it. He recognizes the moral claim upon himself, as he says twice, to 'acknowledge' his bastard; but all this means to him is that he acknowledge that he has a bastard for a son. He does not acknowledge *him*, as a son or a person, with *his* feelings of illegitimacy and being cast out. *That* is something Gloucester ought to be ashamed of; his shame is itself more shameful than his one piece of licentiousness. This is one of the inconveniences of shame, that it is generally inaccurate, attaches to the wrong thing.

In case these remarks should seem inappropriate in view of the moment at which Shakespeare wrote, and someone wishes at this stage to appeal to the conventions of Elizabethan theater according to which a bastard is an evil character, hence undeserving of the audience's sympathy, and thereby suggest that it is unthinkable that Gloucester should feel anything other than a locker-room embarrassment at what has sprung from him, then I should ask that two points be borne in mind: (1) It is a particular man, call him Shakespeare, we are dealing with, and while it is doubtless true that a knowledge of the conventions he inherited is indispensable to the full understanding of his work, the idea that these conventions supply him with solutions to his artistic purposes, rather than problems or media within which those purposes are worked out, is as sensible as supposing that one has explained why a particular couple have decided to divorce by saying that divorce is a social form. (There are, of course, proper occasions for explanations of that kind; for example, an explanation of why separation is not the same as divorce.) Shakespeare's plays are conventional in the way that their language is grammatical, in the way that a football game satisfies the rules of football: One has to know them to understand what is happening, but consulting them will not tell you who plays or speaks well and who mechanically, nor why a given remark or a particular play was made *here*, nor who won and who lost. You have to know something more for that, and you have to look. (2) At the moment at which *King Lear* was written, Sir Robert Filmer was an adolescent. It is hard not to suppose that when this eldest son and pillar of society wrote his defense of patriarchal society, and consequently of primogeniture, he was talking about something which had been problematic since his youth and something which needed his defense in 1630 because it was by then becoming openly questioned.[4] But this is perfectly clear from Edmund's opening soliloquy. The idea that Shakespeare favored primogeniture, or supposed that only a bastard would question it, is one which must come from a source beyond Shakespeare's words. In that soliloquy Edmund rails equally against his treatment as a bastard and as a younger son – as if to ask why a younger son should be treated like a bastard. Both social institutions seem to him arbitrary and unnatural. And nothing in the play shows him to be wrong – certainly not the behavior of Lear's legitimate older daughters, nor of Regan's lawful husband, nor of legitimate King Lear, who goes through an abdication without abdicating, and whose last legitimate act is to banish love and service from his realm. When Shakespeare writes a revenge tragedy, it is *Hamlet*; and when he presents us with a bastard, legitimacy as a whole is thrown into question.

That Gloucester still feels shame about his son is shown not just by his descriptions of himself, but also by the fact that Edmund 'hath been out nine years, and away he shall again' [I i 32], and by the fact that Gloucester has to joke about him: Joking is a familiar specific for brazening out shame, calling enlarged attention to the thing you do not want naturally noticed. (Hence the comedian sports disfigurement.) But if the failure to recognize others is a failure to let others recognize you, a fear of what is revealed to them, an avoidance of their eyes, then it is exactly shame which is the cause of his withholding of recognition. (It is not simply his legal treatment that Edmund is railing against.) For shame is the specific discomfort produced by the sense of being looked at; the avoidance of the sight of others is the reflex it produces. Guilt is different; there the reflex is to avoid discovery. As long as no one *knows* what you have done, you are safe; or your conscience will press you to confess it and accept punishment. Under shame, what must be covered up is not your deed, but yourself. It is a more primitive emotion than guilt, as inescapable as the possession of a body, the first object of shame. – Gloucester suffers the same punishment he inflicts: In his respectability, he avoided eyes; when respectability falls away and the disreputable come into power, his eyes are avoided. In the fear of Gloucester's poor eyes there is the promise that cruelty can be overcome, and instruction about how it can be overcome. That is the content which justifies the scene of his blinding, aesthetically, psychologically, morally.

This raises again the question of the relation between the Gloucester subplot and the Lear plot. The traditional views seem on the whole to take one of two lines: Gloucester's fate parallels Lear's in order that it become more universal (because Gloucester is an ordinary man, not a distant king, or because in happening to more than one it may happen to any); or more concrete (since Gloucester suffers physically what Lear suffers psychically). Such suggestions are not wrong, but they leave out of account the specific climactic moment at which the subplot surfaces and Lear and Gloucester face one another.

> EDGAR I would not take this from report; it is,
> And my heart breaks at it.   [IV vi 142–3]

I have felt that, but more particularly I have felt an obscurer terror at this moment than at any other in the play. The considerations so far introduced begin, I think to explain the source of that feeling.

Two questions immediately arise about that confrontation: (1) This is the scene in which Lear's madness is first broken through; in the next scene he is reassembling his sanity. Both the breaking through and the reassembling are manifested by his *recognizing* someone, and my first question is: Why is it Gloucester whom Lear is first able to recognize from his madness, and in recognizing whom his sanity begins to return? (2) *What* does Lear see when he recognizes Gloucester? What is he confronted by?

1. Given our notion that recognizing a person depends upon allowing oneself to be recognized by him, the question becomes: Why is it Gloucester whose recognition Lear is first able to bear? The obvious answer is: Because Gloucester is blind. Therefore one can be, can only be, *recognized by him without being seen*, without having to bear eyes upon oneself.

Leading up to Lear's acknowledgment ('I know thee well enough') there is that insane flight of exchanges about Gloucester's eyes; it is the only active cruelty given to Lear by Shakespeare, apart from his behavior in the abdication scene. But here it seems uncaused, deliberate cruelty inflicted for its own sake upon Gloucester's eyes.

> GLOU.   Dost thou know me?
> LEAR I remember thine eyes well enough. Dost thou squiny at me?

No, do thy worst, blind Cupid; I'll not love.
Read thou this challenge; mark but the penning of it.

[IV vi 137–40]

(This last line, by the way, and Gloucester's response to it seem a clear enough reference to Gloucester's reading of Edmund's letter, carrying here the suggestion that he was blind then.)

GLOU.   Were all thy letters suns [sons?], I could not see.
LEAR   Read.
GLOU.   What! with the case of eyes?
LEAR   Oh, ho! are you there with me? No eyes in your head, nor no money in your purse? Your eyes are in a heavy case, your purse in a light: yet you see how this world goes.
GLOU.   I see it feelingly.
LEAR   What! art mad? A man may see how this world goes with no eyes. . . .

Get thee glass eyes;
And, like a scurvy politician, seem
To see the things thou dost not.   [IV vi 141–51, 172–4]

Lear is picking at Gloucester's eyes, as if to make sure they are really gone. When he is sure, he recognizes him:

If thou wilt weep my fortunes, take my eyes;
I know thee well enough; thy name is Gloucester.

[IV vi 178–9]

(Here 'take my eyes' can be read as a crazy consolation: Your eyes wouldn't have done you any good anyway in this case; you would need to see what I have seen to weep my fortunes; I would give up my eyes not to have seen it.)

This picking spiritually relates Lear to Cornwall's and Regan's act in first blinding Gloucester, for Lear does what he does for the same reason they do – in order not to be seen by this man, whom he has brought harm. (Lear exits from this scene running. From what? From 'A Gentleman, with Attendants.' His first words to them are: 'No rescue? What! A prisoner?' But those questions had interrupted the Gentleman's opening words to him, 'Your most dear daughter –'. Lear runs not because in his madness he cannot distinguish friends from enemies but because he knows that recognition of himself is imminent. Even madness is no rescue.)

2. This leads to the second question about the scene: What is Lear confronted by in acknowledging Gloucester? It is easy to say: Lear is confronted here with the direct consequences of his conduct, of his covering up in rage and madness, of his having given up authority and kingdom for the wrong motives, to the wrong people; and he is for the first time confronting himself. What is difficult is to show that this is not merely or vaguely symbolic, and that it is not merely an access of knowledge which Lear undergoes. Gloucester has by now become not just a figure 'parallel' to Lear, but Lear's double; he does not merely represent Lear, but is psychically identical with him. So that what comes to the surface in this meeting is not a related story, but Lear's submerged mind. This, it seems to me, is what gives the scene its particular terror, and gives to the characters what neither could have alone. In this fusion of plots and identities, we have the great image, the double or mirror image, of everyman who has gone to every length to avoid himself, caught at the moment of coming upon himself face to face. (Against this, 'take my eyes' strikes psychotic power.)

The identity is established at the end of the blinding scene, by Regan:

> Go thrust him out at gates, and let him smell
> His way to Dover.   [III vii 92–3]

It is by now commonly appreciated that Gloucester had, when that scene began, no plans for going to Dover. Interpreters have accounted for this discrepancy by suggesting that Shakespeare simply wanted all his characters present at Dover for the climax, adding that the repeated question 'Wherefore to Dover?' may have put that destination in Gloucester's mind, which has been kicked out of shape. But this interprets the wrong thing, for it overlooks the more obvious, anyway the first, discrepancy. The question is why *Regan* assumes that he is going to Dover. (Her husband, for example, does not: 'Turn out that eyeless villain.') We may wish here to appeal to those drummed Dovers to explain her mind, and to suppose that she associates that name with the gathering of all her enemies. But the essential fact is that the name is primarily caught to the image of her father. In her mind, the man she is sending on his way to Dover is the man she *knows* is sent on his way to Dover: In her paroxysms of cruelty, she imagines that she has just participated in blinding her father.

And Gloucester apparently thinks so too, for he then, otherwise inexplicably, sets out for Dover. 'Otherwise inexplicably': for it is *no* explanation to say that 'the case-histories of suicides contain stranger obsessive characteristics than this' [Muir, xlix]. There is no reason, at this stage – other than our cultural advantage in having read the play before – to assume that Gloucester is planning suicide. He sets out for Dover because he is *sent* there: by himself, in sending Lear, in whose identity he is now submerged; and by the thrust of Regan's evil and confusion. But he has no *reason* to go there, not even some inexplicable wish to commit suicide there. At the beginning of the plan to go to Dover he says, 'I have no way' [IV i 18]. It is only at the end of that scene that he mentions Dover *cliff* [73]. One can, of course, explain that he had been thinking of the cliff all along. But what the text suggests is that, rather than taking a plan for suicide as our explanation for his insistence on using Dover cliff, we ought to see his thought of the cliff, and consequently of suicide, as *his* explanation of his otherwise mysterious mission to Dover. Better suicide than no reason at all.

When Shakespeare's lapses in plot construction are noticed, critics who know that he is nevertheless the greatest of the bards undertake to excuse him, or to justify the lapse by the great beauty of its surroundings. A familiar excuse is that the lapse will in any case not be noticed in performance. No doubt there are lapses of this kind, and no doubt they can sometimes be covered by such excuses. But it ought also to occur to us that what looks like a lapse is sometimes meant, and that our failure to notice the lapse is just that, our failure. This is what has happened to us in the present scene. We 'do not notice' Regan's confusion of identity because we share it, and in failing to understand Gloucester's blanked condition (or rather, in insisting upon understanding it from our point of view) we are doing what the characters in the play are seen to do: We avoid him. And so we are implicated in the failures we are witnessing; we share the responsibility for tragedy.

This is further confirmed in another outstanding lapse, or crux – Gloucester's appearance, led by an old man, to Edgar–Tom. The question, as generally asked, is: Why does Edgar wait, on seeing his father blind, and hearing that his father knows his mistake, before revealing himself to him? The answers which suggest themselves to that question are sophisticated, not the thing itself. For example: Edgar wants to clear himself in the eyes of the world before revealing himself. (But he could still let his *father* know. Anyway, he does tell his father before he goes to challenge Edmund.) Edgar 'wants to impose a penance on his father, and to guarantee the genuineness and permanence of the repentance' [Muir, 1]. (This seems to me psychologically fantastic; it suggests that the first thing which occurs to Edgar on seeing his father blinded is to exact some further punishment. Or else it makes Edgar into a monster of righteousness; whereas he is merely self-righteous.) Edgar wants to cure his father of his desire to commit suicide. (But *revealing himself* would seem the surest and most immediate way to do that.) And so on. My dissatisfaction with these answers is not that they are psychological explanations, but that they are explanations of the wrong thing, produced by the wrong question: Why does Edgar *delay*? 'Delay' implies he is going to later. But we do not *know* (at this stage) that he will; we do not so much as know that he intends to. In terms of our reading of the play so far, we are alerted to the fact that what Edgar does is most directly described as *avoiding recognition. That* is what we want an explanation for.

And first, this action bears the same meaning, or has the same consequences, it always has in this play: mutilating cruelty. This is explicit in one of Gloucester's first utterances after the blinding, led into Edgar's presence:

> O! dear son Edgar,
> The food of thy abused father's wrath;
> Might I but live to see thee in my touch,
> I'd say I had eyes again.   [IV i 21–4]

So Edgar's avoidance of Gloucester's recognition precisely deprives Gloucester of his eyes again. This links him, as Lear was and will be linked, to Cornwall and the sphere of open evil.

This reading also has consequences for our experience of two subsequent events of the play.

1. In a play in which, as has often been said, each of the characters is either very good or very bad, this revelation of Edgar's capacity for cruelty – and the *same* cruelty as that of the evil characters – shows how radically implicated good is in evil; in a play of disguises, how often they are disguised. And Edgar is the ruler at the end of the play, Lear's successor, the man who must, in Albany's charge, 'the gor'd state sustain.' (A very equivocal charge, containing no assurance that its body may be nursed back to health; but

simply nursed.) If good is to grow anywhere in this state, it must recognize, and face, its continuity with, its location within, a maze of evil. Edgar's is the most Christian sensibility in the play, as Edmund's is the most Machiavellian. If the Machiavellian fails in the end, he very nearly succeeds; and if the Christian succeeds, his success is deeply compromised.

2. To hold to the fact that Edgar is avoiding recognition makes better sense to me of that grotesque guiding of Gloucester up no hill to no cliff to no suicide than any other account I know. The special quality of this scene, with its purest outbreak of grotesquerie, has been recognized at least since Wilson Knight's essay of 1930.[5] But to regard it as *symbolic* of the play's emphasis on the grotesque misses what makes it so grotesque, and fails to account for the fact that Edgar and Gloucester find themselves in this condition. It is grotesque because it is so *literal* a consequence of avoiding the facts. It is not the emblem of the Lear universe, but an instance of what has led its minds to their present state: There are no lengths to which we may not go in order to avoid being revealed, even to those we love and are loved by. Or rather, especially to those we love and are loved by; to other people it is *easy* not to be known. That grotesque walk is not full of promise for our lives. It is not, for example, a picture of mankind making its way up Purgatory,[6] for Gloucester's character is not purified by it, but extirpated. It shows what people will *have* to say and try to mean to one another when they are incapable of acknowledging to one another what they have to acknowledge. To fill this scene with nourishing, profound meaning is to see it from Edgar's point of view; that is, to avoid what is there. Edgar is Ahab, trying to harpoon the meaning of his life into something external to it; and we believe him, and serve him. He is Hedda Gabler, with her ugly demand for beauty. In the fanciful, childish deceit of his plan, he is Tom Sawyer in the last chapters of *Huckleberry Finn*, enveloping Jim's prison with symbols of escape, instead of opening the door.

If one wishes a psychological explanation for Edgar's behavior, the question to be answered is: Why does Edgar avoid his father's recognition? Two answers suggest themselves. (1) He is himself ashamed and guilty. He was as gullible as his father was to Edmund's 'invention.' He failed to confront his father, to trust his love, exactly as his father had failed him. He is as responsible for his father's blinding as his father is. He wants to make it up to his father before asking for his recognition – to make it up instead of repenting, acknowledging; he wants to *do* something instead of stopping and seeing. So he goes on doing the very thing which needs making up for. (2) He cannot bear the fact that his father is incapable, impotent, maimed. He wants his father still to be a father, powerful, so that *he* can remain a child. For otherwise they are simply two human beings in need of one another, and it is not usual for parents and children to manage that transformation, becoming for one another nothing more, but nothing less, than unaccommodated men. That is what Lear took Edgar to be, but that was a mad, ironic compliment; to become natural again, human kind needs to do more than remove its clothes; for we can also cover up our embarrassment by nakedness. We have our inventions, our accommodations.

We learn in the course of Edgar's tale, after his successful duel with Edmund, when it was that he brought himself to allow his father to recognize him:

> Never – O fault! – revealed myself unto him
> Until some half-hour past, when I was arm'd.
>
> [v iii 192–3]

Armed, and with the old man all but seeped away, he feels safe enough to give his father vision again and bear his recognition. As sons fear, and half wish, it is fatal. Now he will never know whether, had he challenged recognition when recognition was denied, at home, both of them could have survived it. That Edgar is so close to the thing love demands contributes to the grotesque air of the late scenes with his father.[7] Love does maintain itself under betrayal; it does allow, and forward, its object's wish to find the edge of its own existence; it does not shrink from recognition that its object is headed for, or has survived, radical change, with its attendant destructions – which is the way love knows that a betrayal is ended, and is why it provides the context for new innocence. But Edgar does not know that love which has such power also has the power to kill, and, in going to the lengths he takes it, must be capable of absolute scrupulousness. It cannot lead, it can only accompany, past the point it has been, and it must feel that point. It is Edgar's self-assurance here which mocks his Christian thoroughness.

We now have elements with which to begin an analysis of the most controversial of the *Lear* problems, the nature of Lear's motivation in his opening (abdication) scene. The usual interpretations follow one of three main lines: Lear is senile; Lear is puerile; Lear is not to be understood in natural terms, for the whole scene has a fairytale or ritualistic character which simply must be accepted as the premise from which the tragedy is derived. Arguments ensue, in each case, about whether Shakespeare is justified in what he is asking his audience to accept. My hypothesis will be that Lear's behavior in this scene is explained by – the tragedy begins because of – the same motivation which manipulates the tragedy throughout its course, from the scene which precedes the abdication, through the storm, blinding, evaded reconciliations, to the final moments: by the attempt to avoid recognition, the shame of exposure, the threat of self-revelation.

Shame, first of all, is the right kind of candidate to serve as motive, because it is the emotion whose effect is most precipitate and out of proportion to its cause, which is just the rhythm of the *King Lear* plot as a whole. And with this hypothesis we need not assume that Lear is either incomprehensible or stupid or congenitally arbitrary and inflexible and extreme in his conduct. Shame itself is exactly arbitrary, inflexible, and extreme in its effect. It is familiar to find that what mortifies one person seems wholly unimportant to another: Think of being ashamed of one's origins, one's accent, one's ignorance, one's skin, one's clothes, one's legs or teeth. . . . It is the most isolating of feelings, the most comprehensible perhaps in idea, but the most incomprehensible or incommunicable in fact. Shame, I've said, is the most primitive of *social* responses. With the discovery of the individual, whether in Paradise or in the Renaissance, there is the simultaneous discovery of the isolation of the individual; his presence to himself, but simultaneously to *others*. Moreover, shame is felt not only toward one's own actions and one's own being, but toward the actions and the being of those with whom one is identified – fathers, daughters, wives. . . . , the beings whose self-revelations reveal oneself. Families, any objects of one's love and commitment, ought to be the places where shame is overcome (hence happy families are all alike); but they are also the place of its deepest manufacture, and one is then hostage to that power, or fugitive. – L. B. Campbell, in *Shakespeare's Tragic Heroes*,[8] collects valuable examples of Renaissance 'doctrine,' and sorts them perspicuously around Shakespeare's topics. But she follows a typical assumption of such investigations – that if Shakespeare's work is to be illuminated by these contemporary doctrines, he must illustrate them. For example:

It must be evident, then, that there was in Shakespeare's day an old and firmly founded philosophy of anger, finding its sources in ancient medicine and ancient philosophy and in the mediaeval makings-over of those ancient sources as well. According to this philosophy, pride or self-esteem is the condition in which anger takes its rise, vengeance becomes its immediate object, and some slight, real or imagined, is its cause. Anger is folly; anger brings shame in its train. The sequence of passions is pride, anger, revenge, and unless madness clouds the reason altogether, shame.

But in *King Lear* shame comes first, and brings rage and folly in its train. Lear is not maddened because he had been wrathful, but because his shame brought his wrath upon the wrong object. It is not the fact of his anger but the irony of it, specifically and above all the *injustice* of it, which devours him.

That Lear is ashamed, or afraid of being shamed by a revelation, seems to be the Fool's understanding of his behavior. It is agreed that the Fool keeps the truth present to Lear's mind, but it should be stressed that the characteristic mode of the Fool's presentation is *ridicule* – the circumstance most specifically feared by shame (as accusation and discovery are most feared by guilt). Part of the exquisite pain of this Fool's comedy is that in riddling Lear with the truth of his condition he increases the very cause of that condition, as though shame should finally grow ashamed of itself, and stop. The other part of this pain is that it is the therapy prescribed by love itself. We know that since Cordelia's absence 'the fool hath much pin'd away' [I iv 78], and it is generally assumed that this is due to his love for Cordelia. That need not be denied, but it should be obvious that it is directly due to his love for Lear; to his having to see the condition in Lear which his love is impotent to prevent, the condition moreover which his love has helped to cause, the precise condition therefore which his love is unable to comfort, since its touch wounds. This is why the Fool dies or disappears; from the terrible relevance, and the horrible irrelevance, of his only passion. This is the point of his connection with Cordelia, as will emerge.

I call Lear's shame a hypothesis, and what I have to say here will perhaps be hard to make convincing. But primarily it depends upon not imposing the traditional interpretations upon the opening events. Lear is puerile? Lear senile? But the man who speaks Lear's words is in possession, if not fully in command, of a powerful, ranging mind; and its eclipse into madness only confirms its intelligence, not just because what he says in his madness is the work of a marked intelligence, but because the nature of his madness, his melancholy and antic disposition, its incessant invention, is the sign, in fact and in Renaissance thought, of genius; an option of escape open only to minds of the highest reach. How then can we understand such a mind seriously to believe that what Goneril and Regan are offering in that opening scene is love, proof of his value to them; and to believe that Cordelia is withholding love? We cannot so understand it, and so all the critics are right to regard Lear in this scene as psychologically incomprehensible, or as requiring from them some special psychological makeup – if, that is, we assume that Lear believes in Goneril and Regan and not in Cordelia. But we needn't assume that he believes anything of the kind.

We imagine that Lear *must* be wildly abused (blind, puerile, and the rest) because the thing works out so badly. But it doesn't *begin* badly, and it is far from incomprehensible conduct. It is, in fact, quite ordinary. A parent is bribing love out of his children; two of them accept the bribe, and despise him for it; the third shrinks from the attempt, as though from violation. Only this is a king, this bribe is the last he will be able to offer; everything in his life, and in the life of his state, depends upon its success. We need not assume that he does not know his two older daughters, and that they are giving him false coin in return for his real bribes, though perhaps like most parents he is willing not to notice it. But more than this: There is reason to assume that the open possibility – or the open fact – that they are *not* offering true love is exactly what he wants. Trouble breaks out only with Cordelia's 'Nothing,' and her broken resolution to be silent. – What does he want, and what is the meaning of the trouble which then breaks out?

Go back to the confrontation scene with Gloucester:

> If thou wilt weep my fortunes, take my eyes.

The obvious rhetoric of those words is that of an appeal, or a bargain. But it is also warning, and a command: If you weep for me, the same thing will happen to me that happened to you; do not let me see what you are weeping for. Given the whole scene, with its concentrated efforts at warding off Gloucester, that line says explicitly what it is Lear is warding off: Gloucester's sympathy, his love. And earlier:

GLOU.   O! Let me kiss that hand.
LEAR   Let me wipe it first, it smells of mortality.

[IV vi 134–5]

Mortality, the hand without rings of power on it, cannot be lovable. He feels unworthy of love, when the reality of lost power comes over him. That is what his plan was to have avoided by exchanging his fortune for his love at one swap. He cannot bear love when he has no reason to be loved, perhaps because of the helplessness, the passiveness which that implies, which some take for impotence. And he wards it off for the reason for which people do ward off being loved, because it presents itself to them as a demand:

LEAR   No. Do thy worst, blind Cupid; I'll not love.

[IV vi 139]

Gloucester's presence strikes Lear as the demand for love; he knows he is being offered love; he tries to deny the offer by imagining that he has been solicited (this is the relevance of 'blind Cupid' as the sign of a brothel); and he does not want to pay for it, for he may get it, and may not, and either is intolerable. Besides, he has recently done just that, paid his all for love. The long fantasy of his which precedes this line ('Let copulation thrive. . . . There is the sulphurous pit – burning, scalding, stench, consumption . . .') contains his most sustained expression of disgust with sexuality (ll. 116ff.) – as though furiously telling himself that what was wrong with his plan was not the debasement of love his bargain entailed, but the fact that love itself is inherently debased and so unworthy from the beginning of the bargain he had made for it. That is a maddening thought; but still more comforting than the truth. For some spirits, to be loved knowing you cannot return that love is the most radical of psychic tortures.

This is the way I understand that opening scene with the three daughters. Lear knows it is a bribe he offers, and – part of him anyway – wants exactly what a bribe can buy: (1) false love and (2) a public expression of love. That is, he wants something he does not have to return *in kind*, something which a division of his property fully pays for. And he wants to *look* like a loved man – for the sake of the subjects, as it were. He is perfectly happy with his little plan, until Cordelia speaks. Happy not because he is blind, but because he is getting what he wants, his plan is working. Cordelia is alarming precisely because he *knows* she is offering the real thing, offering something a more opulent third of his kingdom cannot, must not, repay; putting a claim upon him he cannot face. She threatens to expose both his plan for returning false love with no love, and expose the necessity for that plan – his terror of being loved, of needing love.

Reacting to oversentimental or over-Christian interpretations of her character, interpreters have made efforts to implicate her in the tragedy's source, convincing her of a willfulness and hardness kin to that later shown by her sisters. But her complicity is both less and more than such an interpretation envisages. That interpretation depends, first of all, upon taking her later speeches in the scene (after the appearance of France and Burgundy) as simply uncovering what was in her mind and heart from the beginning. But why? Her first utterance is the aside:

> What shall Cordelia speak? Love, and be silent.

This, presumably, has been understood as indicating her decision to refuse her father's demand. But it needn't be. She asks herself what she can say; there is no necessity for taking the question to be rhetorical. She wants to obey her father's wishes (anyway, there is no reason to think otherwise at this stage, or at any other); but how? She sees from Goneril's speech and Lear's acceptance of it what it is he wants, and she would provide it if she could. But to pretend publicly to love, where you do not love, is easy; to pretend to love, where you really do love, is not obviously possible. She hits on the first solution to her dilemma: Love, and be silent. That is, love *by being* silent. That will do what he seems to want, it will avoid the expression of love, keep it secret. She is his joy; she knows it and he knows it. Surely that is enough? Then Regan speaks, and following that Cordelia's second utterance, again aside:

> Then poor Cordelia!
> And yet not so; since I am sure my love's
> More ponderous than my tongue.   [I i 76–8]

Presumably, in line with the idea of a defiant Cordelia, this is to be interpreted as a reaffirmation of her decision not to speak. But again, it needn't be. After Lear's acceptance of Regan's characteristic outstripping (she has no ideas of her own; her special vileness is always to increase the measure of pain others are prepared to inflict;

her mind is itself a lynch mob) Cordelia may realize that she will *have* to say something. 'More ponderous than my tongue' suggests that she is going to move it, not that it is immovable – which would make it more ponderous than her love. And this produces her second groping for an exit from the dilemma: to speak, but making her love seem less than it is, out of love. Her tongue will move, and obediently, but against her condition – then poor Cordelia, making light of her love. And yet *she* knows the truth. Surely that is enough?

But when the moment comes, she is speechless: 'Nothing, my lord.' I do not deny that this can be read defiantly, as can the following 'You have begot me, bred me, lov'd me' speech. She is outraged, violated, confused, so young; Lear is torturing her, claiming her devotion, which she wants to give, but forcing her to help him betray (or not to betray) it, to falsify it publicly. (Lear's ambiguity here, wanting at once to open and to close her mouth, further shows the ordinariness of the scene, its verisimilitude to common parental love, swinging between absorption and rejection of its offspring, between encouragement to a rebellion they failed to make and punishment for it.) It may be that with Lear's active violation, she snaps; her resentment provides her with words, and she levels her abdication of love at her traitorous, shameless father:

> Haply, when I shall wed,
> That lord whose hand must take my plight shall carry
> Half my love with him.   [I i 100–2]

The trouble is, the words are too calm, too cold for the kind of sharp rage and hatred real love can produce. She is never in possession of her situation, 'her voice was ever soft, gentle and low' [v iii 272–3]; she is young, and 'least' [I i 83]. (This notation of her stature and of the quality of her voice is unique in the play. The idea of a defiant *small* girl seems grotesque, as an idea of Cordelia.) All her words are words of love; to love is all she knows how to do. That is her problem, and at the cause of the tragedy of King Lear.

I imagine the scene this way: The older daughters' speeches are public, set; they should not be said to Lear, but to the court, sparing themselves his eyes and him theirs. They are not monsters first, but ladies. He is content. Then Cordelia says to him, away from the court, in confused appeal to their accustomed intimacy, 'Nothing' – don't force me, I don't know what you want, there is nothing I can say, to speak what you want I must not speak. But he is alarmed at the appeal and tries to cover it up, keeping up the front, and says, speaking to her and to the court, as if the ceremony is still in full effect: 'Nothing will come of nothing; speak again.' (*Hysterica passio* is already stirring.) Again she says to *him*: 'Unhappy that I am, I cannot heave my heart into my mouth' – not the heart which loves him, that always has been present in her voice; but the heart which is shuddering with confusion, with wanting to do the impossible, the heart which is now in her throat. But to no avail. Then the next line would be her first attempt to obey him by speaking publicly: 'I love your Majesty according to my bond; no more or less' – not stinting, not telling *him* the truth (what is the true *amount* of love this loving young girl knows to measure with her bond?), not refusing him, but still trying to conceal her love, to lighten its full measure. Then her father's brutally public, and perhaps still publicly considerate, 'How, how, Cordelia! Mend your speech a little, lest you may mar your fortunes.' So she tries again to divide her kingdom ('. . . that lord whose hand must take my plight shall carry half my love with him'). Why should she wish to shame him publicly? He has shamed himself and everyone knows it. She is trying to conceal him; and to do that she cuts herself in two. (In the end, he faces what she has done here: 'Upon such sacrifices, my Cordelia . . .' Lear cannot, at that late moment, be thinking of prison as a sacrifice. I imagined him there partly remembering this first scene, and the first of Cordelia's sacrifices – of love to convention.)

After this speech, said in suppression, confusion, abandonment, she is shattered, by her failure and by Lear's viciousness to her. Her sisters speak again only when they are left alone, to plan. Cordelia revives and speaks after France enters and has begun to speak *for* her:

> Sure, her offence
> Must be of such unnatural degree
> That monsters it, or your fore-vouch'd affection
> Faln into taint; which to believe of her,
> Must be a faith that reason without miracle
> Should never plant in me.   [I i 218–23]

France's love shows him the truth. Tainted love is the answer, love dyed – not decayed or corrupted exactly; Lear's love is still alive, but expressed as, colored over with, hate. Cordelia finds her voice again, protected in France's love, and she uses it to change the subject, still protecting Lear from discovery.

A reflection of what Cordelia now must feel is given by one's rush of gratitude toward France, one's almost wild relief as he speaks his beautiful trust. She does not ask her father to relent, but only to give France some explanation. Not the right explanation: What has 'that glib and oily art' got to do with it? That is what her sisters needed, because their task was easy: to dissemble. Convention perfectly suits these ladies. But she lets it go at that – he hates me because I would not flatter him. The truth is, she *could* not flatter; not because she was too proud or too principled, though these might have been the reasons, for a different character; but because nothing she could have done would have *been* flattery – at best it would have been *dissembled flattery*. There is no convention for doing what Cordelia was asked to do. It is not that Goneril and Regan have taken the words out of her mouth, but that here she cannot say them, because for her they are true ('Dearer than eye-sight, space and liberty'). She is not disgusted by her sisters' flattery (it's nothing new); but heartbroken at hearing the words she wishes she were in a position to say. So she is sent, and taken, away. Or half of her leaves; the other half remains, in Lear's mind, in Kent's service, and in the Fool's love.

(I spoke just now of 'one's' gratitude and relief toward France. I was remembering my feeling at a production given by students at Berkeley during 1946 in which France – a small part, singled out by Granville-Barker as particularly requiring an actor of authority and distinction – was given his full sensitivity and manliness, a combination notably otherwise absent from the play, as mature womanliness is. The validity of such feelings as touchstones of the accuracy of a reading of the play, and which feelings one is to trust and which not, ought to be discussed problems of criticism.)

It may be felt that I have forced this scene too far in order to fit it to my reading, that too many directions have to be provided to its acting in order to keep the motivation smooth. Certainly I have gone into more detail of this kind here than elsewhere, and I should perhaps say why. It is, first of all, the scene in which the problem of performance, or the performability, of this play comes to a head, or to its first head. Moreover, various interpretations offered of this scene are direct functions of attempts to *visualize* its progress; as though a critic's conviction about the greatness or weakness of the scene is a direct function of the success or unsuccess with which he or she has been able to imagine it concretely. Critics will invariably dwell on the motivations of Lear and Cordelia in this scene as a problem, even while taking their motivation later either as more or less obvious or for some other reason wanting no special description; and in particular, the motives or traits of character attributed to them here will typically be ones which have an immediate visual implication, ones in which, as it were, a psychological trait and its physical expression most nearly coalesce: At random, Lear is described as irascible (Schüking), arrogant, choleric, overbearing (Schlegel); Cordelia as shy, reluctant (Schüking), sullen, prideful (Coleridge), obstinate (Muir). This impulse seems to me correct, and honest: It is one thing to say that Cordelia's behavior in the opening scene is not inconsistent with her behavior when she reappears, but another to *show* its consistency. This is what I have wanted to test in visualizing her behavior in that scene. But it is merely a test, it proves nothing about my reading, except its actability; or rather, a performance on these lines would, or would not, prove that. And that is a further problem of aesthetics – to chart the relations between a text (or score), an analysis or interpretation of it, and a performance in terms of that analysis or interpretation.

The problem is not, as it is often put, that no performance is ideal, because this suggests we have some clear idea of what an ideal performance would be, perhaps an idea of it as embodying all true interpretations, every resonance of the text struck under analysis. But this is no more possible, or comprehensible, than an experiment which is to verify every implication of a theory. (Then what makes a theory convincing?) Performances are actions, and the imitations of actions. As with any action, performance cannot contain the totality of a human life – though one action can have a particularly summary or revelatory quality, and another will occur at a crossroads, and another will spin tangentially to the life and circumstances which call it out, or rub irrelevantly or mechanically against another. Some have no meaning for us at all, others have more resonance than they can express – as a resultant force answers to forces not visible in the one direction it selects. (Then what makes action bearable, or comprehensible?) I cannot at will give my past expression, though every gesture expresses it, and each elation and headache; my character is its epitome, as if the present were a pantomime of ghostly selections. What is necessary to a performance is what is necessary to action in the present, that it have its autonomy, and that it be in character, or out, and that it have a specific context and motive. Even if everything I have said about Cordelia is true, it needn't be registered explicitly in the way that first scene is played – there may, for example, be merit in stylizing it drastically. Only there will be no effort to present us with a sullen or prideful or defiant girl who reappears, with nothing intervening to change her, as the purest arch of love.

Nor, of course, has my rendering of the first scene been meant to bring out all the motivations or forces which cross there. For example, it might be argued that part of Lear's strategy is exactly to put Cordelia into the position of being denied her dowry, so that he will not lose her in marriage; if so, it half worked, and required the magnanimity of France to turn it aside. Again, nothing has been said of the theme of politics which begins here and pervades the action. Not just the familiar Shakespearean theme which opens the inter-play between the public and private lives of the public creature, but the particularity of the theme in this play, which is about the interpenetration and confusion of politics with love; something which, in modern societies, is equally the fate of private creatures – whether in the form of divided loyalties, or of one's relation to the state, or, more pervasively, in the new forms love and patriotism themselves take: love wielding itself in gestures of power, power extending itself with claims of love. *Phèdre* is perhaps the greatest play concentrated to this theme of the body politic, and of the body, torn by the privacy of love; as it is closest to *King Lear* in its knowledge of shame as the experience of unacceptable love. And Machiavelli's knowledge of the world is present; not just in his attitudes of realism and cynicism, but in his experience of the condition to which these attitudes are appropriate – in which the inner and outer worlds have become disconnected, and man's life is all public, among strangers, seen only from outside. Luther saw the same thing at the same time, but from inside. For some, like Edmund, this is liberating knowledge, lending capacity for action. It is what Lear wants to abdicate from. For what Lear is doing in that first scene is trading power for love (pure power for mixed love); this is what his opening speech explicitly says. He imagines that this will prevent future strife now; but he is being counseled by his impo-tence, which is not the result of his bad decision, but produces it: He feels powerless to *appoint* his successor, recognized as the ultimate test of authority. The consequence is that politics becomes private, and so vanishes, with power left to serve hatred.

The final scene opens with Lear and Cordelia repeating or completing their actions in their opening scene; again Lear abdicates, and again Cordelia loves and is silent. Its readers have for centuries wanted to find consolation in this end: Heavy opinion sanctioned Tate's Hollywood ending throughout the eighteenth century, which resurrects Cordelia; and in our time, scorning such vulgarity, the same impulse fastidiously digs itself deeper and produces redemption for Lear in Cordelia's figuring of transcendent love. But Dr Johnson is surely right, more honest and more responsive: Cordelia's death is so shocking that we would avoid it if we could – if we have responded to it. And so the question, since her death is restored to us, is forced upon us: Why does she die? And this is not answered by asking, What does her death mean? (cp. Christ died to save sinners); but by answering, What killed her? (cp. Christ was killed by us, because his news was unendurable).

Lear's opening speech of this final scene is not the correction but the repetition of his strategy in the first scene, or a new tactic designed to win the old game; and it is equally disastrous.

CORD.   Shall we not see these daughters and these sisters?
LEAR   No, no, no, no!   [v iii 7–8]

He cannot finally face the thing he has done; and this means what it always does, that he cannot bear being seen. He is anxious to go off to prison, with Cordelia; his love now is in the open – that much circumstance has done for him; but it remains imperative that it be confined, out of sight. (Neither Lear nor Cordelia, presumably, knows that the soldier in command is Gloucester's son; they feel unknown.) He is still ashamed, and the fantasy expressed in this speech ('We two alone will sing like birds i' the cage') is the same fantasy he brings on the stage with him in the first scene, the thwarting of which causes his maddened destructiveness. There Cordelia had offered him the marriage pledge ('Obey you, love you, and most honor you'), and she has shared his fantasy fully enough to wish to heal political strife with a kiss (or perhaps it is just the commonest fantasy of women):

CORD.   Restoration hang
  Thy medicine on my lips.   [IV vii 26–7]

(But after such abdication, what restoration? The next time we hear
the words 'hang' and 'medicine,' they announce death.) This
gesture is as fabulous as anything in the opening scene. Now, at the
end, Lear returns her pledge with his lover's song, his invitation to
voyage ('. . . so we'll live, and pray, and sing, and tell old tales, and
laugh'). The fantasy of this speech is as full of detail as a daydream,
and it is clearly a happy dream for Lear. He has found at the end a
way to have what he has wanted from the beginning. His tone is not:
We shall love *even though* we are in prison; but: Because we are
hidden together we can love. He has come to accept his love, not by
making room in the world for it, but by denying its relevance to the
world. He does not renounce the world in going to prison, but flees
from it, to earthly pleasure. The astonishing image of 'God's spies'
[V iii 17] stays beyond me, but in part it contains the final emphasis
upon looking without being seen; and it cites an intimacy which
requires no reciprocity with real men. Like Gloucester toward
Dover, Lear anticipates God's call. He is not experiencing reconciliation with a daughter, but partnership in a mystic marriage.
    If so, it cannot be, as is often suggested, that when he says,

           Upon such sacrifices, my Cordelia,
           The Gods themselves throw incense.   [V iii 20–1]

he is thinking simply of going to prison with Cordelia as a sacrifice.
It seems rather that, the lines coming immediately after his love
song, it is their love itself which has the meaning of sacrifice. As
though the ideas of love and of death are interlocked in his mind –
and in particular of death as a payment or placation for the granting
of love. His own death, because acknowledging love still presents
itself to him as an annihilation of himself. And her death, because
now that he admits her love, he must admit, what he knew from the
beginning, that he is impotent to sustain it. This is the other of
Cordelia's sacrifices – of love to secrecy.
    Edmund's death reinforces the juncture of these ideas, for it is
death which releases his capacity for love. It is this release which
permits his final act:

> ... some good I mean to do
> Despite of mine own nature. Quickly send ...
>
> [v iii 243–4]

What has released him? Partly, of course, the presence of his own death; but that in itself need not have worked this way. Primarily it is the fact that all who have loved him, or claimed love for him, are dead. He has eagerly prompted Edgar to tell the tale of their father's death; his reaction upon hearing of Goneril's and Regan's deaths is as to a solution to impossible, or illegitimate, love: 'All three now marry in an instant'; and his immediate reaction upon seeing their dead bodies is: 'Yet Edmund was belov'd.' *That* is what he wanted to know, and he can acknowledge it now, when it cannot be returned, now that its claim is dead. In his following speech he means well for the first time.

It can be said that what Lear is ashamed of is not his need for love and his inability to return it, but of the *nature* of his love for Cordelia. It is too far from plain love of father for daughter. Even if we resist seeing in it the love of lovers, it is at least incompatible with the idea of her having any (other) lover. There is a moment, beyond the words, when this comes to the surface of the action. It is the moment Lear is waking from his madness, no longer incapable of seeing the world, but still not strong enough to protect his thoughts: 'Methinks I should know you and know this man' [IV vii 64]. I take it 'this man' is generally felt to refer to Kent (disguised as Caius), for there is clearly no reason to suppose Lear knows the Doctor, the only other man present. Certainly this is plausible; but in fact Lear never does acknowledge Kent, as he does his child Cordelia.[9] And after this recognition he goes on to ask, 'Am I in France?' This question irresistibly (to me) suggests that the man he thinks he should know is the man he expects to be with his daughter, her husband. This would be unmistakable if he directs his 'this man' to the Doctor, taking him for, but not able to make him out as, France. He finds out it is not, and the next time we see him he is pressing off to prison with his child, and there is no further thought of her husband. It is a standing complaint that Shakespeare's explanation of France's absence is perfunctory. It is more puzzling that Lear himself never refers to him, not even when he is depriving him of her forever. Either France has ceased to exist for Lear, or it is importantly from him that he wishes to reach the shelter of prison.

I do not wish to suggest that 'avoidance of love' and 'avoidance of a particular kind of love' are alternative hypotheses about this play. On the contrary, they seem to me to interpret one another. Avoidance of love is always, or always begins as, an avoidance of a particular kind of love: Human beings do not just naturally not love, they learn not to. And our lives begin by having to accept under the name of love whatever closeness is offered, and by then having to forgo its object. And the avoidance of a particular love, or the acceptance of it, will spread to every other; every love, in acceptance or rejection, is mirrored in every other. It is part of the miracle of the vision in *King Lear* to bring this before us, so that we do not care whether the *kind* of love felt between these two is forbidden according to humanity's lights. We care whether love is or is not altogether forbidden to us, whether we may not altogether be incapable of it, of admitting it into our world. We wonder whether we may always go mad between the equal efforts and terrors at once of rejecting and of accepting love. The soul torn between them, the body feels torn (producing a set of images accepted since Caroline Spurgeon's *Shakespeare's Imagery* as central to *King Lear*), and the solution to this insoluble condition is to wish for the tearing apart of the world.

Lear wishes to escape into prison for another old reason – because he is unwilling to be seen to weep.

> The good years shall devour them, flesh and fell,
> Ere they shall make us weep: we'll see 'em starved first.
>
> [v iii 24–5]

See them shalt thou never. And in the end he still avoids Cordelia. He sees that she is weeping after his love song ('Wipe thine eyes'). But why is she in tears? Why does Lear think she is? Lear imagines that she is crying for the reasons that he is on the verge of tears – the old reasons, the sense of impotence, shame, loss. But *her* reasons for tears do not occur to him, that she sees him as he is, as he was, that he is unable to take his last chance; that he, at the farthest edge of life, must again sacrifice her, again abdicate his responsibilities; and that he cannot know what he asks. And yet, seeing that, it is for him that she is cast down. Upon such knowledge the gods themselves throw incense.

It is as though her response here is her knowledge of the end of the play; she alone has the capacity of compassion Lear will need when we next see him, with Cordelia dead in his arms: 'Howl, howl, howl! O! you are men of stones.' (Cp. the line and a half Dante gives to Ugolino, facing his doomed sons, a fragment shored by Arnold: 'I did not weep, I so turned to stone within. They wept.') Again he begins to speak by turning on those at hand: 'A plague upon you, murderers, traitors all!' But then the tremendous knowledge is released: 'I might have saved her.' From the beginning, and through each moment until they are led to prison, he might have saved her, had he done what every love requires, put himself aside long enough to see through to her, and be seen through. I do not mean that it is clear that he could, at the end, have done what Edmund feared ('pluck the common bosom on his side, And turn our impress'd lances in our eyes'); but it is not clear that he could not. And even if he had not succeeded, her death would not be on his hands. In his last speech, 'No, no, no, no' becomes 'No, no, no life!' His need, or his interpretation of his need, becomes her sentence. This is what is unbearable. Or bearable only out of the capacity of Cordelia. If we are to weep her fortunes we must take her eyes.

Is this a Christian play? The question is very equivocal. When it is answered affirmatively, Cordelia is viewed as a Christ figure whose love redeems nature and transfigures Lear. So far as this is intelligible to me, I find it false both to the experience of the play and to the fact that it *is* a play. *King Lear* is not illustrated theology (anyway, which theology is thought to be illustrated, what understanding of atonement, redemption, etc., is thought to be figured?), and nature and Lear are not touched, but run out. If Cordelia exemplifies Christ, it is at the moment of crucifixion, not resurrection. But the moment of his death is the moment when Christ resembles us, finally takes the human condition fully into himself. (This is why every figure reaching the absolute point of rejection starts becoming a figure of Christ. And perhaps why it is so important to the Christ story that it begins with birth and infancy.) It is in his *acceptance* of this condition that we are to resemble him. If Cordelia resembles Christ, it is by having become fully human, by knowing her separateness, by knowing the deafness of miracles, by accepting the unacceptability of her love, and by nevertheless maintaining her love and the whole knowledge it brings. One can say she 'redeems nature' [IV vi 207], but this means nothing miraculous, only that she shows nature not to be the cause of evil – there is no cause in nature which makes these hard hearts, and no cause outside either. The cause is the heart itself, the having of a heart, in a world made heartless. Lear is the cause. Murderers, traitors *all*.

Another way, the play can be said to be Christian – not because it shows us redemption (it does not) but because it throws our redemption into *question*, and leaves it up to us. But there is no suggestion that we can take it up only through Christ. On the contrary, there is reason to take this drama as an alternative to the Christian one. In the first place, Christianity, like every other vision of the play, is not opted for, but tested. Specifically, as was said earlier, in Edgar's conduct; more generally, in its suggestion that all appeals to gods are distractions or excuses, because the imagination uses them to wish for complete, for final solutions, when what is needed is at hand, or nowhere. But isn't this what Christ meant? And isn't this what Lear fails to see in wishing to be God's spy before he is God's subject? Cordelia is further proof of this: Her grace is shown by the absence in her of any unearthly experiences; she is the only good character whose attention is wholly on earth, on the person nearest her. It is during the storm that Lear's mind clouds most and floods with philosophy; when it clears, Cordelia is present.

These considerations take us back to the set of ideas which see Lear as having arrived, in the course of the storm, at the naked human condition – as if the storm was the granting of his prayer to 'feel what wretches feel.' It may seem that I have denied this in underlining Lear's cruelty to Gloucester and in placing him at the cause of Cordelia's death, because it may feel as if I am blaming Lear for his behavior here.[10] And what room is there for blame? Is he to blame for being human? For being subject to a cosmic anxiety and to fantasies which enclose him from perfect compassion? Certainly blame is inappropriate, for certainly I do not claim to know what *else* Lear might do. And yet I cannot deny that my pain at Lear's actions is not overcome by my knowledge of his own suffering. I might describe my experience of him here as one of unplaceable blame, blame no one can be asked to bear and no one is in a position to level – like blaming heaven. That does not seem to me inappropriate as an experience of tragedy, of what it is for which tragedy provides catharsis. (Neither Kent nor Cordelia requires tragedy for purification; the one preceding, the other transcending personal morality.) What I am denying is that to say Lear becomes simply a man is to say that he achieves the unaccommodated human condition. The ambiguities here stand out in William Empson's suggestion of Lear as scapegoat and outcast.[11] This cannot be wrong, but it can be made too much of, or the wrong thing. We do not want the extremity of Lear's suffering to have gone for nothing, or for too little, so we may imagine that it has made him capable of envisioning ours. But as the storm is ending he is merely humanly a scapegoat, as any man is on the wrong end of injustice; and no more an outcast than any man out of favor. Only at his finish does his suffering measure the worst that can happen to a man, and there not because he is a scapegoat but because he has made a scapegoat of his love. But that Cordelia is Lear's scapegoat is compatible with Lear's being ours. And seeing him as a scapegoat is not incompatible with seeing him as avoiding love – on the contrary, it is this which shows what his connection with us is, the act for which he bears total, sacrificial consequences. If this play contains scapegoats, it is also about scapegoats, about what it is which creates scapegoats and about the cost of creating them. To insist upon Lear as scapegoat is apt to thin our sense of this general condition in his world; and this again would put us in his position – not *seeing* it from his point of view (maintaining ours), but accepting his point of view, hence denying the other characters, and using the occasion not to feel for him (and them) but to sympathize with ourselves.

All the good characters are exiled, cast out – Cordelia and Kent initially, Edgar at the beginning and Lear at the end of Act II, Gloucester at the end of Act III. But there is from the opening lines a literal social outcast of another kind, the bastard, the central evil character. A play which has the power of transforming kings into fools equally has the power of overlapping kings and bastards – the naked human condition is more than any man bargains for. Empson finds Lear's 'most distinct expression of the scapegoat idea' in the lines

> None does offend, none; I say none. I'll able 'em:
> Take that of me, my friend, who have the power
> To seal the accuser's lips.   [IV vi 170–2]

Empson reads: 'The royal prerogative has become the power of the outcast to deal directly on behalf of mankind.' I do not question the presence of this feeling, but it is equivocal. For what is the nature of this new, direct power of sealing lips? The problem is not just that

'None does offend, none; I say none' protests too much, as though
Lear can't quite believe it. The problem is that Edmund also deals
with men to seal their lips, and he can directly, even elatedly, use
this human power because he is an outcast, because judgment has
already been passed upon him. That is the justice of his position.
And he could express himself in the words 'None does offend.' He
would mean, as in his second soliloquy [I ii 124–40], that all are
equally evil and evasive; hence no man is in a position from which to
judge offense in others.

What would this prove, except that the Devil can quote scripture?
But that is proof enough if it proves that the greatest truths are
nothing, mean harm or help or nothing, apart from their application
in the individual case. We see (do we see?) how Edmund's meaning
repudiates the Gospels: He is not speaking on behalf of mankind,
but on his own; and he is not forgoing judgment, but escaping it by
making it indiscriminate, cynicizing it. Then do we see how Lear's
mind, in its rage at injustice, is different from Edmund's? For Lear
too has a private use for this indiscriminate condemnation of the
world. Suppose we see in the progress of Lear's madness a recapitu-
lation of the history of civilization or of consciousness: from the
breaking up of familial bonds and the release of offenses which
destroy the social cosmos [III iv], through the fragile replacement of
revenge by the institution of legal justice [III vi], to the corruption of
justice itself and the breaking up of civil bonds [IV vi]. In raging with
each of these stages in turn, Lear's mind gusts to a calm as the storm
calms, drawing even with the world as it goes (This is why,
adapting Empson's beautiful and compassionate perception, Lear at
this point removes his boots, at home again in the world.) If he is an
outcast, every man is, whose society is in rags about him; if he is a
scapegoat, every man is, under the general shiftings of blame and in
the inaccuracy of justice. Lear has not arrived at the human
condition he saw imaged in poor naked Tom (the sight which tipped
him from world-destroying rage into world-creating madness); but
one could say he now has this choice open to him. He finds himself a
man; so far he has abdicated. But he has not yet chosen his
mortality, to be one man among others; so far he is not at one;
atonement is not complete. He has come to terms with Goneril and
Regan, with filial ingratitude; he has come back from the way he
knew madness lies. But he has not come to terms with parental
insatiability (which he denounced in his 'barbarous Scythian'

speech [I i 116], and which Gloucester renounces in 'the food of thy abused father's wrath' [IV i 22]). He has not come back to Cordelia. And he does not.

Evidence for this in this scene is not solely that his 'None does offend' is said still stranded in madness (nor even in the possible hint of power in the fact that he does not just take off his boots but imagines them removed for him, as by a servant) but in the content of his ensuing sermon ('I will preach to thee'):

> When we are born, we cry that we are come
> To this great stage of fools.   [IV vi 184–5]

This is a sermon, presumably, because it interprets the well-known text of tears with which each human life begins. But, as Empson puts it, 'the babies cannot be supposed to know all this about human affairs.' I think Lear is there feeling like a child, after the rebirth of his senses (children do naturally 'wawl and cry' at injustice); and feeling that the world is an unnatural habitat for man; and feeling it is unnatural because it is a stage. Perhaps it is a stage because its actors are seen by heaven, perhaps because they are seen by one another. Either way, it is Lear (not, for example, Gloucester, Lear's congregation) who sees it there as a stage. But why a stage of fools? There will be as many answers as there are meanings of 'fool.' But the point around which all the answers will turn is that it is when, and because, he sees the world as a stage that he sees it peopled with fools, with distortions of persons, with natural scapegoats, among whom human relationship does not arise. Then who is in a position to level this vision at the world? Not, of course, that it is invalid – no one could deny it. The catch is that there is no one to assert it – without asserting himself a fool. The world-accusing fool, like the world-accusing liar, suffers a paradox. Which is why 'the praise of Folly' must mean 'Folly's praise.' (To say that the theatricalization of others makes them scapegoats is a way of putting the central idea of Part II of this essay.)

But if the sense in which, or way in which, Lear has become a scapegoat is not special about him, he can be said to be special there in his *feeling* that he is a scapegot and in his universal casting of the world with scapegoats. This is an essential connection between him and Gloucester's family: Gloucester is in fact turned out of society, and while he is not left feeling that society has made a scapegoat of him, he has made scapegoats of his sons, deprived each of his birthright, the one by nature and custom, the other by decree. Each reciprocates by casting his father out, in each case by a stratagem, though the one apparently acts out of hatred, the other apparently out of love; and each of the brothers makes a scapegoat of the other, the one by nature and custom, the other by design. Like Edgar, Lear casts himself in the role of scapegoat, and then others suffer for it; like Edmund, he finds himself the natural fool of Fortune, a customary scapegoat, and then kill, kill, kill, kill, kill, kill [cf. IV vi 189] – the mind clawing at itself for a hold. These nests of doublings (and in no play is Shakespeare's familiar doubling of themes so relentless, becoming something like the medium of the drama itself, or its vision of the world) suggest that the dramatic point of Shakespeare's doublings is not so much to amplify or universalize a theme as to focus or individuate it, and in particular to show the freedom under each character's possession of his character. Each way of responding to one's foolishness is tested by every other; each way of accepting one's having been cast out is tested by every other; that Gloucester is not driven mad by filial ingratitude (though he is no stranger to the possibility: His very openness in looking at it ['I'll tell thee, friend, I am almost mad myself' [III iv 169–70]) makes him a sensitive touchstone of normalcy in this) means that there is no necessary route Lear's spirit has followed. One will want to object that from the fact that a route is not necessary to Gloucester it does not follow that it is not necessary to Lear. But that is the point. To find out why it is necessary one has to discover who Lear is, what *he* finds necessary, his specific spins of need and choice. His tragedy is that he has to find out too, and that he cannot rest with less than an answer. 'Who is it that can tell me who I am?' [I iv 238]. At the first rebuff in his new condition, Lear is forced to the old tragic question. And the Fool lets out his astonishing knowledge: 'Lear's shadow.' At this point Lear either does not hear, or he thinks the Fool has *told* him who he is, and takes it, as it seems easy to take it, to mean roughly that he is in reduced circumstances. It would be somewhat harder to take if he heard the suggestion of *shade* under 'shadow'. But the truth may still be harder to be told, harder than anything that can just be told.

Suppose the Fool has precisely answered Lear's question, which is only characteristic of him. Then his reply means: Lear's shadow can tell you who you are. If this is heard, it will mean that the answer to Lear's question is held in the inescapable Lear which is now obscure and obscuring, and in the inescapable Lear which is projected upon the world, and that Lear is double and has a double. And then this play reflects another long curve of feeling about doubling, describing an emphasis other than my recent suggestion that it haunts the characters with their freedom. In the present guise it taunts the characters with their lack of wholeness, their separation from themselves, by loss or denial or opposition. (In Montaigne: 'We are, I know not how, double in ourselves, so that what we believe we disbelieve, and cannot rid ourselves of what we condemn.'[12] By the time of Heine's *Doppelgänger* ['Still ist die Nacht...'], the self is split from its past and from its own feeling, however intimately present both may be.) But in either way, either by putting freedom or by putting integrity into question, doubling sets a task, of discovery, of acknowledgment. And both ways are supported in the moment Lear faces Gloucester and confuses identities with him.

If on a given experience of the play one is caught by the reference to adultery and then to 'Gloucester's bastard son' which launches Lear's long tirade against the foulness of nature and of man's justice, one may find that absent member of the Gloucester family presiding over Lear's mind here. For Lear's disgust with sexual nature is not far from Edmund's early manic praise of it, especially in their joint sense of the world as alive in its pursuit; and Edmund's stinging sensitivity to the illegitimacy of society's 'legitimacy' prefigures Lear's knowledge of the injustice of society's 'justice.' If, therefore, we are to see in this play, in Miss Welsford's fine phrase, the investing of the king with motley, then in this scene we may see the king standing up for bastards – an illegitimate king in an unlawful world. (Edmund has tossed off a prayer for bastards, and perhaps there is a suggestion that the problem with prayers is not that few are answered but that *all* are, one way or another.) As the doublings reflect one another, each character projecting some more or less eccentric angle to a common theme, one glimpses the possibility of a common human nature which each, in his or her own way, fails to achieve; or perhaps glimpses the idea that its gradual achievement is the admission of reflection in oneself of every human theme. As Christ receives reflection in every form of human scapegoat, every way in which one man bears the brunt of another's distortion and rejection. For us the reflection is brightest in Cordelia, because of her acceptance, perhaps because she is hanged; it is present, on familiar grounds, in the mysteries of the Fool. I cannot help feeling it, if grossly, in the figure of the bastard son. I do not press this. Yet it makes us reflect that evil is not wrong when it thinks of itself as good, for at those times it recaptures a craving for goodness, an experience of its own innocence which the world rejects.

There is hope in this play, and it is not in heaven. It lies in the significance of its two most hideous moments: Gloucester's blinding and Cordelia's death. In Gloucester's history we found hope, because while his weakness has left him open to the uses of evil, evil *has* to turn upon him because it cannot bear him to witness. As long as that is true, evil does not have *free* sway over the world. In Cordelia's death there is hope, because it shows the gods more just — more than we had hoped or wished: Lear's prayer is answered again in this. The gods are, in Edgar's wonderful idea, clear. Cordelia's death means that *every* falsehood, every refusal of acknowledgment, will be tracked down. In the realm of the spirit, Kierkegaard says, there is absolute justice. Fortunately, because if all we had to go on were the way the world goes, we would lose the concept of justice altogether; and then human life would become unbearable. Kant banked the immortality of the soul on the fact that in *this* world goodness and happiness are unaligned – a condition which, if never righted, is incompatible with moral sanity, and hence with the existence of God. But immortality is not necessary for the soul's satisfaction. What is necessary is its own coherence, its ability to judge a world in which evil is successful and the good are doomed; and in particular its knowledge that while injustice may flourish, it cannot rest content. This, I take it, is what Plato's *Republic* is about. And it is an old theme of tragedy.

Its companion theme is that our actions have consequences which outrun our best, and worst, intentions. The drama of *King Lear* not merely embodies this theme, it comments on it, even deepens it. For what it shows is that the *reason* consequences furiously hunt us down is not merely that we are half blind, and unfortunate, but that we go on doing the thing which produced these consequences in the first place. What we need is not rebirth, or salvation, but the courage, or plain prudence, to see and to stop. To abdicate. But what do we need in order to do that? It would be salvation.

. . . I pause here to indicate why I am not trying unduly to blur the immodest or melodramatic quality of the claims I have made: that quality will itself be serviceable if it provides further data for investigating the act of criticism.[13] I am assuming, that is, that criticism is inherently immodest and melodramatic – not merely from its temptations to uninstructive superiority and to presumptuous fellow feeling (with audience or artist) but from the logic of its claims, in particular from two of its elements: (1) A critical position will finally rest upon calling a claim *obvious*; (2) a critical discovery will present itself as the *whole* truth of a work, a provision of its total meaning. Taken in familiar ways, these claims seem easily disconfirmable. How can a claim be obvious if not everyone finds it obvious? (And there is always someone who does not – maybe the critic himself won't tomorrow.) And how can a claim to total meaning be correct when so much is left out? (And there is always something.) But if critical judgments are felt to be refuted on *such* grounds, they are not merely intolerant but a little idiotic. (That is the implied claim of such refutations. I don't say it is never justified.) But suppose we hold on to the intolerance and hold off the idiocy for a moment. Then we must ask: How can serious people habitually make such *vulnerable* claims? (Meaning, perhaps, claims so *obviously* false?) But suppose there is another way of taking them; that is, suppose our familiar ways of taking them are what make them seem a bit simple. What are these ways? They take a claim to obviousness as a claim to certainty, and they take the claim to totality as a claim to exhaustiveness. The first of these ways is deeply implicated in the history of modern epistemology, and its effect has been to distrust conviction rather than to investigate the concept of the obvious. (Wittgenstein's later philosophy can be thought of as investigations of obviousness.) The second of these ways expresses the exclusiveness of a lived world, instanced by the mutual offense and the interminable and glancing criticisms of opposed philosophies, and its effect has been to distrust exclusiveness or to attempt exhaustiveness rather than to investigate the concept of totality. It is in the nature of both of these sources of intolerance to appear to be private; because in both one at best has nothing to go on but oneself. (A fashionable liberalism has difficulty telling the difference between seriousness and bigotry. A suggestion of the difference is that the bigot is never isolated. A more ambitious connoisseur will number the differences between seriousness and madness.) This is why a critical discovery is often accompanied by a peculiar exhilaration and why recognition of a critical lapse is accompanied by its peculiar chagrin. One will want to know how (and whether) these emotions differ from the general relish of victory and the general anguish at defeat – say, in science. I do not say that in every case there are differences, but I point to the different ways in which concepts such as 'discovery,' 'advance,' 'talent,' 'professional,' 'insight,' 'depth,' 'competition,' 'influence,' etc. are, or may be, applied in criticism and in science – the different shapes of the arenas in which victory and defeat are determined. It seems difference enough that one imagines a major scientific insight occurring to a person with an impulse to race into the streets with it, out of relief and out of the happy knowledge that it is of relevance to his fellow townsmen; whereas the joy in a major critical insight may be unsharable if one lacks the friends, and even not need to be spoken (while perhaps hoping that another will find it on his or her own). This must go with the fact that the topics of criticism are not objects but works, things which are *already* spoken. And if arrogance is inherent in criticism (and therefore where not in the humanities?), then humility is no less painful a task there than anywhere else. Nor is it surprising that the specific elements of arrogance afflict both criticism and philosophy: If philosophy can be thought of as the world of a particular culture brought to consciousness of itself, then one mode of criticism (call it philosophical criticism) can be thought of as the world of a particular work brought to consciousness of itself. . . .

SOURCE: *Disowning Knowledge* (1987)

NOTES

1. '*King Lear* and the Theory of the Sight Pattern,' in R. Brower and R. Poirier, eds, *In Defense of Reading* (New York, Dutton, 1963), pp. 133–52.

2. Alpers gives the references for the elements of his quotation as follows: J. I. M. Stewart, *Character and Motive in Shakespeare* (New York, Longman, Green, 1949), pp. 20–1; R. B. Heilman, *This Great Stage* (Baton Rouge, Louisiana State University Press, 1948), p. 25; L. C. Knights, *Some Shakespearean Themes* (London, Chatto and Windus, 1959), p. 107; *King Lear*, ed. K. Muir (Cambridge, Harvard University Press, 1952, Arden edition), p. lx.

3. This of course is not to say that such critics have correctly interpreted this feeling of insight, and it does not touch Alpers's claim that such critics have in particular interpreted 'moral insight' as 'the perception of moral truths'; nor, finally, does it weaken Alpers's view of such an interpretation as moralizing, hence evading, the significance of (this) tragedy. I am not, that is, regarding Alpers and the critics with whom, on this point, he is at

odds, as providing alternative readings of the play, between which I am choosing or adjudicating. Their relation is more complex. Another way of seeing this is to recognize that Alpers does not deny the presence of a controlling 'sight' pattern in *King Lear* but that he transforms the significance of this pattern.

4. See the introduction by Peter Laslett to his edition of Filmer's *Patriarcha* (Oxford, Blackwell, 1949).

5. '*King Lear* and the Comedy of the Grotesque,' one of the studies composing *The Wheel of Fire*, originally published by Oxford University Press, 1930; published in the fifth revised edition by Meridian Books (New York, 1957).

6. Suggested by R. W. Chambers, *King Lear*, 1940; cited by Muir, p. 1.

7. The passage from this sentence to the end of the paragraph was added as the result of a conversation with Rose Mary Harbison.

8. New York: Barnes and Noble, 1966; the quotation that follows is from pp. 181–2 of this edition. The book was first published in 1930 by Cambridge University Press.

9. Professor Jonas Barish – to whom I am indebted for other suggestions about this essay as well as the present one – has pointed out to me that in my eagerness to solve all the *King Lear* problems I have neglected trying an account of Kent's plan in delaying making himself known ('Yet to be known shortens my made intent' [IV vii 9]). This omission is particularly important because Kent's is the one delay that causes no harm to others; hence it provides an internal measure of those harms. I do not understand his 'dear cause' [IV iii 52], but I think the specialness of Kent's delay has to do with these facts: (1) It never prevents his perfect faithfulness to his duties of service; these do not require – Kent does not permit them to require – personal recognition in order to be performed. This sense of the finitude of the demands placed upon Kent, hence of the harm and of the good he can perform, is a function of his complete absorption into his social office, in turn a function of his being the only principal character in the play (apart from the Fool) who does not appear as a member of a *family*. (2) He does not delay revealing himself to Cordelia, only (presumably) to Lear. A reason for that would be that since the king has banished him it is up to the king to reinstate him; he will not presume on his old rank. (3) If his plan goes beyond finding some way, or just waiting, for Lear to recognize him first (not out of pride but out of right) then perhaps it is made irrelevant by finding Lear again only in his terminal state, or perhaps it always consisted only in doing what he tries to do there, find an opportunity to tell Lear about Caius and ask for pardon. It may be wondered that we do not feel Lear's fragmentary recognitions of Kent to leave something undone, nor Kent's hopeless attempts to hold Lear's attention to be crude intrusions, but rather to amplify a sadness already amplified past sensing. This may be accounted for partly by Kent's pure expression of the special poignance of the servant's office, requiring a life centered in another life, exhausted in loyalty and in silent witnessing (a silence Kent broke and Lear must mend); partly by the fact that Cordelia has fully recognized him: 'To be acknowledg'd, Madam, is o'er-paid' [IV vii 4]; partly by the fact that when his

master Lear is dead, it is his master who calls him, and his last words are those of obedience.

10. In a detailed and very useful set of comments on an earlier draft of this essay, Professor Alpers mentions this as a possible response to what I had written; and it was his suggestion of Empson's appeal to the scapegoat idea as offering a truer response to Lear's condition that sent me back to Empson's essay (see note 11). It ws as an effort to do justice to Alpers's reaction that I have included the ensuing discussion of scapegoats in *King Lear*. Beyond this, I have altered or expanded several other passages in the light of his comments, for all of which I am grateful.

11. 'Fool in Lear,' in *The Structure of Complex Words* (Ann Arbor, University of Michigan Press [Ann Arbor Paperback], 1967), pp. 145, 157. Because of Empson's espousal of it, George Orwell's essay on Lear may be mentioned here ('Lear, Tolstoy and the Fool,' reprinted from *Shooting an Elephant and Other Essays*, in F. Kermode (ed.), *Four Centuries of Shakespearean Criticism* [New York, Avon Books, 1965], pp. 514–31). It is, perhaps, of the nature of Orwell's piece that one finds oneself remembering the feel of its moral passion and honesty and the clarity of its hold on the idea of *renunciation* as the subject of the play, without being able oneself to produce Orwell's, or one's own, evidence for the idea in the play – except that the meaning of the entire opening and the sense of its consequences assume, as it were, a self-evidence within the light of that idea. It is probably as good a notation of the subject as one word could give, and Orwell's writing, here as elsewhere, is exemplary of a correct way in which the moral sensibility, distrusting higher ambitions, exercises its right to judge an imperfect world, never exempting itself from that world.

12. Auden uses this as the epigraph to *The Double Man*; I have not yet found its context.

13. The facts of intolerance, expressed as part of an examination of their causes and reasons, particularly of the starkness of their appearance in the criticism of modern arts, is the content of Michael Fried's contribution to *Art Criticism in the Sixties* (New York, October House, 1967), four papers that composed a symposium held at Brandeis University in May 1966.

Stephen Greenblatt and the Exorcists

Shakespeare (1988)

I

Between the spring of 1585 and the summer of 1586, a group of English Catholic priests led by the Jesuit William Weston, alias Father Edmunds, conducted a series of spectacular exorcisms, principally in the house of a recusant gentleman, Sir George Peckham of Denham, Buckinghamshire. The priests were outlaws – by an act of 1585 the mere presence in England of a Jesuit or seminary priest constituted high treason – and those who sheltered them were guilty of a felony, punishable by death. Yet the exorcisms, though clandestine, drew large crowds, almost certainly in the hundreds, and must have been common knowledge to hundreds more. In 1603, long after the arrest and punishment of those involved, Samuel Harsnett, then chaplain to the bishop of London, wrote a detailed account of the cases, based on sworn statements taken from four of the demoniacs and one of the priests. It has been recognized since the eighteenth century that Shakespeare was reading Harsnett's book, *A Declaration of Egregious Popish Impostures*, as he was writing *King Lear*.[1]

The relation between these two texts enables us to glimpse with unusual clarity and precision the institutional negotiation and exchange of social energy. The link between *King Lear* and *A Declaration of Egregious Popish Impostures* has been known for centuries, but the knowledge has remained almost entirely inert, locked in the conventional pieties of source study. From Harsnett, we are told, Shakespeare borrowed the names of the foul fiends by whom Edgar, in his disguise as the bedlam beggar Tom, claims to be possessed. From Harsnett too the playwright derived some of the language of madness, several of the attributes of hell, and a number of colorful adjectives. These and other possible borrowings have been carefully cataloged, but the question of their significance has been not only unanswered but, until recently, unasked.[2] For a long time the prevailing model for the study of literary sources, a model in effect parceled out between the old historicism and the new criticism, blocked such a question. As a freestanding, self-sufficient, disinterested art work produced by a solitary genius, *King Lear* has only an accidental relation to its sources: they provide a glimpse of the 'raw material' that the artist fashioned. Insofar as this 'material' is taken seriously at all, it is as part of the work's 'historical back-ground,' a phrase that reduces history to a decorative setting or a convenient, well-lighted pigeonhole. But once the differentiations on which this model is based begin to crumble, then source study is compelled to change its character: history cannot simply be set against literary texts as either stable antithesis or stable background, and the protective isolation of those texts gives way to a sense of their interaction with other texts and hence of the permeability of their boundaries. 'When I play with my cat,' writes Montaigne, 'who knows if I am not a pastime to her more than she is to me?'[3] When Shakespeare borrows from Harsnett, who knows if Harsnett has not already, in a deep sense, borrowed from Shakespeare's theater what Shakespeare borrows back? Whose interests are served by the borrowing? And is there a larger cultural text produced by the exchange?

Such questions do not lead, for me at least, to the *O altitudo!* of radical indeterminacy. They lead rather to an exploration of the institutional strategies in which both *King Lear* and Harsnett's *Declaration* are embedded. These strategies, I suggest, are part of an intense and sustained struggle in late sixteenth- and early seventeenth-century England to redefine the central values of society. Such a redefinition entailed transforming the prevailing standards of judgment and action, rethinking the conceptual categories by which the ruling elites constructed their world and which they attempted to impose on the majority of the population. At the heart of this struggle, which eventuated in a murderous civil war, was the definition of the sacred, a definition that directly involved secular as well as religious institutions, since the legitimacy of the state rested explicitly on its claim to a measure of sacredness. What is the sacred? Who defines and polices its boundaries? How can society distinguish between legitimate and illegitimate claims to sacred authority? In early modern England rivalry among elites competing for the major share of authority was characteristically expressed not only in parliamentary factions but also in bitter struggles over religious doctrine and practice.

Harsnett's *Declaration* is a weapon in one such struggle, the attempt by the established and state-supported Church of England to eliminate competing religious authorites by wiping out pockets of rivalrous charisma. Charisma, in Edward Shils's phrase, is 'awe-arousing centrality,'[4] the sense of breaking through the routine into the realm of the 'extraordinary' to make direct contact with the ultimate, vital sources of legitimacy, authority, and sacredness. Exorcism was for centuries one of the supreme manifestations in Latin Christianity of this charisma: 'In the healing of the possessed,' Peter Brown writes, 'the *praesentia* of the saints was held to be registered with unfailing accuracy, and their ideal power, their *potentia*, shown most fully and in the most reassuring manner.'[5] Reassuring, that is, not only or even primarily to the demoniac but to the community of believers who bore witness to the ritual and, indeed, through their tears and prayers and thanksgiving, partici-pated in it. For unlike the sorcerer who practiced his art most frequently in the dark corners of the land, in remote rural hamlets and isolated cottages, the charismatic healer depended upon an audience: the great exorcisms of the late Middle Ages and early Renaissance took place at the heart of cities, in churches packed with spectators.

'Great troupes did daily flock thither,' writes the Dominican exorcist Sebastian Michaelis about a series of exorcisms he con-ducted in Aix-en-Provence in the early seventeenth century, and they were, he argues, deeply moved by what they witnessed. Thus, for example, from the body of the young nun Louise, the demon Verrine cried out 'with great and ghastly exclamations' that heretics and sinners would be deprived of the vision of God 'for ever, for ever, for ever, for ever, for ever.' The spectators were so 'affrighted' with these words 'that there gushed from their eyes abundance of tears, when they called to remembrance their offences which they had committed.'[6]

As voluminous contemporary accounts declare, then, exorcisms were moving testimonials to the power of the true faith. But by the late sixteenth century in Protestant England neither the *praesentia* nor the *potentia* of the exorcist was reassuring to religious author-ities, and the Anglican church had no desire to treat the urban masses to a spectacle whose edifying value had been called into question. Moving testimonials extorted from the devil himself – praise of the Virgin, awe in the presence of the Eucharist, acknow-ledgment of the authority of the pope – now seemed both fraudulent and treasonous, and the danger was as great when it came not from a Catholic healer but from a stubbornly nonconforming Protestant. Although the latter did not celebrate the power of the Virgin – when someone tried to invoke Mary's name at a Protestant exorcism, the presiding exorcist sternly rebuked him, 'for there is no other name under Heaven, whereby we may challenge Salvation, but th'only name of Jesus Christ'[7] – he exalted the power of fasting and prayer and made it clear that this power did not depend upon a state-sponsored ecclesiastical hierarchy. The authorities could easily close the cathedrals to such sedition, but even relatively small assemblies in obscure private houses far from the cities had come to represent a threat.

In the *Declaration* Harsnett specifically attacks exorcism as practiced by Jesuits, but he had earlier leveled the same charges at a Puritan exorcist. And he does so not, as we might expect, to claim a monopoly on the practice for the Anglican church but to expose exorcism itself as a fraud. On behalf of established religious and secular authority, Harsnett wishes to cap permanently the great rushing geysers of charisma released in rituals of exorcism. Spiritual *potentia* will henceforth be distributed with greater moderation and control through the whole of the Anglican hierarchy, at whose pinnacle sits the sole legitimate possessor of absolute charismatic authority, the monarch, Supreme Head of the Church in England.

The arguments that Harsnett marshals against exorcism have a rationalistic cast that may mislead us, for despite appearances we are not dealing with the proto-Enlightenment attempt to construct a rational faith. Harsnett denies the presence of the demonic in those whom Father Edmunds claimed to exorcise but finds it in the exorcists themselves: 'And who was the devil, the broacher, herald, and persuader of these unutterable treasons, but *Weston* [alias Edmunds] the Jesuit, the chief plotter, and . . . all the holy Covey of the twelve devilish comedians in their several turns: for there was neither devil, nor urchin, nor Elf, but themselves' [154–5]. Hence, writes Harsnett, the 'Dialogue between *Edmunds*, & the devil' was in reality a dialogue between 'the devil *Edmunds*, and *Edmunds* the devil, for he played both parts himself' [86].

This strategy – the reinscription of evil onto the professed enemies of evil – is one of the characteristic operations of religious authority in the early modern period and has its secular analogues in more recent history when famous revolutionaries are paraded forth to be tried as counter-revolutionaries. The paradigmatic Renaissance instance is the case of the *benandanti*, analyzed brilliantly by the historian Carlo Ginzburg.[8] The *benandanti* were members of a northern Italian folk cult who believed that they went forth seasonally to battle with fennel stalks against their enemies, the witches. If the *benandanti* triumphed, their victory assured the peasants of good harvests; if they lost, the witches would be free to work their mischief. The Inquisition first became interested in the practice in the late sixteenth century; after conducting a series of lengthy inquiries, the Holy Office determined that the cult was demonic and in subsequent interrogations attempted, with some success, to persuade the witch-fighting *benandanti* that they were themselves witches.

Harsnett does not hope to persuade exorcists that they are devils; he wishes to expose their fraudulence and relies on the state to punish them. But he is not willing to abandon the demonic altogether, and it hovers in his work, half accusation, half metaphor, whenever he refers to Father Edmunds or the pope. Satan's function was too important for him to be cast off lightly by the early seventeenth-century clerical establishment. The same state church that sponsored the attacks on superstition in *A Declaration of Egregious Popish Impostures* continued to cooperate, if less enthusiastically than before, in the ferocious prosecutions of witches. These prosecutions, significantly, were handled by the secular judicial apparatus – witchcraft was a criminal offense like aggravated assault or murder – and hence reinforced rather than rivaled the bureaucratic control of authority. The eruption of the demonic into the human world was not denied altogether, but the problem would be processed through the proper secular channels. In cases of witchcraft, the devil was defeated in the courts through the simple expedient of hanging his human agents, not, as in cases of possession, compelled by a spectacular spiritual counterforce to speak out and depart.

Witchcraft then was distinct from possession, and though Harsnett himself is skeptical about accusations of witchcraft, his principal purpose is to expose a nexus of chicanery and delusion in the practice of exorcism.[9] By doing so he hopes to drive the practice out of society's central zone, to deprive it of its prestige, and to discredit its apparent efficacy.[10] In late antiquity, as Peter Brown has demonstrated, exorcism was based on the model of the Roman judicial system: the exorcist conducted a formal *quaestio* in which the demon, under torture, was forced to confess the truth.[11] Now, after more than a millennium, this power would once again be vested solely in the state.

Harsnett's efforts, backed by his powerful superiors, did seriously restrict the practice of exorcism. Canon 72 of the new Church Canons of 1604 ruled that henceforth no minister, unless he had the special permission of his bishop, was to attempt 'upon any pretense whatsoever, whether of possession or obsession, by fasting and prayer, to cast out any devil or devils, under pain of the imputation of imposture or cozenage and deposition from the ministry.'[12] Since special permission was rarely, if ever, granted, in effect exorcism had been officially halted. But it proved easier to drive exorcism from the center to the periphery than to strip it entirely of its power. Exorcism had been a process of reintegration as well as a manifestation of authority; as the ethnographer Shirokogorov observed of the shamans of Siberia, exorcists could 'master' harmful spirits and restore 'psychic equilibrium' to whole communities as well as to individuals.[13] The pronouncements of English bishops could not suddenly banish from the land inner demons who stood, as Peter Brown puts it, 'for the intangible emotional undertones of ambiguous situations and for the uncertain motives of refractory individuals.'[14] The possessed gave voice to the rage, anxiety, and sexual frustration that built up easily in the authoritarian, patriarchal, impoverished, and plague-ridden world of early modern England. The Anglicans attempted to dismantle a corrupt and inadequate therapy without effecting a new and successful cure. In the absence of exorcism Harsnett could offer the possessed only the slender reed of Jacobean medicine; if the recently deciphered journal of the Buckinghamshire physician Richard Napier is at all representative, doctors in the period struggled to treat a significant number of cases of possession.[15]

But for Harsnett the problem does not really exist, for he argues that the great majority of cases of possession are either fraudulent or subtly called into existence by the ritual designed to treat them. Eliminate the cure and you eliminate the disease. He is forced to concede that at some distant time possession and exorcism were authentic, for Christ himself had driven a legion of unclean spirits out of a possessed man and into the Gadarene swine [Mark 5:1–19]; but the age of miracles has passed, and corporeal possession by demons is no longer possible. The spirit abroad is 'the spirit of illusion' [*Discovery*, p. A3]. Whether they profess to be Catholics or Calvinists does not matter; all modern exorcists practice the same time-honored trade: 'the feat of juggling and deluding the people by counterfeit miracles' [*Discovery*, p. A2]. Exorcists sometimes contend, Harsnett acknowledges, that the casting out of devils is not a miracle but a wonder – '*mirandum & non miraculum*' – but 'both terms spring from one root of wonder or marvel: an effect which a thing strangely done doth procure in the minds of the beholders, as being above the reach of nature and reason' [*Discovery*, p. A4[r–v]).

The significance of exorcism, then, lies not in any intrinsic quality of the ritual or in the character of the marks of possession but in the impression made upon the minds of the spectators. In *The Discovery of Witchcraft* (1584), a remarkable book that greatly influenced Harsnett, Reginald Scot detailed some of the means used to shape this impression: the cunning manipulation of popular superstitions; the exploitation of grief, fear, and credulity; the skillful handling of illusionistic devices developed for the stage; the blending of spectacle and commentary; the deliberate arousal of anxiety coupled with the promise to allay it. Puritan exorcists throw themselves into histrionic paroxysms of prayer; Catholic exorcists deploy holy water, smoldering brimstone, and sacred relics. They seem utterly absorbed in the plight of the wretches who writhe in spectacular contortions, vomit pins, display uncanny strength, foam at the mouth, cry out in weird voices. But all of this apparent absorption in the supernatural crisis is an illusion; there is nothing real out there on the bed, in the chair, on the pulpit. The only serious action is transpiring in the minds of the audience.

Hence the exorcists take care, notes Harsnett, to practice their craft only when there is 'a great assembly gathered together,' and the ritual is then explicitly presented to this assembly with a formal prologue: 'The company met, the *Exorcists* do tell them, *what a work of God they have in hand,* and after a long discourse, *how Sathan doth afflict the parties,* and *what strange things they shall see*: the said parties are brought forth, as it were a Bear to the stake, and being either bound in a chair, or otherwise held fast, they fall to their fits, and play their pranks point by point exactly, according as they have been instructed' [*Discovery*, p. 62].

What seems spontaneous is in fact carefully scripted, from the shaping of audience expectations to the rehearsal of the performers. Harsnett grants that to those who suspect no fraud the effect is extraordinarily powerful: 'They are cast thereby into a wonderful astonishment' [*Discovery*, p. 70]. Aroused by wonder to a heightened state of both attention and suggestibility, the beholders are led to see significance in the smallest gestures of the possessed and to apply that significance to their own lives. But the whole moving process is a dangerous fraud that should be exposed and punished in the courts.

To substantiate these charges the English church needed, in the language of spy stories, to 'turn' one of the participants in the spectacle of possession and exorcism. In the mid-1590s the authorities were alerted to the activities of a charismatic Puritan healer named John Darrel. Through fasting and prayer he had helped to exorcise one Thomas Darling, popularly known as the Boy of Burton, and had then gone on to a still greater success in a case of mass possession, known as the Seven in Lancashire. Alarmed by this success, the authorities in 1598 found what they were looking for: William Sommers, aged twenty-one, an unstable musician's apprentice in Nottingham who was being exorcized by Darrel in a series of spectacular spiritual encounters. Under great pressure Sommers confessed to imposture and exposed – or claimed to expose – Darrel's secret methods: 'As I did use any of the said gestures,' testified Sommers, recalling his first manifestation in Nottingham of the symptoms of possession,

Oh would M. Darrell say, to the standers by: see you not how he doth thus, and thus? These things signify that such and such sins do reign in this town. They also that were present having heard M. Darrell, would as I tossed with my hands, and tumbled up and down upon my bed presently collect and say: oh, he doth so for this sin, and so for that sin, whereby it came to pass, that I could do nothing in any of my fits, either that night or the day after, either stir my head, or any part of my body: look merrily, or sadly, sit or lie, speak or be silent, open or shut mine eyes, but some would still make an interpretation of it: as to be done by the Devil in me, to declare such sins in Nottingham, as they themselves imagined.   [*Discovery*, p. 117]

Darrel denied ever offering an interpretation of Sommers's gestures, but he confirmed the nature of the performance:

This evening, he acted many sins by signs & gestures, most lively representing & shadowing, them out unto us: as namely brawling, quarreling, fighting, swearing, robbing by the highways, picking and cutting of purses, burglary, whoredom, pride in men and women, hypocrisy, sluggishness in hearing of the word, drunkenness, gluttony, also dancing with the toys thereunto belonging, the manner of Antic dancers, the games of dicing and carding, the abuse of the Viol, with other instruments. At the end of sundry of these, he laughed exceedingly, diverse times clapping his hands on his thighs for joy: percase to shadow out the delight, that both himself, and sinners take in their sins. And at the end of some of them, as killing and stealing, he showed how he brought them to the Gallows, making a sign thereof. [*Discovery*, pp. 118–19]

According to Harsnett, on the Sunday following this display one of Darrel's colleagues delivered from the pulpit an 'authentical reading' of the 'dumb show,' and this reading was in turn followed by a popular ballad: a campaign, in short, to extend the exorcist's influence beyond the immediate circle of beholders to both the elite and the masses. Harsnett, in response, participates in a massive counter-campaign to destroy this influence. Hounding or imprisoning Darrel was not enough, for persecution could easily heighten his popular appeal, and even were he conveniently to disappear, he would be succeeded by others. The exorcist had to be attacked where he had his power: in the minds of beholders or potential beholders.

Accounts of exorcism in the late sixteenth and early seventeenth centuries make it clear that the spectacle of the symptoms of demonic possession had a profoundly disturbing effect on those who witnessed them. The spectacle was evidently more than that of physical or psychic anguish; after all, the men and women of this period would have been accustomed and perhaps hardened to the sight of abject misery. Quite apart from the spectacle of public maimings and executions, an Elizabethan who survived to adolescence must have already been an aficionado of human wretchedness.

Demonic possession was something more: it was utterly strange – a fearful visitation of the perverted spiritual presences of the other world – and at the same time uncannily intimate, for if the demons were exotic tormenters with weird names, the victims were neighbors enduring their trials in altogether familiar surroundings. Hence the testimony taken from those who witnessed the sufferings combines the homely and the bizarre: an evil spirit that appeared in Suffolk became 'a thick dark substance about a foot high, like to a sugar loaf, white on the top',[16] young Mary Glover's voice sounded to one witness like 'the hissing of a violent *Squib*,' to another like a '*Hen* that hath the *squack*,' to a third like 'the loathsome noise that a *Cat* maketh forcing to cast her gorge';[17] William Sommers's 'entrails shot up & down like a weavers shuttle.'[18] Sommers's cries seemed unutterably strange – he shrieked 'with 3 several voices so hideously, and so terribly,' a surgeon reports, 'as they were not like any human creature' – but each of the witnesses seems to have tried immediately to place the extraordinary events in the context of the familiar. William Aldred, a preacher, reports that he stood in a crowd of about one hundred and fifty persons and watched Sommers having his fits. What he noticed was Darrel praying and preaching; 'then the whole congregation breaking their hitherto continued silence cried out all at once as it were with one voice unto the Lord, to relieve the distressed person: and within a quarter of an hour, or thereabouts it pleased God to hear their prayers.' Joan Pie, the wife of Nottingham baker Robert Pie, also saw the fits; what she noticed was that suddenly Sommers 'was plucked round upon a heap, as though his body had lain like a great brown loaf.' Richard Mee, butcher, remarked that Sommers suddenly screeched 'like a swine when he is in sticking.'[19]

The domestication of the demonic (a zany Elizabethan version of *What Do People Do All Day?*) only serves to intensify for most of the witnesses the wonder of the supernatural visitation. Harsnett's task is to demolish this experience of wonder; he seeks to shine the sharp, clear light of ridicule on the exorcist's mysteries and thus to expose them as shabby tricks. Among the demoniac's most frightening symptoms was a running lump – variously described as resembling a kitten, a mouse, a halfpenny white loaf, a goose egg, a French walnut, and a hazelnut – that could be seen under the coverlet, moving across his body as he lay in a trance. One of the bystanders, apparently less awestruck than the rest, impulsively pounced on the lump and found that he had seized Sommers's hand. In his confession Sommers confirmed that he achieved his effect by no more complicated means than moving his fingers and toes under the coverlet. It seems impossible for this miserable expedient to produce so much as a frisson, but a skeptical witness, quoted by Harsnett, tried it out at home: 'And it fell out to be so agreeable with that which the boy did, as my wife being in bed with me, was on the sudden in great fear, that *Somers* spirit had followed me' [*Discovery*, p. 240].

Held up to the light, the devil's coin is a pathetic counterfeit, fit only to frighten women and boys. Yet Harsnett is not content simply to publish Sommers's confession of fraud, in part, perhaps, because there was reason to believe that the confession was forced, in part because even if Sommers were proven to be a mere actor, other demoniacs clearly believed in all sincerity that they were possessed by devils. Moreover, the polemic had to be conducted with an odd blend of rhetorical violence and doctrinal caution. 'If neither possession, nor witchcraft (contrary to that hath been so long generally & confidently affirmed),' wrote Darrel in his own defense, 'why should we think that there are Devils? If no Devils, no God.'[20]

No one in the Anglican church was prepared to deny the existence of Satan, any more than they were prepared to deny the existence of God. What role did Satan play then in the fraudulent dramas in which his name figured so prominently? In the case of Catholic exorcists, Harsnett is prepared to locate the demonic in the very figures who profess themselves to be the agents of God:

Dissemblers, jugglers, impostors, players with God, his son, his angels, his saints: devisers of new devils, feigned tormentors of spirits, usurpers of the key of the bottomless pit, whippers, scourgers, batfoulers of fiends, Pandars, Ganimedeans, enhancers of lust, deflowerers of virgins, defilers of houses, uncivil, unmanly, unnatural venereans, offerers of their own mass to supposed devils, depravers of their own relics, applying them to unspeakable, detestable, monstrous deformities: prostituters of all the rites, ornaments, and ceremonies of their Church to impure villainies: profaners of all parts of the service, worship, and honour of God: violators of tombs, sacrilegious, blasphemers of God, the blessed Trinity, and the virgin *Mary*, in the person of a counterfeit devil: seducers of subjects, plotters, conspirators, contrivers of bloody & detestable treasons, against their anointed Sovereign: it would pose all hell to sample them with such another dozen. [*Declaration*, pp. 160–61]

In short, they were Jesuits. But Darrel was a Protestant and, by all accounts, a man of austere and upright life. If he could not be portrayed as the devil incarnate, where was the devil to be found? One answer, proposed by Harsnett's allies John Deacon and John Walker, was that Satan could produce the *illusion* of demonic possession. 'The *Devil* (being always desirous to work among the dear children of *God* the greatest *disturbance* that may be, and finding withal some such lewd disposed *person* as is naturally inclined to all manner of *knaveries*) he taketh the opportunity of so fit a *subject*, and worketh so cunningly upon the *corruption* of *that lewd persons nature*, as the *party* himself is easily brought to believe, and to bear others also in hand, that he is (in deed and in truth) *essentially possessed of Satan*.'[21]

The problem with this argument is that it undermines the clarity and force of the confession of fraudulence the authorities had worked so hard to obtain. That confession was intended to establish a fixed, stable opposition between counterfeit – the false claim of demonic agency – and reality: the unblinking, disenchanted grasp of the mechanics of illusion mongering. Now after all the devil is discovered hovering behind the demoniac's performance. And if the Prince of Darkness is actually present, then the alleged evidence of fraudulence need not trouble the exorcist. For as Satan in possessing someone has sought to hide himself under the cover of human agency, so when detected he may wish to convince observers that the signs of possession are counterfeits. 'Sathan in his subtlety,' argues Darrel, 'hath done in the boy some sleight and trifling things, at divers times, of purpose to deceive the beholders, and to bear them in hand, that he did never greater things in him: thereby to induce them to think, that he was a counterfeit' [*Discovery*, p. 231].[22]

If Satan can counterfeit counterfeiting, there can be no definitive confession, and the prospect opens of an infinite regress of disclosure and uncertainty. How shall I know that this is thou *William Somers?*' asked Darrel, after the boy confessed to fraud. At first Sommers had been possessed only in body; now, said the exorcist, he is 'also possessed in soul' [*Discovery*, p. 186]. As Harsnett perceives, this 'circular folly' at the heart of the practice of exorcism prevents a decisive judicial falsification. What Harsnett needs is not further evidence of fraud in particular cases – for such evidence can always be subverted by the same strategy of demonic doubt – but a counter-strategy to disclose fraudulence *always and everywhere*: in every gesture of the demoniac, in every word and deed of the exorcist. To demystify exorcism definitively, Harsnett must demonstrate not only why the ritual was so empty but why it was so effective, why beholders could be induced to believe that they were witnessing the ultimate confrontation between good and evil, why a few miserable shifts could produce the experience of horror and wonder. He must identify not merely the specific institutional motives behind exorcism – the treasonous designs of the Catholic church or the seditious mischief of self-styled Protestant saints – but the source of the extraordinary power in exorcism itself, a power that seems to transcend the specific and contradictory ideological designs of its practitioners. He needs an explanatory model, at once metaphor and analytical tool, by which all beholders will see fraud where once they saw God. Harsnett finds that explanatory model in *theater*.[23]

Exorcisms, Harsnett argues, are stage plays, most often tragi-comedies, that cunningly conceal their theatrical inauthenticity and hence deprive the spectators of the rational disenchantment that frames the experience of a play. The audience in a theater knows that its misrecognition of reality is temporary, deliberate, and playful; the exorcist seeks to make the misrecognition permanent and invisible. Harsnett is determined to make the spectators see the theater round them, to make them understand that what seems spontaneous is rehearsed, what seems involuntary carefully crafted, what seems unpredictable scripted.

Not all of the participants themselves may fully realize that they are in a stage play. The account in *A Declaration of Egregious Popish Impostures* presents the exorcists, Father Edmunds and his cohorts, as self-conscious professionals and the demoniacs (mostly impressionable young servingwomen and unstable, down-at-heels young gentlemen) as amateurs subtly drawn into the demonic stage business. Those selected to play the possessed in effect learn their roles without realizing at first that they are roles.

The priests begin by talking conspicuously about successful exorcisms abroad and describing in lurid detail the precise symptoms of the possessed. They then await occasions on which to improvise: a servingman 'being pinched with penury, & hunger, did lie but a night, or two, abroad in the fields, and being a melancholic person, was scared with lightning, and thunder, that happened in the night, & lo, an evident sign, that the man was possessed' [24]; a dissolute young gentleman 'had a spice of the *Hysterica passio*' or, as it is popularly called, 'the Mother' [25],[24] and that too is a sign of possession. An inflamed toe, a pain in the side, a fright taken from the sudden leaping of a cat, a fall in the kitchen, an intense depression following the loss of a beloved child – all are occasions for the priests to step forward and detect the awful presence of the demonic, whereupon the young 'scholars,' as Harsnett wryly terms the naive performers, '*frame* themselves jump and fit unto the Priests humors, to mop, mow, jest, rail, rave, roar, commend & discommend, and as the priests would have them, upon fitting occasions (according to the difference of times, places, and comers in) in all things to play the devils accordingly' [38].

To glimpse the designing clerical playwright behind the performance is to transform terrifying supernatural events into a human strategy. One may then glimpse the specific material and symbolic interests served by this particular strategy, above all by its clever disguising of the fact that it is a strategy.

The most obvious means by which the authorities of the English church and state could make manifest the theatricality of exorcism was the command performance: the ability to mime the symptoms at will would, it was argued, decisively prove the possession a counterfeit. Hence we find the performance test frequently applied in investigations of alleged supernatural visitations. In the 1590s, for example, Ann Kerke was accused of bewitching a child to death and casting the child's sister into a fit that closely resembled that of a demoniac: 'her mouth being drawn aside like a purse, her teeth gnashing together, her mouth foaming, and her eyes staring.'[25] The judge, Lord Anderson, ordered the sister to 'show how she was tormented: she said she could not show it, but when the fit was on her' [100]. The reply was taken to be strong corroboration of the authenticity of the charge, and Ann Kerke was hanged.

A similar, if subtler, use of the performance test occurs in the early 1620s. Thomas Perry, known as the Boy of Bilson, would fall into fits upon hearing the opening verse from the gospel of John; other verses from Scriptures did not have the same effect. Three Catholic priests were called in to exorcise the evil spirit that possessed him. During the boy's fit – watched by a large crowd – one of the priests commanded the devil 'to show by the sheet before him, how he would use one dying out of the Roman Catholic Church?' who very unwillingly, yet at length obeyed, tossing, plucking, haling, and biting the sheet, that it did make many to weep and cry forth.'[26] A similar but still fiercer demonstration was evoked in response to the names Luther, Calvin, and Fox. Then, predictably, the priest commanded the devil 'to show what power he had on a good Catholic that died out of mortal sin? he thrust down his arms, trembled, holding down his head, and did no more' [51].[27] The Catholics triumphantly published an account of the case, *A Faithful Relation.*

English officials, understandably annoyed by such propaganda, remanded Perry to the custody of the bishop of Coventry and Lichfield. To test if the boy was authentically possessed or 'an execrable wretch, who playest the devils part,' the Bishop read aloud the verse that set off the symptoms; the boy fell into fits. When the boy recovered, the bishop told him that he would read the same verse in Greek; once again the boy fell into fits. But in fact the Bishop had not read the correct verse, and the boy had been tricked into performance. Since the Devil was 'so ancient a scholar as of almost 6000 years standing' [59], he should have known Greek. The possession was proved to be a counterfeit, and the boy, it is said, confessed that he had been instructed by an old man who promised that he would no longer have to go to school.

The Protestants now produced their own account of the case, *The Boy of Bilson, or, A True Discovery of the Late Notorious Impostures of Certain Romish Priests in Their Pretended Exorcism.* 'Although these and the like pranks have been hissed of[f] the Stage, for stale and gross forgeries,' the author declares, since the Catholics have ventured to publish their version, it is necessary to set the record straight. A reader of the Catholic account should understand 'that he hath seen a *Comedy*, wherein the Actors, which present themselves, are these, A crafty *old man*, teaching the feats and pranks of counterfeiting a person *Demoniacal* and possessed of the *Devil*; the next, a most docible, subtle, and expert young *Boy*, far more dextrous in the Practique part, than his Master was in the Theory; after him appear three Romish *Priests*, the Authors of seducement, conjuring their only imaginary *Devils*, which they brought with them; and lastly, a *Chorus* of credulous people easily seduced, not so much by the subtlety of those *Priests*, as by their own sottishness'[9].

Performance kills belief; or rather acknowledging theatricality kills the credibility of the supernatural. Hence in the case of William Sommers the authorities not only took the demoniac's confession of fraud but also insisted that he perform his simulated convulsions before the mayor and three aldermen of Nottingham. If he could act his symptoms, then the possession would be decisively falsified. Darrel countered that 'if he can act them all in such manner and form as is deposed, then he is, either still possessed, or more than a man: for no humans power can do the like.'[28] But the officials denied that the original performances themselves, stripped of the awe that the spectators brought to them, were particularly impressive. Sommers's possession, Harsnett had said, was a 'dumb show' that depended upon an interpretive supplement, a commentary designed at once to intensify and control the response of the audience by explicating both the significance and the relevance of each gesture. Now the state would in effect seize control of the commentary and thereby alter the spectators' perceptions. Sommers's audience would no longer see a demoniac; they would see someone playing a demoniac. Demonic possession would become theater.

After the civic officials had satisfied themselves that Sommers's possession was a theatrical imposture, an ecclesiastical commission was convened to view a repeat performance. In a bizarre twist, however, Sommers unexpectedly withdrew his confession before the startled commissioners, and he signaled this withdrawal by falling into spectacular fits before the moment appointed for the performance. The commissioners, unprepared to view these convulsions as a deliberate or self-conscious exhibition, declared that they were evidently of supernatural origin. But in less than two weeks, before the mayor and two justices, the wretched Sommers, under renewed state pressure, reaffirmed his confession of fraud, and a few days later he once again 'proved' his claim by simulating fits, this time before the assize judge. The next step might have been to ask a court of law to determine whether Sommers's expressly simulated fits were identical to those he underwent when he was not confessing imposture. But the authorities evidently regarded this step, which Darrel himself demanded,[29] as too risky; instead, without calling Sommers to appear, they first obtained a conviction of the exorcist on charges of imposture and then launched a national campaign to persuade the public that possession and exorcism were illicit forms of theater.

Sommers's oscillation between the poles of authenticity and illusion are for Harsnett an emblem of the maddening doubleness implicit in the theatricality of exorcism: its power to impose itself on beholders and its half-terrifying, half-comic emptiness. Exorcists could, of course, react by demonizing the theater: Puritans like Darrel argued at length that the playhouse was Satan's temple, while the Jesuit exorcists operating clandestinely in England implied that theatrical representations of the devil in mystery plays were not mere imitations of reality but lively images based on a deep bond of resemblance. When in the 1580s a devil possessing Sara Williams refused to tell his name, the exorcist, according to the Catholic *Book of Miracles*, 'caused to be drawn upon a piece of paper, the picture of a vice in a play, and the same to be burned with hallowed brimstone, whereat the devil cried out as being grievously tormented.'[30] Harsnett remarks in response that 'it was a pretty part in the old Church-plays, when the nimble Vice would skip up nimbly like Jacke an Apes into the devils neck, and ride the devil a course, and belabour him with his wooden dagger, til he made him roar, whereat the people would laugh to see the devil so vice-haunted' [114–15]. Sara's devils, he concludes contemptuously, 'be surely some of those old vice-haunted cashiered wooden-beaten devils, that were wont to frequent the stages . . . who are so scared with the *Idea* of a vice, & a dagger, as they durst never since look a paper-vice in the face' [115]. For Harsnett the attempt to demonize the theater merely exposes the theatricality of the demonic; once we acknowledge this theatricality, he suggests, we can correctly perceive the actual genre of the performance: not tragedy but farce.

The theatricality of exorcism, to which the *Declaration* insistently calls attention, has been noted repeatedly by modern ethnographers who do not share Harsnett's reforming zeal or his sense of outrage.[31] In an illuminating study of possession among the Ethiopians of Gondar, Michel Leiris notes that the healer carefully instructs the *zâr*, or spirit, who has seized on someone how to behave: the types of cries appropriate to the occasion, the expected violent contortions, the 'decorum,' as Harsnett would put it, of the trance state.[32] The treatment is in effect an initiation into the performance of the symptoms, which are then cured precisely because they conform to the stereotype of the healing process. One must not conclude, writes Leiris, that there are no 'real' – that is, sincerely experienced – cases of possession, for many of the patients (principally young women and slaves) seem genuinely ill, but at the same time no cases are exempt from artifice [27–8]. Between authentic possession, spontaneous and involuntary, and inauthentic possession, simulated to provide a show or to extract some material or moral benefit, there are so many subtle shadings that it is impossible to draw a firm boundary [94–5]. Possession in Gondar *is* theater, but theater that cannot confess its own theatrical nature, for this is not 'theater played' (*théâtre joué*) but 'theater lived' (*théâtre vécu*), lived not only by the spirit-haunted actor but by the audience. Those who witness a possession may at any moment be themselves possessed, and even if they are untouched by the *zâr*, they remain participants rather than passive spectators. For the theatrical performance is not shielded from them by an impermeable membrane; possession is extraordinary but not marginal, a heightened but not separate state. In possession, writes Leiris, the collective life itself takes the form of theater [96].

Precisely those qualities that fascinate and charm the ethnographer disgust the embattled clergyman: where Leiris can write of 'authentic' possession in the unspoken assurance that none of his readers actually believe in the existence of 'zârs,' Harsnett, granted no such assurance and culturally threatened by the alternative vision of reality, struggles to prove that possession is by definition inauthentic; where the former sees a complex ritual integrated into the social process, the latter sees 'a *Stygian* comedy to make silly people afraid' [69]; where the former sees the theatrical expression of collective life, the latter sees the theatrical promotion of specific and malevolent institutional interests. And where Leiris's central point is that possession is a theater that does not confess its own theatricality, Harsnett's concern is to enforce precisely such a confession: the last 112 pages of *A Declaration of Egregious Popish Impostures* reprint the 'several Examinations, and confessions of the parties pretended to be possessed, and dispossessed by *Weston* the Jesuit, and his adherents: set down word for word as they were taken upon oath before her Majesty's Commissioners for causes Ecclesiastical' [172]. These transcripts prove, according to Harsnett, that the solemn ceremony of exorcism is a 'play of sacred miracles,' a 'wonderful pageant' [2], a 'devil Theater' [106].

The confession of theatricality, for Harsnett, demolishes exorcism. Theater is not the disinterested expression of the popular spirit but the indelible mark of falsity, tawdriness, and rhetorical manipulation. And these sinister qualities are rendered diabolical by the very concealment of theatricality that so appeals to Leiris. The spectators do not know that they are responding to a powerful, if sleazy, tragicomedy; their tears and joy, their transports of 'commiseration and compassion' [74], are rendered up not to a troupe of acknowledged players but to seditious Puritans or to the supremely dangerous Catholic church. For Harsnett the theatrical seduction is not merely a Jesuitical strategy; it is the essence of the church itself: Catholicism is a 'Mimic superstition' [20].[33]

Harsnett's response is to try to drive the Catholic church into the theater, just as during the Reformation Catholic clerical garments – the copes and albs and amices and stoles that were the glories of medieval textile crafts – were sold to the players. An actor in a history play taking the part of an English bishop could conceivably have worn the actual robes of the character he was representing. Far more than thrift is involved here. The transmigration of a single ecclesiastical cloak from the vestry to the wardrobe may stand as an emblem of the more complex and elusive institutional exchanges that are my subject: a sacred sign, designed to be displayed before a crowd of men and women, is emptied, made negotiable, traded from one institution to another. Such exchanges are rarely so tangible; they are not usually registered in inventories, not often sealed with a cash payment. Nonetheless they occur constantly, for through institutional negotiation and exchange differentiated expressive systems, distinct cultural discourses, are fashioned.

What happens when the piece of cloth is passed from the church to the playhouse? A consecrated object is reclassified, assigned a cash value, transferred from a sacred to a profane setting, deemed suitable for the stage. The theater company is willing to pay for the object not because it contributes to naturalistic representation but because it still bears a symbolic value, however attenuated. On the bare Elizabethan stage costumes were particularly important – companies were willing to pay more for a good costume than for a good play – and that importance in turn reflected the culture's fetishistic obsession with clothes as a mark of status and degree. And if for the theater the acquisition of clerical garments was a significant appropriation of symbolic power, why would the church part with that power? Because for the Anglican polemicists, as for a long tradition of moralists in the West, the theater signifies the unscrupulous manipulation for profit of popular faith; the cynical use of setting and props to generate unthinking consent; the external and trivialized staging of what should be deeply inward; the tawdry triumph of spectacle over reason; the evacuation of the divine presence from religious mystery, leaving only vivid but empty ceremonies; the transformation of faith into bad faith.[34] Hence selling Catholic vestments to the players was a form of symbolic aggression: a vivid, wry reminder that Catholicism, as Harsnett puts it, is 'the Pope's playhouse.'[35]

This blend of appropriation and aggression is similarly at work in the transfer of possession and exorcism from sacred to profane representation. A Declaration of Egregious Popish Impostures takes pains to identify exorcism not merely with 'the theatrical' – a category that scarcely exists for Harsnett – but with the actual theater; at issue is not so much a metaphorical concept as a functioning institution. For if Harsnett can drive exorcism into the theater – if he can show that the stately houses in which the rituals were performed were playhouses, that the sacred garments were what he calls a 'lousy holy wardrobe' [78], that the terrifying writhings were simulations, that the uncanny signs and wonders were contemptible stage tricks, that the devils were the 'cashiered wooden-beaten' Vices from medieval drama [115], and that the exorcists were 'vagabond players, that coast from Town to Town' [149] – then the ceremony and everything for which it stands will, as far as he is concerned, be emptied out. And with this emptying out Harsnett will have driven exorcism from the center to the periphery – in the case of London quite literally to the periphery, where increasingly stringent urban regulation had already driven the public playhouses.

In this symbolically charged zone of pollution, disease, and licentious entertainment Harsnett seeks to situate the practice of exorcism.[36] What had once occurred in solemn glory at the very center of the city would now be staged alongside the culture's other vulgar spectacles and illusions. Indeed the sense of the theater's tawdriness, marginality, and emptiness – the sense that everything the players touch is rendered hollow – underlies Harsnett's analysis not only of exorcism but of the entire Catholic church. Demonic possession is a particularly attractive cornerstone for such an analysis, not only because of its histrionic intensity but because the theater itself is by its nature bound up with possession. Harsnett did not have to believe that the cult of Dionysus out of which the Greek drama evolved was a cult of possession; even the ordinary and familiar theater of his own time depended upon the apparent transformation of the actor into the voice, the actions, and the face of another.

II

With his characteristic opportunism and artistic self-consciousness, Shakespeare in his first known play, *The Comedy of Errors* (1590), was already toying with the connection between theater, illusion, and spurious possession. Antipholus of Syracuse, accosted by his twin's mistress, imagines that he is encountering the devil: 'Sathan, avoid. I charge thee tempt me not' [IV iii 48]. The Ephesian Antipholus's wife, Adriana, dismayed by the apparently mad behavior of her husband, imagines that the devil has possessed him, and she dutifully calls in an exorcist: 'Good Doctor Pinch, you are a conjurer,/Establish him in his true sense again.' Pinch begins the solemn ritual:

> I charge thee, Sathan, hous'd within this man,
> To yield possession to my holy prayers,
> And to thy state of darkness hie thee straight:
> I conjure thee by all the saints in heaven!   [IV iv 54–7]

But he is interrupted with a box on the ears from the outraged husband: 'Peace, doting wizard, peace! I am not mad.' For the exorcist, such denials only confirm the presence of an evil spirit: 'the fiend is strong within him' [IV iv 107]. At the scene's end, Antipholus is dragged away to be 'bound and laid in some dark room.'

The false presumption of demonic possession in *The Comedy of Errors* is not the result of deception; it is an instance of what Shakespeare's source calls a 'suppose' – an attempt to make sense of a series of bizarre actions gleefully generated by the comedy's screwball coincidences. Exorcism is the straw people clutch at when the world seems to have gone mad. In *Twelfth Night*, written some ten years later, Shakespeare's view of exorcism, though still comic, has darkened. Possession now is not a mistaken 'suppose' but a fraud, a malicious practical joke played on Malvolio. 'Pray God he be not bewitch'd!' [III iv 101] Maria piously exclaims at the sight of the cross-gartered, leering gull, and when he is out of earshot, Fabian laughs: 'If this were play'd upon a stage now, I could condemn it as an improbable fiction' [III iv 127–8].[37] The theatrical self-consciousness is intensified when Feste the clown is brought in to conduct a mock exorcism: 'I would I were the first that ever dissembled in such a gown' [IV ii 5–6], he remarks sententiously as he disguises himself as Sir Topas the curate. If the jibe had a specific reference for the play's original audience, it would be to the Puritan Darrel, who had only recently been convicted of dissembling in the exorcism of Sommers. Now, the scene would suggest, the tables are being turned on the self-righteous fanatic. 'Good Sir Topas,' pleads Malvolio, 'do not think I am mad; they have laid me here in hideous darkness.' 'Fie, thou dishonest Sathan!' Feste replies; 'I call thee by the most modest terms, for I am one of those gentle ones that will use the devil himself with courtesy' [IV ii 29–33].

By 1600, then, Shakespeare had clearly marked out possession and exorcism as frauds, so much so that in *All's Well That Ends Well* a few years later he could casually use the term *exorcist* as a synonym for illusion monger: 'Is there no exorcist/Beguiles the truer office of mine eyes?' cries the King of France when Helena, whom he thought dead, appears before him; 'Is't real that I see?' [V iii 304–6]. When in 1603 Harsnett was whipping exorcism toward the theater, Shakespeare was already at the entrance to the Globe to welcome it.

Given Harsnett's frequent expressions of the 'antitheatrical prejudice,' this welcome may seem strange, but in fact nothing in *A Declaration of Egregious Popish Impostures* necessarily implies hostility to the theater as a professional institution. It was Darrel, not Harsnett, who represented an implacable threat to the theater, for where the Anglican polemicist saw the theatrical in the demonic, the Puritan polemicist saw the demonic in the theatrical: 'The Devil,' wrote Stephen Gosson, 'is the efficient cause of plays.'[38] Harsnett's work attacks a form of theater that pretends it is not entertainment but sober reality; his polemic virtually depends upon the existence of an officially designated commercial theater, marked off openly from all other forms and ceremonies of public life precisely by virtue of its freely acknowledged fictionality. Where there is no pretense to truth, there can be no *imposture*: this argument permits so ontologically anxious a figure as Sir Philip Sidney to defend poetry – 'Now for the poet, he nothing affirms, and therefore never lieth.'

In this spirit Puck playfully defends *A Midsummer Night's Dream*:

> If we shadows have offended,
> Think but this, and all is mended,
> That you have but slumb'red here
> While these visions did appear.
> And this weak and idle theme,
> No more yielding but a dream.   [v i 423–8]

With a similarly frank admission of illusion Shakespeare can open the theater to Harsnett's polemic. Indeed, as if Harsnett's momentum carried *him* into the theater along with the fraud he hotly pursues, Shakespeare in *King Lear* stages not only exorcism, but Harsnett *on* exorcism: 'Five fiends have been in poor Tom at once: of lust, as Obidicut; Hobbididance, prince of dumbness; Mahu, of stealing; Modo, of murder, Flibbertigibbet, of mopping and mowing, who since possesses chambermaids and waiting-women' [IV i 58–63].[39]

Those in the audience who had read Harsnett's book or heard of the notorious Buckinghamshire exorcisms would recognize in Edgar's lines an odd joking allusion to the chambermaids, Sara and Friswood Williams, and the waiting woman, Ann Smith, principal actors in Father Edmunds's 'devil Theater.' The humor of the anachronism here is akin to that of the Fool's earlier quip, 'This prophecy Merlin shall make, for I live before his time' [III ii 95–6];

both sallies of wit show a cheeky self-consciousness that dares deliberately to violate the historical setting to remind the audience of the play's conspicuous doubleness, its simultaneous distance and contemporaneity.

A Declaration of Egregious Popish Impostures supplies Shakespeare not only with an uncanny anachronism but also with the model for Edgar's histrionic disguise. For it is not the *authenticity* of the demonology that the playwright finds in Harsnett – the usual reason for authorial recourse to a specialized source (as, for example, to a military or legal handbook) – but rather the inauthenticity of a theatrical role. Shakespeare appropriates for Edgar a documented fraud, complete with an impressive collection of what the *Declaration* calls 'uncouth non-significant names' [46] that have been made up to sound exotic and that carry with them a faint but ineradicable odor of spuriousness.

In Sidney's *Arcadia*, which provided the outline of the Gloucester subplot, the good son, having escaped his father's misguided attempt to kill him, becomes a soldier in another land and quickly distinguishes himself. Shakespeare insists not only on Edgar's perilous fall from his father's favor but upon his marginalization: Edgar becomes the possessed Poor 'Tom, the outcast with no possibility of working his way back toward the center. 'My neighbors,' writes John Bunyan in the 1660s, 'were amazed at this my great conversion from prodigious profaneness to something like a moral life; and truly so well they might for this my conversion was as great as for a Tom of Bethlem to become a sober man.'[40] Although Edgar is only a pretend Tom o' Bedlam and can return to the community when it is safe to do so, the force of Harsnett's argument makes mimed possession even more marginal and desperate than the real thing.

Indeed Edgar's desperation is bound up with the stress of 'counterfeiting,' a stress he has already noted in the presence of the mad and ruined Lear and now, in the lines I have just quoted, feels more intensely in the presence of his blinded and ruined father. He is struggling with the urge to stop playing or, as he puts it, with the feeling that he 'cannot daub it further' [IV i 52]. Why he does not simply reveal himself to Gloucester at this point is unclear. 'And yet I must' is all he says of his continued disguise, as he recites the catalog of devils and leads his despairing father off to Dover Cliff.[41]

The subsequent episode – Gloucester's suicide attempt – deepens the play's brooding upon spurious exorcism. 'It is a good *decorum* in a Comedy,' writes Harsnett, 'to give us empty names for things, and to tell us of strange Monsters within, where there be none' [142]; so too the 'Miracle-minter' Father Edmunds and his fellow exorcists manipulate their impressionable gulls: 'The priests do report often in their patients hearing the dreadful forms, similitudes, and shapes, that the devils use to depart in out of those possessed bodies. . . : and this they tell with so grave a countenance, pathetical terms, and accommodate action, as it leaves a very deep impression in the memory, and fancy of their actors' [142–3]. Thus by the power of theatrical suggestion the anxious subjects on whom the priests work their charms come to believe that they too have witnessed the devil depart in grotesque form from their own bodies, whereupon the priests turn their eyes heavenward and give thanks to the Blessed Virgin. In much the same manner Edgar persuades Gloucester that he stands on a high cliff, and then, after his credulous father has flung himself forward, Edgar switches roles and pretends that he is a bystander who has seen a demon depart from the old man:

> As I stood here below, methought his eyes
> Were two full moons; he had a thousand noses,
> Horns welk'd and waved like the enridged sea.
> It was some fiend; therefore, thou happy father,
> Think that the clearest gods, who make them honors
> Of men's impossibilities, have preserved thee.

> [IV vi 69–74]

Edgar tries to create in Gloucester an experience of awe and wonder so intense that it can shatter his suicidal despair and restore his faith in the benevolence of the gods: 'Thy life's a miracle' [IV vi 55], he tells his father.[42] For Shakespeare as for Harsnett this miracle minting is the product of specifically histrionic manipulations; the scene at Dover is a disenchanted analysis of both religious and theatrical illusions. Walking about on a perfectly flat stage, Edgar does to Gloucester what the theater usually does to the audience: he persuades his father to discount the evidence of his senses – 'Methinks the ground is even' – and to accept a palpable fiction: 'Horrible steep' [IV vi 3]. But the audience at a play never absolutely accepts such fictions: we enjoy being brazenly lied to, we welcome for the sake of pleasure what we know to be untrue, but we withhold from the theater the simple assent we grant to everyday reality. And we enact this withholding when, depending on the staging, either we refuse to believe that Gloucester is on a cliff above Dover Beach or we realize that what we thought was a cliff (in the convention of theatrical representation) is in reality flat ground.

Hence in the midst of the apparent convergence of exorcism and theater, we return to the difference that enables *King Lear* to borrow comfortably from Harsnett: the theater elicits from us complicity rather than belief. Demonic possession is responsibly marked out for the audience as a theatrical fraud, designed to gull the unsuspecting: monsters such as the fiend with the thousand noses are illusions most easily imposed on the old, the blind, and the despairing; evil comes not from the mysterious otherworld of demons but from this world, the world of court and family intrigue. In *King Lear* there are no ghosts, as there are in *Richard III, Julius Caesar,* or *Hamlet*; no witches, as in *Macbeth*; no mysterious music of departing daemons, as in *Antony and Cleopatra.*

King Lear is haunted by a sense of rituals and beliefs that are no longer efficacious, that have been *emptied out.* The characters appeal again and again to the pagan gods, but the gods remain utterly silent.[43] Nothing answers to human questions but human voices; nothing breeds about the heart but human desires; nothing inspires awe or terror but human suffering and human depravity. For all the invocation of the gods in *King Lear,* it is clear that there are no devils.

Edgar is no more possessed than the sanest of us, and we can see for ourselves that there was no demon standing by Gloucester's side. Likewise Lear's madness has no supernatural origin; it is linked, as in Harsnett, to *hysterica passio,* exposure to the elements, and extreme anguish, and its cure comes at the hands not of an exorcist but of a doctor. His prescription involves neither religious rituals (as in Catholicism) nor fasting and prayer (as in Puritanism) but tranquilized sleep:

> Our foster-nurse of nature is repose,
> The which he lacks; that to provoke in him
> Are many simples operative, whose power
> Will close the eye of anguish.   [IV iv 12–15][44]

King Lear's relation to Harsnett's book is one of reiteration then, a reiteration that signals a deeper and unexpressed institutional exchange. The official church dismantles and cedes to the players he powerful mechanisms of an unwanted and dangerous charisma; in return the players confirm the charge that those mechanisms are theatrical and hence illusory. The material structure of Elizabethan and Jacobean public theaters heightened this confirmation; unlike medieval drama, which was more fully integrated into society, Shakespeare's drama took place in carefully demarcated playgrounds. *King Lear* offers a double corroboration of Harsnett's arguments. Within the play, Edgar's possession is clearly designated as a fiction, and the play itself is bounded by the institutional signs of fictionality: the wooden walls of the play space, payment for admission, known actors playing the parts, applause, the dances that followed the performance.

The theatrical confirmation of the official position is neither superficial nor unstable. And yet, I want now to suggest, Harsnett's arguments are alienated from themselves when they make their appearance on the Shakespearean stage. This alienation may be set in the context of a more general observation: the closer Shakespeare seems to a source, the more faithfully he reproduces it on stage, the more devastating and decisive his transformation of it. Let us take, for a small initial instance, Shakespeare's borrowing from Harsnett of the unusual adjective *corky* – that is, sapless, dry, withered. The word appears in the *Declaration* in the course of a sardonic explanation of why, despite the canonist Mengus's rule that only old women are to be exorcised, Father Edmunds and his crew have a particular fondness for tying in a chair and exorcising young women. Along with more graphic sexual innuendos, Harsnett observes that the theatrical role of a demoniac requires 'certain actions, motions, distortions, dislocations, writhings, tumblings, and turbulent passions . . . not to be performed but by suppleness of sinews. . . . It would (I fear me) pose all the cunning Exorcists, that are this day to be found, to teach an old corky woman to writhe, tumble, curvet, and fetch her morris gambols' [23].

Now Shakespeare's eye was caught by the word 'corky,' and he reproduces it in a reference to old Gloucester. But what had been a flourish of Harsnett's typically bullying comic style becomes part of the horror of an almost unendurable scene, a scene of torture that begins when Cornwall orders his servant to take the captive Gloucester and 'Bind fast his corky arms' [III vii 29]. The note of bullying humor is still present in the word, but it is present in the character of the torturer.

This one-word instance of repetition as transvaluation may suggest in the smallest compass what happens to Harsnett's work in the course of *Lear*. The *Declaration*'s arguments are loyally reiterated, but in a curiously divided form. The voice of skepticism is assimilated to Cornwall, to Goneril, and above all to Edmund, whose 'naturalism' is exposed as the argument of the younger and illegitimate son bent on displacing his legitimate older brother and eventually on destroying his father. The fraudulent possession and exorcism are given to the legitimate Edgar, who is forced to such shifts by the nightmarish persecution directed against him. Edgar adopts the role of Poor Tom not out of a corrupt will to deceive but out of a commendable desire to survive. Modo, Mahu, and the rest are fakes, exactly as Harsnett said they were, but Edgar's impostures are the venial sins of a will to endure. And even 'venial sins' is too strong: the clever inventions enable a decent and unjustly persecuted man to live. Similarly, there is no grotesque monster standing on the cliff with Gloucester – there is not even a cliff – but only Edgar, himself hunted down like an animal, trying desperately to save his father from suicidal despair.

All of this has an odd and unsettling resemblance to the situation of the Jesuits in England, if viewed from an unofficial perspective.[45] The resemblance does not necessarily resolve itself into an allegory in which Catholicism is revealed to be the persecuted legitimate elder brother forced to defend himself by means of theatrical illusions against the cold persecution of his skeptical bastard brother Protestantism. But the possibility of such a radical undermining of the orthodox position exists, and not merely in the cool light of our own historical distance. In 1610 a company of traveling players in Yorkshire included *King Lear* and *Pericles* in a repertoire that included a 'St. Christopher Play' whose performance came to the attention of the Star Chamber. The plays were performed in the manor house of a recusant couple, Sir John and Lady Julyan Yorke, and the players themselves and their organizer, Sir Richard Cholmeley, were denounced for recusancy by their Puritan neighbor, Sir Posthumus Hoby.[46] It is difficult to resist the conclusion that someone in Stuart Yorkshire believed that *King Lear*, despite its apparent staging of a fraudulent possession, was not hostile, was strangely sympathetic even, to the situation of persecuted Catholics. At the very least, we may suggest, the current of sympathy is enough to undermine the intended effect of Harsnett's *Declaration*: an intensified adherence to the central system of official values. In Shakespeare, the realization that demonic possession is a theatrical imposture leads not to a clarification – the clear-eyed satisfaction of the man who refuses to be gulled – but to a deeper uncertainty, a loss of moorings, in the face of evil.

'Let them anatomize Regan,' Lear raves, 'see what breeds about her heart. Is there any cause in nature that makes these hard hearts?' [III vi 76–8]. We know that there is no cause *beyond* nature; the voices of evil in the play – 'Thou, Nature, art my goddess'; 'What need one?'; 'Bind fast his corky arms' – do not well up from characters who are possessed. I have no wish to live in a culture where men believe in devils; I fully grasp that the torturers of this world are all too human. Yet Lear's anguished question insists on the pain this understanding brings, a pain that reaches beyond the king. Is it a relief to understand that the evil was not visited upon the characters by demonic agents but released from the structure of the family and the state by Lear himself?

Edgar's pretended demonic possession, by ironic contrast, is homiletic; the devil compels him to acts of self-punishment, the desperate masochism of the very poor, but not to acts of viciousness. Like the demoniacs who in Harsnett's contemptuous account praise the Mass and the Catholic church, Poor Tom gives a highly moral performance: 'Take heed o' th' foul fiend. Obey thy parents, keep thy word's justice, swear not, commit not with man's sworn spouse, set not thy sweet heart on proud array. Tom's a-cold' [III iv 80–3]. Is it a relief to know that Edgar only mimes this little sermon?

All attempts by the characters to explain or relieve their sufferings through the invocation of transcendent forces are baffled. Gloucester's belief in the influence of 'these late eclipses in the sun and moon' [I ii 103] is dismissed decisively, even if the spokesman for the dismissal is the villainous Edmund. Lear appeals almost constantly to the gods:

> O Heavens!
> If you do love old men, if your sweet sway
> Allow obedience, if you yourselves are old,
> Make it your cause; send down, and take my part.
>
> [II iv 189–92]

But his appeals are left unanswered. The storm in the play seems to several characters to be of more than natural intensity, and Lear above all tries desperately to make it *mean* something (as a symbol of his daughters' ingratitude, a punishment for evil, a sign from the gods of the impending universal judgment), but the thunder refuses to speak. When Albany calls Goneril a 'devil' and a 'fiend' [IV ii 59, 66], we know that he is not identifying her as a supernatural being – it is impossible, in this play, to witness the eruption of the denizens of hell into the human world – just as we know that Albany's prayer for 'visible spirits' to be sent down by the heavens 'to tame these vile offenses' [IV ii 46–7] will be unanswered.

In *King Lear*, as Harsnett says of the Catholic church, 'neither God, Angel, nor devil can be gotten to speak' [169]. For Harsnett this silence betokens a liberation from lies; we have learned, as the last sentence of his tract puts it, 'to loathe these despicable Impostures and return unto the truth' [*Declaration*, p. 171]. But for Shakespeare the silence leads to the desolation of the play's close:

> Lend me a looking-glass,
> If that her breath will mist or stain the stone,
> Why then she lives.   [v iii 262–4]

The lines voice a hope that has repeatedly tantalized the audience: a hope that Cordelia will not die, that the play will build toward a revelation powerful enough to justify Lear's atrocious suffering, that we are in the midst of what the Italians called a *tragedia di fin lieto*, that is, a play in which the villains absorb the tragic punishment while the good are wondrously restored.[47] Lear appeals, in effect, to the conventions of this genre. The close of a tragicomedy frequently requires the audience to will imaginatively a miraculous turn of events, often against the evidence of its senses (as when the audience persuades itself that the two actors playing Viola and Sebastian in *Twelfth Night* really *do* look identical, in spite of the ocular proof to the contrary, or when at the close of *The Winter's Tale* the audience accepts the fiction that Hermione is an unbreathing statue in order to experience the wonder of her resurrection). But the close of *King Lear* allows an appeal to such conventions only to reverse them with bitter irony: to believe Cordelia dead, the audience, insofar as it can actually see what is occurring onstage, must work against the evidence of its own senses. After all, the actor's breath would have misted the stone, and the feather held to Cordelia's mouth must have stirred. But we remain convinced that Cordelia is, as Lear first says, 'dead as earth'.

In the wake of Lear's first attempt to see some sign of life in Cordelia, Kent asks, 'Is this the promis'd end?' Edgar echoes the question: 'Or image of that horror?' And Albany says, 'Fall, and cease!' By itself Kent's question has an oddly literary quality, as if he were remarking on the end of the play, either wondering what kind of ending this is or implicitly objecting to the disastrous turn of events. Edgar's response suggests that the 'end' is the end of the world, the Last Judgment, here experienced not as a 'promise' – the punishment of the wicked, the reward of the good – but as a 'horror'. But like Kent, Edgar is not certain about what he is seeing: his question suggests that he may be witnessing not the end itself but a possible 'image' of it, while Albany's enigmatic 'Fall, and cease!' empties even that image of significance. The theatrical means that might have produced a 'counterfeit miracle' out of this moment are abjured; there will be no imposture, no histrionic revelation of the supernatural.

Lear repeats this miserable emptying out of the redemptive hope in his next lines:

> This feather stirs, she lives! If it be so,
> It is a chance which does redeem all sorrows
> That ever I have felt.　　　　　　　[v iii 266–8]

Deeply moved by the sight of the mad king, a nameless gentleman had earlier remarked,

> 　　　　　　　Thou hast one daughter
> Who redeems nature from the general curse
> Which twain have brought her to.　　[iv vi 205–7]

Now in Lear's words this vision of universal redemption through Cordelia is glimpsed again, intensified by the king's conscious investment in it.

What would it mean to 'redeem' Lear's sorrows? To buy them back from the chaos and brute meaninglessness they now seem to signify? To reward the king with a gift so great that it outweighs the sum of misery in his entire long life? To reinterpret his pain as the necessary preparation – the price to be paid – for a consummate bliss? In the theater such reinterpretation would be represented by a spectacular turn in the plot – a surprise unmasking, a sudden reversal of fortunes, a resurrection – and this dramatic redemption, however secularized, would almost invariably recall the consummation devoutly wished by centuries of Christian believers. This consummation had in fact been represented again and again in medieval Resurrection plays, which offered the spectators ocular proof that Christ had risen.[48] Despite the pre-Christian setting of Shakespeare's play, Lear's craving for just such proof – 'This feather stirs, she lives!' – would seem to evoke precisely this theatrical and religious tradition, but only to reveal itself, in C. L. Barber's acute phrase, as 'post-Christian.'[49] *If it be so*: Lear's sorrows are not redeemed; nothing can turn them into joy, but the forlorn hope of an impossible redemption persists, drained of its institutional and doctrinal significance, empty and vain, cut off even from a theatrical realization, but like the dream of exorcism, ineradicable.

The close of *King Lear* in effect acknowledges that it can never satisfy this dream, but the acknowledgment must not obscure the play's having generated the craving for such satisfaction. That is, Shakespeare does not simply inherit and make use of an anthropological given; rather, at the moment when the official religious and secular institutions are, for their own reasons, abjuring the ritual they themselves once fostered, Shakespeare's theater moves to appropriate it. Onstage the ritual is effectively contained in the ways we have examined, but Shakespeare intensifies as a theatrical experience the need for exorcism, and his demystification of the practice is not identical in its interests to Harsnett's.

Harsnett's polemic is directed toward a bracing anger against the lying agents of the Catholic church and a loyal adherence to the true established Church of England. He writes as a representative of that true church, and this institutional identity is reinforced by the secular institutional imprimatur on the confessions that are appended to the *Declaration*. The joint religious and secular apparatus works to strip away imposture and discover the hidden reality that is, Harsnett says, the theater. Shakespeare's play dutifully reiterates this discovery: when Lear thinks he has found in Poor Tom 'the thing itself,' 'unaccommodated man,' he has in fact found a man playing a theatrical role. But if false religion is theater, and if the difference betwen true and false religion is the presence of theater, what happens when this difference is enacted in the theater?

What happens, as we have already begun to see, is that the official position is *emptied out*, even as it is loyally confirmed. This 'emptying out' resembles Brecht's 'alienation effect' and, even more, Althusser and Macherey's 'internal distantiation.' But the most

fruitful terms for describing the felt difference between Shakespeare's art and the religious ideology to which it gives voice are to
be found, I think, in the theological system to which Harsnett
adhered. What is the status of the Law, asks Hooker, after the
coming of Christ? Clearly the Savior effected the 'evacuation of the
Law of Moses.' But did that abolition mean 'that the very name of
Altar, of priest, of Sacrifice itself, should be banished out of the
world'? No, replies Hooker; even after evacuation, 'the words which
were do continue: the only difference is, that whereas before they
had a literal, they now have a metaphorical use, and are as so many
notes of remembrance unto us, that what they did signify in the
letter is accomplished in the truth.'[50] Both exorcism and Harsnett's
own attack on exorcism undergo a comparable process of evacuation
and transformed reiteration in *King Lear*. Whereas before they had a
literal, they now have a literary use and are as so many notes of
remembrance unto us, that what they did signify in the letter is
accomplished – with a drastic swerve from the sacred to the secular
– in the theater.

Edgar's possession is a theatrical performance exactly in Harsnett's terms, but there is no saving institution, purged of theater,
against which it may be set, nor is there a demonic institution that
the performance may be shown to serve. On the contrary, Edgar
mimes in response to a free-floating, contagious evil more terrible
than anything Harsnett would allow. For Harsnett the wicked are
corrupt individuals in the service of a corrupt church; in *King Lear*
neither individuals nor institutions can adequately contain the
released and enacted wickedness; the force of evil in the play is
larger than any local habitation or name. In this sense, Shakespeare's tragedy reconstitutes as theater the demonic principle
demystified by Harsnett. Edgar's fraudulent, histrionic performance
is a response to this principle: evacuated rituals, drained of their
original meaning, are preferable to no rituals at all.

Shakespeare does not counsel, in effect, that for the dream of a
cure one accept the fraudulent institution as true – that is the
argument of the Grand Inquisitor. He writes for the greater glory
and profit of the theater, a fraudulent institution that never pretends
to be anything but fraudulent, an institution that calls forth what is
not, that signifies absence, that transforms the literal into the
metaphorical, that evacuates everything it represents. By doing so
the theater makes for itself the hollow round space within which it

survives. The force of *King Lear* is to make us love the theater, to seek out its satisfactions, to serve its interests, to confer on it a place of its own, to grant it life by permitting it to reproduce itself over generations. Shakespeare's theater has outlived the institutions to which it paid homage, has lived to pay homage to other, competing, institutions that in turn it seems to represent and empty out. This complex, limited institutional independence, this marginal and impure autonomy, arises not out of an inherent, formal self-reflexiveness but out of the ideological matrix in which Shakespeare's theater is created and re-created.

Further institutional strategies lie beyond a love for the theater. In a move that Ben Jonson rather than Shakespeare seems to have anticipated, the theater itself comes to be emptied out in the interests of reading. In the argument made famous by Charles Lamb and Coleridge, and reiterated by Bradley, theatricality must be discarded to achieve absorption, and Shakespeare's imagination yields forth its sublime power not to a spectator but to one who, like Keats, sits down to reread *King Lear*. Where institutions like the King's Men had been thought to generate their texts, now texts like *King Lear* appear to generate their institutions. The commercial contingency of the theater gives way to the philosophical necessity of literature.

Why has our culture embraced *King Lear's* massive display of mimed suffering and fraudulent exorcism? Because the judicial torture and expulsion of evil have for centuries been bound up with the display of power at the center of society. Because we no longer believe in the magical ceremonies through which devils were once made to speak and were driven out of the bodies of the possessed. Because the play recuperates and intensifies our need for these ceremonies, even though we do not believe in them, and performs them, carefully marked out for us as frauds, for our continued consumption. Because with our full complicity Shakespeare's company and scores of companies that followed have catered profitably to our desire for spectacular impostures.

And also, perhaps, because the Harsnetts of the world would free us from the oppression of false belief only to reclaim us more firmly for the official state church, and the solution – confirmed by the rechristening, as it were, of the devil as the pope – is hateful. Hence we embrace an alternative that seems to confirm the official line, and thereby to take its place in the central system of values, yet at the same time works to unsettle all official lines.[51] Shakespeare's theater empties out the center that it represents and in its cruelty – Edmund, Goneril, Regan, Cornwall, Gloucester, Cordelia, Lear: all dead as earth – paraodixcally creates in us the intimation of a fullness that we can savor only in the conviction of its irremediable loss:

> we that are young
> Shall never see so much, nor live so long.

SOURCE: *Shakespearean Negotiations* (1988).

NOTES

1. Samuel Harsnett, *A Declaration of egregious Popish Impostures, to withdraw the harts of her Maiesties Subjects from their allegeance, and from the truth of Christian Religion professed in England, under the pretence of casting out deuils* (London, Iames Roberts, 1603). Harsnett's influence is noted in Lewis Theobald's edition of Shakespeare, first published in 1733. Shakespeare is likely to have known one of the principal exorcists, Robert Dibdale, the son of a Stratford Catholic family linked to the Hathaways.

On the clandestine exorcisms I am particularly indebted to D. P. Walker, *Unclean Spirits: Possession and Exorcism in France and England in the Late Sixteenth and Early Seventeenth Centuries* (Philadelphia, University of Pennsylvania Press, 1981).

2. A major exception, with conclusions different from my own, has recently been published: John L. Murphy, *Darkness and Devils: Exorcism and 'King Lear'* (Athens, Ohio University Press, 1984). Murphy's study, which he kindly allowed me to read in galleys after hearing the present chapter delivered as a lecture, argues that exorcism is an aspect of clandestine political and religious resistance to Queen Elizabeth's rule. For thoughtful comment on Murphy's book by an expert on Harsnett, see F. W. Brownlow's review in *Philological Quarterly*, 65 (1986), 131–3. See also, for interesting reflections, William Elton, *'King Lear' and the Gods* (San Marino, Calif., Huntington Library, 1966). For useful accounts of Harsnett's relation to *Lear*, see *Narrative and Dramatic Sources of Shakespeare*, 8 vols, ed. Geoffrey Bullough (London, Routledge and Kegan Paul, 1958–75), 7, 299–302; Kenneth Muir, 'Samuel Harsnett and *King Lear*,' *Review of English Studies*, 2 (1951), 11–21, and Muir's edition of *Lear*, New Arden text (Cambridge, Mass., Harvard University Press, 1952), pp. 253–6.

3. Michel de Montaigne, 'Apology for Raymond Sebond', in *Complete Essays*, trans. Donald M. Frame (Stanford, Stanford University Press, 1948), p. 331.

4. Edward Shils, *Center and Periphery: Essays in Macrosociology* (Chicago, University of Chicago Press, 1975), p. 257.

5. Peter Brown, *The Cult of the Saints: Its Rise and Function in Latin Christianity* (Chicago, University of Chicago Press, 1981), p. 107.

6. Sebastian Michaelis, *The Admirable Historie of the Possession and Conversion of a Penitent Woman*, trans. W. B. (London, William Aspley, 1613), p. 21. Mass exorcism was a particularly important phenomenon in sixteenth- and early seventeenth-century France. See Michel de Certeau, *La Possession de Loudun*, Collection Archive Series no. 37 (Paris, Gallimard, 1980); Robert Mandrou, *Magistrats et sorciers en France au XVIIe siècle* (Paris, Seuil, 1980); Robert Muchembled, *La Culture populaire et culture des élites* (Paris, Flammarion, 1977); Jonathan L. Pearl, 'French Catholic Demonologists and Their Enemies in the Late Sixteenth and Early Seventeenth Centuries,' *Church History*, 52 (1983), 457–67; Henri Weber, 'L'Exorcisme à la fin du seizième siècle, instrument de la Contre Réforme et spectacle baroque,' *Nouvelle Revue du seizième siècle*, 1 (1983), 79–101. For a comparison between exorcism in France and in England, see D. P. Walker, *Unclean Spirits* and my own article, 'Loudun and London,' *Critical Inquiry*, 12 (1986) 326–46. I have incorporated some pages from this article in the present chapter.

7. *A Booke Declaringe the Fearfull Vexasion of one Alexander Nyndge. Beynge moste Horriblye tormented wyth an euyll Spirit* (London, Thomas Colwell, 1573), p. Biiii^r.

8. Carlo Ginzburg, *I benandanti: Recerche sulla stregoneria e sui culti agrari tra cinquecento e seicento* (Turin, Einaudi, 1966).

9. For Harsnett's comments on witchcraft, see *Declaration*, pp. 135–6. The relation between demonic possession and witchcraft is complex. John Darrel evidently had frequent recourse, in the midst of his exorcisms, to accusations of witchcraft whose evidence was precisely the demonic possessions; Harsnett remarks wryly that 'of all the partes of the tragicall Comedie acted between him and *Somers*, there was no one Scene in it, wherein *M. Darrell* did with more courage and boldnes acte his part, then in this of the discouerie of witches' (*A Discovery of the Fraudulent Practises of J. Darrel . . . concerning the pretended possession and dispossession of W. Somers, etc.* [1599], p. 142). There is a helpful discussion of possession and witchcraft, along with an important account of Harsnett and Darrel, in Keith Thomas, *Religion and the Decline of Magic* (London, Weidenfeld and Nicolson, 1971).

10. I borrow the phrase 'central zone' from Edward Shils, for whom it is coterminous with society's central value system, a system constituted by the general standards of judgment and action and affirmed by the society's elite [*Center and Periphery*, p. 3]. At the heart of the central value system is an affirmative attitude toward authority, which is endowed, however indirectly or remotely, with a measure of sacredness. 'By their very possession of authority,' Shils writes, elites 'attribute to themselves an essential affinity with the sacred elements of their society, of which they regard themselves as the custodians' [5].

11. Brown, *Cult of the Saints*, pp. 109–11.

12. Thomas, *Religion and the Decline of Magic*, p. 485. 'This effectively put an end to the practice,' Thomas writes, 'at least as far as conforming members of the Anglican Church were concerned.'

13. S. M. Shirokogorov, *The Psycho-Mental Complex of the Tungus* (Peking, Routledge, 1935), p. 265.

14. Brown, *Cult of the Saints*, p. 110.

15. Michael MacDonald, *Mystical Bedlam* (Cambridge, Cambridge University Press, 1981). See also MacDonald's 'Religion, Social Change, and Psychological Healing in England, 1600–1800,' in *The Church and Healing*, ed. W. J. Shiels, Studies in Church History 19 (Oxford, Basil Blackwell, 1982); H. C. Erik Midelfort, 'Madness and the Problems of Psychological History in the Sixteenth Century,' *Sixteenth Century Journal*, 12 (1981), 5–12.

16. *A Report Contayning a brief Narration of certain diuellish and wicked witcheries, practized by Olisse Barthram alias Doll Barthram in the Country of Suffolke*, bound with *The Triall of Maist. Dorrell, or A Collection of Defences against Allegations not yet suffered to receiue convenient answere* (1599), p. 94.

17. Iohn Swan, *A True and Briefe Report. of Mary Glovers Vexation* (1603), p. 42.

18. *The Triall of Maist. Dorrell*, p. 29.

19. Quoted in [John Darrel,] *A Briefe Narration of the possession, dispossession, and repossession of William Sommers* (1598), pp. Diiv, Ciiiiv.

20. *The Triall of Maist. Dorrell*, p. 8.

21. John Deacon and John Walker, *A Summarie Answere to al the material points in any of Master Darel his bookes* (London, George Bishop, 1601), pp. 237–8.

22. Harsnet sees this argument as a variant on the exorcists' general rule that 'when deuilles are cast out of man, they endeuoure by all the means they can, to perswade, that hee was neuer in them: that so the partie being vnthankeful to God for his deliuerance, they might the better reenter into him' [*Discovery*, p. 72]. Harsnett cites the important exorcism manual by R. F. Hieronymus Mengus [Girolamo Menghi], *Flagellum Daemonum* (Bologna, 1582).

23. In 1524 Erasmus satirized exorcism by depicting it not simply as a fraud but as a play in five acts (*Exorcismus, sive spectrum*, in *The Colloquies of Erasmus*, trans. Craig R. Thompson [Chicago, University of Chicago Press, 1965], pp. 231–7). The play, in Erasmus's account, is an elaborate practical joke played on a character called Faunus, a gullible and pretentious parish priest who is cleverly induced to be an unwitting actor in an outlandish and grotesque theatrical performance. The representation of the demonic is spurious, but its effect on the victim of the joke is alarmingly real: 'So thoroughly did this fancy obsess him that he dreamt of nothing but specters and evil spirits and talked of nothing else. His mental condition carried over into his very countenance, which became so pale, so drawn, so downcast that you would have said he was a ghost, not a man' [237]. A successful demon play can fashion the dreams of its victims, and illusions can inscribe themselves in the very bodies of those who believe in them. The colloquy ostensibly celebrates the histrionic cunning of the jokers, but Erasmus makes it clear that there are larger institutional implications: a gifted director, an unscrupulous actor who has 'perfect control of his expression,' and a few props suffice not only to create an intense illusion of

the demonic among large numbers of spectators but also to entice the gullible into participating in a play whose theatricality they cannot acknowledge. The defense against such impostures is a widespread public recognition of this theatricality and a consequent skepticism: 'Up to this time I haven't, as a rule, had much faith in popular tales about apparitions,' one of Erasmus's speakers concludes, 'but hereafter I'll have even less' [237].

24. See Edmund Jorden, *A briefe discourse of a disease Called the Suffocation of the Mother* (London, 1603).

25. *A Report Contayning a brief Narration of certain diuellish and wicked witcheries*, pp. 99–100.

26. [Richard Baddeley,] *The Boy of Bilson, or A True Discovery of the Late Notorious Impostvres of Certaine Romish Priests in their pretended Exorcisme, or expulsion of the Diuell out of a young Boy, named William Perry, sonne of Thomas Perry of Bilson* (London, F. K., 1622), p. 51. Baddeley is quoting from the Catholic account of the events, which, in order to dispute, he reprints: *A Faithful Relation of the Proceedings of the Catholicke Gentlemen with the Boy of Bilson; shewing how they found him, on what terms they meddled with him, how farre they proceeded with him, and in what case, and for what cause they left to deale further with him* [in Baddeley, pp. 45–54].

27. In both England and France the reliability of the devil's testimony was debated extensively. 'We ought not to beleeue the Diuell,' writes the exorcist and inquisitor Sebastian Michaelis, 'yet when hee is compelled to discourse and relate a truth, then wee should feare and tremble, for it is a token of the wrath of God' [*Admirable Historie of the Possession and Conversion of a Penitent Woman*, p. C7v]. Michaelis's long account of his triumph over a devil named Verrine was published, the translator claims, to show 'that the Popish Priests, in all Countries where men will beleeue them, are vniforme & like vnto themselues, since that which was done couertly in England, in the daies of Queene *Elizabeth* by the Deuils of *Denham* in *Sara Williams* and her fellowes, is now publikely taken vp elsewhere by men of no small ranke' [A4r]. This seems to me a disingenuous justification for publishing, without further annotation or qualification, over five hundred pages of Catholic apologetics, but obviously the Jacobean licensing authorities accepted the explanation.

28. [Darrel] *A Briefe Narration of the possession, dispossession, and repossession of William Sommers*, p. Biiv.

29. 'Let him be brought before some indifferent persons, let the depositions be read, and let him act the same in such manner, and forme as is deposed, by naturall, or artificiall power, then Mr. Dorrell will yeeld that he did conterfeit. If he cannot, (as vndoubtedlie he cannot,) then pleade no longer for the Deuill; but punish that imp of Satan as a wicked lier, and blasphemer of the mightie worke of God' [*Briefe Narration*, p. Biiv].

30. *Booke of Miracles*, quoted in Harsnett, *Declaration*, pp. 113–14.

31. In Haiti, for example, an individual possessed by a *loa*, or spirit, is led to the vestry of the sanctuary, where he chooses the costume appropriate to the particular spirit that has possessed him; dressed in this costume – for Baron Saturday, a black suit, starched cuffs, top hat, and white gloves; for

the peasant god Zaka, a straw hat, pouch, and pipe; and so forth – he returns to the clearing and performs for the assembled crowd the appropriate mimes, monologues, and dances (Alfred Metraux, 'Dramatic Elements in Ritual Possession,' *Diogenes*, 11 [1964], 18–36). In Sri Lanka, exorcisms integrate feasting, the making of ritual offerings, dancing, the singing of sacred texts, drumming, masking, and the staging of improvised, frequently obscene, comedies. The comedies are at once explicitly theatrical and integral to the healing process.

In a major study of exorcism rituals performed in and near the town of Galle in southern Sri Lanka, Bruce Kapferer observes that demons in Sinhalese culture are understood to operate by means of illusions; the disorder and suffering that these illusions occasion are combated by spectacular demystifying counter-illusions. Hence exorcists 'consider their healing rites to be elaborate tricks which they play on demons': to induce demons to treat the illusory as reality is to gain control over them (Bruce Kapferer, *A Celebration of Demons: Exorcism and the Aesthetics of Healing in Sri Lanka* [Bloomington Indiana University Press, 1983], p. 112). Demonic possession has disturbed a hierarchical order that must be restored by humiliating the demons and returning them to their rightful subordinate position in the order of things. This restoration is achieved through ceremonies that 'place major aesthetic forms into relation and locate them at points when particular transformations in meaning and experience are understood by exorcists to be occurring or are to be effected' [8]. The ceremonies transform demonic identity into normal social identity; the individual is returned to himself and hence to his community whose solidarity is not only mirrored but constituted by the aesthetic experience. Exorcists then are 'the masters of illusion' [113], and their histrionic skills do not arouse doubts about their authenticity but heighten confidence in their powers.

For further reflections on demonic possession, see Ernst Arbman, *Ecstasy or Religious Trance* (Norstedts, Svenska Bokförlaget, 1963), 3 vols, esp. chapter 9; *Disguises of the Demonic: Contemporary Perspectives on the Power of Evil*, ed. Alan M. Olson (New York, Association Press, n.d.); I. M. Lewis, *Ecstatic Religion: An Anthropological Study of Spirit Possession and Shamanism* (Harmondsworth, Penguin, 1971).

32. Michel Leiris, *La Possession et ses aspects théâtraux chez les Ethiopiens de Gondar* (Paris, Plon, 1958).

33. This argument has the curious effect of identifying all exorcisms, including those conducted by nonconformist preachers, with the pope. On attacks on the Catholic church as a theater, see Jonas Barish, *The Antitheatrical Prejudice* (Berkeley, University of California Press, 1981), pp. 66–131 passim.

34. At least since Plato there has been a powerful tendency to identify the stage with unreality, debased imitation, and outright counterfeiting. Like the painter, says Socrates in the *Republic*, the tragic poet is an imitator of objects that are themselves imitations and hence 'thrice removed from the king and from the truth' [597e]. Though this position had its important Christian adherents, it is not, of course, the only intellectual current in the

West; not only do medieval mystery plays depend upon a conviction that dramatic performance does not contradict religious truth, but the Mass itself appears to have been conceived by several important medieval thinkers as analogous to theatrical representation. For further discussion, see my 'Loudun and London', pp. 328–9.

35. *Discovery*, p. A3r. As Catholic priests 'have transformed the celebrating of the Sacrament of the *Lords supper* into a *Masse-game*, and all other partes of the *Ecclesiasticall service* into *theatricall sights*,' writes another sixteenth-century Protestant polemicist, 'so, in steede of *preaching the word*, they caused it to be played' (John Rainolds, cited in Barish, *The Antitheatrical Prejudice*, p. 163).

36. Harsnett was not alone, of course. See, for example, John Gee: 'The Jesuits being or having Actors of such dexterity, I see no reason but that they should set up a company for themselves, which surely will put down The Fortune, Red-Bull, Cock-pit, and Globe' (John Gee, *New Shreds of the Old Snare* [London, 1624]). I owe this reference, along with powerful reflections on the significance of the public theater's physical marginality, to Steven Mullaney.

37. This sentiment could serve as the epigraph to both of Harsnett's books on exorcism; it is the root perception from which most of Harsnett's rhetoric grows.

38. Stephen Gosson, *Plays Confuted in Five Actions* (c. 1582), cited in E. K. Chambers, *The Elizabethan Stage*, 4 vols (Oxford, Clarendon, 1923), 4, 215.

39. These lines were included in the quarto but omitted from the folio. For the tangled textual history, see Michael J. Warren, 'Quarto and Folio *King Lear*, and the Interpretation of Albany and Edgar,' in *Shakespeare: Pattern of Excelling Nature*, ed. David Bevington and Jay L. Halio (Newark, University of Delaware Press, 1978), pp. 95–107; Steven Urkowitz, *Shakespeare's Revision of 'King Lear'* (Princeton, Princeton University Press, 1980); and Gary Taylor, 'The War in *King Lear*,' *Shakespeare Survey*, 33 (1980), 27–34. Presumably, by the time the folio appeared, the point of the allusion to Harsnett would have been lost, and the lines were dropped.

40. John Bunyan, *Grace Abounding to the Chief of Sinners*, ed. Roger Sharrock (London, Clarendon Press, 1966), p. 15.

41. Edgar's later explanation – that he feared for his father's ability to sustain the shock of an encounter – is, like so many explanations in *King Lear*, too little, too late. On this characteristic belatedness as an element of the play's greatness, see Stephen Booth, *'King Lear,' 'Macbeth,' Indefinition, and Tragedy* (New Haven, Yale University Press, 1983).

42. On 'counterfeit miracles' produced to arouse awe and wonder, see especially Harsnett, *Discovery*, Epistle to the Reader.

43. Words, signs, gestures that claim to be in touch with super-reality, with absolute goodness and absolute evil, are exposed as vacant – illusions manipulated by the clever and imposed on the gullible.

44. This is, in effect, Edmund Jorden's prescription for cases such as Lear's, in *A briefe discourse of a disease*.

45. 'It is even possible,' writes Peter Milward, S.J., 'that the lot of such

priests as Weston and Dibdale provided Shakespeare with a suggestion for his portrayal of Edgar in hiding' (*Shakespeare's Religious Background* [London, Sidgwick and Jackson, 1973], p. 54). But I cannot agree with Milford's view that Shakespeare continually 'laments the plight of his poor country" since the day Henry VIII decided to break with Rome' [224].

46. On the Yorkshire performance, see John Murphy, *Darkness and Devils*, pp. 93–118.

47. In willing this disenchantment against the evidence of our senses, we pay tribute to the theater. Harsnett has been twisted around to make this tribute possible. Harnett several times characterizes exorcism as a 'tragicomedy' [*Discovery*, p. 142; *Declaration*, p. 150]. On Harsnett's conception of tragicomedy, see Herbert Berry, 'Italian Definitions of Tragedy and Comedy Arrive in England,' *Studies in English Literature*, 14 (1974), 179–87.

48. O. B. Hardison, Jr., *Christian Rite and Christian Drama in the Middle Ages: Essays in the Origin and Early History of Modern Drama* (Baltimore, Johns Hopkins University Press, 1965), esp. pp. 220–52.

49. C. L. Barber, 'The Family in Shakespeare's Development: Tragedy and Sacredness,' in *Representing Shakespeare: New Psychoanalytic Essays*, ed. Murray M. Schwartz and Coppélia Kahn (Batimore, Johns Hopkins University Press, 1980), p. 196.

50. Richard Hooker, *Laws of Ecclesiastical Polity*, 1, 582–3. This truth, which is the triumph of the metaphorical over the literal, confers on the church the liberty to use certain names and rites, even though they have been abolished. The entire passage in Hooker is powerfully suggestive for understanding the negotiation between the domain of literature and the domain of religion:

They which honour the Law as an image of the wisdom of God himself, are notwithstanding to know that the same had an end in Christ. But what? Was the Law so abolished with Christ, that after his ascension the office of Priests became immediately wicked, and the very name hateful, as importing the exercise of an ungodly function? No, as long as the glory of the Temple continued, and till the time of that final desolation was accomplished, the very Christian Jews did continue with their sacrifices and other parts of legal service. That very Law therefore which our Saviour was to abolish, did not *so soon* become unlawful to be observed as some imagine; nor was it afterwards unlawful *so far*, that the very name of Altar, of Priest, of Sacrifice itself, should be banished out of the world. For though God do now hate sacrifice, whether it be heathenish or Jewish, so that we cannot have the same things which they had but with impiety; yet unless there be some greater let than the only evacuation of the Law of Moses, the names themselves may (I hope) be retained without sin, in respect of that proportion which things established by our Saviour have unto them which by him are abrogated. And so throughout all the writings of the ancient Fathers we see that the words which were do continue; the only difference is, that whereas before they had a literal, they now have a metaphorical use, and are so many notes of remembrance unto us, that what they did signify in the letter is accomplished in the truth. And as no man can deprive the Church of this liberty, to use names whereunto the Law was accustomed, so neither are we generally forbidden the use of things which the Law hath; though it neither command us any particular rite, as it did the Jews a number and the weightiest which it did command them are unto us in the Gospel prohibited. [4.11.10]

For the reference to Hooker I am indebted to John Coolidge.

51. 'Truth to tell,' writes Barthes, 'the best weapon against myth is perhaps to mythify it in its turn, and to produce an *artificial myth:* and this reconstituted myth will in fact be a mythology' (Roland Barthes, *Mythologies*, trans. Annette Lavers [New York, Hill and Wang, 1972], p. 135).

SELECT BIBLIOGRAPHY

(Books from which extracts are taken are omitted.)

EDITIONS

The Arden Shakespeare, ed. Kennth Muir (Methuen and Harvard U.P., 1952)
New Shakespeare Series, ed. G. I. Duthie and J. Dover Wilson (Cambridge U.P., 1960).
Penguin Shakespeare, ed. G. K. Hunter (Penguin, 1972).
The Complete King Lear, ed. Michael Warren (University of California Press, 1990).

STUDIES

Paul Alpers, '*King Lear* and the theory of the sight patterns', in R. Brower and R. Poirier (eds), *In Defense of Reading* (New York, E. F. Dutton, 1962), pp. 133–52.
W. H. Clemen, *The Development of Shakespeare's Imagery* (Methuen and Harvard U.P., 1951).
William Empson, *The Structure of Complex Words* (Chatto & Windus and New Directions, 1951) ch. 6.
Barbara Everett, '*King Lear*: Loving', in *Young Hamlet: Essays on Shakespeare's Tragedies* (Oxford University Press, 1989), pp. 59–82.
Terence Hawkes, *Shakespeare and the Reason* (Routledge & Kegan Paul, 1964; Humanities, 1965).
R. B. Heilman, *This Great Stage* (Louisiana State U.P., 1948; University of Washington P., 1963).
   The most extensive study of thematic and image patterns in the play.
Ernst Honigmann, *Shakespeare: Seven Tragedies* (Macmillan, 1976).
H. Granville-Barker, *Prefaces to Shakespeare* (1927, Princeton, N.J., 1946, 1959; Batsford, 1963) II 1–85.
L. C. Knights, *Some Shakespearean Themes* (Chatto & Windus, 1959; Stanford U.P., 1966).
Wyndham Lewis, *The Lion and the Fox* (Grant Richards and Harper, 1927; Methuen, 1951).
   Eccentric and various in approach, but basically concerned with Shakespeare's reaction to the Machiavellian opposition – reconciliation between nobility and cunning, and his attitude to kings and heroes. No lengthy treatment of *Lear*, but will be stimulating to students of that play.
N. Maclean, 'Episode, Scene, Speech, and Word: The Madness of Lear', in *Critics and Criticisms*, ed. R. S. Crane (University of Chicago Press, 1957).

An example of the Chicago 'neo-Aristotelian' approach, which emphasises the sequential rather than the 'spatial' aspect of the plot.

Kenneth Muir and Stanley Wells, *Aspects of King Lear* (Cambridge University Press, 1982). Includes a survey of criticism, by G. R. Hibbard, and other articles.

J. Middleton Murry, *Shakespeare* (Cape, 1936; Hillary, 1965).
A sensitive but hostile account.

Ruth Nevo, *Tragic Form in Shakespeare* (Princeton, Princeton University Press, 1972).

Marvin Rosenberg, *The Masks of King Lear* (Berkeley, Cal., University of California Press, 1972).

Arthur Sewell, *Character and Society in Shakespeare* (Oxford and New York, 1951).
The heroes (Lear and others) represent a striving for ordered vision and society.

NOTES ON CONTRIBUTORS

A. C. BRADLEY (1851–1935): Professor of Literature at Liverpool and Glasgow Universities, Professor of Poetry at Oxford; author of *Shakespearean Tragedy* (1904) and *Oxford Lectures on Poetry* (1909).

STANLEY CAVELL: Professor of Philosophy, Harvard University, author of *Must We Mean What We say?*, *Disowning Knowledge* (1987) and many other books.

S. T. COLERIDGE (1772–1834): Coleridge's Shakespeare criticism was done either as marginalia or lectures, which others took down and later transcribed. There are also passages in *Biographia Literaria* (1817).

W. R. ELTON: Professor of English, City University of New York.

BARBARA EVERETT: Senior Research Fellow of Somerville College, Oxford, author of *Young Hamlet: Essays on Shakespeare's Tragedies* (1989) and other critical works.

STEPHEN GREENBLATT: Professor of English Literature at the University of California, Berkeley, author of *Renaissance Self-Fashioning* (1980) and *Shakespearean Negotiations* (1988).

R. B. HEILMAN: formerly Professor of English Literature, University of Washington; author of *This Great Stage* (1948) and *Magic in the Web* (1956) on *Othello*.

JOHN HOLLOWAY: Professor Emeritus, Cambridge University, author of *The Victorian Sage* (1953), *The Charted Mirror* (1960), *The Story of the Night* (1961) and many other books.

SAMUEL JOHNSON (1709–84): first published a prospectus for a new edition of Shakespeare in 1745, but did not begin it till 1756. After a long interruption he resumed work in 1763 and this edition, with the Preface and Notes, appeared in 1765.

G. WILSON KNIGHT: Professor Emeritus, Leeds University, pioneer of Shakespearian 'interpretation'. Among his many books on Shakespeare are *The Wheel of Fire* (1930), *The Imperial Themes* (1931), *Principles of Shakespearian Production* (1936, 1949) and *The Crown of Life* (1947).

MAYNARD MACK: Professor of English at Yale, biographer of Pope, editor and Shakespearian critic. *King Lear in Our Time* (1965) is his only book on Shakespeare.

GEORGE ORWELL: (pseudonym of Eric Hugh Blair: 1903–50), author of several novels including *Animal Farm* (1945) and *Nineteen Eighty-four* (1949), and many essays on social, political, and literary themes.

A. W. SCHLEGEL (1767–1845): German critic and translator; Professor of Literature at Jena and Bonn, and most famous of Shakespeare's German translators. His lectures on *Dramatic Art and Literature* were published in 1811 and translated into English in 1815.

P. B. SHELLEY (1792–1822): *A Defence of Poetry* was published posthumously in 1840.

NAHUM TATE (1652–1715): Poet Laureate, playwright.

ENID WELSFORD: author of *The Court Masque* (1927) and *The Fool* (1935).

INDEX

NOTE: For obvious reasons, characters in *King Lear* are not included in the index, nor are references to the play.